Islam in the Eyes of the West

From the terrorist attacks of September 11, 2001, in New York to the Madrid and London bombings of 2004 and 2005, the presence of Muslim communities in the West has generated security issues and major political concern. Governments, the media, and the general public have raised questions regarding potential links between Western Muslims, radical Islam and terrorism. This speculation has given rise to popular myths concerning the Islamic world and led to a host of illiberal measures such as illegal warranting, denial of *habeas corpus*, "black prisons", and extreme torture throughout the democratic world. *Islam in the Eyes of the West* challenges the authenticity of these myths and examines the ways in which they have been used to provide an ideological cover for the "war on terror" and the subsequent Iraq War. It argues that they are not only unfounded and hollow, but have also served a dangerous purpose, namely war-mongering and the empowerment of the national-security state. It further considers the origin and transmission of these myths, focusing on media, government policy, and popular discourse.

Tareq Y. Ismael is Professor of Political Science at the University of Calgary, Canada. He is the Editor of the *International Journal of Contemporary Iraqi Studies*; his most recent publications include *The Rise and Fall of the Communist Party in Iraq* and *Cultural Cleansing in Iraq: Why Museums were Looted, Libraries Burned and Academics Murdered.*

Andrew Rippin is Professor of Islamic History at the University of Victoria, British Columbia, Canada. Elected Fellow of the Royal Society of Canada in 2006, his publications include *Muslims: Their Religious Beliefs and Practices*, and *The Islamic World* (both published by Routledge).

Durham Modern Middle East and Islamic World Series

Series Editor: Anoushiravan Ehteshami,
University of Durham

Islam in the Eyes of the West

Images and realities in an age of terror

**Edited by
Tareq Y. Ismael
and Andrew Rippin**

LONDON AND NEW YORK

First published 2010
by Routledge
2 Park Square, Milton Park, Abingdon, Oxon, OX14 4RN

Simultaneously published in the USA and Canada
by Routledge
270 Madison Avenue, New York, NY 10016

*Routledge is an imprint of the Taylor & Francis Group,
an informa business*

Typeset in Times New Roman by Glyph International
Printed and bound in Great Britain by CPI Antony Rowe,
Chippenham, Wiltshire

British Library Cataloguing in Publication Data
A catalogue record for this book is available from the British Library

Library of Congress Cataloging in Publication Data
Islam in the eyes of the West: images and realities in an age of
terror / edited by Tareq Y. Ismael and Andrew Rippin.
    p. cm. – (Durham modern Middle East and Islamic world series)
Includes bibliographical references and index.
1. Islam–Relations. 2. Islam–Public opinion. 3. East and West.
4. Terrorism–Religious aspects–Islam. 5. War on Terrorism, 2001–
6. Jihad. I. Ismael, Tareq Y. II. Rippin, Andrew, 1950–
BP170.I845 2010
297.09'0511–dc22   2009040882

ISBN 13: 978-0-415-56414-4 (hbk)
ISBN 10: 0-415-56414-X (hbk)

ISBN 13: 978-0-203-85438-9 (ebk)
ISBN 10: 0-203-85438-1 (ebk)

Contents

Contributors

Raymond W. Baker, Professor, Department of International Relations, Trinity College, Connecticut, USA, and Adjunct Professor, Department of Political Science, American University in Cairo.

Shadia Drury, Professor of Philosophy and Political Science, University of Regina, Saskatchewan, Canada.

Alexander Henry, graduate student, Social Theory, University of Chicago, USA.

Tareq Y. Ismael, Professor, Department of Political Science, University of Calgary, Alberta, Canada.

Dietrich Jung, Head of the Centre for Contemporary Middle East Studies, University of Southern Denmark.

Karim H. Karim, Professor, School of Journalism and Communication, Carleton University, Ontario, Canada.

Norton Mezvinsky, Professor Emeritus, Department of History, Central Connecticut State University, USA.

Glenn E. Perry, Professor, Department of Political Science, Indiana State University, USA.

Andrew Rippin, Professor, Department of History, University of Victoria, British Columbia, Canada.

Keiko Sakai, Professor of Middle Eastern Studies, Tokyo University of Foreign Studies, Japan.

Fuad Shaban, Dean of Graduate Studies and Research, Yarmouk Private University, Damascus, Syria.

Abdel Salam Sidahmed, Associate Professor, Department of Political Science, University of Windsor, Ontario, Canada.

Patrick Smith, Professor, Department of Political Science, Simon Fraser University, British Columbia, Canada.

Janice J. Terry, Professor Emeritus, Department of History, Eastern Michigan University, USA.

Sunera Thobani, Associate Professor, Centre for Women's and Gender Studies, University of British Columbia, Canada.

Preface

These essays had their origin in a conference that was organized by the International Centre of Contemporary Middle Eastern Studies and the University of Victoria, entitled "The Muslim World and the West: Emerging Avenues for Convergence" and was held in Victoria, British Columbia, Canada, 28–30 March 2008.

At its core, the conference sought to examine the relationship between the Muslim world and the West which has been fraught with negative tension since the Crusades. Focusing on the clash of civilizations, contemporary discourse has largely concentrated on the confrontational dimension of relations between the Muslim world and the West. This conference was convened to provide an interdisciplinary forum to examine the other side of the coin with an emphasis on exploring emerging patterns of interaction and the synergies they generate.

Acknowledgements

A conference of this magnitude would not have been successful without the efforts of so many people, the organizing committee composed of scholars who dedicated so much time into bringing the idea of a conference to fruition – we would be remiss if we did not acknowledge Dr. Budd Hall, Dr. Gordon Smith, the Programme Committee and the Canadian and International advisory boards. In addition, we must also extend our gratitude to Candice M. Juby and Christopher Langille who worked relentlessly in the preparation of the conference, as onsite staff and as editorial assistants for this volume. This conference would not have taken place without the generous support of the International Development Research Centre of Canada and the Social Sciences and Humanities Research Council of Canada and the many participants who travelled from all over the world, each of whom contributed in so many ways to the discussion and this final work.

The Editors
Calgary, Alberta, and Victoria, British Columbia
August 2009

Introduction

The "West" and the Islamic world: patterns of confrontation and paths to reconciliation

Tareq Y. Ismael and Andrew Rippin

The contemporary relationship between the Western and the Islamic world is a relationship between the strong and the weak, whose markers have been bloodshed, cultural misunderstanding, and domination. This modern predicament was presaged over millennia of reciprocal (though, for the past two centuries, frequently uneven) warfare, religious rivalry, and the establishment of vast, self-serving colonial empires. Given this long and unpropitious history, projects of reconciliation and understanding – however noble – are often met with suspicion and preconceived ideological baggage.

The contemporary scene is especially fraught with danger and tension, as the United States – the world's hegemon – began the twenty-first century with a project of global militarism, thus bringing the Western and the Muslim world on an acute collision course. The rise of global militarism, whether labelled as neo-conservatism or otherwise, seems to be waning with the end of the Bush Presidency and the Republican Party majority in the House and Senate, but the poisonous fruits of its labour remain. The persisting occupation of Muslim lands is a reminder of the ill-fated path of the United States.

Popular discourses based upon the Bernard Lewis/Samuel Huntington "clash of civilizations" view form the intellectual and cultural backdrop of the world we inhabit, and thus, the theme of this book which surveys the various dimensions of Western-Islamic world relations: military and economic, cultural and intellectual, confrontational and reconciliatory. The most prominent themes of this book focus on Western-Islamic conflict and the negative representation of the Islamic 'Other' in the "Western mind", although throughout the chapters, the authors attempt to survey alternative forms of relations, both real and possible.

Prior to proceeding with an introduction to the chapters in this volume, it is useful to brief the reader on the contemporary and historical context of Western-Islamic relations, first surveying the meaning of potential shifts within the political culture of the American hegemon.

The present context

With the wounds of the George W. Bush presidency still festering, the commencement of the Obama Presidency was met with significant domestic goodwill and exuberance as well as a sense of cautious hope in the world at large. The Bush Presidency, which was inaugurated in controversy and disrepute, suitably concluded with the exiting President facing record levels of public disapproval and scrutiny. In the Muslim world, people saw the Bush Presidency as an era of American domination, occupation of Muslim lands, indulgence of Israeli assaults on the Palestinians, and a general spirit of confrontation and belligerence. It was during this time that Western-Islamic relations reached another historical nadir:

> Not only had the world turned sharply against the United States by tragically failing to resolve the festering Arab-Israeli conflict, a primary generator of what we call terrorism, the Bush administration ensured such violence would persist. But it was the administration's clumsy, ultimately catastrophic efforts to dominate global energy resources by invading Afghanistan and Iraq that led to a head-on confrontation with the Muslim world. A confrontation, one must assume, in which the Rasputin-like figure of Vice-President Dick Cheney and his neoconservative Praetorian Guard took full advantage of the president's simplistic, biblical view of the Mideast, and his limited knowledge of history and foreign affairs, to advance their aggressive imperial agenda.[1]

The beginnings of the Obama presidency were instead marked by lofty rhetoric and an often-conciliatory tone, which suggested to the world a break from the past and a possible new direction forward. This spirit of change and reconciliation under the new President was initiated with a formal order to close Guantanamo Bay and the ban on waterboarding, both of which had been powerful emblems of America's wayward direction. While these executive orders had powerful symbolic value, the sincerity of their application is clouded in ambiguity. Such is also the case with President Obama's rhetorical appeals to the Muslim world. Obama's inaugural address, while dressed in the typical clichés of American exceptionalism, nevertheless revealed suggestions of a new path forward in the Muslim world, one "based on mutual interest and mutual respect".[2] Likewise, in an interview granted to *al Arabiya* on 26 January 2009, Obama repeated this promise of a 'new path', and moreover attempted to connect personally to the Islamic world, noting the "Muslim members" of his family and his experience of having "lived in Muslim countries".

Since his inauguration as President, Barack Obama has made further rhetorical appeals to the Muslim world, notably his speech to the Turkish parliament and – later – his Cairo address, a speech to the Muslim world suitably entitled "A New Beginning". His speech to the Turkish parliament, while largely focused on matters of American-Turkish bilateral cooperation (economic and security cooperation) and pro forma flattery of the Turkish republic, nevertheless addressed issues of larger concern. In Obama's support for Turkey's entry into the European Union lies a latent endorsement of a notion that the 'Islamic world' and 'West' represent pieces of an interconnected world, rather than opposing spheres of existence. Moreover, President Obama referenced Muslim-Americans as having made enriching contributions to the United States, while casting his life experience (with members of his family being Muslim) as an example of a bridge between the West and Islamic world.[3]

President's Obama subsequent Middle East speech, his Cairo "A New Beginning" address, expanded upon these themes. At the rhetorical level, Obama's speech acknowledged Muslim grievances against the United States, specifically referencing America's participation in the 1953 overthrow of Iran's Mossadegh regime – making himself the first American president to do so; likewise, though not unique in this regard, Obama spoke of his desire to see a Palestinian state, acknowledged the suffering of Palestinians living under occupation, and denied the legitimacy of Israeli settlements. As with his previous speech, President Barack Obama paid tribute to Muslim contributions, both in the general sense (algebra, arts, architecture, etc.) and in the more American sense: American Muslims having "fought in our wars … served in our government … stood for civil rights … started businesses … won the Nobel Prize … been elected to [our] congress …".[4] The thrust of the speech, while not especially remarkable at the policy level (indeed President George W. Bush had spoken of a Palestinian state) lacked the rhetorical harshness and perceived arrogance of the preceding administration, and from that perspective, carried a measure of sincerity.

A speech remains mere rhetoric, however, and a common refrain in reaction to the speech was a desire to have the conciliatory rhetoric matched by policy. Indeed, against the backdrop of Obama's beneficent language, America continues its occupation of two Muslim countries, Afghanistan and Iraq. On the matter of Afghanistan, Obama in fact appears more dedicated to the military occupation than even his predecessor, promising an infusion of 30,000 American troops and an acceleration of the "war on terror" in the Afghan/Pakistan theatre. As for Iraq, he began his path to the Presidency as a critic of the war, and remains rhetorically dedicated to the phased withdrawal of American troops. However, it is useful to note that the timetable of Obama's withdrawal seems to roughly correspond with the terms of withdrawal that had been earlier established by the US-Iraq Status of Forces Agreement (SOFA), approved in late 2008; which prescribes the exit of American troops from Iraqi cities by June 2009 and a complete withdrawal by December 2011. It nevertheless appears that Obama's plan for Iraq neatly dovetails with what had already been prescribed by the Bush administration.

The primary Middle East flashpoint under the Obama Presidency remains the conflict between Israel and Palestine. In his 26 January 2009 interview with *al Arabiya*, Obama reiterated hope for a comprehensive peace settlement and a Palestinian state, as had his predecessor George W. Bush. If he aspires to succeed in the very place where his predecessors failed, his statements and actions on the matter must coalesce. The Israeli assault of December 2008–January 2009 on the people of Gaza was met with a general silence from then President-Elect Obama who, in deference to the policy of "one President at a time", offered no significant comment.

In his Presidential term, Obama appointed former Senator George Mitchell as his Middle East Peace Envoy, instructed – as revealed in the *al Arabiya* interview – to "start by listening, because all too often the United States starts by dictating". Yet, George Mitchell – for all his laudable diplomatic talents – and Obama – for all his lofty rhetoric and honorable intentions – are doomed to failure so long as American policy remains uncritical towards Israeli militarism and its refusal to recognize the legitimate rights of Palestinian nationhood. Obama's 30 January 2009 authorization of US$20 million in aid to the Palestinians in Gaza, while helpful, was a proportional pittance compared to the efforts of other nations. Moreover, it is grimly ironic that the estimated US$1.4 billion in damages wreaked on Gaza was inflicted by American-supplied arms.[5] In this case, optimism within the Muslim world towards Obama is measured by realism.

Moreover, whatever the intentions of Obama and his Envoy, Mitchell, any plan for a 'two-state solution' – or any other peaceful settlement – is severely limited by the political climate that has emerged in Israel. Parliamentary elections in February 2009 resulted in a virtual tie between the right-wing Likud and the nominally 'centrist' Kadima, with the quasi-fascist party of Avigdor Lieberman, *Yisrael Beiteinu* [*Israel is Our Home*], emerging as kingmaker. *Yisrael Beiteinu*, which styles itself as the heir to Zev Jabotinsky's radical project of revisionist Zionism, emerged from the wilderness with appeals to anti-Arab racism and the stigmatization of Arab parties, including a demand that Israeli Arabs provide a humiliating oath of loyalty to the Israeli state under threat of stripping their citizenship. That a party as radical as *Yisrael Beiteinu* could win 15 parliamentary seats in the Israeli Knesset does not bode well for any future peace prospects.

Such is the world at present; numerous violent flashpoints between the West and the Muslim World, and the now receding and unpopular face of American belligerence, George W. Bush, giving way to the humane façade of President Barack Hussein Obama, who, though rhetorically rejecting the legacy of his predecessor, called for a return to the "traditional bipartisan realistic policy of George Bush's father, of John F. Kennedy, of, in some ways, Ronald Reagan",[6] and appears to share the fundamental assumptions of America's right to domination and unilateral violence. Indeed, the 'traditional' foreign policy that Obama appears to endorse is not viewed by the peoples of the Muslim world as a golden age in Western-Islamic relations; nor should one treat the era of George W. Bush as a total historical aberration detached from its Presidential predecessors, but instead, it should be seen as a culmination of an already established American policy. In associating himself with this American tradition, Obama has not promised a 'new' American policy, but a rejection of the bombast and extremism of George W. Bush. Despite everything positive he represents, he has so far positioned his Presidency as a continuation of American grand strategy.

An editorial in *Al Hayat* commented on Obama's conciliatory discourse toward the Arab and Muslim world, and adequately reflects Middle Eastern political views:

> Obama has to carefully watch his time, as time will steal the sparkle from his attractiveness. Appeal does not have a long shelf life in the Middle East.

It has to be fortified with substance to fulfil hope ... [However,] the experience of the last few months gives strong indications that there are many who are angry with America and those who loathe America are not few in number; the number of those who are disappointed with [the US] is likewise not small. However, there is the most certain [longing] for a different America, realistic and minimally fair. Obama's vision of America benefited directly from the mistakes of George W. Bush's world view. Bush's Iraqi adventure destabilized the entire region and served [in the final analysis] all those who dreamt of weakening the US ... Obama needs to move the [Arab-Israeli] peace process forward before he loses his attractiveness ... and quickly move to reinvigorate the hope for peace ... Obama's chance to change the environment in the Middle East will soon be gone, which means more extremism and hopelessness if he fails, and a return to a policy of retaliation. This is why Obama is required to be decisive, which will help the people of the area to take similarly difficult decisions. The key to convincing the Arabs that there is change in American policy is to see a change in America's approach toward Israel.[7]

An article written two weeks later echoes the same theme:

The time has come to save the reputation of the Barack Obama Administration and to save US leadership from falling into a situation where doubts are raised over its sincerity, competence and credibility, as well as over its determination to achieve the qualitative shift it has promised – not because of the absence of Arab normalization procedures, but rather because it continued Israeli procedures that negate international law without being accountable. The time has come for a policy of immediate US "interference" to force the two sides, Palestinian and Israeli, to implement their commitments as per the Road Map to the two-state solution, Palestine alongside Israel.[8]

Cultural representations of the 'Other'

Undergirding the long history of violent conflict between the West and the Islamic world is a reservoir of cultural suspicions and clichés, and mutually serving representations that divide the two worlds into separate, irreconcilable, peoples. From the Western vantage point, contempt for the East has a long heritage. Indeed, from the early spread of Islam, the religion of an eventual billion plus, its prophet Muhammad had been viewed as an imposter. In the medieval era, Muhammad was represented as a "deceiving prophet", who provided "nothing true" except "human bloodshed".[9] Muhammad was frequently represented as a failed Cardinal, who formed the Islamic faith to compensate for his thwarted aspirations within the Roman Church. Appropriate to the medieval mindset, the Italian poet Dante Aligheri provided the most memorable medieval treatment of the Islamic prophet, dooming him and his son-in-law Ali to eternal punishment by demons:

> See how maimed Mohammad is! And he
> who walks and weeps before me is Ali
> whose face is opened wide from chin to forelock.[10]

Representations of such tortures would be reproduced by popular illustrator Gustave Doré, the poet William Blake, and later, the surrealist Salvador Dali. Indeed, medieval representations of this sort continued to cause tension even as late as 2002, when complaints and threats arose concerning Giovanni de Modena's *The Last Judgement*, an Italian fresco depicting Islam's prophet facing hellish torments.[11]

Contemporary representations of the Prophet of Islam tend to be removed from medieval sentiments, though the religious component has continued. At the popular, demagogic level, televangelist Jerry Falwell commented: "I think Muhammad was a terrorist."[12] At the more elevated level, Pope Benedict XVI quoted a medieval dialogue recounted by Byzantine emperor Manuel II Paleologus: "Show me what Muhammad brought that was new and there you will find things only evil and inhuman, such as his command to spread by the sword the faith he preached."[13] The Pope's ill-conceived comments, part of an academic treatise criticizing violence in the name of religion – all religions – nevertheless provoked a backlash, revealing the continuing resonance of religious tension and rivalry.

Popular representations of the 'other', detached from theology, are plenty and potent. A series of post-September 11th cultural conflagrations erupted, including the Danish "cartoon controversy", the Sudan "teddy bear" case, Theo Van Gogh and Ayaan Hirsi Ali's *Submission*, right-wing Danish politician Geert Wilders' *Fitna*, "human rights" lawsuits in Canada, and so on. In popular film, threatening representations of Arabs and Islam date as early as George Melford's *The Sheik* (1921) and George Fitzmaurice's *Son of the Sheik* (1926) – films from the silent era – that raised the spectre of Arab 'defilement' of white women, to much consternation. Like the standard of 'blackface' in racist minstrel acts, the 'Sheik' of these films was played in stereotyped Arab dress by the decidedly non-Arab Rudolph Valentino, a sex symbol of that era. Arab terrorists and villains have become stock characters in popular Hollywood films,[14] and similar representations are replicated in more modern media, notably video games, where the player is instructed in cultural stereotypes by slaughtering waves of gibberish-shrieking and faceless 'terrorists'.

In the absence of historical context, the cultural eruptions that have become a feature of the twenty-first century, largely attributed to the supposed fanaticism of Muslims, have been difficult for many to understand. Impetuous reaction from some quarters of Muslim societies to these various preferred cultural insults have only encouraged further provocations, stimulating a market of anti-Islamic polemics and paying dividends to xenophobic political parties in continental Europe.

Complicating these recurring cultural collisions are widespread beliefs in the Muslim world that attribute religious motives to Western foreign policy, and the direct assault upon the religious traditions of the Islamic world. According to data collected by *World Public Opinion*/University of Maryland in February 2007 – polling Morocco, Egypt, Pakistan, and Indonesia – vast majorities believe that US actions in the Muslim world are 'definitely/probably' intended to 'weaken and divide Islam':

- 78 per cent in Morocco
- 92 per cent in Egypt
- 73 per cent in Pakistan
- 73 per cent in Indonesia

Moreover, significant majorities further believe that US actions are 'definitely/probably' intended to 'spread Christianity':

- 67 per cent in Morocco
- 64 per cent in Pakistan
- 61 per cent in Indonesia.[15]

In concert, the recurrence of cultural conflicts and the negative perceptions of Muslim majorities tend to be treated in the West as, first, a reflection of the supposed defects of Islam and Muslim peoples, and, second, of the presumed paranoia that 'infects' Muslim thought. Neither of these popular explanations provides any solution to the imposed "clash of civilizations". Only in an understanding of history and power relations – an understanding sorely lacking in much of Western society – might one see some way of untangling the woeful state of West-Muslim world relations.

The historical context

A millennium of inter-cultural conflict and Western domination reached its apex in the aftermath of World War I as the dismemberment of the Ottoman Empire marked the formal end of Islamic power and the emergence of a modern Middle East under the stewardship of Western colonial powers. The Sykes–Picot Agreement of 1916 defined the colonial spheres of influence among the colonial powers of the United Kingdom, France, and Imperial Russia; while the Balfour Declaration of 1917 – in contravention of the Hussein–McMahon Correspondence among others – founded the eventual emergence of the Zionist colonial project in Palestine which was formalized in 1948.

Europe's colonial projects in the Middle East relied upon imperial paraphernalia of rule by quiescent satraps, and the privileging of ethnic minorities as a way of divide-and-rule, but, more crucially, was the use of mass violence against the population to achieve submission. Colonial projects, however brutal, engendered resistance and Western colonial projects in the Muslim world were no different.

Resistance to colonization in the Middle East took multiple forms; in an early example that presaged the later emergence of Islamic resistance movements, imperial Britain was scandalized by the emergence of the 'Mahdi movement' in nineteenth-century Sudan; the simple cleric, Mohammed Ahmed al-Mahdi, backed by his band of "dervishes" (as termed in Britain), declared a national liberation struggle in Sudan, waylaid British-Egyptian expeditionary forces, and, in 1885, ultimately besieged the capital Khartoum and killed the colonial general, Sir Charles Gordon.[16]

The event horrified Victorian Britain, rendering Gordon a virtual Christian saint, a devout bulwark against the 'barbarous' natives led by the "Mad Mahdi", "a man driven to lunacy by the malevolent intoxication of Islam [that] would deny the manifest benefits of British rule and Christian redemption".[17] This tone should be familiar to the reader; in the context of Iraq, where America's parade of villains – like the British before them – came to be represented in the popular press as forces of pure atavism and fanaticism, ungracious to the benefits of American civilization. In the case of General Gordon, as with subsequent heroes of 'civilization' at war with 'barbarians', the relationship between politics and art was manifest. Gordon was romanticized in George William Joy's painting *General Gordon's Last Stand*, and even as late as 1966, the colonial travails of Gordon were lionized in the popular film *Khartoum*, starring Charlton Heston as Gordon. In any case, the Mahdi revolt was brutally put down in 1898 by British forces, where over 11,000 "Dervish" warriors were machine-gunned to death in Omdurman. Nevertheless, the incident powerfully presaged later colonial revolts.

Notable for its historical resonance and contemporary relevance is the Great Iraqi Revolt of 1920 where British colonial dominion over Iraq – strewn from the Ottoman *vilayets* of Baghdad, Mosul, and Basra, but representing a historically contiguous region – was affirmed in 1920 at the San Remo Conference. Rejecting this 'allocation', the Revolt broke out, drawing on multiple quarters of Iraqi society, notably Arab nationalist and Shi'i-led elements. The British forces temporarily staved off the Revolt, both through mass violence and the investment in local elites. The British colonial project in Iraq, nonetheless, ultimately collapsed.

At the end of World War II, Turkey and Saudi Arabia were independent Middle Eastern states, and through a wave of decolonization, the colonial possessions of Great Britain and France – whether official or *de facto* – broke free; these newly free nations took on progressive-nationalist forms in Egypt (1952) and Iraq (1958) and more traditional forms elsewhere. In the context of the Cold War, however, with the European powers weakened, and the newly emerged superpowers, the United States and the Soviet Union, engaged in a crucial global struggle, the Middle East fell into a pattern of intrusion and domination by both camps.

The United States, which proved to be the more enduring of the competing superpowers, established its regional influence early by engaging in several Cold War policies that have decisively shaped the contemporary Middle East:

- In February 1945, a meeting between US President Franklin Delano Roosevelt and Saudi King Ibn Saud set the contours of what is often labelled an 'oil-for-protection' pact, whereby Saudi Arabia guaranteed the cheap and undisturbed flow of petrol to the US in exchange for security guarantees against regional challengers. These challenges have taken the various forms of Pan-Arabism, Progressive movements, and Islamic forces. American-Saudi regional coordination peaked with its joint anti-Soviet venture in Afghanistan. The depth and extent of these concerted Saudi-American policies resulted in an American military presence in Saudi Arabia and consequently the emergence of al-Qaeda.

- The United States officially recognized Israel in 1948 and gradually accelerated US military aid for that project (particularly after 1967). At present, the United States guarantees Israel's security as its chief outpost in the region, and as of 2008, Israel was provided an estimated US$2.4 billion in military aid, scheduled for annual adjustments, plus additional funds in non-military support.[18] As a consequence of this relationship, the United States – inspite of all its pretenses of "fair brokerage" – has put itself in direct opposition to the national aspirations of the Palestinian people, who are bombarded by American-supplied arms. This has been a primary source of popular opposition to the United States in the region. In 1978, Israel and Egypt – under American auspices – signed the Camp David Accords, formalizing peace between Israel and Egypt and ending Egypt's aspirations of Arab leadership, a mantle that Iraq would attempt to inherit. Presently, the Egyptian autocracy is the second largest recipient of American military aid.

- In 1953, the CIA, in concert with Britain's MI6, overthrew the nationalist government of Mohammed Mosaddeq in Iran, inadvertently setting into motion the Islamic revolution in 1979.

- The United States has engaged in a long and unhappy relationship with Iraq. In 1963, General Abdul Karim Qasim's nationalist regime was overthrown by a Ba'athist-led coup, "Almost certainly a gain for our side," wrote Robert Komer, an NSS aide to President Kennedy. Little remarked at the time, the historical record reveals CIA backing for the coup.[19] Ali Saleh Sa'adi, the former Ba'ath Party Secretary, stated as much, "We came to power on a CIA train." In the 1980s, as is well known, the US backed Iraq in its brutal war with neighboring Iran, with the dead exceeding – in some estimates – over a million. This was followed by the reversal of Iraq's conquest of Kuwait with the 1991 Gulf War, which was followed, in turn, by a brutal regime of economic sanctions that, according to a 1995 estimate by the UN Food and Agriculture Organization (FAO), resulted in the deaths of 567,000 children, a "price" that US Secretary of State Madeline Albright deemed "worth it".[20] Whatever the final toll, the nation of Iraq was left crippled and unprepared for the 2003 Anglo-American invasion that cruelly followed.

All these measures, alongside "lesser" interventions as in Lebanon, have subverted and deformed the democratic development capital of the Middle Eastern countries. Given its role in perpetuating this order though vigorous support of what was described as its "moderate" allies (pro-American dictatorships), the United States – as the heir to previous empires – is viewed very poorly by the Arab masses. Further, notwithstanding the official narrative in the US media, this hostility has little to do with the 'innate' characteristics of the region or its religious practice. In fact, extensive polling concluded over six years reveals that the Muslim masses are overwhelmingly supportive of democratic principles. Support for the principle of 'free speech' – for example – extends as far as "99% in Lebanon, 94% in Egypt, 92% in Iran ... Support is also strong in most Muslim majority nations for freedom of religion and freedom of assembly."[21]

The Middle East, at present, faces a legitimacy crisis, and a confounding future. The American occupation of Iraq, currently in its sixth year, has capsized the foundation of Iraq's secular state-building project, empowered sectarian-minded parties, and brought a death toll estimated to range from hundreds of thousands to over a million.[22] In the Israeli assault on Gaza during January 2009, over 1,300 were killed, half of them civilians, with an estimated 5,450 wounded.[23] With the failure of the Arab system to engineer democratic state-building projects, or successfully stave off foreign domination, Islamic-based parties have emerged as potent regional players, with Hamas in the Palestinian territories, Hezbollah in Lebanon, the Muslim Brotherhood in Egypt and beyond, and in an especially perverse form, the multitude of sectarian militia parties in occupied Iraq. The Middle East, with the American hegemon as an unwilling participant, is in the state of disarray and tyranny that they have predominantly been responsible for.

Overview of the book

This volume's collection of chapters begins with those that focus on the origins, concepts and realities of the two worlds – Muslim and the West – interacting on various levels. This is followed by a triad of essays that direct attention to the manner in which the Muslim world is conveyed and portrayed through the mass media, in the West, including Japan. The concluding four chapters are enlightening, instructive and forward-thinking, at the same time demonstrating that we can, in fact, understand one another and cooperate on various levels.

Chapter 1, Dietrich Jung's "The common origin of Difference: Edward Said, Michael Foucault and the modern image of Islam" commences with Edward Said's claim to have been inspired by the work of Foucault, in particular by his *Archaeology of Knowledge* and *Discipline and Punish*. In taking Said's claim as its departure point, this chapter criticizes the theoretical framework of *Orientalism* from a sociological perspective. Thereby, it takes up Sadik al-Azm's argument that Said was blind to the phenomenon of "Orientalism in reverse": the incorporation of Orientalist concepts in the ideological constructions of both Islamist and Arab Nationalist thinkers. The chapter argues that in taking Foucault's theoretical position seriously, Said should have been aware of the reciprocal power of discourses in shaping this essentialist image of Islam.

In Chapter 2, Shadia B. Drury's "Demonizing the enemy in the War on Terror" proposes that the conflict between the United States and its Muslim 'enemies' represents a conflict between competing chauvinisms, each claiming the side of

God, while claiming its enemies represent absolute evil. The infusion of these theological assumptions into politics does not augur well for the world; these religious ideas lead to the demonization of the enemy, which in turn makes war more vicious, intractable, and oblivious to all prudential considerations. Drury concludes by arguing that the Barack Obama administration must take the lead in abandoning the "war on terror".

Chapter 3, Norton Mezvinsky's "Islam and Muslims as seen by the Christian Zionists" evaluates the phenomenon of "Christian Zionism" and the movement's role in the post-September 11th "war on terror". Mezvinsky categorizes and evaluates the movement's stated hostility to Islam, and its favorable orientation towards Israel. He then tracks the lobbying activities of the Christian Zionist network, pinpointing the ideology and main points of the Christian Zionist platform, while revealing its major figures.

Chapter 4, Sunera Thobani's "Vigilante masculinity and the 'War on Terror'" examines the historical relationship between masculinity, the nation and war, in light of the post-September 11, 2001 world. Analyzing mainstream media, documentaries and popular Hollywood films, Thobani argues that the war has enabled emergent vigilante masculinity – exceptional in the support it has received from the institutions of the state (the Presidency, the Supreme Court, the Attorney General's Office, the Joint Chiefs of Staff, etc.) – to become dominant in North American political life. Exulting in its demonization of Islam as innately prone to violence, and of Muslim men as inherently misogynist, this vigilante form has successfully merged with a more traditional militaristic masculinity, and in the process, garnered significant support for itself in the cause of 'protecting' Western 'civilization' against its 'Islamic' Other.

Following this, Chapter 5, Fuad Shaban's "Islam in the US: the contemporary scene" argues that the September 11th attacks invited a mass of hostile condemnations and representations of Islam from American society, attacks that had been previously limited to the religious and political far right. In the present, Islamophobia has become an accepted practice by the media, politicians, and by public figures to express open suspicion, outright prejudice and religious profiling of Muslims.

Chapter 6, Abdel Salam Sidahmed's "'Jihadiology' and the problem of reaching a contemporary understanding of Jihad" critically assesses some of the scholarly, policy, and journalistic Western writings on jihad, noting that in most of these writings the word jihad became more or less synonymous with terrorism, hatred and destruction. This chapter surveys Western media and populist writings on jihad. It concludes by arguing that contemporary Jihadism figures as an inspiration, a component of the Salafist ideology of global radical Islamism.

Chapter 7, Keiko Sakai's "Islam, Muslims, neighbors in Asia? The transformation of Japan's perceptions of Islam as depicted in its media" tracks Japanese perspectives of Islam in terms of imported Western philosophies, and Japan's regional interests and the idea of Asianism. The former model encouraged Orientalist and prejudiced treatments of Islam, while the latter encouraged cynical policies intended to manipulate Muslim communities for the benefit of

Japanese imperialism. Finally, the author considers more contemporary treatments of Islam and Muslims in Japan in terms of the transformation of the perception of Japan's own position in Asia and in the West.

Chapter 8, Janice J. Terry's "U.S. politics, media and Muslims in the post-9/11 era" highlights media and public treatment of Muslims and Arab Americans since the events of September 11th. Negative stereotypes of Arabs and Muslims are deeply embedded in US culture, and have been reinforced by special interest groups, pro-Zionist lobbyists, neo-conservatives, and Evangelicals. Campaigns to limit or prevent objective discussions on issues involving Islam, the Arab-Israeli conflict, and the Arab world within the academic community have been particularly troublesome, and this chapter describes the origins of these campaigns and their impacts.

Chapter 9, Karim H. Karim's "Self and Other in a time of terror: myth, media and Muslims" considers the division of "good" violence and "bad" violence within dominant media discourses, in the context of Western 'self' versus the Muslim 'other'. Karim argues that the mainstream media, largely adhering to the interpretations of events offered by ruling elites, are drawing on polarizing tendencies of myth to shape the public understanding of terrorism. They seem to disregard completely another aspect of the myths of Self and Other that present them as fundamentally interconnected with each other.

In Chapter 10, Raymond W. Baker and Alexander Henry's "Understanding the Muslim world: we *can* do better", the authors provide an alternative to cultural relativism for interpreting the non-West. It argues that the same measures used to explain and appraise one another's actions in our own culture are more than sufficient in interpreting people from other cultures – including Islamic ones – provided we perform the necessary translations. Drawing on recent work in the American philosophical tradition of pragmatism, the authors describe interpretation and evaluation in terms of the attribution of commitments, where the content of a commitment is a pattern of activity: certain things done in certain contexts. The authors draw out the methodological implications of this approach for the analysis of Islam as a culture, focusing on the interpretation of centrist Islamism and of terrorism.

Chapter 11, Patrick Smith's "Applying the 'McCarthy Test' to Canadian and American security legislation: a 10-year retrospective on the impact of September 11, 2001 on privacy rights" examines the state of American and Canadian security legislation in the decade following the events of September 11th, 2001. It poses this analysis in the context of what might be termed the 'McCarthy Test'. Like those who now look back on the McCarthy era – in the US and its equivalent iterations in Canada and elsewhere – there is no more important question to ask. The answer suggested in this reflection is that collective security has trumped the very rights it is intended to protect.

Chapter 12, Glenn Perry's "Huntington's 'clash of civilizations': rumours and clarification" reevaluates Samuel P. Huntington's "clash of civilizations" and the criticism that followed. Perry argues that the Huntington thesis is not an *incitement to* a clash of civilisations but rather a *warning of* such a clash.

While Huntington emphasizes the importance of culture, this is argued to refer to identity with one's own civilisation (civilisations as "super-tribes", as he puts it) rather than a broader ethnocentrism. Instead of calling for a belligerent Western policy toward other civilisations, Huntington is warning that Western supremacy has been a temporary phenomenon that we must not try to perpetuate.

Rounding off this collection is Chapter 13, Raymond W. Baker's "Getting it wrong, yet again: America and the Islamic mainstream" where the author argues that the United States, in particular, but the West generally, has failed to integrate the Islamic mainstream as a potential partner in struggles towards peace, freedom, and economic justice. Increasingly across the Arab Islamic world, these struggles are waged under the banner of the Islamic centre. In their aspirations, they are consonant with American democratic traditions. Yet, as a consequence of US policies during the George W. Bush years, the United States has alienated potential democratic allies, thrusting them into the 'enemy' column. While it is unlikely that the most damaging US foreign policies will be reversed any time soon, even with the Obama administration, there are openings now for Western civil society institutions with democratic *and* anti-imperial orientations to offset the damaging consequences of US policies and to create cooperative openings to the Islamic mainstream.

Notes

1 Eric S. Margolis *American Raj: Liberation or Domination? Resolving the Conflict between the West and the Muslim World*, Toronto: Key Porter Books Ltd., 2008, p. 37.
2 President Barack Obama, Inaugural Address, 20 January 2009.
3 President Barack Obama's address to the Turkish National Assembly, 6 April 2009. Available at: www.cspan.org/Watch/watch.aspx?MediaId=HP-R-17163, accessed April 2009.
4 President Barack Obama, *Remarks by the President on a New Beginning*, 4 June 2009. Available at: www.whitehouse.gov/the_press_office/Remarks-by-the-President-at-Cairo-University-6-04-09/, accessed June 2009.
5 Karin Laub, "First Gaza Damage Estimate: $1.4 billion", *Associated Press*, 14 January 2009.
6 28 March 2008, campaign speech in Greensburg, Pennsylvania.
7 *Al Hayat*, editorial, 30 July 2009.
8 Raghida Dergham, "What is Required of the Obama Administration Today …", *Al Hayat*, 14 August 2009. Available at: www.daralhayat.com/portalarticlendah/47392, accessed August 2009.
9 Walter Emil Kaegi, Jr., "Initial Byzantine Reactions to the Arab Conquest", *Church History*, 38(2) (June 1969): 139–149, pp. 139–142, quoting from *Doctrina Jacobi nuper baptizati*, pp. 86–87.
10 Dante Aligheri, "Inferno", *Divine Comedy*, canto XXVIII, pp. 31–33.
11 Frank Bruni, "Italy Arrests 5; Fresco Showing Muhammad is Issue", *New York Times*, 21 August 2002.
12 In a 6 October 2002 appearance on CBS' *60 Minutes*.
13 Speech by Pope Benedict at the University of Regensburg, *Faith, Reason and the University Memories and Reflections*, 12 September 2006. Available at: www.vatican.va/holy_father/benedict_xvi/speeches/2006/september/documents/hf_ben-xvi_spe_20060912_university-regensburg_en.html, accessed June 2009.

14 See Jack Sheehan, *Reel Bad Arabs: How Hollywood Vilifies a People*, New York: Olive Branch Press, 2001.
15 Stephen Kull *et al.*, "Muslim Public Opinion on US Policy, Attacks on Civilians and al Qaeda", 24 April 2007, Program on International Policy Attitudes at the University of Maryland. Available at: www.worldpublicopinion.org/pipa/articles/brmiddleeastnafricara/346.php?lb=brme&pnt=346&nid=&id, accessed June 2009.
16 Margolis, op. cit., pp. 71–75.
17 Ibid., p. 74.
18 BBC, "Israel Hails US Military Aid Rise", 29 July 2007. Available at: www.news.bbc.co.uk/2/hi/middle_east/6920988.stm, accessed June 2009.
19 Roger Morris, "A Tyrant 40 Years in the Making", *New York Times*, 14 March 2003.
20 Rahul Mahajan, "We Think the Price Is Worth it", *Fairness & Accuracy in Reporting* (November/December 2001). Available at: www.fair.org/index.php?page=1084, accessed June 2009.
21 John L. Esposito and Dalia Mogahed, "Who Will Speak for Islam?", *World Policy Journal*, 25(3) (Fall 2008): 47–57.
22 Opinion Research Business, "January 2008 – Update on Iraqi Casualty Data", *Opinion Research Business*, January 2008. Available at: www.opinion.co.uk/Newsroom_details.aspx?NewsId=88, accessed June 2009.
23 Conn Hallinan, "Gaza: Death's Laboratory", *Foreign Policy in Focus*, 11 February 2009. Available at: www.fpif.org/fpiftxt/5862, accessed June 2009.

1 The origin of difference

Edward Said, Michel Foucault and the modern image of Islam

Dietrich Jung

When taking up the theme of Islam and the West, Edward Said's book *Orientalism* is an almost obligatory reference. First published in 1978, the book represents a milestone in the field of cultural studies. It triggered ongoing scholarly debates and stimulated the exploration of new avenues of research in fields such as post-colonial and colonial discourse studies. Not that Edward Said's argument was entirely new. The theme of Islam and the West had a series of predecessors in the decades before Said's publication.[1] Rather, the outstanding success of *Orientalism* was due to the particular political, societal and scholarly context in which it appeared. The learned polemic of a "Western scholar with Oriental roots", was written in the new language of so-called post-structuralist criticism and surfed on the political waves of Third-Worldism.

Said based the general argument in *Orientalism* on the analysis of academic and literary texts about the Orient. In this body of literature, he discerned both ontological and epistemological differences that distinguish an unchanging Orient from an absolutely different and dynamic West.[2] Based on this binary code of difference between East and West, according to Said, the European Orientalists produced a hegemonic discourse over the Orient. They not only created an exotic Other, but they also legitimized the colonial oppression of the East by Western powers. Referring to the work of Michel Foucault, Said viewed the birth of the 'Oriental' as the result of a specific nexus of power and knowledge which has characterized the relationship of the East, in particular the Muslim world, with the leading powers of the West. In producing an "imaginative geography", Orientalist scholars have invented and constructed a geographical space that provided the necessary knowledge for "the mapping, conquest, and annexation of territory".[3] In this way, the scholarly and literary representation of the Orient by the texts of Orientalists became an imperial institution, facilitating and justifying colonial domination. In clear distinction to the mere disciplinary content of the terms "Orientalist" and "Orientalism" in the nineteenth century, Said extended their notion enormously. Once the designations for an academic avant-garde, Said's book turned them into pejorative labels for stereotypical Western thinkers and concepts that claim the absolute superiority of the West over the East. In short, in Said's writing, Orientalism became an all-encompassing and ideological concept for the oppression of the Orient by the West.

There is no doubt that contemporary debates about Islam and the West are still informed by some of the stereotypes which *Orientalism* so aptly described. The modern image of Islam has been, until now, dominated by the essentialist assumption according to which Islamic societies rest on a unified and unchangeable codex of religious, juridical, and moral rules, supposedly regulating the life of both the individual Muslim and the Islamic community in all its aspects. Presenting the Muslim religion as a holistically closed system, as a social and cultural unity resisting historical change, this essentialist image of Islam has trickled down into society at large. Even more important, it has become a building block of globally shared public knowledge about Islam in the Western and Muslim worlds alike. This is apparent in the fact that both Western Orientalists and contemporary Islamists conceptualize Islam as an all-encompassing, determinant, and unchanging cultural entity that is intrinsically different from the modern democratic culture of the West.

In a response to *Orientalism*, the Syrian philosopher Sadik al-Azm criticized Edward Said for being blind to this form of "Orientalism in reverse", the apparent self-application of Orientalist stereotypes in the ideologies of both Islamists and Arab nationalists.[4] Indeed, in Said's book, the application of the essentialist image of Islam and of the foundational dichotomy between East and West by Muslim thinkers is almost completely absent. The partisan purpose of his book probably made Said blind to the phenomenon of Orientalism in reverse. Yet in order to understand the relationship between images and realities in the contemporary discourse about Islam and the West, it is important to inquire into the origins of this mutually reinforcing assumption of fundamental cultural difference. Why do Orientalists and Islamists define Islam similarly as an all-encompassing religious, political and social system?

In order to answer this question, I will start with a critique of Edward Said's application of Foucault. I will argue that in taking Foucault seriously, this reciprocal imaging of Islam by Orientalists and Islamists, whose world-views have emerged from the very same "discursive formation" (Foucault), should not have escaped Said's attention. In a second step, I shall analyze the phenomenon of Orientalism in reverse, based on a brief assessment of Sadik al-Azm's arguments. Then, I take the life and work of Ernest Renan (1823–1892) as my point of departure to show in which ways Orientalists and Muslim intellectuals were closely knitted together by a web of discursive and social ties. The chapter concludes with a theoretically inspired interpretation of the common origin of the modern essentialist image of Islam in this network of Orientalists and Islamic reformers in the late nineteenth and early twentieth centuries.

Discourse theory and the "real Orient"

In his introduction to his Reader containing core texts on the *Orientalism* controversy, editor A.L. Macfie indicated that a number of Said's critics, in particular historians of the Middle East, were "firmly wedded to a traditional (realist) approach to the writing of history". Insisting on the mere validity of so-called historical facts, these historians were, according to Macfie, as a result of their methodological positions, not really able to communicate with Said, who approached his subject with the assistance of postmodern philosophy.[5] Indeed, given the various audiences that Said's book addressed, it is not surprising that a good deal of critique was also related to misunderstandings and particularistic readings of *Orientalism*. Yet some of his theoretically more versed critics raised the question of whether Said himself really understood the theoretical approach he claimed to use in *Orientalism*.[6]

This question specifically has been posed concerning Said's application of Michel Foucault's discourse theory.[7] Said claimed to write from a Foucauldian perspective and, on the surface, he seemingly did so in two ways: first, in framing the field of Orientalism as a discursive institution with a holistic and determining character; second, in analyzing the Oriental discourse through the inseparable relationship between structures of social power and structures of knowledge. Contrary to the approach of Foucault, however, Said's method is characterized by a firm subjectivist component. His strong sense of "humanism"[8] clearly contradicts the fundamentals of Foucault's anti-subjectivist and anti-humanist philosophy. For Said, individual writers play an eminent if not determining role in shaping the discursive field of Orientalism, which he analyses "as a dynamic exchange between individual authors and the large political concerns shaped by the three great empires – British, French, American".[9] We will see that this deliberate deviation from Foucault's discourse theory created some confusion on the side of Said's reviewers, but also in the argumentation of the book itself.

Edward Said claimed to borrow his "Foucauldian perspective" from *The Archaeology of Knowledge* and from *Discipline and Punish*.[10] Like *The Order of Things, The Archaeology of Knowledge* belongs to the early works of Michel Foucault, which in my reading are of a structuralist rather than a post-structuralist nature. In these works, discourses have an almost autonomous character. They are not mentally anchored but they exist in historically specific discursive practices which are not the result of intersubjective exchanges but, rather, are the conditions for them.[11] In *The Order of Things*, Foucault developed his discourse theory with respect to changing bodies of knowledge. He was concerned with the phenomenon of three totally different systematizations of knowledge that separate the *epistemé* of modern times from previous epochs. In classical times, according to his analysis, knowledge built on a universal science of measurement and order with regard to the relationship between things, a relationship that classical knowledge methodologically ordered according to the intrinsic categories of identity and difference. The classical *epistemé*, therefore, did not assign a role to the ordering perspective of an observer. Modern knowledge, however, shows a completely different logic. In the patterns of meaning in modernity, the subject enters the field and becomes both observer and observed, that is to say, both the subject and object of knowledge. The modern *epistemé* introduced the ordering subject into a world of objects.[12]

However, it would be absolutely wrong to consider this introduction of the subject into modern knowledge as coming a step closer to "scientific truth".

For Foucault, the appearance of man at the centre of modern epistemology only indicates a radical change in the historically specific but unconsciously applied discursive structures on which human knowledge generally rests. In this sense, the move from classical to modern knowledge should not be misunderstood as a process of scientific progress. Foucault did not interpret the ontological and epistemological priority of the subject in modern knowledge in terms of a progress of reason, but simply as a historical change in forms of *episteme* in modern times. In Foucault's eyes, both subjects and objects of knowledge are only results of discursive practices. Theoretically, individual actors are nothing more than "discursive effects".[13] Consequently, there is no progress in human knowledge and human actors themselves are a product of the unconscious application of historically different, discursive paradigms of knowledge. In *The Order of Things*, Foucault focused on the order of "networks of concepts", whereas *The Archaeology of Knowledge* had the discursive regularities of their formation as its topic.[14]

Against this theoretical background, Edward Said did more than deviate from Foucault. In prioritizing the individual and adding a voluntary component to his approach, he actually undermined the whole theoretical edifice of the French scholar. Aijaz Ahmad clearly pointed to this problem in his critique:

> In the Foucaultian definitions, representations cannot be referred back to any truth outside or beyond themselves, nor to the intentionality of the representer, because the structure of the representation is already inscribed in and always regulated by the power of discourse. Representations correspond thus not to an external object, a truth, a subjectivity, a purpose, a project, but to the discursive regularity alone.[15]

From a Foucauldian perspective, Orientalists cannot deliberately invent an Orient in order to provide the necessary knowledge for "the mapping, conquest, and annexation" of a geographical space. The Orientalist observer and the Oriental observed are discursive effects of the very same fundamental structure. When Said presents Oriental scholarship in terms of the intended actions of rational actors, he definitely cannot base this thesis about the close strategic cooperation of Orientalists and colonizers on Foucault. Rather, Said's approach reflects the tradition of critique of ideologies which goes back to Karl Marx and Ludwig Feuerbach. While it might be possible to view Foucault's critique of the human sciences as an extension of this line of scholarly tradition,[16] the nature of his critique is fundamentally different. Foucault aims not to reveal hidden interests and institutional rationalities, but to understand the deep structures on which the whole edifice of social interests, institutions, and knowledge rests. The archaeological method tries to discover the regularities of discursive practices that give rise to a corpus of knowledge and therewith to the emergence of various but distinct "scientific disciplines".[17] *Orientalism* analytically remains on the level of the analysis of a concrete disciplinary discourse, whereas *The Archaeology of Knowledge* attempts to discover the intrinsic regularities of general discursive practices out of which the different sciences of man emerged.[18]

Said's introduction of voluntarist components into a structuralist body of theory caused further confusion with regard to the question of the "real Orient". In keeping with his Foucauldian approach, Said insists throughout the book that neither the West nor the East have any kind of "ontological stability".[19] At several points in *Orientalism* he emphasizes that he does not want to suggest something like the existence of a "real Orient".[20] This position, however, is often contradicted by Said only a few pages later on. In labeling Orientalism as "distorted knowledge"[21] or in accusing scholars such as Bernard Lewis of "distorting the truth",[22] Said himself implies the existence of something "real" to be distorted. The consequent application of a Foucauldian framework would have excluded this dichotomy of distorted and true realities that, despite Said's defense, nevertheless runs throughout the whole book. Following Foucault, the distorted Orient is real!

Islamist ideologies as a form of "Orientalism in reverse"

Said's tendency to neglect the reciprocity in processes of stereotyping the self and the other[23] by describing the relationship between Orientalists and Orientals merely as a one-way street has raised another set of critical questions which are epitomized in Sadik al-Azm's postulation of an "Orientalism in reverse". It was al-Azm who first argued that Orientals not only perceive Western people through similar stereotypical lenses, but that they also even have firmly incorporated some of the Orientalist stereotypes in their self-image.[24] In the second part of his critique, *Orientalism in Reverse*, Al-Azm applauds the "most prominent and interesting accomplishments of Said's book", the deconstruction of the still-powerful Orientalist pretensions of a principal epistemological and ontological difference between the East and the West. This essentialist image of the Orient (Islam), as I designated it, al-Azm labels as "Ontological Orientalism", as the firm belief in the enduring cultural essence, the fundamental and unchangeable attributes of the Orient or Islam.[25] In light of Said's warning not to apply the readily available stereotypes of Orientalism to themselves, Al-Azm contends that these applications "not only did take place, but are continuing on a fairly wide scale".[26] He discerns these self-applications of Orientalist concepts in both Arab nationalist and Islamist ideologies.

In his analysis of Arab nationalist ideologies, al-Azm finds particularly striking the way in which the "Orientalist obsession with language, texts and philology" made its inroads into the ideological cosmos of Arab nationalism. He accuses Arab nationalists of "obediently and uncritically" adopting the textual attitude of Orientalists to human reality. Employing the fashion of Renan's Semitic studies, based on the "Indo-European Hypothesis",[27] Arab nationalist ideologues discover the 'Arab mind' in the vocal and grammatical structures of the Arabic language. Yet, contrary to Renan's negative verdict on Semitic culture, they do not conclude that the Arab mind is inferior to the thought processes of Indo-European culture. According to al-Azm, the philological and linguistic studies of Arab nationalists try to prove the superiority of Arab civilization over the West.[28] As early as

Muhammad Abduh (1849–1905), a leading figure of the Islamic reform movement in the nineteenth century and a controversial Sheikh at the Egyptian Al-Azhar University who later became Great Mufti of Egypt, referred in his defense of Islam to this reversed form of Renan's thesis,[29] a thesis which had turned into one of the popular truisms of nineteenth-century thinking. A similar form of Ontological Orientalism characterizes Islamist thinking in which not Arab culture, but the religious factor, Islam, becomes the central variable for the factual superiority of Muslim over Western culture. Both Arab nationalists and Islamists work with essentialist images of monolithic, hermetically closed and unique cultures, eternally different and distinct from the West. In Al-Azm's words, they "simply reproduce the whole discredited apparatus of classical Orientalist doctrine concerning the difference between the East and West, Islam and Europe".[30]

There is no doubt that the field of Islamic studies has experienced important changes with regard to objects and methods within recent decades. This is true even for the period before the publication of *Orientalism*. Nevertheless, the essentialist tradition has visibly maintained its strength in Western scholarship. In light of Edward Said's critique, this continuing strand of essentialist scholarship has been branded as "New Orientalism".[31] In taking up questions of democratization and modernization in the Muslim world, the new Orientalists have perpetuated the approach of their predecessors and still perceive Islam as the determining explicative variable for the understanding of Muslim societies. From this perspective, for instance, they almost naturally associate the large absence of democratic rule in Muslim countries with the specific role of the Islamic religion.[32]

In a similar manner, Western scholarship on Islam has maintained a visible tendency to view societal developments in Muslim countries as determined by the normative power of the revealed scriptures of Islam. A perfect example of this bias toward sacred texts is demonstrated in a book by the Swiss professor Johann Christoph Bürgel. He identifies in the concept of God's omnipotence the trans-historical principle which has determined the course of Islamic history until today. In basing his research on the revealing power of scriptural sources, Bürgel discovers in the 'experience' of this divine omnipotence the essence of the Islamic world-view. In his conclusion, based on textual analysis alone, he defines the omnipotence of God as the fundamental collective and individual experience in the lives of Muslims.[33] Consequently, Bürgel asserts that for the analysis of Islamic history, sociological or economic explanations necessarily remain on the surface. He works with a concept of religion seemingly far detached from social practices. In his opinion, only the exegesis of revealed texts is able to disclose the true deep structures on which the history of Islamic civilization has rested.[34]

Turning toward Muslim intellectual traditions, we find strong parallels to the essentialist concepts of Western Orientalism in the broad range of so-called Islamist or neo-fundamentalist ideologies.[35] Since the early twentieth century, the development of Islamist ideologies has been anchored in the same themes of difference to the West and of the intrinsic unity of religion and politics in Islam. Islamists also frame Islam as being more than a mere religion, as representing a holistic civilization based on sacred texts. Moreover, Orientalists and Islamists share the interpretation of Islamic history as a history of decline.[36] With respect to the theme of a confrontation between Islam and the West, Huntington's scenario of a clash between civilizations has found its most audible echo in the ideologies of militant transnational Islamists such as Osama bin Laden.[37]

In his *Letter to the Pakistani Muslims*, bin Laden took up the clash of civilization motif and presented the world as divided between two camps, "one under the banner of the cross, ... and one under the banner of Islam".[38] In radical ideologies of the al-Qaeda type, Islam is under siege and Bernard Lewis' worldwide expansion of the Judeo-Christian heritage[39] is interpreted as a total war against Islam. The chief ideologues of a "global *jihad* for the defense of Islam" underpin their world-view with rather randomly chosen and often de-contextualized quotes from the Qur'an. They like to relate their cause to the classical reformer Ibn Taymiyya (1263–1328) and his struggle against Mongol occupation.[40] While their ideological constructs provide a religiously justified platform for rallying followers behind their militant cause, their propagation of the establishment of a just Islamic society profoundly lacks any kind of elaborate ideas about the institutional setting on which this Islamic order should rest.

More sophisticated versions of the essentialist image of Islam and its religio-political order can be found in the ideologies of political movements which have their origins in the various branches of the Muslim Brotherhood. Their political ideologies share, in principle, the idea of a revealed, trans-historical Islamic system. The political Charter of the Palestinian Hamas, for instance, is inspired by this essentialist conceptualization of Islam. In the tradition of the Muslim Brotherhood, Hamas' political agenda presents a typical fusion of nationalist, societal, and religious aims. In the very first chapter, the Charter exposes a holistic concept of Islam as an all-encompassing program (*manhaj*) for the organization of human life.[41] Hamas anchors the struggle for Palestine historically in the religious narratives about early Islam and the Charter's political strategy is predicated on the supposedly inseparable unity of religion and politics in Islam. Consequently, the Charter leaves no room for territorial concessions in the Israeli-Palestinian conflict, as this would mean compromising Islam itself.[42]

One of the most elaborate forms of Islamist political theory, however, has been developed within the intellectual environment of Shi'ite theology. In his theory of the *vilayet-e faqih*, Ayatollah Khomeini combined the essentialist unity of religion, politics, and social order with some specifically Shi'ite ideas of divinely sanctioned leadership. Like the mainstream of Sunni Islamists, Khomeini views Islam as a comprehensive and all-encompassing way of life, as a systematic order that has to be implemented by an Islamic government. Yet Sunni versions of Islamist political thinking often lack precise ideas about the appropriate institutional forms of political leadership in an Islamic state. Khomeini, in contrast, drew heavily on an elaborate reinterpretation of Shi'ite traditions and the Shi'ite teachings about the role of the Imamate in defining the legitimate leadership of an Islamic state. In *Islam and Revolution*, Khomeini developed an institutional setting for an Islamic government in which he designates the religious jurists (*fuqaha*, sing. *faqih*) to be the true rulers.[43] Some representatives of the conservative Islamist political establishment in Iran closely follow Orientalist stereotypes in their interpretation of the *vilayet-e faqih* and even declare the Iranians as, in principle, ill-suited for democracy.[44]

Against this background of mutually shared and reinforcing stereotypes, Al-Azm accused Edward Said of not grasping the "interactive process of the Orientalist discourse".[45] The fact is that, despite all asymmetric power relations, discursive structures do not function as a one-way street; that is to say they do not simply impose the stereotypes of the more powerful side on the weaker other. Therefore, following David Kopf, Said also misunderstood the nature of Orientalism in South Asia, the "intercivilizational encounter between the European and Asian intelligentsia" manifested in the historical fact that "British Orientalism gave birth to the Bengal Renaissance".[46] In a similar way, the cultural encounter between East and West in the Middle East has never been one of "Oriental silence" and "Western writing" as, for instance, the factually "dialogic relationship" between writers from Iran and Europe shows.[47] Another example is the advocacy of Chinese cultural uniqueness by the People's Republic of China's Communist regime. Chinese intellectuals took part in a discursive practice in which they creatively appropriated and constructed both "Occidentalist" images of the West and "Orientalist" images of China's past.[48, 49] The stereotyping of the Other is apparently not only a general feature of cross-cultural perceptions, but these perceptions are themselves derived from a rather invisible discursive formation on which processes of intercultural exchange rest. It is this intercultural exchange between the Muslim and the Western worlds which is at the heart of our problem: the continuing and mutually reinforcing dominance of a holistic and systemic modern image of Islam. Sadik al-Azm's thesis of an Orientalism in reverse is therefore perfectly suited to complement the rather one-sided analysis of Said.

Without a doubt, if Edward Said had followed Foucault more closely, the various forms of reciprocity in the shaping of stereotypical images would not have escaped his attention. In a purely Foucauldian sense, however, it is not the reciprocity of actors, but the creative power of the invisible structures of a discursive formation that generates a phenomenon like Orientalism in reverse. To stress this theoretically essential point again, in Foucauldian terms: Orientalists and Islamists are discursive effects based on the very same *episteme*. Conditioned by the asymmetric power structures of European imperialism, they both contributed in constructing and spreading the modern essentialist image of Islam. A short excursion into the relationship between Orientalists, departing from Ernest Renan, and some prominent representatives of the Islamic reform movement will show in which ways Orientalists and Muslim intellectuals were inseparable parts of the discursive formation from which the modern essentialist image of Islam evolved.

Ernest Renan, European Orientalism and Islamic reform

In *Orientalism*, Edward Said declared Ernest Renan's *Histoire générale et systéme comparé des langues sémitiques* (1855) to be the chief instance of the Orientalist scientific project. Said assigned Renan a foundational role in the field of Oriental studies, labeling him the systematizer in the Orientalist project [50] who was instrumental in giving the Oriental subject matter its scholarly coherence.[51] This prime role of Renan in Said's argumentation sharply contrasts with the factual role which the French scholar played in the intellectual history of nineteenth-century Europe. Certainly Renan was an Orientalist, but Oriental studies in the more narrow sense are comparatively marginal in his work. Renan was not only known as an Orientalist but also as a historian, a philologist, a philosopher, a novelist, a poet, an autobiographer and a moralist.[52] In writing on religion, history, philosophy, modern life, as well as on social and political questions of France and Europe, Renan was a writing celebrity. His work clearly transcended the field of Oriental studies and Renan was able to win the largest audience among educated Europeans by a living French author in the second part of the nineteenth century.[53]

Typically for his times, Ernest Renan found his way into Orientalism from theology. Aiming at the philological exegesis of the Bible, he became a scholar of Semitic languages, excelling in Hebrew; however, according to his own judgment he remained mediocre in Arabic throughout his life.[54] His scholarly knowledge of Islam predominantly rested on two sources: the reading of second-ary sources and the observations he made in Egypt and the Levant. In particular, he learned from the situation he had experienced during 1860–1861 when he traveled under the protection of French troops in Lebanon and Palestine in the aftermath of the Druze rebellion. Generally speaking, Renan's pejorative picture of Islam was built upon the well-known sample of anti-Muslim stereo-types prevalent in Europe. It was the combination of his general reputation as a scholar of religion, as a prime representative of French nineteenth-century literature, and as an authority on "having been there" rather than any kind of Orientalist erudition which gave him enormous power in spreading an essentialist and anti-modern image of Islam in Europe.

In Renan's well-known lecture *Islamism and Science* (1883), Islam played the world historical role of being the religious counterpart to secular civilization and progress. Stressing the then apparent political inferiority of Muslim coun-tries, Renan began his lecture with a cascade of denigrating statements about Islam. In his opinion, Muslims have "the most profound disdain for instruction, for science, for everything that constitutes the European spirit". Islam as a reli-gion turns the believer into a "fanatic", into a believer foolishly proud of holding the absolute truth and completely incapable of acquiring new knowledge. The conversion to Islam eradicates all differences among people, producing this "intellectual nullity" and "decadence", observable in the countries governed by Islam.[55] The whole lecture is an attempt to prove the incompatibility of Islam with the modern world and to show his audience that the former flourishing of science and philosophy under Muslim rule was not due to the Islamic religion but was an achievement of other forces against it.[56] In addressing a French audience in 1883, which was predominantly concerned with the political struggle of the Third Republic, Renan turned Islam into a synonym for orthodox religion and supernatural beliefs in general: "Western theology has not persecuted less than that of Islamism; only it has not been successful, it has not crushed out the modern spirit, as Islamism has trodden out the spirit of the lands it has conquered."[57]

Putting it into historical context, we easily can translate the title of Renan's lecture *Islamism and Science* into "Religion and Science", taking Islam as the foil on which to discuss the harm that orthodox religion can do to science and human progress. To be sure, given Renan's socialization in the Catholic milieu of Brittany, as well as his apologist mission of reconciling positivist science with a kind of "secularized" and sensualist Christianity, he certainly was at ease in choosing Islam as his prime target. Nevertheless, his lecture must also been understood as a vocal petition for curtailing further the worldly and ecclesiastical powers of the papacy in Rome, for a strict separation of state and church and for the promotion and implementation of national, secular state education which finally took place in France under the Ferry Laws in 1905.

The reputation of French scholarship, Renan's prominent role among European intellectuals and his topical themes might explain the resonance which his work also found in the Muslim world. Like their European counterparts, Muslim intellectuals tried to comprehend the modern transformation in discussing the role of religion in the structural context of emerging societal subsystems such as law, state, science and education. The Islamic reform movement was not separated from European discourses. On the contrary, Muslim reformers articulated their concerns based on the same modern *episteme* as European intellectuals did, yet combining the very same general themes relating to the role of religion in the modern world with their historically specific experiences, narratives and traditions. Consequently, they engaged in both social and discursive interaction with Orientalists such as Ernest Renan, shaping together with them the modern images of Islam.

Ernest Renan's lecture on Islam and Science, for instance, triggered immediate responses from the Pan-Islamist Jamal al-Din al-Afghani (1838–1897) and the Ottoman intellectual Namik Kemal (1840–1888). Both defended Islam against Renan's accusations, however, in different ways. While Afghani conceded a certain incompatibility between traditional religion and modern science, Namik Kemal completely refuted Renan's denigrating picture of Islam from an apologetic perspective.[58] The relationship between modern science and religion was also a central issue discussed by other Muslim intellectuals. As in Europe, we can observe in these discussions a variety of opinions between the opposite poles of positivist and apologetic argumentations. In particular among leading bureaucrats and intellectuals of the Ottoman Empire, positivist attitudes became enormously attractive and traditional Islam was perceived as "a major obstacle to social progress".[59] Similar to Renan, they firmly based their world-view on the idealization of modern science. They expressed strong anti-clerical tendencies and aimed at a separation of political and religious institutions. Abdullah Cevdet (1869–1932), a graduate of the Ottoman Royal Medical Academy and a leading intellectual behind the Young Turk Movement, even translated an essay of Reinhard Dozy (1820–1883) in which the Dutch Orientalist associated the Islamic revelation with Muhammed's alleged mental disease.[60] Yet this radical stance against traditional religion did not necessarily lead to a total rejection of Islam. Another Young Turk leader, Ahmet Riza (1859–1930), for instance, combined his anticlericalism with an idea of "pure Islam" which would be compatible with the modern scientific world-view and could serve as a moral means for cohesion in modern social life.[61]

From the very different position of the Arab Muslim apologist Muhammad Abduh, came ideas of the unity of Islam, science and modern education. Abduh combined his erudition in Islamic sciences with the reading of European authors such as Comte, Guizot, Spencer, Renan, Rousseau and Tolstoy. He was convinced that a rational interpretation of Islamic tradition would open the way for the integration of the economic, political and scientific achievements of Europe in a Muslim context. For Abduh, modern science and faith were not opposite but mutually reinforcing sources of knowledge. In his intellectual history of the nineteenth-century Middle East, Albert Hourani tells us about Muhammad Abduh's strong interest in the work of European intellectuals and his contacts with them. Moreover, Abduh examined the critical approaches of Christian theology,[62] and the personal library of this Azhar Sheikh included several books by Ernest Renan as well as a copy of David Friedrich Strauss' *Life of Jesus*.[63] In his lectures at the Azhar, Abduh reconstructed Islam as a civilization with reference to François Guizot's (1787–1884) apologetic *History of Civilization in Europe*, apparently attracted by the historical philosophy of this French historian and statesman. Guizot, who belonged to France's Protestant minority, played an important role in fighting French positivism, together with the Bishop of Orleans who once facilitated Renan's theological studies with a scholarship.[64]

As for the Muslim reform movement of South Asia, Muhammad Iqbal is an excellent example of the discursive and social integration of Muslim intellectuals into what I would call an emerging global public sphere. In his modern revitalization of Islam, Iqbal was not only "deeply influenced" by the work of Nietzsche,[65] but he also studied at Cambridge and submitted his PhD on Persian metaphysics to the philosophical faculty of the Ludwig Maximilian University in Munich. Deeply inspired by Goethe and Rumi, Iqbal represents the fusion of European and Muslim thinking. In social and intellectual terms, he was very close to his teacher Thomas Arnold, whom he met at the Government College in Lahore. Arnold himself was a scholar of modern Islam and received his training in Oriental Studies from William Robertson Smith at Cambridge.[66] Before moving to Lahore, he was a professor among the first generation of scholars who taught at the Muhammadan Anglo-Oriental College of Aligarh (Aligarh Muslim University) which was founded by the famous Indian Muslim reformer Sayyid Ahmad Khan in 1875.[67] Studying philosophy, English literature and Arabic, Iqbal was encouraged by Arnold to come to Europe and to engage more deeply with Western literature and philosophy.

These examples may suffice to indicate that European Orientalists and Muslim intellectuals developed their ideas within a discursive setting which hardly can be reduced to the idea of colonial imposition. In addition to the fusion of discursive intellectual milieus, there existed numerous direct social ties between leading representatives from both camps and the knowledge of European Orientalists was requested by some new Muslim institutions of higher education. One of the founding fathers of modern Islamic studies, for example, the Hungarian Ignaz Goldziher (1850–1921) called Jamal al-Din al-Afghani his friend. Goldziher first met him on his trip to Egypt in 1873–1874. In Cairo, he joined Afghani and his group of Egyptian students, discussing for a couple of months political and religious matters related to Islam. Later Goldziher visited both Renan and Afghani in Paris.[68] Although he never traveled in the Middle East, Goldziher's teacher in Arabic philology, Heinrich Leberecht Fleischer (1801–1888), conducted a regular exchange of letters with Butrus Bustani (1819–1883) and other Arab reformists in Beirut.[69] In his *Oriental Diary*, Ignaz Goldziher mentioned the almost "religious" reverence with which the Christian-Arab scholars around Bustani referred to the German Arabist.[70] After the foundation of Cairo University in 1908, both Goldziher and his Dutch friend and colleague Christiaan Snouck Hurgronje (1857–1936) were invited to take up academic chairs in Cairo.[71] A final example is the German Orientalist and later Prussian minister of education, Carl-Heinrich Becker, who personally met Muhammad Abduh in 1901 and turned down the offer of a chair in Arabic at Aligarh in 1906.[72] The modern images of Islam emerged in close discursive and social exchanges between the East and the West, rather than in the isolated colonial mindset of Western scholarship. They were a product of an emerging global public sphere where Muslims and non-Muslims shaped Islam as a modern religion. To be sure, this public sphere was permeated by asymmetric power relations and a far cry from the ideal role the public sphere plays in liberal political theories such as developed by Jürgen Habermas.[73] Yet, following Edward Said's thesis too closely not only compromises Foucault's theory, but also deprives Muslim intellectuals of their role in shaping the modern images of Islam. The phenomenon of Orientalism in reverse is the result of a still ongoing process of negotiating Islam as a modern religion among a variety of global actors.

Conclusion: from Islamic reform to Islamist revolution

In spite of all waves of often harsh and substantial criticism, *Orientalism* undoubtedly has its lasting merits. With its huge popularity Said's book set a new agenda for studying phenomena such as representation, identity construction, the emergence of bodies of knowledge, and the relationship between knowledge and power. His particular reading of "the Orient" engendered the emergence of a vast field of critical studies in domains such as literature, theatre, music, architecture, science, politics, journalism, and travel accounts.[74] Said popularized the understanding of academic knowledge as developing within a context of social power and he showed the paths of its dissemination in society at large.

Looking at Orientalist stereotypes in the world-view of poets, novelists, politicians and journalists, Said emphasized the traffic of ideas between academic and common-sense knowledge. This perspective is crucial not only with regard to the trivialization and spread of Orientalist knowledge in the West, but also in particular to the appropriation and simplification of Orientalist concepts and ideas by Islamist ideologues. This becomes apparent from a theoretical perspective which can be derived from a more precise reading of Foucault.

Against the background of the above arguments, I would conclude that the essentialist image of Islam as an all-encompassing social system has to be understood within the theoretical framework of an emerging global modernity.[75] The origins of this image can be traced back to both the emergence of the academic discipline of Islamic studies in the late nineteenth century and the parallel rise of Islamic modernism, representing an amalgam of various teachings of Islamic reform, of the encounter with indigenous and colonial faces of modernization, as well as of the intellectual debates about scholarly and literary interpretations of Islamic culture by the West. This amalgam of ideas became a fundament of modern knowledge about Islam, based on the reinterpretation of Islamic tradition through the modern lenses of so-called Western cognitive and political concepts such as state, law, secularism, religion, culture, authenticity, and so forth. In emphasizing the transcendence and unity of God, the search for authenticity in a "golden age", and the focus on normative elements of Islam, reformers such as Afghani and Abduh re-interpreted pre-modern ways of Islamic thinking which John Voll summarized as the fundamentalist traditions in Islam.[76] In doing so, they underpinned the Islam contained in the interpretations of Western Orientalists who also stressed dogmatic and legal dimensions of Islam at the expense of other traditions such as mysticism or heterodox forms of religious belief and practices.[77]

In this way, Orientalists and Islamic reformers re-constructed Islamic traditions as a modern religion in a very selective way. Their way of imaging Islam, then, has been further developed and transformed by Islamist movements in the twentieth century. In particular the ideologies of religio-social movements such as the Muslim Brotherhood founded by Hasan al-Banna (1909–1949) or the South-Asian Jamaat-i Islami of Abu Ala Mawdudi (1903–1979) were key forces in transforming the intellectual heritage of Orientalists and Islamic reformers into the essentialist concepts which even today dominate the modern image of Islam. This gradual transformation from ideas of Islamic reform to ideologies of Islamist revolution took place within a social field whose major coordinates were the structures of international and national power politics, the processes of decolonization and regional state formation, and the changing character of a global public sphere whose modern infrastructure facilitated the gradual popularization, trivialization, and dissemination of a previously rather elitist discourse on Islam and the West.

Notes

1 Prime among them are: Norman Daniel, *Islam and the West: The Making of an Image*, Edinburgh: Edinburgh University Press, 1960; R. N. Frye (ed.) *Islam and the West*,

The Hague: Mouton and Co., 1957; Philip K. Hitti, *Islam and the West: A Historical Cultural Survey*, Princeton, NJ: Van Nostrand, 1962; Maxime Rodison, "The Western Image and Western Studies of Islam", in Joseph Schacht and C. E. Bosworth (eds), *The Legacy of Islam*, Oxford: Oxford University Press, 1974; Raymond Schwab, *La Renaissance Orientale*, Paris: Payot, 1950; R. W. Southern, *Western Views of Islam in the Middle Ages*, Cambridge, MA: Harvard University Press, 1962; A. L. Tibawi, "English-Speaking Orientalists: A Critique of Their Approach to Islam and Arab Nationalism", *The Muslim World*, 53(3) (1963): 185–204; and Montgomery W. Watt, *The Influence of Islam on Medieval Europe*, Edinburgh: Edinburgh University Press, 1972.

2 Edward W. Said, *Orientalism*, New York: Vintage, 1978, p. 96.
3 Edward W. Said, "Invention, Memory, and Place", *Critical Inquiry*, 26(Winter) (2000): 181.
4 Sadik Jalal Al-Azm, "Orientalism and Orientalism in Reverse", *Khamsin* 8 (1981), reprinted in A. L. Macfie (ed.) *Orientalism: A Reader*, Edinburgh: Edinburgh University Press, 2000.
5 A. L. Macfie (ed.) "Introduction", in Macfie (ed.), op. cit.
6 Cf. Aijaz Ahmad, "Between Orientalism and Historicism", 1991, reprinted in A. L. Macfie (ed.), op. cit.; Homi Bhaba, "The Other Question" (1983), in Padmini Mongia (ed.) *Contemporary Postcolonial Theory: A Reader*, London and New York: Arnold, 1997; Robert Irwin, *For Lust of Knowing: The Orientalists and their Enemies*, London: Penguin Books, 2006; Jürgen Osterhammel, "Edward W. Said und die 'Orientalismus'-Debatte: Ein Rückblick", *Asien, Afrika, Lateinamerika*, 25 (1997): 597–607; Michael Richardson, "Enough Said: Reflections on Orientalism", *Anthropology Today*, 6(4), 1990.
7 Said applies a broad and multiple usage of the concept. Therewith, he follows the "widespread consensus" of relating the origin of this broad usage of discourse to Foucault's work. However, Keith Sawyer shows convincingly that this usage of discourse theory does actually not originate with Foucault and largely contradicts the theoretical quality of Foucault's "more limited technical usage" of discourse. (Keith R. Sawyer, "A Discourse on Discourse: An Archeological History of an Intellectual Concept", *Cultural Studies* 16(3), 2002: 435).
8 Cf. Edward W. Said, *Humanism and Democratic Criticism*, London and New York: Palgrave Macmillan, 2004.
9 Said 1978, op. cit., p. 14.
10 Ibid., p. 3.
11 Although Foucault dissociated himself strongly from a structuralist approach, especially in the conclusions of *The Archaeology of Knowledge*, where he also remarked on not having used the word "structure" a single time in his previous *The Order of Things* (Michael Foucault, *Archaeology of Knowledge*, London and New York: Routledge, 1989, p. 221), his "archaeological method" and concepts such as discursive formations, positivities, and episteme are, in my opinion, of a structuralist nature. In my interpretation, Foucault is not distancing himself from a structural approach, but rather from the French schools of structuralist analysis in the tradition of Saussure and Lévi-Strauss, with their trans-historical and mentalist pretension. Foucault locates meaning not in universal mental structures, but in historically specific codes observable in texts.
12 Michael Foucault, *The Order of Things*, London and New York: Routledge, 1994.
13 Andreas Reckwitz, *Die Transformation der Kulturtheorien. Zur Entwicklung eines Theorieprogramms*, Weilerswist: Velbrück Wissenschaft, 2000, p. 282.
14 Foucault 1989, op. cit., p. 72.
15 Ahmad, op. cit., p. 292.
16 Urs Marti, *Michel Foucault*, München: C.H Beck, 1988, p. 36.
17 Foucault 1989, op. cit., p. 210.

18 Ibid., p. 69.
19 Said 1978, op. cit., p. xvii.
20 Even in his last book, published post mortem, Edward Said reiterated:

> My critique was premised on the flawed nature of all representations and how
> they are intimately tied up with worldliness, that is, with power, position, and
> interests. This required saying explicitly that my work was not intended as a
> defense of the real Orient or that it even made the case that a real Orient
> existed.
>
> (Said, 2004, p. 48)

21 Ibid., p. xxii.
22 Edward W. Said, "Afterword", in *Orientalism*, New York: Vintage, 1994, p. 331.
23 Cf. Richardson, op. cit.
24 See Fred Halliday, "Orientalism and Its Critics", *British Journal of Middle Eastern
    Studies*, 20(2), 1993: 145–163; Emmanuel Sivan, *Interpretations of Islam: Past and
    Present*, Princeton, NJ: The Darwin Press, 1985, and Nevzat Soguk, "Reflection on the
    'Orientalized Orientals'", *Alternatives* 18 (1993): 363–364.
25 Al-Azm, op. cit., p. 230.
26 Ibid., p. 231.
27 This hypothesis bestowed the polytheistic culture of Indo-Europeans with a progress-
    ing character, whereas declaring the monotheistic Semites as immobile in time and
    space, hardly being able to contribute to universal historical progress. Maurice
    Olender, *The Languages of Paradise: Race, Religion, and Philology in the Nineteenth
    Century*, Cambridge, MA: Harvard University Press, 1992, p. 12.
28 Ibid., pp. 231–233.
29 Yvonne Haddad, "Muhammad Abduh: Pioneer of Islamic Reform", in Ali Rahnena
    (ed.) *Pioneers of Islamic Revival*, new edn, London: Zed Books, 2005.
30 Al Azm, op. cit., p. 234. Despite the example of Ayatollah Khomeini, Al-Azm does
    not refer to typically Islamist thinkers, but to what he calls representatives of an
    "Islamanic trend". The most prominent figures of this trend, according to his analysis,
    come from the ranks of the former Arab left and he quotes, for example, the Lebanese
    writer Adonis.
31 Yahya Sadowski, "The New Orientalism and the Democracy Debate", *Middle East
    Report*, 183 (1993): 14–21.
32 For an example of this debate about the relationship between Arab or Muslim culture
    and democratic rule in the post-September 11 era, see the debate in *Journal of
    Democracy*, 15(4), October 2004.
33 Johann Christoph Bürgel, *Allmacht und Mächtigkeit. Religion und Welt des Islam*,
    München: C.H. Beck, 1991, p. 43.
34 Ibid., p. 361.
35 I normally use the term "Islamist" instead of the also frequently used term "fundamen-
    talist", which serves much more comparative purposes and does not necessarily refer
    to the politicization of religion in the way "Islamist" does.
36 Akbar S. Ahmed, *Discovering Islam: Making Sense of Muslim History and Society*,
    revised edn (first edn 1988), London: Routledge, 2002, p. 30.
37 In fact, Huntington took up this theme from Bernard Lewis who had, already in the
    1960s, referred to a clash between civilizations in Arab-Western relations. Cf. Jeremy
    Salt, *The Unmaking of the Middle East: A History of Western Disorder in Arab Lands*,
    Berkeley, CA: University of California Press, 2008, pp. 18–19.
38 Osama bin Laden, *Letter to the Pakistani Muslims*, 2001. Available at: www.news.
    bbc.co.uk/2/hi/world/monitoring/media_reports/1633204.stm, accessed 13 September
    2006.
39 Bernard Lewis, "The Roots of Muslim Rage", *The Atlantic Monthly*, 266(3), 1990: 60.

40 Cf. *Global Jihad*, "In the words of Osama Bin Laden", ed. Ayman Al Zawahiri abd Musab Al Zarqawi, Philadelphia, PA: Pavilion Press, 2006.

41 Abdallah Azzam, *Hamas: al-judur at-tarikhiya wa al-mithaq* [Hamas: The Historical Roots and the Manifesto], Amman, 1990, p. 119.

42 Ibid., p. 129. It goes without saying that this non-compromising ideology does not necessarily reflect factual policies. Also Hamas has in rhetoric and in action shown a propensity to come to pragmatic solutions if they serve the organization's interests. As an ideological framework, the Charter of Hamas is in principle as open to negotiation and revision as the National Charter of the Palestinian Liberation Organization (PLO) has been. Regarding this complex dynamics of Palestinian politics, see Dietrich Jung, "Global Conditions and Global Constraints: The International Paternity of the Palestine Conflict", in Dietrich Jung (ed.) *The Middle East and Palestine: Global Politics and Regional Conflict*, New York: Palgrave, 2004.

43 A. R. Khomeini, *Islam and Revolution: Writings and Declarations of Imam Khomeini*, trans. Hamid Algar, Berkeley, CA: Mizan Press, 1981, p. 60.

44 Ali M. Ansari, *Iran under Ahmadinejad: The Politics of Confrontation*, Adelphi Paper No. 393, London: IISS, 2007, p. 24.

45 Lata Mani and Ruth Frankenberg, "The Challenge of Orientalism", *Economy and Society*, 14(2) (1985): 177. If *Orientalism* is read carefully, this accusation is not entirely just. There are a few pages in *Orientalism* where Said implies the self-reception of the Orientalist stereotypes by the Orientals. He mentions that "the Orientalist notions influenced the people who were called Orientals as well as those called Occidental" and that Orientalism exerted its force "on the Orient, on the Orientalist, and on the Western 'consumer' of Orientalism". Moreover, Said seemed to be aware of the fact that Arab authors also took up stereotypical discourses about Islam and the "Arab mind". However, this awareness remained at the margins of his argumentation and he never elaborated further on the aspect of the Oriental adoption of Orientalist stereotypes. Said, 1978, op. cit., pp. 42, 67, 322.

46 David Kopf, "Hermeneutics versus History," *Journal of Asian Studies*, 39(3) (1980): 501–502.

47 Targhi Mohamad Tavakoli, "Orientalism's Genesis Amnesia", *Comparative Studies of South Asia, Africa and the Middle East*, 16(1) (1996): 1–14.

48 Xiaomei Chen, *Occidentalism: A Theory of Counter-Discourse in Post-Mao China*, Oxford: Oxford University Press, 1995, p. 5.

49 For the phenomenon of "Occidentalism", see Ian Buruma and Avishai Margalit, *Occidentalism*, London: Atlantic Books, 2004, and James G. Carrier (ed.) *Occidentalism: Images of the West*, Oxford: Clarendon Press, 1995.

50 Said, 1978, op. cit., p. 130.

51 Ibid., p. 140.

52 Henri Peyre, *Renan*, Paris: Presses Universitaires de France, 1969, p. 22, and David C.J. Lee, *Ernest Renan: In the Shadow of Faith*, London: Duckworth, 1996, p. 19.

53 J.M. Robertson, *Ernest Renan*, London: Watts & Co., 1924, pp. 1 and 29.

54 Ernest Renan, *Souvenirs d'enfance et de jeunesse*, Paris: Nelson and Calmann-Lévy, 1936, p. 210.

55 Ernest Renan, "Islamism and Science – 1883", in *Poetry of the Celtic Races, and Other Essays by Ernest Renan*, London and New York: The Walter Scott Publishing Co (no printing date), p. 85.

56 Ibid., p. 98.

57 Ibid.

58 Nikki R. Keddie, *An Islamic Response to Imperialism: Political and Religious Writings of Sayyid Jamal ad-Din al-Afghani*, Berkeley, CA: University of California Press, 1983, and Namik Kemal, *Renan Müdafaanamesi (Islamiyet ve Maarif)*, Ankara: Milli Kültür Yayinlari, 1962.

59 Sükrü Hanioglu, *The Young Turks in Opposition*, Oxford: Oxford University Press, 1995, p. 28.

60 Ibid., p. 50.

61 Jan-Erik Zürcher, "Ottoman Sources of Kemalist Thought", in Elisabeth Özdalga (ed.) *Late Ottoman Society: The Intellectual Legacy*, London and New York: Routledge, 2005, p. 17. The resurrection of Islam by Ottoman positivists is very reminiscent of the French resurrection of Christianity as a religion of humanity as it appears in the works of Renan and Durkheim. Durkheim's sociology of religion made also a strong impact on Ziya Gökalp, one of the leading Turkish nationalists who tried to synthesize Turkism with Islam. Ibid., pp. 200, 204, 233.

62 Albert Hourani, *Arabic Thought in the Liberal Age, 1798–1939*, reissued with a new preface, 1983, Cambridge: Cambridge University Press, 1962, p. 135.

63 In 1835/36, David Friedrich Strauss published the "scandalous" *Das Leben Jesu* [The Life of Jesus], a book in which he applied the critical method to the New Testament and presented Jesus Christ as nothing more than a human being. This publication made Strauss the best-known German theologian in Europe and he triggered a Europe-wide life-of-Jesus-debate that lasted until the 1870s.

64 Robertson, op. cit., p. 5.

65 Annemarie Schimmel, "Muhammad Iqbal 1873–1938: The Ascension of the Poet", *Die Welt des Islams*, III(2) (1954): 153.

66 Katherine Watt, "Thomas Walker Arnold and the Re-Evaluation of Islam, 1864–1930", *Modern Asian Studies*, 36(1) (2002): 7–8.

67 Cf. David Lelyveld, *Aligarh's First Generation: Muslim Solidarity in British India*, New Delhi: Oxford University Press, 1996.

68 Ignaz Goldziher, "Heinrich Leberecht Fleischer", in *Allgemeine Deutsche Biographie*, vol. 9 (1904), p. 108.

69 Ibid., p. 198. Butrus al-Bustani (1819–1893) was a leading figure in the Christian Arab Awakening throughout the nineteenth century (cf. Hisham Sharabi, *Arab Intellectuals and the West: The Formative Years, 1875–1914*, Baltimore, MD: Johns Hopkins University Press, 1970, Chapter IV). Fleischer was a student of de Sacy in Paris and established at Leipzig University a philological school of Arabism that became a centre for Semitic studies in the nineteenth century which attracted students from all over the world.

70 Raphael Patai, *Ignaz Goldziher and His Oriental Diary: A Translation and Psychological Portrait*, Detroit: Wayne University Press, 1987, p. 109.

71 Donald Malcolm Reid, *Cairo University and the Making of Modern Egypt*, Cambridge: Cambridge University Press, 1990.

72 Guido Müller, *Weltpolitische Bildung und akademische Reform. Carl Heinrich Beckers Wissenschafts- und Hochschulpolitik, 1908–1930*, Cologne: Böhlau Verlag, 1991.

73 Jürgen Habermas, *Strukturwandel der Öffentlichkeit*, [1962], 1990, Frankfurt a.M.: Suhrkamp.

74 Cf. Thomas Scheffler, "Exotismus und Orientalismus", *KulturRevolution*, 32/33 (1995).

75 For an elaboration of this theoretical framework, see Dietrich Jung, "The Political Sociology of World Society", *European Journal of International Relations*, 7(4) (2001): 443–474.

76 John Voll, "The Sudanese Mahdi: Frontier Fundamentalist", *International Journal of Middle East Studies*, 10 (1979): 145–166.

77 Cf. Joseph E. B. Lumbard (ed.) *Islam, Fundamentalism, and the Betrayal of Tradition: Essays by Western Muslim Scholars*, Bloomington, IN: World Wisdom, 2004.

2   Demonizing the enemy in the War on Terror

Shadia Drury

The conflict between the United States and its Muslim enemies is a confrontation between two equally chauvinistic cultures cut from the same cloth; each believes itself to be on the side of God, while its enemies are the incarnation of evil. The infusion of these theological assumptions into politics does not augur well for the world. In this chapter, I will argue that these religious ideas lead to the demonization of the enemy, which in turn makes war more vicious, intractable, and oblivious to all prudential considerations. I will also give reasons for why the administration of Barack Obama must take the lead in abandoning the 'War on Terror' begun by his predecessor.

The infantilism of the War on Terror

There is something infantile about the War on Terror. Why is it necessary to coin a new term for what is politics as usual? After all, the 'War on Terror' is nothing other than the use of terror on a large scale (American) to fight terror on a smaller scale (that which is initiated by al-Qaeda, for example). Seen from the perspective of political realists from Saint Augustine to Thomas Hobbes, Carl Schmitt, Hans Morgenthau, and Henry Kissinger, big thugs are necessary to keep the plurality of little thugs in check.[1] So, what is called the 'War on Terror' is just politics as usual.

St Augustine tells the story of a pirate who was brought before Alexander the Great to be punished. Alexander asked the pirate, "What do you think you are doing?" The pirate responded:

> I am doing exactly what you are doing. Just because you do it with a great fleet and I do it with a little ship, they call you emperor and bow down before you. As for me, I am condemned and reviled as a criminal and the worst of the worst. In truth, the difference between us is a question of magnitude; you are a bandit on a grand scale!

Augustine was very impressed by the pirate; after all, "What are kingdoms but great robberies?" he added.[2] For political realists, the pirate speaks the truth about politics. However, what he does not understand is that little thugs like him must nevertheless be punished. Political order and stability require that the big thugs keep the plethora of little thugs in check. Human beings are, on the whole, better off when big thugs are in control. From the realist point of view, the war on terror is simply politics as usual.

Even though I am inclined to endorse the political realist perspective, I do think it is in need of some modification. The world is not that simple. Justice remains an important factor in the human equation. Despite the fact that people are inclined to tolerate a great deal of injustice, there comes a breaking point. As such, big thugs must beware that they do not overstep those hazy and intangible boundaries. As the sole superpower, the United States under the administration of George W. Bush overstepped these boundaries. It not only riled the downtrodden and disenfranchised with its aggressive wars, but also with its bombastic rhetoric. In my view, the real source of that imprudent rhetoric is not the legendary incompetence of the Bush administration, but its repudiation of political realism. The only political realist in that administration was Colin Powell, who was sidelined, isolated, and forced to resign.

In coining the term 'War on Terror', the Bush administration abandoned political realism in favor of a new holy war where American terror represents the divine wrath against evil. Thus understood, the 'War on Terror' is a just war against the malevolence of the enemy. The same biblical rhetoric is used by America's Islamic enemies. In this way, the dualistic and Manichean aspects of biblical religion are reintroduced into politics. We are confronted with a clash between two enemies who believe that they are custodians of the one and only truth – divine, singular, unassailable, eternal, and unchanging. In a struggle with pure evil, there can be no compromise, no negotiation, and no mutual co-existence. The result is the eclipse of politics understood as plurality, diplomacy, and compromise. Instead of the language of politics, the administration adopted the rhetoric of God.

There is a sense in which the biblical God provides the model for American self-understanding. He poses as a universal god, supreme among all others – a god for all humanity. In truth, he turns out to be a parochial and tribal god. He leads the Israelites out of Egypt and to the Promised Land that is supposed to be flowing with milk and honey. After trudging through the desert for 40 years, the Israelites finally arrive to find, much to their surprise, that the Promised Land is heavily populated. They would have been happy to live on the other side of the river, but God orders them to cross the river and kill every man, woman, child, ox, and every other living thing. Being decent and reasonable men, the Israelites were reluctant to follow these orders. Besides, the Canaanites (those whom they were ordered to slaughter) seemed rather large and formidable. However, the Israelites had the sort of god that refuses to take no for an answer; they knew that his wrath was sure to descend upon those who disobey him for generations to come. Naturally, they were afraid; but God told them not to worry; he would ensure their success. True to his word, he threw huge boulders from the sky, and more of the Canaanites died of his boulders than died from the swords of the Israelites.[3]

Far from being the god of all humanity, the biblical God turns out to be a small and tribal god – the god of the Israelites. He confuses the tribal with the universal, insists on his global dominance, and declares those opposed to his projects to be evil and deserving of death. The same errors have been replicated by the rhetoric of the War on Terror – confusing the tribal with the universal, insisting on global dominance, imagining that this unrivaled supremacy will benefit the world, and defining all opposition as evil to be destroyed.

After the collapse of the Soviet Union, the United States became so intoxicated with power that it mirrored the narcissism of the biblical god. The infamous think-tank 'Project for the New American Century' (or PNAC), provides a chilling vision of the dream of American global dominance. It defines all states opposed to America's global supremacy as 'rogue states' destined for 'regime change' by military means, i.e., destined for destruction.

Those who coined the term 'War on Terror' intended it to be a war against evil–defined as all those who oppose American global supremacy. Books by authors such as David Frum and Richard Perle, *An End to Evil: How to Win the War on Terror*[4] allowed the administration of George W. Bush to imagine that it was possible to live in a world without enemies – enemies that could present obstacles to the realization of the mad dream of 'full spectrum dominance'. Some of the neo-conservatives were certain that there is nothing to fear from American global hegemony, because America is a "Behemoth with a conscience".[5] Like the biblical God, they confused their tribal ambitions with the good of humanity. This way of thinking allowed them to see their enemies as demons to be destroyed, and not as competitors worthy of respect. Since they alone are good, their enemies must be evil. They imagined that the world would be better off as a result of American domination. This allowed them to endorse a double standard for America and the world. For example, America should have a huge nuclear arsenal, but should not allow anyone who is hostile to its plans to have any weapons of mass destruction of any sort. Anyone who thwarts (or shows any sign of wishing to thwart) America's plans for the world, must pay the ultimate price.

The current economic crisis may hamper America's ability to launch new aggressive wars. However, it will not dampen the narcissism of the American psyche. America has always had a grandiose image of itself as the 'city on the hill', the New Jerusalem, the Zion that will light up the world. Americans have always believed that they have a divine calling, and a manifest destiny to be servants of truth and justice—a beacon of freedom for the world.

This sort of narcissism fuels brutality – not only American brutality, but also the brutality of its enemies. A superpower upholding a single ideal, a single way of life, no matter how appealing, is bound to be hated and resisted, even by those it has liberated from despotism. As Hannah Arendt has rightly pointed out, a conception of politics devoid of all plurality is the hallmark of totalitarianism. No matter how just or free, a totalitarian global culture is bound to incite rage because it spells the end of all diversity. It insists that only one flower can bloom – an idea that triggers a stupefying impotence. Totalitarianism breeds a nihilistic melancholy, which manifests itself in senseless violence, anarchy, and terrorism. Totalitarianism and terror are twins – like God and Satan.

In short, the 'War on Terror' bears all of the hallmarks of political infantilism, which is to confuse tribal ambitions with universal human happiness and prosperity. It is to define our plans and ambitions as good, and those who thwart them or refuse to endorse them as evil; to believe that it is possible to live in a world without 'evil' defined as those who would resist our policies, especially when these policies involve the subordination of all.

Gratuitous evil

At the heart of the rhetoric of the 'War on Terror' is the biblical conception of evil as completely gratuitous, purposeless, irrational, incomprehensible, and inscrutable. In the Bible, political enemies are portrayed as Satan was portrayed—he hated God, not because he was an overbearing autocrat, but because he was good, wise, merciful, and just.[6] Like Satan, America's enemies supposedly hate America not because of anything it has done, not because of its policies in the Middle East, not because its multinational corporations get wealthy on the backs of the poor of the world, not because its economy depends on producing and exporting weapons of mass destruction, not because it intends to dominate the globe, not because it launches aggressive wars, and not because it is the biggest exporter of pornography. They hate America because it is good and noble. They hate it because, being evil, they hate everything that is good—they hate freedom, democracy, prosperity, truth, and justice. They will have none of it. Like Satan, the wickedness of America's enemies is unfathomable.

After the attacks of September 11, 2001, the American inclination to demonize their Muslim enemy became more radical. Secretary of Defense, Donald Rumsfeld proclaimed that America's enemies were "the worst of the worst". They were terrorists, thugs, criminals, and dead-enders, with no legitimate claims, no hopes, dreams, or aspirations – only a vision of darkness. Torture, extraordinary rendition, and indefinite detention are appropriate for them, even if they are only 'suspected' terrorists. With such creatures, there can be no holds barred. A special facility was created in Guantanamo Bay (Cuba) to house America's prisoners of war along with any 'suspected' enemies. The Bush administration refused to grant them the courtesy of being treated according to the rules of war ratified by the Geneva Conventions. They refused to grant them the status of soldiers; instead they were dubbed 'unlawful combatants'. The implication here is that no one can legitimately fight against American aggression; to take up arms against America is to be so evil as to be unworthy of the basic rules of war.

In light of this, it is useless to ask "Why do they hate us?" It is equally useless to ask "Have we done anything to rile them?" These are irrelevant questions because the wickedness of the enemy has absolutely nothing to do with anything that America has done. Preeminent scholars such as Bernard Lewis convinced the administration of George W. Bush that the attacks of September 11th were the result of the failure of the Muslim world to deal with globalization and modernization.[7] Victor Davis Hanson also claimed that striking at America was merely an expression of the frustration that is the result of that failure, and their corresponding envy of Western culture.[8] There is no sense in thinking that we were "in any way culpable for past transgressions".[9] The US was attacked because they were an obstacle to Bin Laden's ambitions and "mad dreams of grandeur", in virtue of Western freedom, democracy, and success.[10] In other words, America's enemies do not hate it for its foreign policy in the Middle East. They do not hate the insidious imperialism, which America portrays as the irreversible juggernaut of modernity and globalization. The 737 military bases around the world are not the problem.[11] None of these things have anything to do with the attacks of September 11, 2001. Osama bin Laden's desire for a caliphate modeled on life in the Middle Ages is one of those "mad dreams of grandeur", but America's ambition to rule the world is not a mad dream. American neo-conservatives did not invent these fantasies, but they have pushed them to new heights. When it comes to absolute evil, the only logical thing to do with such an enemy is to destroy it.

Demonizing the enemy is a pre-requisite to justifying its annihilation. Even though Iraq had nothing to do with September 11th, its strategic location and oil reserves made it an irresistible piece of real estate for an empire eager to dominate the globe. However, Americans could not simply invade Iraq. They had to justify the invasion with the claim that Iraq was a threat to the civilized world, that it had weapons of mass destruction, and was linked to the terrorist attacks of September 11, 2001. All this was false. Nevertheless, all these lies were necessary to demonize the regime of Saddam Hussein.

The demonization of Iraq in general and of Saddam Hussein in particular, started long before September 11th. In August 1990, Saddam Hussein invaded Kuwait. The liberation of Kuwait from Saddam Hussein's army was not the sort of thing that Americans would willingly die for. Kuwait did not have a democratically elected regime that deserved to be liberated. So, a propaganda campaign was necessary to convince Americans that this was a war worthy of their blood and treasure. On 10 October 1990, a teenage Kuwaiti girl, whose true identity had to be kept secret for security reasons, appeared before the Congressional Human Rights Caucus and described the atrocities perpetrated by Saddam Hussein and his soldiers on her country. In an emotional and tearful voice, she described the army marching into the Al-Adan Hospital in Kuwait City and throwing premature infants out of their incubators. She claimed that she saw at least 15 babies snatched out of their incubators and left to die on the floor. She was visibly shaken and crying as she mentioned her nephew who was born premature and could have been killed. Clearly, an evil of that magnitude had to be stopped.

As it turned out, the teenage girl did not live in Kuwait. She lived in Washington DC. She was 15-year-old Nariyah al Sabah, who was the daughter of the Kuwaiti ambassador to the US. She had not been in Kuwait for many years and had not witnessed any of the atrocities she described to Congress. The whole story was a fabrication, but it had a huge influence on the decision to go to war.[12] The attack on premature infants became the paradigmatic evil of the Saddam Hussein regime–he was a baby killer who had to be stopped. However, no one paused to ask why Saddam Hussein was interested in killing babies. Nor did anyone stop to ponder what possible threat premature infants might pose to Hussein and his conquering army or investigate the strategic importance of the incubator babies to the conquest of a country such as Kuwait. In a Christian culture, the wholly gratuitous nature of the evil enemy is taken for granted. The enemy is the embodiment of the metaphysical and unfathomable wickedness of humanity. It inflames the emotions while silencing reason. And that is what propaganda is supposed to accomplish. By the time the falsehood was discovered, the war was over.

America is not alone in demonizing its enemies. Canada has fallen into the same habit. In an effort to lend a helping hand to the American 'War on Terror', Canadians have become embroiled in the project of exterminating the Taliban enemy in Afghanistan. Brigadier General Tim Grant, the head of the Canadian troops in Afghanistan, was asked by a Canadian Broadcasting Corporation (CBC)[13] reporter if the abduction of 20 Christian Korean aid-workers by the Taliban in 2006 and the killing of two of the hostages would have a negative impact on the reconstruction of the country. He responded that it would indeed have a negative impact because it would drive other non-governmental organizations (NGOs) out of the country and that this would slow down reconstruction, disabling the delivery of the aid needed by the Afghani people. This was an obvious answer to a banal question. However, the General added that such an outcome was precisely what the Taliban are aiming at – their goal is to rebuff all of the beneficence of aid workers; they intend to deprive the people of all the good things that the NGOs can offer; they want the people to suffer.

This is a classic expression of the gratuitous wickedness of the enemy. It makes the enemy incomprehensible, making the goals and motives of the enemy completely inscrutable. It also makes it very difficult to rationally analyze, much less understand, the enemy. The gratuitous wickedness of an enemy that desires the suffering of its own people as an end in itself makes no sense. Wanting their people to suffer can only be a means to some other end. What is that other end? Understanding this is a critical step in determining how to deal with the enemy in a way that is likely to be more successful than focusing simply on the endless task of extermination.

In light of the radical evil of the enemy, it makes no sense to ask why the Taliban might wish to drive the foreign troops out of their country. Is it surprising that they wish to keep out foreign troops who are killing many civilians and wedding parties (even if that is 'accidental')? Is it surprising that they wish to keep Christian organizations and missionaries out of their country?[14] Surely, their hostility to an invading army is understandable. There are things that the West has done that have sparked their legitimate anger—invading their country, removing their government, and installing a Western puppet regime. To acknowledge this is to admit that the West is not exactly innocent. Admitting one's guilt means that the conflict cannot be depicted as a clash of good against evil. If we have the magnanimity to acknowledge that the enemy has some legitimate claims, some meaningful aspirations, some understandable desires, some genuinely human objectives, then a compromise may be possible. However, an enemy that is pure wickedness, has no rational goals, no comprehensible desires, and no legitimate grievances is one that no one can negotiate with. The only thing to do with such an enemy is to exterminate it. No questions asked.

God bless America

The other side of demonizing one's enemies is insisting on one's own innocence, goodness, and justice. Questioning America's innocence is not only taboo among the neo-conservatives, the Bush administration, and the blindly patriotic; it is regarded as treason even in the supposedly liberal mainstream media. The 'scandal' involving Reverend Jeremiah Wright is a case in point. Wright is a black minister whose church has for long been attended by President Barack Obama. In one of his 'controversial' sermons, Wright declared that the attacks of September 11, 2001 were payback for America's activities abroad. America was not innocent – it was not the representative of truth and justice in the world. All of these appeals to God to bless America are misguided. Why should God bless America? It would be more truthful to say, along the rest of the world, "God damn America! God damn America!"

That speech was regarded with such alarm that most political pundits expected it to bring Obama's presidential candidacy to an end. What is interesting is that the horror with which the speech was regarded was such that the mainstream American media could not repeat what he said when they reported the story. They interviewed one pundit after another eager to analyze the implications of the sermon and predict the political fall-out. One after another, they referred to the dreadful and distasteful comments of Reverend Wright. One after another, the political commentators emphasized the need for the candidate to distance himself from the obscene, hateful, and offensive statements, as well as from the individual who uttered them – otherwise, the candidacy of this brilliant politician was bound to be extinguished. There was no debate or discussion of what the reverend said. Everyone agreed that what the reverend said was treasonous and that a presidential candidate could not be a party to such treasonous conduct without the collapse of his campaign. As the backdrop to all the punditry, CNN showed footage of the reverend ranting and raving in the course of delivering his impassioned speech, but without sound. Anyone eager to find out what all the fuss was about had to go online or tune to the CBC to discover what was so dreadfully treasonous and offensive about the speech.

In a brilliant political speech, Obama distanced himself from the statements of Reverend Wright. He declared that the statements were offensive and unacceptable, but did not say what they were. He maintained that what the reverend said was wrong because America has progressed. He attributed the reverend's statements to the real anger and frustration of an earlier generation that has suffered the effects of the long legacy of racism. He refused, however, at least initially, to distance himself from the reverend, whom he considered akin to a family member. In this way, Obama opened the door to the intelligent discussion of the content of the speech, but the media continued to discuss the political effects of the Reverend Wright 'scandal' without discussing or debating the substance of what he said.

America's insistence on its innocence, goodness, and justice, is nothing new. The tradition of American Exceptionalism has always allowed America to see itself as God's country, with a special obligation to fight on behalf of the almighty God against the forces of evil. During the Civil War, the *Battle Hymn of the Republic* identified the Union Army at the Potomac with "the glory of the coming of the Lord", whose "truth is marching on". The army is God's instrument, with which he will crush the serpent once and for all. As such, the neo-conservatives of the Bush administration are not unusual, they have simply pushed the tradition of American Exceptionalism to new heights.

Conclusion

Even though the strident chauvinism that characterizes American imperialism is more than matched by the chauvinism of its Muslim enemies, I believe that the administration of Barack Obama must be assiduous in keeping biblical religion and imagery out of its foreign policy. It must take the lead in abandoning the infantile rhetoric of the 'War on Terror' and bridling the excesses of American Exceptionalism. Why should the United States take the lead?

In the first place, the Unites States is heir to the benefits of modernity. In the West, modernity has been a long and gradual triumph over the forces of religion, radicalism, and irrationality. It has triumphed over papal tyranny and the deadly wars of religion that followed the Reformation. It has provided the West with the political sobriety, moderation, and constitutional governments that paved the way for prosperity and freedom. The War on Terror threatens these achievements. There is absolutely no reason for the United States to wallow in this sort of atavism. In contrast to the West, the relationship of the Muslim world with modernity is entirely different. Modernity did not come to the Muslim world as a liberator; and it did not come gradually. It came suddenly in the form of colonialism and foreign occupation. In the post-colonial era, modernity has been associated with the corrupt and murderous dictators propped up by the West. It is no wonder that Islam has great appeal; it promises virtue in public life, and a regard for social justice and the Islamic values of the past.

In the second place, being wealthier and more powerful, America has more to lose, and therefore has more reason for abandoning the War on Terror, since it has deleterious political as well as military (not to mention moral) ramifications. Politically speaking, when the enemy is the incarnation of gratuitous wickedness, there is no possibility of compromise or negotiation; as a result, the political is disabled. Militarily speaking, when enemies are demonized, they cannot be regarded as worthy opponents, but only as demons to be destroyed. All wars become wars of extermination, which transforms life into a ghastly quagmire of endless slaughter. Since wars of extermination do not distinguish between combatants and non-combatants, war ceases to be a triumph over a worthy and capable opponent; it becomes indistinguishable from crime. So, the idea that we can use armies to stop terrorists is laughable. Terrorism is the killing of innocent and unarmed civilians. Whether this is done by Islamic terrorists or by American or Israeli men and women in uniform with B-52 bombers is irrelevant. These are some of the reasons why the United States must take the lead in abandoning the infantilism and moral self-righteousness implicit in the biblical rhetoric of the 'War on Terror'.

Notes

1 See, for example, Hans J. Morgenthau, *Scientific Man vs. Power Politics*, Chicago: University of Chicago Press, 1946.
2 Saint Augustine, *City of God*, trans. Henry Bettenson, London: Penguin Books, 1980, Book. IV, Chapter 4.
3 Joshua 10:11.
4 David Frum and Richard Perle, *An End To Evil: How to Win the War on Terror*, New York: Ballantine Press, 2004.
5 Robert Kagan, *Of Paradise and Power*, New York: Alfred A. Knopf, 2003, p. 41.
6 Elaine H. Pagels, *Adam, Eve and the Serpent*, New York: Random House, 1988.
7 Bernard Lewis, *The Crisis of Islam: Holy War and Unholy Terror*, New York: The Modern Library, 2003, and Bernard Lewis, *What Went Wrong? The Clash Between Islam and Modernity*, New York: HarperCollins, 2002.
8 Victor Davis Hanson, *An Autumn of War*, New York: Anchor Books, 2002, p. xiv. Hanson is believed to be a favorite of Dick Cheney and George W. Bush. See Michiko Kakutani, "How Books Have Shaped U. S. Policy", *New York Times*, 5 April 2003.
9 Davis Hanson, op. cit., p. xvi.
10 Ibid., p. xvi.
11 Chalmers Johnson, *Nemesis: The Last Days of the American Republic*, New York: Metropolitan Books, 2006, p. 138.
12 John R. MacArthur, "Remember Nayirah, Witness for Kuwait?" *The New York Times Op-Ed*, Monday, 6 January 1992. The claim that Iraqi soldiers removed Kuwaiti babies from incubators and left them to die on hospital floors was shown to be almost certainly false by an ABC reporter, John Martin, in March 1991, after the liberation of Kuwait. He interviewed hospital doctors who had stayed in Kuwait throughout the occupation.
13 Canada's national broadcaster.
14 As the Aga Khan (leader of the Ismaili Muslims and supposedly the descendant of the Prophet Muhammad) pointed out in an interview on CBC Television's *One on One with Peter Mansbridge*, how would the Europeans and Americans feel if a Muslim army entered Northern Ireland and replaced the government with its own puppet regime? Consider the mayhem.

3 Islam and Muslims as seen by the Christian Zionists

Norton Mezvinsky

Scholars representing a variety of academic disciplines, including theology, history, anthropology, sociology, and political science, as well as popular writers have produced a multitude of articles and books about the Christian Right in the United States. Too often, the Christian Right has been – and still is – depicted in an over-generalized manner. The many and varied individuals and groups who allegedly constitute the Christian Right disagree with one another about numerous, significant political, economic, and social issues. In adequately discussing the Christian Right, or any part of it, it is first of all necessary to identify specifically those individuals and/or groups with whom we are dealing.

In this chapter, I shall limit my definition of the Christian Right to just one group: evangelical Christian Zionists. From my perspective, evangelical Christian Zionists are the most significant grouping of the Christian Right. Although Christian Zionists do not fully agree with one another in regard to all issues, they do mostly believe in, reiterate and seek to instill in society the same basic – and what they consider to be essential – theological beliefs.

Christian Zionism itself is not limited to evangelicals. Ministers, lay leaders and congregants of many so-called mainline churches deserve to be called Christian Zionists; they believe and advocate that the political Zionism of the State of Israel's character is legitimate, is moral, is authorized and authenticated by holy scripture and should be supported and maintained. These mainline Christian Zionists differ from one another in their perceptions of Islam and Muslims. The focus of this chapter is, however, not upon these mainline Christian Zionists but rather upon evangelical Christian Zionists.

Not all evangelicals in the United States are Christian Zionists. Some evangelicals, e.g. the noted leader and speaker Tony Compolo, publicly oppose the Christian Zionist theology that emphasizes the necessity of the State of Israel's being under the control of Jews and that attacks Islam and Muslims in numerous ways. The large majority of evangelical Christian leaders and their followers in the United States, nevertheless, are Christian Zionists.

The actual number of evangelical Christian Zionists in the United States in 2009 is difficult to assess accurately. Before he died, the Reverend Jerry Falwell, one of the best known American evangelical leaders, bragged that the number of evangelical Christian Zionists in the United States exceeded one hundred million.

Falwell exaggerated; the number in 2009, determined from consideration of many sources and studies, is probably in the 50–60 million range. Clearly, the number is sufficiently large to suggest by itself pragmatic importance.

The theological basis of Christian Zionism is Christian fundamentalism. Christian Zionists believe literally in the Bible; they believe that the texts of the Old and New Testaments are divine. Christian Zionism asserts without question that Jews need to be and shall be in control, if not the sole inhabitants, of the Holy Land and some surrounding territory before the Second Coming of Jesus Christ, the Messiah.

Christian Zionists additionally believe and state unequivocally that Armageddon, the "mother of all holocausts", will occur before the Second Coming. During Armageddon only the real believers in the divine word, i.e. the true followers of Jesus including only 144,000 Jews who had converted, will be raptured up in the air. Everyone else will perish for having followed a false Messiah, the anti-Christ. Regardless of the forthcoming Armageddon, during which all but 144,000 Jews will be saved, Christian Zionists believe they need to give full support and backing to the current Zionist Jewish state; they believe that they need to do whatever they can to support Israeli Jews against their major enemies: the people and governments of Arab nation-states and Palestinians. To reiterate, evangelical Christian Zionists believe that the 'Holy Land', must be controlled by Jews and must have at least a majority Jewish population before the Second Coming of Jesus Christ.

Within the past quarter of a century, Christian Zionist leaders, with a large number of followers behind them, have developed one of the most powerful and influential lobbies in the United States. This lobby, which constitutes a major function of what many commentators refer to as the Christian Right, has exerted, and does exert, at least as much influence as does the much emphasized Israel lobby. In addition to and often within the context of its support for Israel as a Jewish state and for Zionist principles and practices, many, but not all, spokespeople for and advocates of Christian Zionism have been and presently are outspoken and blunt publicly and privately in their antagonism to Islam and Muslims. These spokespeople see George W. Bush's declared 'War on Terror' to be primarily a war not only against so-called Islamic fundamentalism and Muslim extremists but rather a war against Islam as an evil religion and against its Muslim adherents. At first glance such an assertion about such Christian Zionist assertions may seem over-stated. The evidence for this assertion, however, is voluminous, and overwhelming.

Beginning in the middle of the 1970s, evangelical Christian Zionists began to focus attention on Islam and its expanding role in world affairs. Motivated by the belief that OPEC was largely responsible for an oil crisis in 1973, John F. Walvoord of the Dallas Seminary reflected the concern about Islam in his book, *Armageddon, Oil and the Middle East Crisis*, which sold over 750,000 copies.[1] Other Christian Zionist writers soon began to focus more and more upon Islam. The 1979 revolution in Iran, led by Ayatollah Khomeini, motivated additional concern. Some writers, such as Lester Sumrall who wrote *The Holy War Jihad: The Destiny of Iran and the Muslim World*, predicted that Islamic fundamentalist

Iran would join with the Soviet Union in a final war against Israel. That Shi'ite Muslims were then opponents of the Soviets because of the Soviet Union's invasion of Afghanistan mattered little in this kind of reasoning.[2] What Christian Zionists regarded as the Ayatollah's ruthlessness simply convinced them of what would develop. In 1989, Jim McKeevey typically predicted that Islam was more dangerous than most people then believed. He wrote: "The Muslims have declared war on the West, the United States and especially the Christians ... The Muslim faith ... could turn out to be the 'best system'."[3]

That same year, 1989, Pat Robertson, who started the *Christian Broadcasting Network* (CBN) and was voted the Christian broadcaster of the year, stated that Israel and America were automatically on God's side against 'evil Islam'. Robertson claimed that here he was speaking for 1600 Christian radio and television broadcasters with a combined audience of 141 million or almost one half of the total population of the United States.

Iraq's invasion of Kuwait, beginning in August 1990, almost immediately motivated more readership and increased sales of earlier published Christian Zionist books. These books contained biblical prophecy of what would befall this world in the end time.[4] Such biblical prophecy not only connected Iraq to pending doom but also provided more background to and a broader basis for antagonism to Islam and Muslims. Christian Zionist preachers and teachers, who emphasized such biblical prophecy, suddenly appeared regularly as scheduled interview guests on radio and television. John Walvoort, for example, was interviewed 65 times during 1990 and 1991 on CNN, CBS and CBN. The *New York Times* reported in 1991 that the general concern about such biblical prophecy was at "fever pitch".[5]

The 1990 Gulf War convinced Christian Zionist preachers and teachers that Iraq was the *Book of Revelation*'s Babylon. In Chapters 17 and 18 of the *Book of Revelation*, John recounted his encounter with a woman sitting "upon a scarlet covered beast, full of names and blasphemy, having seven heads and ten horns" (17:3). The woman, dressed in purple and scarlet and covered with jewels, held a golden cup filled with "abominations and the filthiness of her fornication" (17:45). Written on her forehead was: "Mystery, Babylon the Great, the Mother of Harlots and Abominations of the Earth" (17:5). The woman was drunk "with the blood of the saints, and with the blood of the martyrs of Jesus" (17:6).

The standard dispensationalist or Christian Zionist interpretation of the "great whore of Babylon" in symbolic terms appeared in the *Scofield Reference Bible*:

> There are two forms which Babylon is to have in the end-time: political Babylon (Rev. 17:8–17) and ecclesiastical Babylon (Rev. 17:1–7, 18; 18:1–24). Political Babylon is the beast's confederated empire, the last form of Gentile world dominion. Ecclesiastical Babylon is all apostate Christendom, in which the Papacy will undoubtedly be prominent; it may very well be that this union will embrace all the religions of the world. Although some hold to a literal rebuilding of the city of Babylon ... the evidence seems to point to the symbolic use of the name here ... Ecclesiastical Babylon is the "great harlot" (Rev. 17:1) and is to be destroyed by political Babylon.[6]

Most Christian Zionist preachers and teachers came to regard political Babylon as the anti-Christ's revived Roman Empire and to regard ecclesiastical Babylon as the apostate religion. Many believed, based upon reports that Saddam Hussein planned to rebuild the ancient city of Babylon, that the Book of Revelations' references to Babylon should be interpreted literally and that indeed Babylon should be reconstructed. The leading advocate for rebuilding of Babylon was Charles Dyer of the Dallas Seminary; he argued that Saddam should rebuild Babylon so that the returning Christ could destroy it.

Many Christian Zionists spokespeople did not regard Saddam Hussein as the anti-Christ or the Gulf War as Armageddon. They were nevertheless convinced that this was a step towards the end-time, which they believed was fast approaching. Charles Taylor concluded, as did most other Christian Zionist spokespeople: "That which is transpiring is a shifting of the nations to get them in proper position" for events leading to the return of Christ.[7]

The outbreak of the Second Gulf War, which began when the United States invaded Iraq in March 2003, produced mixed reactions from evangelical Christian Zionist preachers, teachers and writers. Some were more restrained than they and their colleagues had been in 1990 about prophetic connections to the end-time. Others reacted in the same manner and sometimes even more strongly than they and their colleagues had reacted earlier. Irvin Baxter, founder of *End-time Magazine*, for example, argued that this later war with Iraq would claim the deaths of millions, because Iraq would use weapons of mass destruction against its neighbors and the United States. Baxter also maintained that other nations would use the Iraqi diversion to accomplish their own ends; China would attempt to regain Taiwan; India would go after Kashmir. The nuclear exchange, moreover, according to Baxter, would result in the deaths of one-third of the world's population.

Michael Evans, a Texas-based Christian Zionist author and preacher who is a passionate advocate of waging war for Jesus, wrote a book, published in 2003 entitled *Beyond Iraq: The Next Move – Ancient Prophecy and Modern-Day Conspiracy Collide*, in which he pinpoints an American plan for global hegemony in the guise of a holy global war. The major players in this 'divine' plot allegedly include the CIA, the United States Government and Army, the government of Israel and various Christian Zionist groups. In his book, Evans fervently welcomes the US invasion of Iraq in 2003 and pleads that the invasion should be expanded into other Muslim countries. The killing of people and destruction wrought in Iraq are for Evans the price that God exacts from Muslims for having been coerced by Satan to loathe the Jews, God's chosen people. Evans claims that the invasion of Iraq was demanded by God. Branding Muslims, especially the Arabs, as virtually agents of the devil, Evans argues that the United States, as the self-appointed agent of Christ, should have no qualms about going further and invading oil-rich lands. This supposedly would break the dependence upon Muslim countries for oil. Evans sees the invasion and occupation as the unfolding of God's plan and as a 'spiritual battle' between Christianity and Satanic forces and demons, represented by Muslims and some other non-Christians.

In short, Evans insists that Iraq, Islam and Muslims are the modern-day representatives of the forces of Satan and, as ordered by God, must be crushed. They are connected to ancient Babylon, a once great city that turned evil and was hence destroyed. The 2003 invasion of Iraq by the United States is for Evans a prelude to the coming Armageddon, the mother of all holocausts.

In his book, Evans focuses even more in-depth on Arabs and Muslims. He argues that they must be humiliated and subjugated before finally being crushed and killed. He quotes the Bible and says God blessed Isaac and his descendants, the Jews, but had a different plan for the Arabs, descendants of Ishmael, Abraham's other son. Evans quotes the Bible's description of Ishmael as a 'wild man' whose hand will be raised against all persons. Evans calls Muhammad a 'proto-terrorist', who banished and killed Jews for not believing in him and for spawning Muslim terrorists with Islam. Terrorism, claims Evans in his book, is a logical consequence of Islam. He argues that the Qadafis, Khomeinis, Arafats, bin Ladens and Husseins of the modern day are disciples of Muhammad and Islam. From Evans' perspective, Islam is a "malevolent manifestation of religion conceived in the pit of hell". Evans equates Islam with the anti-Christ, against whom all Christians must fight with all the resources at their command.[8]

Michael Evans is a widely acclaimed Christian Zionist spokesperson. He is not only a best-selling author; he has appeared on the BBC and US major television network shows and has published articles in the *Wall Street Journal* and the *Jerusalem Post*. He founded the Jerusalem Prayer Team, which included at its inauguration other leading Christian Zionists, e.g. Franklin Graham, Pat Robertson and Jerry Falwell as well as US Representative Dick Armey and former Israeli Prime Minister Benjamin Natanyahu. Evans received the Ambassador Award from the Israeli government and has been a confidant and advisor to numerous Israeli prime ministers and mayors of Jerusalem. The jacket of Evans' book, *Beyond Iraq: The Next Move – Ancient Prophecy and Modern-Day Conspiracy Collide* contains a quotation from Benjamin Natanyahu praising him for having "consistently demonstrated the moral clarity that is necessary to defend Israel from the lies and distortions of its enemies".

Many other major evangelical Christian Zionist leaders echoed the themes expressed by Evans. They often used the term 'militant Islam' negatively to portray Islam in general. John Hagee, founder and pastor of the Cornerstone Church in San Antonio, Texas, repeatedly in speeches and in writing reiterated the alleged connections between ancient Babylon, Iraq and Islam. Hagee, who by the beginning of the twenty-first century had become one of the most influential Christian Zionists leaders, has, to date, consistently emphasized in his books, articles and radio and television interviews that Islam is an evil and dangerous religion and that militant Muslims are committed to wage holy war in the Middle East and throughout the world against non-Muslim enemies. The Muslim aim, according to Hagee, is to expand the Islamic religious-political empire and to eliminate all enemies. Hagee has consistently maintained that the Islamic aim is to triumph over all religions.[9]

Hagee, in line with Evans and other Christian Zionist leaders, has severely and specifically criticized Islam, Muslims and Arabs for targeting and attacking Jews and Judaism. In his book, *Beginning of the End* (1996), Hagee typically asserts: "The conflict between Arabs and Jews goes deeper than disputes over land. It is theological. It is Judaism verses Islam."[10] The origin of this conflict, according to Hagee, is the biblical rivalry between Isaac and Ishmael.[11] This rivalry allegedly expanded to the point that militant Islamists hate and want to kill the Jewish people.[12] Hagee considers Hamas and Iran the leaders in this attempt to kill the Jews, and he sees a reborn Russia conspiring with Islam in a campaign against the State of Israel and the West.[13] Hagee believes Christian Zionists are obligated to support and defend the State of Israel and Jews against the onslaught of Islam and the Muslims.

In 2003, Richard Cizik, vice-president for governmental affairs at the National Association of Evangelicals, succinctly stated what had been and remained the post-Cold War evangelical Christian Zionist anti-Muslim position: "The Muslims have become the modern-day equivalent of the Evil Empire."[14] For Cizik and other evangelical Christian Zionists, Samuel Huntington's clash of civilizations theory, expounded first in a 1993 seminal article in *Foreign Affairs* and then more fully later in a best-selling book, provided a contextual framework for recognition of the threat and fear of Islam. In his article, Huntington wrote: "The centuries-old military interaction between the West and Islam is unlikely to decline. It could become more virulent."[15] Evangelical Christian Zionists have concluded and reiterated that Huntington's prediction was a truism.

Again and again, Christian Zionists have maintained that the State of Israel, as previously indicated, stands as a Judeo-Christian fortress, surrounded by evil Muslim nation-states and threatened by Muslim terror. From the Christian Zionist perspective, Israel remains an important outpost of the West in the post-Cold War struggle of civilizations. The antagonism towards Islam exploded after September 11, 2001. For evangelical Christians generally, the clash of civilizations threat had become a hot war. The role of Israel thus became more important in this developing war, and the Christian Zionist support for Israel increased and became more intense. Gary Bauer, a political activist who was formerly on President Ronald Reagan's staff, is a Christian Zionist leader who considers himself a soldier in the clash between civilizations. Bauer has to date consistently argued that the United States and Israel are "twin pillars of the West" and that any harm to Israel would be "a disaster for Western civilization". Bauer has asserted that the United States and Israel are under attack from the same enemy. In reference to what he terms radical Islam, Bauer has stated:

> It is the same philosophy that motivates the government of Sudan to kill 5 million Christians in the last decade. It inspires the gunmen with AK47s who run into churches in Pakistan and open fire on women and children. It inspires the kidnappers of Daniel Pearl who tormented him on video tape, forcing him to say over and over again "I am a Jew" before they decapitated him and sent the picture of his severed head throughout the Middle East as a

recruiting tool. This philosophy causes the Palestinian mother to leap with joy at the news her teenage son has blown himself up as long as she is assured he killed Jews in the process.[16]

Other Christian Zionists after September 11th reiterated the same theme about the dual threat of Islam and Muslims to Israel, the United States and the world:

> What is at stake in the Middle East is not just the survival of Israel, although the menace to Israel is real and immediate. If we learned anything on September 11th, then we should have learned that what is finally at stake in this confrontation is the survival of us all.[17]

Numerous Members of Congress, acknowledging their evangelical Christian Zionist beliefs, emphasized as well the Islamic threat and the need of the United States to stand with "its close ally", the State of Israel, in opposing this threat.

On 23 July 2003, the then House of Representatives Majority Leader Tom DeLay, in his speech to an American Israel Public Affairs Council (AIPAC) Leadership Summit, stated:

> America's victory in our war on terror relies on Israel's victory in its war on terror. The common destiny of our two nations is not an artificial alliance dictated by our leaders, or a partisan political calculation. It is a heartfelt friendship between the citizens of two democracies at war, bound by the solidarity of freedom.[18]

After September 11, 2001, President George W. Bush declared, in discussing his war against terror, that Islam was "a peaceful religion" and that al-Qaeda did not represent Islam's true nature or character. Condoleezza Rice, the then National Security Adviser, reiterated the president's view numerous times.[19] Within a few weeks after the September 11th attacks President Bush invited representatives of American Muslim and Islamic organizations to meet him and to celebrate Ramadan at the White House.[20]

Many evangelical Christian Zionists were upset by the president's remarks. Jerry Falwell, who founded the Moral Majority, the leading Christian Right group of the 1980s, called Mohammad, Islam's prophet, a terrorist. Jerry Vines, the former president of the Southern Baptist Convention, said Mohammad was "demon possessed". Franklin Graham stated clearly and publicly on behalf of numerous Christian Right leaders: "We're not attacking Islam, but Islam has attacked us ... I believe it is a very evil and wicked religion."

Franklin Graham is the son of the famous evangelist preacher Billy Graham, who had converted George W. Bush to evangelical Christianity. Franklin Graham delivered the benediction at both the 1996 and 2000 Republican National Conventions, gave the invocation at George W. Bush's presidential inauguration and often was invited to lead prayers at the Pentagon. President Bush disapproved of the Graham attack upon Islam, and White House press releases said the president viewed "Islam as a religion that preaches peace".

The president's disapproval of Franklin Graham's statements in turn antagonized many other Christian Right leaders. Pat Robertson, the founder of the Christian Coalition, the most important Christian Right organization of the 1990s, took issue with the president's description of Islam as peaceful. Robertson declared that Islam was not peaceful and did not believe in coexistence with other religions. Islam, according to Robertson, sought ultimately "to control, dominate, and then if need be to destroy".[21] Robertson's reaction reflected the sentiments of other prominent Christian Zionists from the 1990s onward. Hal Lindsey has been one of the most renowned Christian Zionist spokespersons. As a writer and lecturer, he has enthralled millions of people who have listened to him and/or read his writings. Lindsey's book, *The Late Great Planet Earth*, has been on the best-seller list for more than thirty years and has sold tens of millions of copies. During George W. Bush's presidency Lindsey often told audiences that he loved the president as a Bible-believing Christian but that he heartily wished Bush better understood and realized that Islam without question is "violent to the core" and must be opposed.

At times a few evangelical Christian Zionist leaders have been critical to some extent of their colleagues. Even these evangelical Christian Zionist leaders, however, have often made negative comments about Islam. Richard Land, the president of the Southern Baptist Convention's Ethics and Religious Liberty Commission, for example, declared that he had no problem seeing Islam as a great religion. At a meeting to discuss how Christians should treat Islam, co-sponsored by the National Association of Evangelicals, Land and others stated that the comments made by Graham, Robertson, and others did not represent the true evangelical view of Islam.

Land and most of the evangelical leaders who had participated in this meeting, nevertheless, were upset by a comment made by President Bush at a press conference in Britain in late 2003. Bush made the following response to a question about Islam and Muslims: "I believe we worship the same God." Land, on behalf of himself and numerous colleagues, publicly replied that President Bush was "simply mistaken".[22]

Earlier during 2003 a new controversy concerning Islam and Muslims erupted in many evangelical churches. General William C. Boykin, a Special Forces veteran whom Bush had appointed Deputy Under-Secretary of Defense for Intelligence, delivered a series of speeches in evangelical churches in which he said that George W. Bush was president because God had put him there to defeat terrorists in the name of Christ. Boykin specified terrorists by displaying photographs of Mogadishu, the Somali capital. Boykin asserted that a black mark in the sky, visible in the photographs, illustrated a "demonic presence" over the city. In conjunction with this description, Boykin related an incident in which a leading Somali fighter had declared on television that Allah protected him. After the capture of this fighter, Boykin said he knew that "my God was bigger than his".[23] Although President Bush said Boykin's remarks did not express the views of his administration, both the Secretary of Defense, Donald Rumsfeld, and the chairman of the Joints Chief of Staff defended Boykin publicly. (Rumsfeld had earlier convinced Boykin to accept his appointment by Bush.)

During the right years of his presidency, George W. Bush consistently called Islam a religion of peace and warned against anti-Muslim prejudice. He, however, also embraced evangelical Christian Zionist leaders who publicly labeled Islam an evil religion and blamed terrorism upon Muslims. Bush, obviously influenced by Christian Zionist and certain Jewish Zionists, appointed to high positions in his two administrations many individuals who considered Islamic fundamentalism to be the gravest threat to national security.

Among the many examples of such individuals was Daniel Pipes, appointed by Bush to the United States Peace Institute over the objections of numerous Members of Congress, Muslim leaders, and others. Pipes had enraged Muslims by arguing that mosques are breeding grounds for terrorists and that Muslims, occupying government and military positions, should receive special attention and scrutiny as security risks.

John L. Esposito, a professor of religion and international affairs at Georgetown University, expressed the sentiments of many Muslim leaders and scholarly commentators on Islam when in April 2003, he was quoted in a *New York Times* Op-Ed piece:

> President Bush has clearly tried to make a distinction between Islam the religion and actions of Muslim extremists, but there's a difference between what the president says and what his domestic and international policies have been. The president most probably might feel uncomfortable with some of the statements that have been made about Islam by leaders of the Christian Right and neoconservatives [but] this is his constituency.[24]

The tone and substance of antagonism to Islam and Muslims among evangelical Christian Zionists in the United States consistently grew and increased from September 11, 2001 until the end of 2008. Sermons of ministers, written statements in articles and books, comments made in media and television programs and speeches delivered at conferences and other gatherings provide ample documentation. In addition to what has already been presented in this chapter, two more examples will further illustrate this point.

The first of these two additional examples is the clear, precise and oft-repeated position of Rod Parsley, who has become one of the major evangelical Christian Zionist ministers in the United States and who has provided leadership for many of his evangelical colleagues.

The Reverend Rod Parsley is the leader of the World Harvest Church of Columbus, Ohio, a supersize Pentecostal institution with a 12,000-member congregation, a 5200-seat sanctuary, a television studio where Parsley tapes a widely listened to weekly show and a 122,000 sq ft Ministry Activity Center. Parsley has written many widely read books and articles in which he warns (as he does in his sermons and broadcasts) of the grave threats to the United States and American society. One of the most profound of these threats, according to Parsley, is the religion of Islam. Similar in many ways to another extremely influential and well-known Christian Zionist evangelical leader, John Hagee, Parsley maintains that the Christian civilization is in a war against the evil Islamic civilization. What Parsley wrote in his book, *Silent No More*, typifies what he has often reiterated. In a chapter entitled "Islam: The Deception of Allah", Parsley wrote:

> I cannot tell you how important it is that we understand the true nature of Islam, that we see it for what it really is. In fact, I will tell you this: I do not believe our country can truly fulfill its divine purpose until we understand our historical conflict with Islam. I do not shrink from its implications. The fact is that America was founded, in part, with the intention of seeing this false religion destroyed, and I believe September 11, 2001, was a generational call to arms that we can no longer ignore ... We find we have no choice. The time has come ... We may already be losing the battle. As I scan the world, I find that Islam is responsible for more pain, more bloodshed and more devastation than nearly any other force on earth at this moment.[25]

Parsley asserts in *Silent No More*, as he maintains in other writings and speeches, that Islam is an "anti-Christ religion" and is based upon deception. "The Muslim prophet Muhammad received revelations from demons and not from the true God ... Allah was a demon spirit."[26] Making no distinction between violent Islamic extremists and other Muslims, Parsley maintains:

> There are some, of course, who will say the violence I cite is the exception and not the rule. I beg to differ. I will counter, respectfully, that what some call "extremists" are instead mainstream believers who are drawing from the well at the very heart of Islam.[27]

For Parsley, the spirit of Islam is hostility. Islam, according to Parsley, inspired the attacks on 9/11. Parsley is disturbed that tens of thousands of Americans have converted to Islam and that there are 1209 mosques in the United States. Parsley, in a cautioning tone, says that "Islam is a faith that fully intends to conquer the world through violence. [The United States] has historically understood herself as a bastion against Islam, but history is crashing in upon us."[28] Finally, Parsley calls for a crusade against Islam.

Parsley's views about Islam both reflect and influence many other evangelical Christian Zionist ministers, leaders, and followers. Parsley and his church, moreover, have already demonstrated that they have political clout. His World Harvest Church and a group affiliated with his church, Reformation Ohio, have registered voters in Ohio and will probably do so again. On 26 February 2008, during the presidential electoral campaign John McCain, who became the presidential candidate of the Republican Party, appeared at a campaign rally in Cincinnati with Rod Parsley; McCain hailed Parsley as a "spiritual advisor".

(McCain later said he did not agree with all the views of Parsley and/or of Hagee, but he did not renounce Parsley and/or Hagee's endorsements.) The Parsley type of anti-Islam and anti-Muslim sentiment is certainly evident within evangelical ranks in the United States. Although difficult to gauge, the political impact of this sentiment is also evident.

The second illustrative example is taken from an article by a less well-known minister. The importance of the following excerpts from this article, which was written by a pastor of a suburban church and was published in a local newspaper with relatively small circulation, is that it is typical and representative in tone and substance of a large and increasing number of other articles published and sermons delivered locally throughout the United States.

In reaction against Methodist, Catholic, and Episcopalian Churches hosting so-called interfaith Church sessions on Islam, Bim Rowley, Senior Pastor of the Truth Baptist Church in South Windsor, Connecticut, wrote his article entitled, "Strange Alliances", that was published on 9 October 2008, in the *East Hartford Gazette*. In his article, Rowley began by asserting that Islam, and its prophet, Mohammad, were unclean and connected to Satan, therefore being unfit for Christian contact. Rowley pointed out that Mohammad had 11 wives, one of whom was 9 years old when the wedding was consummated. Rowley then maintained that in the second period of his life, when his movement was expanding by use of the sword, Mohammad became intolerant of and violent towards Jews and Christians, because they would not recant and become Muslims. Whenever Islam becomes the primary or dominant religion in a country, according to Rowley, followers of other religions are persecuted. As Rowley wrote:

> Islam is more than a "religion," it is a "state" that becomes less and less tolerant as it gains more clout. Where Moslems gain the majority, the laws and traditions of patriotism along with the cultural values of the host country are overthrown and their own laws and culture are instituted. Say good-bye to first amendment rights in Islamic countries especially for women and those of another religion ... A quick search of what is being taught in Islamic schools around the world as well as in America reveals an indoctrination of anti-Semitism and a blind allegiance to religious leaders that control the minds and hearts of its adherents.[29]

Rowley concluded by asking churches "to rethink their alliances with and implicit promotion of Islam".[30] It is worth reiterating that Rowley's and Parsley's arguments are not limited to an extreme, small minority grouping of evangelical Christian Zionist religious leaders, churches, and congregations. Rather, they are representative and indicative of a growing trend of thought and advocacy within the so-called and significant Christian Right faction of American society.

Evangelical Christian Zionist antagonism to Islam and Muslims constitutes a grave danger in the United States for both Muslims and for American society in general. This antagonism is deep-seated. For evangelical Christian Zionists, Israel is a front-line ally, an outpost of Judeo-Christian civilization surrounded on all sides by Muslim nations and under siege from Muslim terror. This view of Israel as a lonely outpost of the West adds a strategic rationale to the theological reasons for supporting the State of Israel and opposing Islam and Muslims. This is one aspect. Even more serious is the conviction that Islam and Muslims threaten all Christendom and the non-Muslim world. Because of this larger threat, many Christian Zionists believe Islam and Muslims need to be obliterated. The danger here is real for four inter-connected reasons: (1) The clear indication is that most evangelical Christian Zionists sincerely believe that their antagonism is based upon correct interpretations of God's word and God's will. Given such a belief, it would be difficult, if not impossible, for other human beings, who did not so believe, to convince those Christian Zionists otherwise. (2) This antagonism among evangelical Christian Zionists has substantially increased from the end of the 1980s to date. (3) There are, as previously noted, at least 50 million Christian Zionists in the United States, most of whom are most likely extremely antagonistic towards Islam and Muslims. This number is sufficiently large to be potentially dangerous. (4) Christian Zionists have become more politically active since the end of the 1980s and have infiltrated local, state and the national governments. This suggests that the potential danger is becoming more of a real danger.

The danger stems from the fact that most Christian Zionist leaders and followers believe sincerely that their antagonism to the 'evils' of Islam and Muslims is derived from God's word. These Christian Zionists base their attitudes and actions upon what they believe God has directed them to think and to do. Their motivation is clear and simple.

It would be extremely difficult for other human beings to convince Christian Zionists to change or even to question seriously their views of Islam and Muslims. After all, God's word, for those who believe they know and wish to follow it, clearly supersedes the word of any person in this world.

To counter Christian Zionism's assault upon Islam and Muslims requires understanding of Islam and of Christian Zionism's essence. Widespread, sophisticated discussion of these topics in public forums, in sermons and in the mass media is needed. This discussion should include learned Christian, theological refutation of Christian Zionism's essence. The best study of this theology is Steven R. Sizer's book, *Christian Zionism: Road-Map to Armageddon?*[31] The discussion should also include the positive, humanitarian aspects of Islam. Such discussion could seriously limit the proselytizing effect and further spread of Christian Zionism and its assault against Islam and Muslims.

Notes

1 John F. Walvoord, *Armageddon, Oil and the Middle East*, Grand Rapids, MI: Zondervan, 1973.
2 Lester Sumrall, *The Holy War Jihad: The Destiny of Iran and the Muslim World*, Tulsa: Harrison House, 1980.
3 Jim McKeever, quoted in Paul Boyer, *When Time Shall Be No More: Prophecy Belief in Modern American Culture*, Cambridge, MA: Harvard University Press, 1992, p. 327.

4 Zondervan Publishing Company reported an 83 percent increase in 1990–1991 of Hal Lindsey's 1970 best-selling book, *The Late Great Planet Earth*. Bantam Books reported that its "hottest religious title" in the Fall of 1990 was Grant Jeffrey's *Armageddon: Appointment with Destiny*. John F. Walvoord's books, *Prophecy Knowledge Handbook* and *Armageddon, Oil and the Middle East*, surged in sales.

5 See Paul Boyer, op. cit., pp. 327–330.

6 C. I. Scofield (ed.) *The New Scofield Reference Bible*, New York: Oxford University Press, 1967, pp. 1369–1370.

7 Charles Taylor, quoted in Tim LeHaye and Jerry B. Jenkins, *Tribulation Force*, Wheaton, IL: Tyndale, 1996, p. 328.

8 Bill Broadway, "Priest of Predictions for War in Iraq: End-Time Interpreters See Biblical Prophecies Being Fulfilled", *Washington Post*, March 8, 2003, B09. See Michael Evans, *Beyond Iraq: The Next Move – Ancient Prophecy and Modern-day Conspiracy Collide*, Lakeland: White Stone Books, 2003.

9 See John Hagee, *Beginning of the End*, Nashville, TN: Nelson, 1996, pp. 23–25.

10 Ibid., p. 24.

11 Ibid., p. 26.

12 Ibid., p. 144.

13 Ibid., pp. 143–151.

14 Laurie Goodstein, "Seeing Islam as 'Evil' Faith, Evangelicals Seek Converts", *New York Times*, 27 May 2003.

15 Samuel Huntington, "The Clash of Civilizations", *Foreign Affairs*, 72(3) (1993): 22–49.

16 Gary Bauer, speech to AIPAC Policy Conference, Washington, DC, 30 March 2003.

17 Alan Keyes, "Standing Firm for Israel", *World Net Daily*, posted April 29, 2002. Available at: www.worldnetdaily.com/index.php?fa=PAGE.printable&pageId=13720.

18 Tom DeLay, speech to AIPAC Leadership Summit, Washington, DC.

19 See Rice "War on Terror Is Not War on Islam", *NewsMax.com Wires*, 23 October 2003. Available at: www.archive.newsmax.com/archives/articles/2003/10/19/131240.shtml.

20 Franklin Foer, "Grover Norquist's Strange Alliance with Radical Islam", *New Republic*, 12 November 2001.

21 See Dennis Hoover, "Choosing Up Sides in the Middle East", *Religion in the News*, 5(3) (Fall 2002); Michelle Little, "Bible Brigade", *New Republic*, 21 April 2003; Ken Garfield, "Graham Stands by Comments on Islam", *Charlotte Observer*, 19 November 2001; Alan Cooperman, "Robertson Calls Islam a Religion of Violence, Mayhem", *Washington Post*, 22 February 2002.

22 See Alan Cooperman, "Bush's Remark about God Assailed", *Washington Post*, 22 November 2003, p. 11; "Secular Media Wrong about Meeting with Muslims?" *Marantha Christian Journal* (online magazine), 12 May 2003, available at: www.mcjonline.com/news03a/20030512e.shtml.

23 William M. Arkin, "The Pentagon Unleashes a Holy Warrior", *The Los Angeles Times*, 16 October 2003, p. 1.

24 As quoted in John W. Stevenson, "Aftereffects; Washington Memo; For Muslims a Mixture of White House Signals", *New York Times*, 28 April 2003, p. 24.

25 Rod Parsley, *Silent No More*, New York: Frontline, 2005.

26 Ibid.

27 Ibid.

28 Ibid.

29 Bim Rowley, *East Hartford Gazette*, 9 October 2008, p. 6.

30 Ibid.

31 Steven R. Sizer, *Christian Zionism: Road-Map to Armageddon?* Leicester: InterVarsity Press, 2004.

4 Vigilante masculinity and the 'War on Terror'

Sunera Thobani

Introduction

In a video posted on *YouTube*, a young white man, claiming to be an American soldier who served as a guard at Abu Ghraib prison, boasts about having engaged in the torture of Iraqis and the rape of a 15-year-old girl.[1] "What's the big deal in making a haji walk around like a dog and bark?" the young man asks his companion, who urges him to describe his experiences. Laughing, and saying that he did not expect anybody to be upset by his actions, the soldier/rapist describes wrapping plastic around "their necks until they start to choke". Alleging that "the CIA showed us a lot of shit, man", he continues, "As far as I am concerned, they are all guilty. They should have kicked Saddam Hussein out themselves. Instead we are doing the job. We are losing men ... Anyone with a fucking rag on their head is fair game."

When the young man is asked about the 'most fun thing' he did, he responds without hesitation, "Definitely the women ..." He then describes a 15-year-old girl who had not been "touched", who was "fucking prime" ("she was hot too ...") and claims that he "fucked" and then pimped her for $50 dollars to other soldiers, collecting $500. The young woman later committed suicide by hanging herself, he tells his companion. Both men laugh, and the soldier/rapist explains that because rape is shunned in Iraqi society, the girl would have been shamed if it had became public knowledge: "She would have been stoned to death anyway", he states.

It would, of course, be preposterous to suggest that one accept this young man's claims that he served in the US Army, was a guard at Abu Ghraib, or even that he participated in any of the activities he describes simply on the basis of this video posting. However, it would be just as problematic to ignore the similarities between the claims he makes and the case of a 22-year-old American soldier who was found guilty of the rape and murder of a 14-year-old Iraqi girl in Mahmudiya. That young soldier, along with four of his comrades, was found guilty of the rape and also of four murders, that of the young Iraqi woman who was raped, her younger sister and their parents.[2] The veracity of the *YouTube* posting requires investigation, but the similarity of the claims that are described there to the actions of the young American soldier convicted of rape and murder cannot be dismissed lightly. It is to be hoped that the *YouTube* posting is not a recounting of actual events. If that is the case, then the video posting serves as a chilling demonstration of how the 'War on Terror' is feeding the fertile imaginations and fantasy lives of young American men who articulate their desires within the context of the actual events taking place in the war being waged by their country-men and women. It also demonstrates how deeply intertwined are the racial and sexual aspects of such male desires and fantasies: the racialized construct of Muslim societies as misogynist ("she would have been stoned anyway") is used to rationalize the sexual violence that is said to have caused the death of the young Iraqi woman. To treat the violence valorized in the *YouTube* posting as an isolated case is to miss the point that this violence contributes to, and is sustained by, the violence that the United States and its partners have defined as necessary to safeguard their national interests.

In his study of the fictional and non-fictional narratives of the Freikorps, the German volunteer army that decimated the revolutionary German working class and later became the core of the Nazi SA and the SS, Klaus Theweleit describes how deeply these narratives were shaped by the men's fear and hatred of sexual-ity and women's bodies.[3] Theweleit argues that the men's actions cannot be simply attributed to a repressed sexuality. Rather, they have to be treated as an expression of the actual violent desires of the men themselves. Taking Theweleit's point seriously, it can certainly be argued that the racialized/sexualized fantasy-desires of young American men like the ones featured in the *YouTube* posting cannot be taken simply as expressions of wishful (essentially benign, even if disturbing) fantasy lives. For Abu Ghraib demonstrates graphically that when such men – and women – are given the power to act out these fantasies, many do not hesitate to do so in the most wanton manner. Indeed, when the young 'hero' of the *YouTube* video comments that as far as he is concerned "they are all guilty", he serves to remind the viewer that in his case at least, the step from justifying violence against those Iraqis directly engaged in attacks on the American occupation forces to justifying violence, including sexual violence, against all of "them" has already been taken. The rationale articulated by the young man for his acts of violence, i.e. that 'their' society is barbaric ('they' stone women to death), that 'we' had to step in because 'they' cannot take care of 'their' own problems ('they' should have rid themselves of Saddam Hussein), 'they' are treacherous instead of being grateful ('they' attack us while 'our' young men are dying for 'them'), is a key feature of the imperialist ideology that has shaped North American public discussions about the invasion and occupation. This rationale is widely disseminated by the mainstream media in most Western societies in their reporting of the Afghanistan and Iraq wars.

In a provocative argument, Theweleit goes on to claim that the "fantasies and affect" to be found in the narratives of the Freikorps are not the purview of any particular class of men:

> To make the point even clearer, any male reading the texts of these soldier males – and not taking immediate refuge in repression – might find in them

a whole series of traits he recognizes from his own past or present behaviour, from his own fantasies.[4]

Be that as it may, the relation between the disciplinary ethos of the hegemonic masculinity that is critical to the effective functioning of the US military in times of war and the 'normal' forms of masculinity prevalent within that society has been found to be symbiotic.[5]

Moreover, male fantasies and desires of rape and torture are not the only ones being inspired by the violence being waged in Afghanistan and Iraq, for no less potent are the dreams and longings for other articulations of Western power and white supremacy. In the wake of the publication of the Abu Ghraib torture photographs, members of the US Congress conducted hearings on the revelations of the use of torture by American servicemen and women, hearings that were televised live on CNN and other news networks. Here, confronted with the graphic images of the various forms of sadistic violence perpetrated on incarcerated Muslim male bodies, many Members of Congress, news reporters and political commentators made the very holding of such public hearings into a demonstration of the 'open' and 'democratic' nature of American society. The hearings thus became yet another occasion for the assertion of the 'superiority' of Western/American values. In this case, the torture depicted in the Abu Ghraib photographs fed the fantasy/desires of superiority of the governing systems and cultural values of the nation in whose name the torture was being perpetrated. In a truly perverse manner, the claims of American – and Western – superiority were sustained, rather than eroded, by the public exposure of the torture. The debate whether the use of torture is in accordance with American values continues to rage on at the time of writing this paper, as does the torture, if the graphic accounts of those being subjected to it are to be treated seriously.

In the following sections, I begin with a theoretical discussion of the forms of masculinities dominant within American society in the last decades of the twentieth century and then trace the emergence of the vigilante form within the War on Terror. Although an angry masculinity was central to the male backlash of the culture wars of the last decades of the twentieth century, it nevertheless remained marginal in mainstream society. With the launching of the War on Terror, however, this form of masculinity became refashioned into a vigilante form in direct relation to the 'Islamic' threat to ascend to the centre of American political life. In the final section, I make the case that the very violence that marks the vigilante form also undermines its ongoing reproduction. As scholars of masculinity have argued, if war serves as the defining marker of masculine valour, it is also the terrain which reveals the hollowness of their masculinity as men come face to face with the utter vulnerability of their bodies to injury and death.

Popular cultural masculinities

The crisis of white masculinity in North America was a recurring feature in popular media, as it was in political life, in the decades preceding the attacks of

September 11, 2001. A number of scholars have argued that American masculinity, unsettled by the gains of the feminist and civil rights movements of the 1960s and 1970s, and the US defeat in Vietnam, was increasingly resurgent during the 1980s and 1990s through a decidedly anti-feminist and racist politics.[6] A similar anti-feminist and anti-immigrant backlash could also be traced in Canada, where, as was the case in the United States, women were often vocal supporters of this backlash.[7]

Masculinity is, Homi Bhabha explains, "the 'taking up' of an enunciative position, the making up of a psychic complex, the assumption of a social gender, the supplementation of a historic sexuality, the apparatus of a cultural difference".[8] Noting that masculinity is, among other things, a 'choice' which gives rise to particular forms of anxiety ("Are you a Man or a Mouse?" Bhabha recounts his father asking him) and speaks to a "lack-in-being", Bhabha argues that what is required is to "disturb its manifest destiny – to draw attention to it as a prosthetic reality – a prefixing of the rules of gender and sexuality".[9]

A number of scholars of masculinity have sought to do just that, that is, 'disturb' masculinity by theoretically rupturing the equation of masculinity with men and male bodies.[10] They have also critically examined the challenges posed to dominant forms of masculinity by the rise of feminist, anti-racist and queer movements. In so doing, these scholars have drawn attention to the rise of the men's rights organizations of the 1980s and 1990s, which they define as part of the response to these movements. Such men's rights groups, Gardiner notes, "[N]otoriously bewail[ed] male victimization ... the 'masculinist' men's movement argued in favour of male dominance and blamed widespread psychological and social problems on feminist attacks and men's loss of status."[11]

Soloman-Godeau complicates the analysis of the masculinist backlash by arguing that various forms of "radically different and equally widespread expressions of idealized masculinity" coexist in the same historical moment. Asking "which variant of masculinity is to be understood as a manifestation [of] crisis",[12] she sounds a cautionary note and rejects "formulations that imply some utopic or normative masculinity outside crisis". Instead, she argues "that masculinity, however defined, is, like capitalism, *always* in crisis. And the real question is how both manage to restructure, refurbish, and resurrect themselves for the next historical turn."[13] It is this "next historical turn" that is the concern of this chapter.

Targeting 'femi-nazis', 'political correctness', 'gay rights', and the 'reverse racism' of anti-discrimination policies, the resurgent backlash masculinity articulated an anger that was directed specifically towards ending women's access to abortion rights, destroying affirmative action policies, gaining custody rights for fathers, de-legitimizing women's charges of sexual assault by promulgating the notion of 'false memory syndrome', and opposing same-sex marriage, among a host of other issues. The men's rights movements also had to contend with other forms of masculinity that had become dominant – such as the masculinity of the liberal 'sensitive' and 'new age' man – some even pro-feminist – born out of the counter-cultural and peace movements, and of the 'sexual revolution', of the 1960s.

(While beyond the scope of the present chapter, it should be noted that one variant of this form of masculinity is clearly evident in the spectacular rise of Senator Barack Obama to the presidency of the US.)

The highly politicized issues that were the focus of the activism of the men's rights groups discussed above could also be found within popular cinema. Big-budget Hollywood productions, including films like *Basic Instinct* and *Disclosure*, articulated this retrograde masculinist politics. Starring the urbane Michael Douglas as the protagonist in both films, the elite white women who were the antagonists were presented as threatening both the sexual prowess and the economic status of the hard-done-by heroic male. Douglas, who can be described as the 'thinking' man's man (he has been called "one of the most sought-after actors in Hollywood)"[14] and who, as such, appeals to more sophisticated and elite tastes, performed to perfection this wounded masculinity, compelled to fight back in its castrating interactions with strong and powerful, but ultimately vengeful, women.

The status and power said to have been lost to white men had resulted in limited gains for most women and racial minorities, having largely benefited a class of elite white women in their climb up the professional and financial ladder. But this was less visible in the 'backlash' genre of films than the allegation that women were emasculating men, ruining decent American families, and contributing in no small measure to increased crime and delinquency. A return to family values, and the nuclear patriarchal family, as the means to restore order to the nation and its families was the populist ideology on which the Republican Party rode to power as it played to its religious and conservative political base. Presidents Reagan, George Bush and George W. Bush all effectively galvanized this Republican constituency, even as their presidencies significantly boosted the strength and reach of fundamentalist Christian and neo-conservative political forces. In Canada, the parallel could be found in the rise of the Reform Party on an anti-immigrant, anti-feminist and 'pro' family values platform in the 1990s, after which it merged with the Conservative Party to subsequently come to power as the Progressive Conservative Party, reflecting a similar, albeit somewhat muted, politics.

But the resurgence of the angry white male, who provided the model for what became the signature role for Douglas during this period, had more to contend with than might appear at first sight. As mentioned above, along with the rise of feminism, the anti-Vietnam War and the Civil Rights movements of the 1960s, a new ideal of masculinity had also acquired considerable prominence: the angry white male of the 'backlash' era had to contend with the 'new age' sensitive man, defined as more liberal in political outlook and more accommodating of the claims of marginalized others within American society, be they the claims of women or those of racial minorities. In addition to the critique of patriarchy developed by feminism, many men also rebelled against the patriarchal casting of rigid masculine roles.[15] Defined primarily as the 'breadwinner' for the family, many men found their attempts to emulate this role crippling: "Traditional Masculinity", Ehrenreich argues, "is a particularly strenuous act", making men subservient to a capitalism which they, too, found constraining, if not altogether debilitating.[16] Bill Clinton's presidency in the US provides an example of the prominence acquired by this 'new' masculinity. The flamboyant Pierre Trudeau's reign as Prime Minister in Canada might also be seen as reflective of the rise to hegemonic status of the suave charmer of the 'new' man, who, instead of being threatened by the professional status and political participation of women and of people of colour, seemed to actually welcome it. The angry white male variant of masculinity was certainly a significant force in North American politics during this period, but it clearly remained eclipsed. Despite the significant presence of the angry white masculinity propelling the male backlash, popularized through films like *Rambo, Rocky* and *Terminator*, this form of masculinity did not dominate mainstream public and political life. While such action heroes certainly inspired many young men to emulate them as role models, this genre of action films with their archetypal 'warrior' figure of a robust masculinity nonetheless remained outside the purview of social and political respectability. The heroes of such films were as much the objects of ridicule in the respectable press, and in the writings of feminists, as they were the subject of veneration by their largely male audiences. Despite their popularity and box office success, such films rarely moved out of their action film status.

One film stands out as emblematic of this clash of mainstream masculinities in pre-September 11th American society, and seems an eerie foretelling of the role Guantanamo Bay was to play in the War on Terror. In *A Few Good Men*, the challenge presented to the masculinity of the angry white male by the 'new' sensitive masculinity is played out in particularly stark fashion Tom Cruise, who plays the role of a US Navy lawyer, Daniel Kafee, determined to bring to justice two Marines and, through them, an American general, Colonel Nathan Jessep (played by Jack Nicholson), personifies this ideal of a more sensitive and compassionate masculinity. Jessep has ordered his men to give a 'code red' to Santiago, a soldier unable to make the grade at the US Naval base in Guantanamo Bay, Cuba. 'Code red' is a hazing ritual that evokes images of torture, and is not officially condoned in the Marine Corps. Following Jessep's order, the two young marines give Santiago, their friend, a 'code red', which leads to his accidental death. Daniel Kafee, along with Lt. Cdr. JoAnn Galloway (Demi Moore) and Lt. Sam Weinberg (Kevin Pollak) are attorneys assigned to investigate the case.

The masculinity that Tom Cruise, the hero of the film, represents – Harvard educated, sensitive to women, cosmopolitan and polished – is determined to take on Nicholson's angry, white vigilante masculinity over the lawlessness of the act he has ordered in that quintessential masculinist institution, the US Marine Corps. If there ever was a prosthetic masculinity, it certainly can be said to be exhibited *par excellence* in institutions like the navy, army and other defence forces. Writing before the attacks of September 11th 2001, Judith Halberstam treats the 'prosthetic' masculinity of the action hero as outdated, and her disdain for this figure, now in the role of the Marine, is reflected in *A Few Good Men*.[17] In a highly charged courtroom scene, Colonel Jessep (Nicholson) lambasts Tom Cruise as weak and ineffectual:

> You can't handle the truth! Son, we live in a world that has walls. And those walls have to be guarded by men with guns. Who's gonna do it? You? You, Lt. Weinberg? I have a greater responsibility than you can possibly fathom. You weep for Santiago and you curse the Marines. You have that luxury. You have the luxury of not knowing what I know: that Santiago's death, while tragic, probably saved lives. And my existence, while grotesque and incomprehensible to you, saves lives ...You don't want the truth. Because deep down, in places you don't talk about at parties, you want me on that wall. You need me on that wall. We use words like honor, code, loyalty ... we use these words as the backbone to a life spent defending something. You use 'em as a punchline. I have neither the time nor the inclination to explain myself to a man who rises and sleeps under the blanket of the very freedom I provide, then questions the manner in which I provide it! I'd rather you just said thank you and went your way. Otherwise, I suggest you pick up a weapon and stand a post. Either way, I don't give a damn what you think you're entitled to![18]

The effect when Jack Nicholson delivers the above dialogue is to reveal the violence that lies at the heart of the Marine Corps as an institution, and to reveal the thuggish, boorish and bullying nature of the masculinity which feels itself compelled to lawlessness in the name of national security. Face to face with Tom Cruise, who is driven by his respect for the rule of law, Jack Nicholson seems all bluster and blubber. Tom Cruise and his team watch stunned as Jessep is taken away, as does the audience, shaken by the seemingly outlandish ranting of an outdated masculinity they have been shocked to have witnessed. All this was to change quite dramatically after the September 11th attacks on the United States, as the bankrupt rationale proffered by Jessep for his "grotesque and incomprehensible existence" moved to claim centre stage in American politics.

Before I move on to examine the impact of the September 11th, 2001 attacks on this clash of masculinities, one more detail about *A Few Good Man* requires attention. The film is based on a real incident of hazing in the US Marines. The character of the young lawyer played by Tom Cruise is based on that of a Latino US Attorney, David C. Iglesias. The film thus replaces a 'heroic' Latino man with a white one, cinematically recasting the racialized identity of the heroic 'American' masculinity committed to justice and the rule of law. It is surely an irony of history that Iglesias was one of the eight attorneys working as prosecutors for the US Justice Department allegedly fired by then Attorney General, Antonio Gonzales, for purely partisan political reasons. Gonzales, appointed Attorney General by President Bush, is also a Latino and the alleged author of the infamous 'torture' memo authorizing the interrogation methods used on detainees at Abu Ghraib and Guantanamo Bay.

Vigilantism: a 'new' masculinity for the 'new' Islamic threat

Even before the dust had begun to settle on the ruins of the Twin Towers, three male figures emerged out of the rubble who were to become emblematic of post-September 11th 'heroic' American masculinity: the policeman, the soldier, and the fire fighter. Potent signifiers of the prosthetic nature of masculinity, armed as they are with their guns, bombs and hoses, these figures came to embody the masculinity that quickly became defined by the state as absolutely vital to protecting the nation in an unprecedented moment of global crisis. These three figures of male/state authority had come under considerable criticism in the period before the September 11th attacks. In the case of police forces, they had come under considerable scrutiny in large North American cities, including New York City,[19] Los Angeles,[20] Toronto,[21] and Saskatoon[22] for their brutal treatment of people of colour, and particularly for their violence against Black and Aboriginal men. The highly publicized sexual harassment charges recently brought by women in the US Army had demystified the 'heroic' nature of the American soldier, and the beating to death of Shidone Arone, a Somalian teenager by Canadian soldiers had likewise revealed the violence that underpinned the activities of soldiers in their 'humanitarian' role as 'peacekeepers'.[23] As for fire fighters, a number of sexual harassment cases brought by women fire fighters had lifted the curtain on the sexism rampant within the intensely male work culture that was the fire station. All these concerns were swept under the rug as media coverage of the September 11th attacks lionized these figures as the triumvirate of heroism, dedicated to saving the lives of their fellow Americans from *all* their enemies.[24] The public veneration of these three figures was also subsequently carried into Iraq, where each branch of the US Military – the Army, Air Force, Marines and Navy – had its seal displayed on a different corner of a mural in the palace housing American officials in Baghdad.[25] This high-profile veneration of phallic masculinity overwhelmed other variants of masculine responses to the crisis.

The response of the Bush Administration to the attacks rallied the nation behind this phallic masculinity, and in the process, sought to suture the deep cleavages that had previously riven the nation. Voices of dissent were drowned out by the mainstream media's support of the war, and American masculinity, presented as wounded by the seemingly inexplicable nature of the attacks, was projected onto the global stage as signifying both American victimhood and innocence. The media's frequent repetition of the question, 'Why do they hate us?' at once erased the history of the violence of US foreign policy and projected an American persona innocent of any intimation of why it could possibly have been attacked. As other scholars have noted, the question shifted attention away from the realities of geo-politics and towards speculation about the emotional and psychological motives – and makeup – of the attackers.[26]

With the US being defined as having inexplicably come under attack, and with President Bush declaring that the nation was called upon by events and by 'history' to protect Western civilization, the nation's 'wounded' masculinity was called into action. The deeply traumatic effect of the collapse of the Twin Towers became a literal symbol of the emasculation of the nation by its enemies, the media's relentless repetition of the image only further compounding this symbolic castration of the most potent symbol of the nation's economic power. The relationship between masculinity and the nation has historically been deeply significant, with the ultimate mark of masculine valour being the willingness of men to die in the service of the nation, sacrificing their own lives to protect its interests.[27] The Administration's launching of the war thus provided fertile terrain for spurring on the angry masculinity, now officially sanctioned to wage violence in order to recoup the nation's stature.

Osama bin Laden and the al-Qaeda network (rapidly to be joined by Saddam Hussein) were quickly held responsible for what was defined as an unprecedented 'terrorist' attack on American soil.[28] As the definition of Muslims as the most urgent threat to Western civilization gained ground, the media ridiculed the futile attempts of the Taliban to negotiate with the US to turn over Bin Laden to a third (Muslim) country upon presentation of evidence of his involvement in the September 11th attacks, when such efforts were reported on at all. Constituted in the deeply colonialist trope of the barbaric Other, this racialization of Bin Laden and other Jihadis in the media successfully drew upon the racial and gendered divides within the global order that had historically constituted the West as different from, and whose interest were incommensurable with, those of the 'rest'. The construction of the Jihadis as medieval fanatics who opposed – not US foreign policy, as they themselves declared – but 'western' civilization, reinvigorated the Orientalism that was central to the historical development of Euro-American societies and the white masculinities that have shaped them. The media's focus on Bin Laden's Saudi/Arab/Muslim origins, in tandem with a language that dehumanized him and his followers, helped to reconstruct the religious category Muslim as a religio-racial one.

Media representations of Bin Laden continue to remain contradictory: he is simultaneously constructed in hyper-masculine terms as evil incarnate, almost demonic in his maniacal desire to destroy human progress. The most recurrent images in news reports show him riding on a horse, loading a gun, talking on a communications device in what looks like an obvious battle zone, or hiking in the rugged mountains of Afghanistan. In these settings, his long beard, Arab headdress and the gun (or horse or communication device) become accentuated as the markers of an equally harsh and rugged form of 'traditional' Muslim masculinity. Frequently shown loading a rifle, or seated next to a Kalashnikov, his role as a combatant is repeatedly underscored. Conversely, Bin Laden is also presented as a highly feminized figure, with news reports often drawing attention to his poetic style, his soft-spoken manner and the long robes he wears. So, for example, Bin Laden's 'limp' handshake has been the subject of much comment.[29] The 'limp' handshake comes to stand in for a limp masculinity, more feminine than masculine. He is also said to hide in caves, the implication being that he flees the battleground and does not stand and fight like a 'real' man. Through the feminization of the figure of Bin Laden, the Jihadi 'enemy' has become likewise constructed as feminized, or effeminate, enabling the 'wounded' and angry American masculinity to funnel its previous misogynist anger against feminists and women towards these Muslim men who dress, and act, like women. Yet, feminine and/or effeminate as Bin Laden has come to be defined in the Western social imaginary, the effectiveness of the attacks al-Qaeda has repeatedly launched against the US and its allies bespeak a rather different reality than the word 'limpness' might suggest. Moreover, Bin Laden's implied impotence is also challenged by his familial relations: he is reported to have four wives and a number of sons.

On the extremely rare occasions when Bin Laden has been interviewed by Western journalists, he has presented himself in a manner that clearly undermines the media's constant demonization and feminization of Jihadis. His views are well articulated and carefully crafted for their impact. He is described, even by many of his foes, as poetic and charismatic in style. In his dealings with the media, Bin Laden has certainly proven himself extremely adept. As Peter Bergen, one of the leading 'experts' on Bin Laden, recognizes, "Al Qaeda has long understood that propaganda is one of the keys to its success."[30] Yet, notwithstanding Bin Laden's acknowledged media "savvy",[31] news reports continue to discount such acknowledgements by defining Jihadis as 'pre-modern' and 'irrational': "I think their media capability is sophisticated as ever", says Bruce Hoffman, a terrorism expert and professor at Georgetown University in Washington D.C. "It shows how this group with 7th century ideology is exploiting 21st century media capabilities."[32]

Bin Laden's piety and dedication to his cause have also been acknowledged by those who have met him, including men who fought with him in the Afghan jihad against the Soviets, journalists who have interviewed him, and American experts who have followed his career.[33] His austere lifestyle evokes respect, as does his turning away from his family's fortunes. He is said to adhere to Islamic practice even in his conduct of the attacks on the US. For example, he issued public warnings to Americans before Al-Qaeda first attacked the US embassies in Kenya and Tanzania, warning American civilians to leave the Middle East if they wanted to avoid becoming targets. Indeed, he is reported to even have issued an offer of a truce with the US after the war on Afghanistan began in response to criticism he received from other Islamic leaders for the attacks of September 11th. Such details, however, remain contained within a handful of documentaries that have featured interviews with him. These details are restricted from filtering into public awareness as they are not used to inform the extensive media reporting of the War on Terror and the 'real' motives of the Jihadis. Instead, the Taliban, al-Qaeda and Iraqi fighters are routinely defined as cowardly and unmanly: 'they' are said to hide under women's burqas and conceal themselves among civilians, unlike American men who fight like real men. Consequently, the suicide bomber, the mad mullah, the corrupt and self-indulgent oil sheikh, and the misogynist 'honour' killer remain the archetypal images of Muslim men in the Western media, against which the measure of American heroic masculinity is defined.

Facile and distorted media reports of Jihadis represent their motives as irrational, their behaviour as impossible to reason with. They are regularly described as 'evildoers' and 'scumbags', more demonic than human.[34] Such representations intersect with the legal categories developed by the Bush Administration such as "enemy combatant" or "unlawful enemy combatant" to reduce these men to bare life, in the sense discussed by Agamben, stripping them of all rights. With the US having claimed the power to detain or kill any 'suspected terrorist', regardless of their citizenship, the American men and women who hold these people are enabled to claim the power of life or death over them, a form of power defined as 'necropower' by Achille Mbembe. The use of spectacular violence against the Jihadis becomes all the more readily acceptable to North American populations in this manner. Moreover, the exaggeration of the Jihadis' prowess (state legislatures, airports, border crossings, bridges, shopping malls, sports stadiums, schools, including other public places have all been put on high security alert at some point or other all over North America) serves to keep these populations in a recurring state of fear and anxiety.

Face to face with the resistance of Jihadis to American domination of the Middle East and Central Asia, the majority of American and Canadian men and women have sought refuge in a reinvigorated alliance with their ruling elites against those they came to accept as their common enemy; the reproduction of the racialized division between the 'West' and 'Islam' is the precondition for this white gender/class alliance. In a gesture reminiscent of the masculinist men's movements, Americans and Canadians have positioned themselves as 'victims', not of feminists and anti-racist activists this time, but of Muslims, who are imagined as fuelled only by their incomprehensible hatred of women and the West.

Out of such castings of the American nation (and other Western nations) as 'terrorized' by the immeasurably weaker Jihadi groups like Al-Qaeda, and endangered by impoverished states like the Taliban regime in Afghanistan, the previously marginalized white angry masculinity ascended to the centre of political life and state institutions, presenting itself in its vigilante form as indispensable to protecting Americans and their national interests. Drawing on older discourses of Western civilizational superiority and Islamic barbarism, the post-September 11th claiming of national victimhood helped to obfuscate and justify the violence that this newly emboldened masculinity was to use to reassert itself as the only viable 'heroic' masculinity.

Defining itself in relation to the masculinity and femininity of Muslims, the vigilante masculinity could now transcend its previous identification with the misogynist backlash through its claims to be concerned with the rights of oppressed Muslim women: the war is "a hell of a hoot", a three-star Marine is reported as saying.

> It's fun to shoot some people …You go into Afghanistan, you got guys who slapped women around for five years because they didn't wear a veil. You know guys like that ain't got no manhood left anyway. So it's a lot of fun to shoot them.[35]

This merging of military masculinity with vigilantism acquired greater sanction as independent contractors became a key component of the American war strategy. These contractors and soldiers were not subject to Iraqi law.

White racial solidarity, articulated in the discourse of vulnerable Western national securities, and white racial benevolence, in the shared project of saving Muslim women, enabled the American nation to overcome the gender and culture wars of the previous decades in a manner that allowed white women to come together with white men in facing a common national enemy – Islam and the radical Jihadis. Post September 11th, white American masculinity came to re-cast itself as manly primarily in relation to the Muslim men whom it sought to defeat, and the Muslim women whom it claimed to 'save'. Charges of sexism and racism in North America could now be rebutted by white men by recourse to the project of 'saving' Muslim women. In this manner, white American masculinity re-defined itself in the changed global order: the vigilante form was fed by fantasies of Islam as violent, and hence *requiring* a greater violence to be vanquished.

The "shock and awe" war strategy, designed to demonstrate overwhelming US military power and thereby overwhelm Afghan and Iraqi populations into submission, made the exercise of spectacular violence the most salient feature of the war: raining down terror on civilian populations was deemed by Americans and their allies to be the most effective manner in which a wounded masculinity was to be redeemed and Western control was to be asserted. The use of violence by military forces is usually represented as a "violence born of exceptional circumstance", Sherene Razack has noted. "The violence of military men is naturalized as an inevitable by-product of war and of place, that is, as a response to a legitimate external threat, and as a response to a cruel environment."[36] However, in the case of the War on Terror, the violence was presented not only as inevitable, but as something that was to be spectacularized. The public valorization of the 'shock and awe' strategy, and the bypassing of the institutions upholding the rule of law at the international level facilitated the rise of the vigilante masculinity. President Bush's bravado in his orders to US troops to capture Osama Bin Laden "Dead or Alive', and his infamous challenge to Iraqi insurgents to "Bring them on" reflected how cavalierly his Administration was to spur on this vigilantism. If Bush's cowboyish flaunting of American might are dismissed as trite and unfitting, as many commentators do today, the sombre Vice President, Dick Cheney, argued the same point in a somewhat more refined vocabulary. What was required in the post-September 11th period, Cheney stated, was the "rule of men", not the "rule of law".[37]

American, Canadian and other allied soldiers are regularly shown on news networks including CNN, the BBC, and the CBC – with little self-reflexivity – whooping and cheering as the rockets they launch and the guns they fire are successful in finding their targets. Shouting victoriously, images showing them greeting each other with high fives and bear hugs are pervasive. Reporters and news anchors rarely remark about the disturbing nature of the images of these men, armed to the hilt, cheering the blowing up of mud homes and compounds in Afghanistan, or of residential buildings and neighbourhoods in Iraq.

The racialized dehumanization of Muslim men as so irrational and full of hatred that they can only understand the language of violence, and the racialized exalting of Americans, British and Canadians for the laudable goal of bringing 'freedom' to a region not used to it, frame the reporting of such unrestrained use of violence. In their study of Brazilian policemen who tortured and murdered civilians during military rule in that country (1969–1979), Huggins and Haritos-Fatouros found that these men blamed their victims for provoking the very violence to which they were subjected.[38] A similar move shapes media reporting of the War as the insurgents themselves are blamed for bringing on the violence to which they are subjected.

As it would turn out, the step from the widespread public acceptance of the 'shock and awe' strategy to the use of torture was to be a short one. Unrestrained by the rule of law, American and other troops were emboldened to inflict violence at will, and the numerous cases of civilian deaths and torture of detainees that continued to come to light prompted few shifts in this use of violence. Such revelations only provoked debates about how to make the use of violence more effective. The mere allegation of being a 'terrorist' was enough for widespread public acceptance of Muslims being rounded up, detained, incarcerated, tortured, or even targeted for assassination.

Further, the use of unrestrained violence by American independent contractors was also virtually underwritten by the Bush Administration.[39] These contractors, who played a major role in the war, were given free rein for their activities, which are not accountable either under US or Iraqi law: "Hired to protect US diplomats, private security companies like Blackwater can own their own helicopters, buy their own body armor and set their own rules of engagement. Their guards don't answer to the US military, or as recent cases suggest, anyone else."[40]

The partnership between military and vigilante masculinity has come to subordinate and marginalize all other variants, so that these other forms are increasingly being compelled to prove their virility in relation to their willingness to be 'tough' on terrorists. The power of the vigilante masculinity is reflected in the changed political culture, in the changes to laws and state practices, and also in popular culture. These changes have been supported and enacted by different political parties, by many intellectuals, by mainstream society and even by those constituencies who might have opposed it in the past, such as women and feminists.

Not all men, however, have been able to successfully access the vigilante form of masculinity promoted by the War. President Bush, for example, found his earlier attempts to perform this masculinity initially lauded as the coming of age of a strong leader. But these performances were ultimately met with ridicule once the insurgencies in both Afghanistan and Iraq made impossible the easy victories promised by his Administration. Despite the President's resort to the accoutrements of military life (prematurely appearing on a naval base in a pilot's uniform with a helmet in his hands, under a banner that read, "Mission Accomplished", to announce the cessation of hostilities in Iraq), even such props of prosthetic masculinity failed to establish the phallic masculinity he attempted to claim.

While this event was initially celebrated in the media, it later came to be ridiculed as an empty gesture as the war in Iraq continued to rage on. The vigilante form of masculinity did not stick to the figure of the President, for hegemonic masculinity has to deliver what it promises if it is to remain effective. It is in this failure to deliver that the potential resides for the undermining of the vigilante masculinity.

Vulnerable men, insecure masculinity

Scholars of masculinity have pointed out that if war is the pre-eminent site for the celebration of masculine valour, war also reveals the fragility of the male body and psyche.[41] In addition to the millions left dead and maimed during the First World War (1914–1918), "the new phenomenon of shell-shock left men witless, amnesiac, nervous, prone to break down at the least noise or stress".[42] The two World Wars, as well as the Vietnam War, deeply undermined the ideal of masculine invincibility as many soldiers returned from the battlefield scarred and wounded. A new vocabulary, including terms such as 'battle fatigue' and 'post-traumatic stress disorder', emerged to describe their condition. This vocabulary draws attention to the immense vulnerability of soldiers.

In her study of a group of Vietnam veterans diagnosed with post-traumatic stress disorder, Karner points out that "questions of what it means to be a man, how masculinity should be displayed, and where the appropriate social avenues are for its expression are, underlie the veteran's words".[43] Although the reasons for the men's enlistment varied, she found that all of them had been deeply influenced as young boys by the war films they had watched: all had bought into the "mystique" of the army as "glamorous".[44] If Karner's study underscores the importance of war films on shaping the desires of these men to live out the 'glamorous' life of what they imagined to be heroic soldiers, the current generation of American and Canadian soldiers serving in the War on Terror have been raised not only on a steady diet of the genres of war and action films discussed earlier in this chapter, but also of video games, among which war video games have gained considerable popularity. The power of such cinematic images can be easily recognized in President Bush's attempt to fashion himself after the Tom Cruise character in the film, *Mission Impossible*, when he appeared on the battle cruiser under the banner, *Mission Accomplished*, kitted out in full pilot gear, helmet in hands.

However, like the two real life World Wars and the war in Vietnam, the 'War on Terror' has also revealed the conflicts and contradictory impulses with which soldiers live. Desiring the 'glamour' and mystique of war to prove their masculinity, yet vulnerable to their corporeality as men of flesh and blood, these men understand that they are as likely to be killed and maimed themselves as they are to perpetrate the violence for which they have been trained.

In this last section, I focus on two key factors that have emerged as challenges to the successful reproduction of the vigilante American masculinity, and as such, have great potential to stem its ongoing domination. The first is the strength and resilience of the resistance movements that the US and allied forces have met in both Afghanistan and Iraq. The second is the human frailty of the American, Canadian and other soldiers, who are constantly confronted not only with the counter-violence of the insurgencies' resistance, but also by the effects of the violence they themselves expend.

Perhaps the more important of the factors destabilizing the vigilante masculinity is the resistance of the Taliban, al-Qaeda and other insurgents in Afghanistan and Iraq. By all accounts, resistance from an 'enemy' that the white vigilante masculinity has defined as effeminate, cowardly and easily conquerable, has been strong enough to foil American attempts to assert their control over these two countries. Seven years after the launch of the War on Terror, the al-Qaeda network is reported to be growing stronger and "once again on the move".[45] The network is also said to have increased its recruiting potential and is alleged to run training camps in the borderlands between Pakistan and Afghanistan. In his fiftieth year, Bin Laden, as Peter Bergen notes, "has much to celebrate".[46]

American soldiers were led to believe they would enjoy easy victories in both countries; Canadian and British soldiers were likewise led to believe they would be lauded as benefactors of the Afghan and Iraqi populations, especially the women. Instead, these forces have been met with roadside bombs, suicide bombers and mortar attacks. Indeed, the resistance has been so strong that many experts and high-ranking US and British officials predict that the chances of US victory in either country are extremely slim.[47]

The superior weaponry and air power of the US created a sense of the inevitability of American victory, feeding the fantasies of soldiers of their own invincibility. However, such fantasies seem to have dissolved into dread, guilt and anxiety, as the comments of many returning soldiers reveal. Although the weaponry and ferocious air power of American forces signify their military might, the bombs they drop often miss their targets and kill civilians, or even worse from the perspective of the soldiers, kill their fellow soldiers.[48] And despite what is presented to the soldiers as sound intelligence, they often find themselves firing on, and killing, civilians, including children, in the raids that they conduct in search of insurgents.

Calling the debate about Iraq in Washington "surreal", a statement published by a group of seven US soldiers who had served in Iraq reveals the cynicism of many soldiers: "We are skeptical of recent press coverage portraying the conflict as increasingly manageable and feel it has neglected the mounting civil, political and social unrest we see every day." Describing an incident where they witnessed the death of an American soldier and the wounding of two more, they expressed their distress and went on to state:

> Yes, we are militarily superior, but our successes are offset by failures elsewhere. What soldiers call the "battle space" remains the same, with changes only at the margins ... we operate in a bewildering context of determined enemies and questionable allies.[49]

Many of the soldiers report being traumatized and sickened by the deaths they witness, of their fellow soldiers as well as of civilians, and by the violence they themselves perpetrate. Soldiers talk of crying when they see little children terrified of them, many are sickened by the way in which they humiliate Iraqi and Afghan men in front of their families, round them up for no reason, and take them away for further abuse and incarceration.

Interviews with veterans of Iraq and Afghanistan reveal that many of these soldiers (and even independent contractors) clearly recognize that military victory is not viable in the absence of a political resolution in either country.[50] Nor can the futility of the battles engaged in by the soldiers be fully hidden from the general population. Fallujah, for one stark example, was won and then lost by American soldiers to Iraqi insurgents a number of times. In another example, a British unit engaged in a battle to take over a compound controlled by the Taliban was featured in a documentary broadcast on CBC. After a fire-fight with the Taliban, the unit took over the compound. But as soon as they started moving away from it, they heard a report broadcast on the local radio that the Taliban had already re-taken it.[51] The senselessness of their fighting is not lost on these soldiers as was recognized by a British soldier who said of the Taliban, "They're never going to go away."[52] Defeat in any war is difficult enough to accept, but defeat at the hands of enemies who are defined as infinitely weaker (in terms of material resources) and who have been ideologically cast as pre-modern 'killers' and 'scumbags' can certainly be anticipated to be much harder to accept for the US.

The racialized construct of the 'enemy' fighters as not man enough to fight cleanly and openly ('they' hide themselves under women's burqas, 'they' hide themselves among civilian populations) also seem to crumble in a most disturbing manner when American, Canadian, British and other soldiers encounter these 'feminized' men on the ground. For example, the British soldiers featured in the BBC documentary referred to above reluctantly admitted that the Taliban fighters, who were presented largely as a ragtag army, were staunchly dedicated to their cause. They were determined fighters and fought bravely (heroically?) against a far superior military power. Neither the Afghan nor the Iraqi insurgents have access to airpower, although American, Canadian and British soldiers are provided air cover by Apache helicopters and Hellfire missiles. In the documentary, a British commander radios for air support several times in the battle with Taliban fighters, and a helicopter drops a 500 lb bomb on the compound his battalion are fighting to take over from the Taliban. But the helicopter misses its target, and yet another bomb has to be dropped.[53] What is more, the Taliban soldiers fight to the end even in this battle where they faced clear and certain defeat.

The recognition by American and other soldiers of the strength and determination of the 'enemy', however reluctantly conceded, inevitably masculinizes the Afghan and Iraqi insurgents, for the resistance of these fighters speaks to the American soldiers in their own language of what constitutes 'heroic' masculinity. Whatever their attempts at denial, American soldiers are compelled to recognize the masculinity of the 'enemy' as similar in tone and timbre to their own, and in this, they are compelled to recognize the common humanity – *as men* – shared between themselves and their demonized Other.

Some soldiers are also found to be hostile to the presence of the independent contractors who are paid far more for their services and who conduct their operations without being subject to US military or Iraqi laws. These contractors have also killed civilians indiscriminately, and yet have gone unpunished. In the words of one US Marine, the war is a "war of words and manipulated emotions", and his anger at independent contractors such as Blackwater is palpable: "Don't call them security contractors," he said.

> They are cowboys …They are the worst kind of mercenaries. They are not beholden to any laws. They're not held accountable to the Uniform Code of Military Justice. They're not held accountable by U.S. law. And they are not accountable by Iraqi law. The role they play is criminal.

This ex-Marine served in Iraq, but turned into an anti-war activist and is now a member of the group, Iraq Veterans Against the War. "They never really say who is resisting in Iraq", he explains. While there are numerous names to refer to their opponents, "the enemy, terrorists, al-Qaida, foreign fighters and insurgents", this man has come to understand that the "Iraqi people are in the resistance". Strategic concerns and need for oil are reasons for war, he says, and then asks, "I should die for lies?" He comes to condemn his own conduct in a visceral manner: "Every Iraqi has eyes filled with fear, frustration, anger and hopelessness and no amount of body armor I was wearing could protect me from their eyes."[54] With every gesture that humanizes the 'enemy', some American soldiers seemingly become compelled to recognize their own inhumanity.

Moreover, many US soldiers have to train, work with, and fight alongside, their Afghan and Iraqi counterparts. How can their contempt for Muslims, and their mistrust of Muslim men, not be transferred onto these Afghan and Iraqi allies? Some American and other Western soldiers live in close proximity with these Muslim men, share their lives and combat experiences. But their socialization as Westerners has also taught them a revulsion of Muslim culture, and of the level of (under)development in countries like Afghanistan.

Some American soldiers report seeing Muslim civilians at close range, they see the fear on the faces of the children, they hear these children cry. These soldiers recount being reduced to tears as they remember their own children and sometimes even hear their children's voices in the cries of these 'enemy' children. These soldiers are also reminded of a shared humanity, a humanity that the architects of the war seek to deny. Many soldiers also report their distress at witnessing some of their comrades perpetrate acts of senseless brutality and humiliation. Such incidents increase the revulsion they sometimes feel against their own comrades, against their political elites who have enabled such violence to go uncontrolled and unpunished, and also at themselves for being unable to stop it. Such circumstances will, ultimately, undermine the will of many of the American soldiers on the ground, who, in addition to dealing with the Afghans and Iraqis, also have to dealing with the consequences of their actions.

Conclusion: winning a lost war?

Although the brutal violence of the War on Terror is presented as resulting from the actions of a few irresponsible individuals acting outside the law, mainstream consensus exists among the political elite in North America that such violence is necessary, and that it is the only way to deal with Jihadi fanatics. The torture, murder and rape of Afghans and Iraqis by American soldiers have gone largely unpunished, and the withdrawal of the law from these practices allows the vigilante masculinity full rein to operate. However, the opposition of the insurgent movements, with the growing support of their civilian populations, against the Americans and their allies have thus far ensured that the white vigilante masculinity remains unable to deliver on its promise of victory. The American led wars have to be won, if this masculinity is to remain viable and become hegemonic.

The resistance to the occupations of Iraq and Afghanistan also ensures that American and other allied soldiers live and operate in intensely hostile environments. Soldiers live in heavily fortified bases and centres, and have little everyday interaction with the local populations. The indiscriminate killing of civilians by these soldiers ensures that these populations will not accommodate themselves to the occupation.[55] Consequently, American solders are constantly in a state of heightened anxiety. Their racism means that most of them cannot distinguish friend from foe, even as they will have to increasingly rely on the Iraqis and Afghan soldiers and police they manage to 'train'.

The public comments and interviews of American soldiers in Iraq and Afghanistan reveal their ambiguity. Caught between exhilaration and fear, between mastery and insecurity, hatred and compassion, the effects of the war are likely to be of lasting duration. The sense of betrayal expressed by many of the soldiers whose narratives I have examined in this chapter centres on the incompetence of the architects of the war strategy, on the inadequacy of the material support provided to the soldiers, on the lies emanating from the US Administration about the causes of the war, on the immense amounts of money going to independent contractors and corrupt local elites, and on the overstretching of the troops who find themselves on long tours of duty. Soldiers are also being sent to the war without adequate equipment or body protection armour. Although miniscule in comparison to the Afghans, Iraqis and other Muslims being killed, a significant number of American and allied soldiers are also being killed, wounded, and maimed. In the US, these soldiers come back to find inadequate health care and financial support for their families. Many are penalized if they try to leave the army.

Soldiers are also aware of the huge profits being reaped by corporations such as Blackwater, Haliburton, Exxon, Chevron, and even the Bush family. The opportunism and corruption of their political leaders cannot be hidden from them. Nor can the worldwide revulsion that followed the revelation of torture at Abu Ghraib. It is inconceivable that such revelations have not deeply affected the soldiers' perceptions of themselves and their actions. They have also come to learn that the top ranks of their leadership will not be punished for such violence, but the lower ranks will be, if such abuses continue to be brought to light. Some soldiers are not only defecting from the US Army, but are also leaving the US altogether and applying for refugee status in Canada. The US military now also has the highest rate of suicides in decades.

The Vietnam War proved to be a national trauma for the Americans, whose soldiers returned to a population that did not support them and, instead of treating them like heroes, wanted them to disappear quietly. North American populations had an appetite for war as they supported their political leaders in launching and quickly winning the first Gulf War, and then the War on Terror. However, as the resistance to the US- led occupations of Afghanistan and Iraq is proving to be explosively effective, these populations are losing their stomach for the killing and chaos. Caught up in the current climate of vigilantism, American and Canadian soldiers in the War on Terror may yet encounter a fate similar to that of the Vietnam veterans.

Acknowledgments

This chapter is based on research conducted as part of a project on Masculinities at the International Centre for Ethnic Studies in Colombo, Sri Lanka.

Notes

1 The video is entitled, "I've tortured and raped in Iraq", and the text describes the contents as follows: "An American soldier boasts of having tortured Iraqis and making a 15 year old Iraqi girl commit suicide after she had been raped". Available at: www. youtube.com/watch?j=qFOF-jv32dA, accessed 3 August 2007.
2 Reuters, "US Soldier Is Convicted of Raping Iraqi Girl and Killing Her and Kin", reported in *The New York Times*, Sunday, 5 August 2007, p. 11.
3 Klaus Theweleit, *Male Fantasies*, vol. 1, Minneapolis: University of Minnesota Press, 1987.
4 Ibid, p. 89.
5 Susan Brownmiller, *Against Our Will: Men, Women and Rape*, New York: Bantam Books, 1975; Cynthia Enloe, *Maneuvers: The International Politics of Militarizing Women's Lives*, Berkeley, CA: University of California Press, 2000.
6 See Susan Faludi, *Backlash: The Undeclared War Against American Women*, New York: Crown Publishers, Inc., 1991; Judith Regan Gardiner, *Masculinity Studies and Feminist Theory: New Directions*, New York: Columbia University Press, 2002, and Robyn Wiegman, 'Whiteness Studies and the Paradox of Particularity', *Boundary 2*, 26(3) (1999): 115–150.
7 Donna Laframboise, *The Princess at the Window: A New Gender Morality*, Toronto: Penguin Books, 1996, and Danielle Crittenden, *What Our Mothers Didn't Tell Us: Why Happiness Eludes the Modern Woman*, New York: Touchstone, 2000.
8 Homi K. Bhabha, "Are You a Man or a Mouse?" in Maurice Berger, Brian Wallis, Simon Watson and Carrie Weems (eds) *Constructing Masculinity*, New York: Routledge, 1995, pp. 57–58.
9 Ibid.
10 See Gardiner, op. cit.; Judith Halberstam, *Female Masculinity*, Durham, NC: Duke University Press, 1998.
11 Gardiner, op. cit.

12 Abigail Solomon-Godeau, "Male Trouble", in Berger *et al. Constructing Masculinity*, p. 70.

13 Ibid.

14 See Michael Douglas' profile on Wikipedia. Available at: www.en.wikipedia.org/wiki/Michael_Douglas

15 Barbara Ehrenreich, *The Hearts of Men*, New York: Anchor Press, 1983.

16 Ibid., p. 170.

17 Based on a play by Aaron Sorkin, *A Few Good Men* was directed by Rob Reiner and starred a host of popular Hollywood actors, including Jack Nicholson, Tom Cruise, Demi Moore, Kevin Bacon, Kiefer Sutherland, Cuba Gooding Jr. and Kevin Pollak. Made in 1992, the film was nominated for four Oscars and five Golden Globe Awards. See www.en.wikipedia.org/wiki/A_Few_Good_Men, accessed 27 September 2007.

18 Ibid.

19 In February 1999, Amadou Diallo, a West African immigrant man, was shot 41 times by the New York police. See *The Washington Post*, www.washingtonpost.com/wp-dyn/nation/specials/aroundtheworld, accessed 23 December 2007.

20 Speeding on a California highway in 1991, Rodney King, a Black man, was chased and stopped by the California Highway Patrol. He was then tasered and beaten by police from the Los Angeles Police Department. The beating was captured on video, and despite this evidence, the policemen involved were acquitted by an all white Jury. The acquittal sparked riots in Los Angeles. See Madison Gary, "The LA Riots: 15 Years After Rodney King", *Time*. Available at: www.time.com/time'specials/2007/la_riot/article/0,28804,161411, accessed 23 December 2007.

21 In May 2000, the Jamaican-Canadian Association held a public forum to question the Toronto Police Chief on the "disproportionately high number of young Black men shot and killed by the Police". Some 200 people from the Black community attended the forum. See "Toronto's Black Community Grills Fantino", CBC News, 5 May 2000. Available at: www.cbc.ca/news/story/2000/05/05/000505fantino.html, accessed 23 December 2007.

22 Neil Stonechild, a 17-year-old Aboriginal man was alleged to have been left by the police to freeze to death. In the wake of his death, the Saskatoon Police Department ame under scrutiny as it emerged that other Aboriginal men had received similar treatment. See "Who was Neil Stonechild", CBC News Online, 3 November 2005. Available at: www.cbc.ca/news/background/stonechild/, accessed 23 December 2007.

23 Sherene Razack, *Dark Threats and White Knights: The Somalia Affair, Peacekeeping and the New Imperialism*, Toronto: University of Toronto Press, 2004.

24 Six years after the attacks on September 11th, President Bush attended a ceremony to honour 87 firefighters in Denver, Colorado. Defining them as heroes, the President lauded their "dedication and service to the nation". Citing September 11th and Hurricane Katrina, the President stated, "there were firefighters from around the country there to help". Natasha Metzier, "Remembering the Fallen", *Rocky Mountain News*, Monday, 8 October 2007, p. 2.

25 In his reporting of American life inside the Green Zone in Baghdad, Rajiv Chandrasekaran describes the following fixtures in one of the Palaces in Baghdad in which American officials work:

> A mural of the World Trade Center adorned one of the entrances. The Twin Towers were framed within the outstretched wings of a bald eagle. In the middle were the logos of the New York Police and Fire Departments, and atop the towers were the words THANK GOD FOR THE COALITION FORCES & FREEDOM FIGHTERS AT HOME AND ABROAD.
> (Rajiv Chandrasekaran, *Imperial Life in the Emerald City*, New York: Vintage Books, 2007, p. 10)

26 See Mamdani, Mahmood, *Good Muslim, Bad Muslim: America, the Cold War and the Roots of Terror*, New York: Pantheon, 2004; and Ziauddin Sardar and Maryl Wynn Davies, *Why Do People Hate America?* Cambridge: Icon, 2002.

27 Graham Dawson, *Soldier Heroes: British Adventure, Empire and the Imagining of Masculinities*, London and New York: Routledge, 1994; David Buchbinder and Jon Robert Adams, *Male Armor: The Soldier-Hero in Contemporary American Culture*, Charlottesville, VA: University of Virginia Press, 2008.

28 In 1921, white American citizens took over planes from an army base there to fire-bomb a Black neighbourhood. Yet, September 11th became defined as the first terrorist air attack on American soil. Lightweis-Goff argues that this definition demonstrates the racialization of the category "terrorist". See Jennie Lightweis-Goff, 'Blood at the Root: Lynching, Memory, and Freudian Group Psychology', *Psychoanalysis, Culture & Society*, 12 (2007): 288–295.

29 *In the Footsteps of Bin Laden*, documentary by Christianne Amanpour, broadcast on CNN, 17 August 2007.

30 Peter Bergen, "Where You Bin? The Return of Al Qaeda", *The New Republic*, 236(5) (30 January 2007): 16–19.

31 Anna Johnson, *The New York Times*, 20 December 2007.

32 Ibid.

33 Bin Laden gave interviews to CNN, to Abdel Bari Atwan of Al Quds Al Arabi, as well as to Hamid Mir, a Pakistani journalist who is writing his authorized autobiography. Also see Amanpour, op. cit.

34 While President Bush constantly refers to 'terrorists' as 'evildoers', General Rick Hillier, the head of the Canadian Defence Forces constantly refers to al-Qaeda, the Taliban and other insurgents as 'scumbags' and 'murderers'.

35 Paul Watson, *Where War Lives*, Toronto: McClelland & Stewart, 2007, p. xii.

36 Razack, op. cit., p. 57.

37 See documentary, *Cheney's Law*, PBS, Frontline, 16 October, 2007. Available at: www.pbs.org/wgbh/pages/frontline/cheney/etc/synopsis.html.

38 Martha K. Huggins, and Mika Haritos-Fatouros, "Bureaucratizing Masculinities Among Brazilian Torturers and Murderers", in Lee H. Bowker (ed.) *Masculinities and Violence*, Thousand Oaks, CA: Sage Publications, 1998.

39 For example, Blackwater, a security firm that has been one of the major contractors providing security, is reported to have 2,300 soldiers working for the US government in nine countries. It has a database of 21,000 former Special Forces troops and operates its own air fleet, including helicopter gunships. For more information on this corporation, see Jeremy Scahill, *Blackwater: The Rise of the World's Most Powerful Mercenary Army*, New York: Nation Books, 2007.

40 The utter lawlessness within which private security firms operate in Iraq has received much attention after guards working for Blackwater were alleged to have indiscriminately opened fire and killed 17 Iraqi civilians in September, 2007. These killings sparked such outrage in Iraq that the US Congress was "aroused" to pass legislation to make independent contractors "subject to prosecution by US courts". Paul Bremer had earlier signed an order when he was the US appointed governor of Iraq giving independent contractors immunity from Iraqi law. See Anne Flaherty, 'Security Firms Lose Immunity', *Rocky Mountain News*, Friday, 5 October 2007, p. 38. The Iraqi authorities have ordered Blackwater out of Iraq in six months and have asked for $136 million dollars be paid in compensation for the killings. Steven R. Hurst and Qassim Abul-Zahra, "Iraq Seeks $136 million in shootings", *Rocky Mountain News*, Tuesday, 9 October 2007, p. 27.

41 David Buchbinder, *Masculinities and Identities*, Victoria: Melbourne University Press, 1994; Buchbinder and Adams, op. cit., and Dawson, op. cit.

42 Buchbinder, op. cit., p. 9.

43 Tracy Xavia Karner, "Engendering Violent Men: Oral Histories of Military Masculinity", in Bowker (ed.), *Masculinities and Violence*, p. 197.
44 Ibid., p. 213.
45 Bergen, op. cit., pp. 16–19.
46 Ibid.
47 For example, the British Ambassador in Afghanistan was reported as saying there is no military solution in Afghanistan. See *Taking on the Taliban: The Soldier's Story*. The Senlis Council was warned that increased Taliban control in southern Afghanistan means that "a de facto Taliban/Al Qaeda state is on the verge of emerging in southern Afghanistan, straddling the Afghan border into Pakistan". Senlis Council News Release, "Manley Panel Urged to Recommend Canada Call for Emergency Meeting", 5 December 2007. Available at: www.press@senliscouncil.net, accessed 5 December 2007.
48 A number of Canadian soldiers have been killed by 'friendly fire' from US soldiers. See Graeme Smith, 'U.S. Error Kills Canadian, Stalls Attack on Taliban', *The Globe and Mail*, 5 September 2006.
49 Buddika Jayahama, Wesley D. Smith, Jeremy Roebuck, Omar Mora, Edward Sandmeier, Yante T. Gray and Jeremy A. Murphy. Op-Ed contributors, "The War as We Saw It", *New York Times*, 19 August 2007.
50 See interviews with American soldiers returning from Iraq. Laila al Arian and Laura Hanna, "Winter Soldier", *The Nation*, 2008. Available at: www.thenation.com/doc/20080407/wintersoldier
51 BBC documentary, *Taking on the Taliban: The Soldier's Story, Panorama*, broadcast on 10 November 2007.
52 Ibid.
53 Ibid.
54 GI Resistance, "One Veteran's View of the Conflict in Iraq", posted on NYC Labor Against the War (NYCLAW) listserve, 27 October 2007. Available at: http://nyclaw01. wordpress.com/, accessed 13 November 2007.
55 Naomi Wolf reports that 800 investigations have been undertaken of mainly low-ranking soldiers for torture after the revelation of the Abu Ghraib photos. Further action was taken in only 250 cases, resulting in 89 convictions. Some 14 out of 34 soldiers suspected of killing prisoners have been sentenced, with five months imprisonment being the "toughest" sentence. See Naomi Wolf, *The End of America: Letter to a Patriot*. Vermont: Chelsea Green Publishing, 2007, pp. 67–68.

5 Islam in the US

The contemporary scene

Fuad Shaban

September 11, 2001 was not the only factor which caused some Americans to openly attack Islam and the Prophet of Islam. Nor was this act of terror the main cause for the hatred of Islam that has been expressed in some American circles. September 11th, in my opinion, was the catalyst which opened the floodgate for centuries-old anti-Islamic sentiments which had been articulated before, but in limited forums and many times in indirect ways. After September 11, 2001, the right-wing in America – political and religious – gained the upper hand, and moderate voices became almost muffled.

Immediately following the September 11th attacks, President Bush prudently came out to warn his countrymen against renting their anger on Islam as a religion and particularly against American Muslims. Islam, he said, is a religion of peace, and he repeated this statement a number of times. He continued the tradition, started by President Clinton, to host a Ramadan dinner – breaking of the fast – in the White House. He also persisted in voicing this opinion about Islam in the face of mounting pressure from some of his allies and supporters.

A couple of months before the end of his presidency, Bush again told *Al-Arabia Television* that all religions pray to the same God and that "I believe Islam is a great religion that preaches peace."[1] This was his calm reaction to the interviewer, Elie Nakouzi's, provocative question:

> But I want to tell you – and I hope this doesn't bother you at all – that in the Islamic world they think that President Bush is an enemy of Islam – that he wants to destroy their religion, what they believe in. Is that in any way true, Mr. President?[2]

The President elaborated on this firm belief by saying:

> Well, first of all, I believe in an Almighty God, and I believe that all the world, whether they be Muslim, Christian, or any other religion, prays to the same God. That's what I believe. I believe that Islam is a great religion that preaches peace. And I believe people who murder the innocent to achieve political objectives aren't religious people, whether they be Christian who does that – we had a person blow up our – blow up a federal building in

Oklahoma City who professed to be a Christian, but that's not a Christian act to kill innocent people.

And I just simply don't subscribe to the idea that murdering innocent men, women and children – particularly Muslim men, women and children in the Middle East – is an act of somebody who is a religious person.[3]

As late in his second term of office as 5 December 2008, President Bush continued to call for a tolerant stand towards Islam and Muslims. In an interview with MBCTV (Middle East Broadcasting Center), Bush repeated that he continues to tell people this, that I do believe there is a universal God, and a gift of that Almighty to all of us – whether we be Methodists or Muslims or nothing – is freedom. And so freedom is a great alternative.[4]

With these remarks Bush stirred a good deal of anger and disputation among his core Christian Right supporters. One prominent representative of this constituency and a declared enemy of Islam and the Quran, Pat Robertson, tried to rationalize and explain away the President's comments. Appearing on ABC's *This Week*, Robertson said that Bush did not want to wage war on Muslims around the world or to make it look like a holy war. Instead, he said: "He's playing geopolitics and in that case he is very smart." And although Robertson repeated the view that Islam is "violent at its core", he added that "I'm one of his big supporters. I think I played a significant role in getting him elected … One little dispute doesn't separate friends."[5]

Another right-wing Christian, Jen Shroder (founder of Blessed Cause), explained Bush's repeated positive opinion of Islam by referring to 'Saudi Arabian pressure'; the use of oil to put "a knife to its [US] throat and Bush knows it. So he stepped up to the microphone and began to talk of a peaceful Islam, most likely choking on the words."[6]

Daniel Pipes, a neo-con not known for his sympathy with Islam, was more acid and desperate in his criticism. In *The New York Times*, Pipes referred to Bush's speech at the Islamic Center in Washington, DC, as "platitudinous, apologetic references to Islam as the 'religion of peace' ". Pipes then resigned himself to the fact that:

> As columnist Diana West puts it, "Nearly six years after September 11 – nearly six years after first visiting the Islamic Center and proclaiming 'Islam is peace' – Mr. Bush has learned nothing." But we now harbor fewer hopes than in 2001 that he still can learn, absorb, and reflect an understanding of the enemy's Islamist nature.[7]

In another attempt to dissociate himself from these remarks by supporters, and perhaps to provide American Muslims with some assurance of security from bias, Bush responded to the Christian Right's attacks on Islam by telling reporters that "Some of the comments that have been uttered about Islam do not reflect the sentiments of my government or the sentiments of most Americans."[8] At a meeting with United Nations Secretary General Kofi Annan on 13 November 2003, the President said: "By far, the vast majority of American citizens respect the Islamic people and the Muslim faith. After all, there are millions of peaceful-loving Muslim Americans."[9]

Other Christian Right leaders were not so kind and forgiving. Richard Land, President of the Southern Baptist Convention, said that when President Bush concludes that Muslims and Christians worship the same God, he "is simply mistaken". He added: "There is only one true God and this is Jehovah, not Allah."[10] The President of the National Association of Evangelicals, Ted Haggard, commented: "The Christian God encourages freedom, love, forgiveness, prosperity and health. The Muslim god appears to value the opposite. The personalities of each god are evident in the cultures, civilizations and dispositions of the peoples that serve them."[11]

The voice of the President and those of many American moderates were drowned by a propaganda campaign that continues until today and that seems to be an orchestrated effort by many political and religious organizations.

And even the President, like many of his predecessors, occasionally gave mixed signals – consciously or not – regarding his stand towards attacks on Islam in the US. The invitation to the Reverend Franklin Graham to deliver the convocation at the National Cathedral inauguration service in 2004; his playing up to the extreme Christian Right community, especially the missionary establishment in America; and the appointment of openly anti-Islam persons in key government positions – Richard Pearle, Douglas Feith and William Boyken – are some examples that readily come to mind.

One of the stark contrasts to President Bush's objectivity is his reception of the two missionaries, Heather Mercer and Dayna Curry, on their release from detention in Afghanistan. The two young ladies' denials while under detention of any missionary activities was followed on their return to the US by confessions of – indeed, pride in – their missionary goals and their undercover missionary activities in Afghanistan. In the White House the two missionary ladies were given a red-carpet reception and meetings with top officials, and during a photo-op with them, the President had this to say of their activities in his remarks to the media:

> Heather Mercer and Dayne Curry decided to go to help people who needed help. Their faith led them to Afghanistan. One woman who knows them best put it this way: they had a calling to serve the poorest of the poor, and Afghanistan is where that calling took them.[12]

Bush was probably not aware of the insult Muslims felt as a result of missionaries' opportunistic use of the hardships and desperation caused by war, especially waged by the USA, to prey on people's weakness in the name of 'serving the poorest of the poor'. Even at this writing, Heather Mercer is 'serving the poor' in Iraq in her persistent efforts to pursue her missionary zeal.

One of many recent developments relevant to the theme 'Islam in the US: The Contemporary Scene' is the sudden injection of Islam in the debates of the recent presidential campaign in the US. I will focus on this aspect of the campaign and then try to provide a historical backdrop that I hope will show that this contemporary debate over Islam is an old theme in American political and religious history.

In the thick of the battle for the American presidency, the public was treated to another 'smear' leveled against Barack Obama: His middle name is 'Hussein'.

> But "What's in a name?" asked Juliet, and she proceeded to answer:
> "What's in a name? That which we call a rose
> By any other name would smell as sweet?"
> True, but not if your name is Barack HUSSEIN Obama, and you are running
> for President of the United States of America.

Obama's response was measured; he categorically denied that he is a Muslim, emphasized his 20-year membership in the United Church of Christ in Chicago, and declared his firm belief in the Bible. Obama stated again on his website that he "is not and never has been a Muslim." And in a speech – significantly addressing a Jewish audience – on 27 February, he said emphatically: "If anyone is still puzzled about the facts, in fact I have never been a Muslim."[13]

Yet, with all the denials by Obama and his staff, the 'smear' is still reverberating in political and media circles. On websites, on talk shows, in printed journals and magazines and other media outlets, we read and hear expressions like 'White House mosque', 'Obama and Islam forever', and 'Barack HUSSEIN Obama'. In fact, one commentator was astonished that Obama would even think of running for President:

"Once a Muslim, always a Muslim", read a headline in the 18 December issue of *Column* by Debbie Schlussel (a right-wing political commentator), adding

> So, even if he identified strongly as a Christian … is a man who Muslims
> think is a Muslim, who feels some sort of psychological need to prove
> himself to his absent Muslim father, and who is now moving in the direction
> of his father's heritage, a man we want as President when we are fighting the
> war of our lives against Islam? Where will his loyalties be?[14]

Schlussel's final comment at the end of her remarks was the question whether Obama would even be acceptable as vice president. Her answer was the irreverently sarcastic: "NO WAY, Jose; or, is that HUSSEIN?"

The 'smear' became so widespread that *Time* magazine covered it in its online issue of 28 February 2008, where *Time* said: "Barack Obama has been confronted for the second time in 48 hours with efforts by conservative Republicans to convince voters that he is a Muslim and anti-Semite."[15] In fact, Senator McCain had to reproach Bill Cunningham for emphatically repeating the name "Barack Hussein" three times in an election rally which McCain himself addressed later. We have seen the pictures of Obama in a Somali chief dress published on a Republican Party website, and thereafter picked up by many media outlets.

This subject of Islam in the presidential campaign is of a special relevance to the topic at hand for two reasons: first, although the other candidates, mainly McCain and Clinton, either distanced themselves from or did not approve of the statements linking Obama to Islam, the story took on a life of its own and has been the subject of debate on all levels and for a long time.

Second, and more importantly, the term 'smear' has often been carelessly – and sometimes intentionally – used to refer to the Islam charge by many moderate media persons and politicians. In the debate over Obama's 'Islamic heritage,' very few people came out to denounce the description of Islam as a 'smear'.

Obama, his campaign staff, and his supporters were forced to deny time after time that he is a Muslim, thus indirectly confirming the ever-growing perception of Islam as a demon. Confirming the notion of Islam as a smear, or at least acknowledging it, Obama was forced to reply to a question by *60 Minutes'* Steve Kroft over rumours "that you're a Muslim", by saying: "You know, this has been a systematic e-mail smear campaign that's been going on since actually very early in this campaign. I have never been a Muslim, am not a Muslim … It plays into, obviously, a certain fear-mongering there."[16]

ABC News reported on Friday, 3 June 2008, that Obama had to launch a "website to dispel rumors about his faith and patriotism and his wife's views on race that have dogged his candidacy for more than a year". The Obama site insisted in face of the persistent Islam smear that "Senator Obama has never been a Muslim, was not raised as Muslim and is a committed Christian."[17] The site also carries a picture of Obama holding a Bible during his swearing in as Senator.

Even some of those who defended Obama against the Islam smear – one such person is Daniel Pipes – posed more serious questions to taint his image and religious identity. In a piece entitled "Was Barack Obama a Muslim?" in *Front Page Magazine* on 24 December 2007, Pipes quoted Obama's "If I were a Muslim I would tell you", and said: "and I believe him". However, Pipes continued in a left-handed pitch to express another fear which Obama's faith might bring about. He said:

> In fact, he is a practicing Christian, a member of the Trinity United Church of Christ. He is not now a Muslim. But was he ever a Muslim or seen by others as a Muslim? More precisely, might Muslims consider him a murtadd (apostate), that is, a Muslim who converted to another religion and, therefore, someone whose blood may be shed?[18]

Pipes then quoted a statement made by Obama on 22 December 2007 in Oskaloosa, Iowa, in reply to a question about his 'Muslim heritage':

> My father was from Kenya, and a lot of people in his village were Muslim. He didn't practice Islam. Truth is, he wasn't very religious. He met my mother. My mother was a Christian from Kansas, and they married and then divorced. I was raised by my mother. So, I've always been a Christian. The only connection I've had to Islam is that my grandfather on my father's side

came from that country. But I've never practiced Islam ... For a while, I lived in Indonesia because my mother was teaching there. And that's a Muslim country. And I went to school. But I didn't practice. But what I do think it does is it gives me insight into how these folks think, and part of how I think we can create a better relationship with the Middle East and that would help make us safer if we can understand how they think about issues.[19]

Pipes, nevertheless, insisted on posing the questions: "What is Obama's true connection to Islam and what implications might this have for an Obama presidency?" He then persisted to ask these questions in two more sections of his piece with these titles "Was Obama Ever a Muslim?" and "Implications of Obama's Conversion". The significance of Pipes' goal in the whole piece is not only in the repeated suspicion over Obama's assertion, but also the outlandish fear of 'a Muslim's right to change religion'. For a President of the United States in 2009, who would be considered an apostate by Muslims, Pipes predicted:

One must assume that some Islamists would renounce him as a *murtadd* [apostate] and would try to execute him. Given the protective bubble surrounding an American president, though, this threat presumably would not make much difference to his carrying out his duties. More significantly, how would more mainstream Muslims respond to him, would they be angry at what they would consider his apostasy? That reaction is a real possibility, one that could undermine his initiative towards the Muslim world.[20]

One of the tactics used to frighten voters away from Obama is the use of terror-loaded words in the context of the 'Islamic terrorism'. One such word is 'madrassa'. As a young boy, Obama was said to have attended a madrassa in Indonesia. A typical question asked by Obama's critics is one that begins an article in insightmag.com on 16–22 January 2007: "Are the American people ready for an elected president who was educated in a Madrassa as a young boy and has not been forthcoming about his Muslim heritage?" To add to the suspicion over Obama's faith, the article even went as far as to involve the United States intelligence community which "has determined that today most of these schools are financed by the Saudi Arabian government and they teach a Wahhabi doctrine that denies the rights of non-Muslims".[21]

Although the article mentions Obama's statements to the contrary in his autobiography, prominence is given to this notion that he was, and perhaps still is, a Muslim.

In the face of this propaganda campaign, Obama and his supporters had to spent a great deal of time and energy correcting what became a public perception and in setting the record straight.

The traditional as well as electronic media were flooded with a discussion of Obama's faith, and denial after denial had to be issued by Obama and his campaign, in addition to moderate investigations such as that done by CNN.

But local newspapers, especially those leaning towards the Christian Right, carried the story and drew tremendous public blogging, thus increasing the perception of Obama's Muslim 'heritage'. One example of what was written on the topic is the op-ed by Gary Sillett in *The Ottawa Herald*. The *Community Viewpoint* op-ed by Sillett was entitled "Don't Betray Your Heritage for Obama's 'Change'". The piece strongly warned that "To elect Barack Obama to the highest office in the land would be nothing less than spitting on the graves of the victims of 9/11." Emphasizing the 'fact' of Obama's concealed religion, Sillett said that "The Democratic Party actually intends to put a Muslim fundamentalist in the White House."[22]

Not only did Obama have to issue a number of statements denying the 'Islam smear'; he and his campaign aides had to ignore the Muslim minority in the United States and to avoid any open association with them. This policy of ignoring American Muslims prompted Andrea Elliot to write in *The New York Times* (23 June 2008) that "Muslims feel snubbed by Obama". Elliot related an incident where Keith Ellison

> believed that Mr. Obama's message of unity resonated deeply with American Muslims. He volunteered to speak on Mr. Obama's behalf at a mosque in Cedar Rapids, one of the nation's oldest Muslim enclaves. But before the rally could take place, aides to Mr. Obama asked Mr. Ellison to cancel the trip because it might stir controversy. Another aide appeared at Mr. Ellison's Washington office to explain.[23]

The writer comments on this that:

> While the senator has visited churches and synagogues, he has yet to appear at a single mosque. Muslim and Arab-American organizations have tried repeatedly to arrange meetings with Mr. Obama, but officials with those groups say their invitations – unlike those of their Jewish and Christian counterparts – have been ignored. Last week, two Muslim women wearing head scarves were barred by campaign volunteers from appearing behind Mr. Obama at a rally in Detroit.[24]

Senator Clinton's position on the charge was made in a shrewdly ambivalent response to the question put to her by a reporter. "No, he is not a Muslim", she said, and added, "as far as I know."[25]

McCain's behaviour during the campaign was much less subtle concerning the Islam 'smear' and the fear tactics used against Obama. One example of this behaviour is his abrupt response to questions posed by the audience at a Minnesota town-hall meeting. One member of the audience said that he had read about him – Obama – and he was scared of what his election would do to America, and an older lady confirmed this by stating that "He's an Arab that I cannot trust. Well, isn't he?" she asked. In an obviously nervous reaction, McCain yanked the microphone from her and corrected her: "No, Ma'am, no, Ma'am. He's a decent family man, a citizen, that I just happen to have disagreements with on fundamental issues and that's what this campaign is all about."[26]

After September 11th, it was an open season for unchecked attacks on Islam and Muslims. The attacks included American Muslims as well as Muslims throughout the world, and some of the diatribes were purely racist and ethnic vilifications.

A catalogue of the persons – clergyman, politicians, media and public figures – who took part in this anti-Islam campaign and of the literature cannot be accommodated here. The following brief account is limited only to some of the relevant materials connected with the September 11th, 2001 attacks and the presidential elections.

During the presidential campaign, one of Rudolph Guiliani's aides, Daniel Pipes, said in an article that "the ultimate goal of militant Islam ... in the US [is] to replace the Constitution with the Quran".[27] And in Pipes' scheme of things, US Muslims had among them many radicals who agreed with this agenda.

Just one month after the September 11th attacks, Pipes was able to gauge the public opinion among "the Moslem population in this country" and concluded in November 2001 that this population

> is not like any other group, for it includes within it a substantial body of people – many times more numerous than the agents of Osama bin Ladin – who share with the suicide hijackers a hatred of the United States and the desire, ultimately, to transform it into a nation living under the strictures of militant Islam.[28]

Pipes bemoaned the fact that "the idea of an Islamist takeover remains unrecognized in establishment circles in the US government, the old media, the universities, the mainline churches".[29]

But some persons, like the other Giuliani aide, John Deady, did recognize the threat, and suggested that the election of his boss would be the remedy. Not limiting his remarks, as Pipes did, to 'militant Islam', Deady included in the warning all Muslims, suggesting that his boss has

> got, I believe, the knowledge and the judgment to attack one of the most difficult problems in current history and that is the rise of the Muslims, and make no mistake about it, this hasn't happened for a thousand years. These people are very, very dedicated and they're also very smart, in their own way. We need to keep the feet to the fire and keep pressing these people until we defeat or chase them back to their caves – or in other words get rid of them.[30]

With the increasing numbers of illegal immigrants in the United States (some 12 million), questions of how to deal with them became a major election issue, which also led to the larger issue of immigration in general. And whereas all candidates, when dealing with this issue, tried not to appear prejudiced against minorities, especially Latin Americans – sometimes even including illegal immigrants – no such deference was paid to the Muslim minority. In fact, in the heated debate on the war on terror, Muslim immigration, small as it is, became a potential danger to American security, perhaps even a possible factor that could destroy American civilization. In a piece by Lewis Loflin entitled "Muslim Immigration Must Be Halted", under a picture of a group of austere threatening bearded faces of Muslim clerics flanked by endless rows of young men with Islamic head bands all raising their right arms in a Nazi-like salute, Loflin warned:

> Massive Muslim immigration to the West is becoming a growing danger and must be halted. It must be halted until Muslims can come to grips with reality and at least stop killing each other. Muslims also tend to gather in large, self-imposed ghettos trying to bring many of the barbaric customs with them. ... Until they prove they accept Western ideals on democracy, separation of mosque/state, reject slavery, polygamy, abuse of women and girls, and religious freedom for non-Muslims, they should be barred from any further immigration into the West. (Don't try political correctness or racism crap with me.)[31]

The lines have been systematically blurred between Islam, Muslims and Muslim countries, and terrorism and extremism. Generic terms such as 'murderous cult', 'people who hate us' have been used to point to Islamic terrorists in contexts that may also be applied to all Muslims, including American Muslims. One example of this trend is what Ann Coulter wrote in her editorial in *NRO* two days after the September 11th terrorist strike:

> The nation has been invaded by a fanatical, murderous cult. And we welcome them. We are so good and so pure we would never engage in discriminatory racial or 'religious' profiling.
>
> People who want our country destroyed live here, work for our airlines, and are submitted to the exact same airport shakedown as a lumberman from Idaho. This would be like having the Wehrmacht immigrate to America and work for our airlines during World War II. Except the Wehrmacht was not so bloodthirsty.[32]

Muslim communities felt threatened by the racism of extreme political and religious public figures. There were those who felt that there are 'too many mosques' in America, and that Muslims constituted 'dangerous neighborhoods'. Islam and Muslims were lumped together with 'Islamic terrorism' and al-Qaeda. In the wake of September 11, 2001, Ann Coulter passionately warned Americans against allowing Muslims into the United States without special scrutiny, perhaps even profiling. She also advised that "We should invade their [terrorists'] countries, kill their leaders and convert them to Christianity."[33] Even in 2007, Representative Peter King (Rep., N. Y.), the ranking Republican on the House Homeland Security Committee, said that there are "too many mosques in this country" in an interview with *Politico* on 19 September 2007. As a member of the Homeland Security committee, King referred to the Muslim community, saying: "There are too many people sympathetic to radical Islam … We should be looking at them more carefully and finding out how we can infiltrate them." Explaining what he meant, King added: "I think there has been a lack of full cooperation from too many people in the Muslim community."[34] According to King, in a statement made to Sean Hannity, 85 percent of the mosques in the United States were controlled by extremist leadership.

US policy on Muslim immigration suddenly became the top issue for many politicians and commentators. Governor Mike Huckabee, while running for president, expressed fear that Muslim terrorists might sneak through the borders with Mexico.

The issue by the US Postal Service of an Eid Stamp (to commemorate the Muslim feast of breaking the fast) drew severe criticism from many quarters where Islam, Muslims and the September 11th terrorists were lumped together as one and the same. The Eid Stamp was not selling well, but Paul Weyrich, President of the Free Congress Foundation, wrote to Congressional leaders to "suggest that the current stamps be withdrawn, to be overprinted with the image of the Twin Towers and then reissued". Wyerich added, tying Islam as a religion to the September 11, 2001 terrorists, "I have no doubt a majority of Americans would find the altered stamps a more appropriate commemoration of Islam than the current celebratory version."[35] A response came quickly from one sympathetic blogger under a title "US New Stamp":

> Remember the Muslim bombing of the American Embassies in Africa! Remember the Muslim bombing of the USS Cole! Remember the Muslim attack on the Twin Towers on 9/11/2001!
>
> Remember all the American lives that were lost in those vicious Muslim attacks! Remember the beheadings at the hands of Muslim's!!!!!!!! Now the United States Postal Service remembers and honors the Eid Muslim holiday season with a commemorative first class holiday postage stamp. Remember to adamantly and vocally boycott this stamp when purchasing your stamps at the post office. To use this stamp would be a slap in the face to all those Americans who died at the hands of those whom this stamp honors. Remember to pass this along to every patriotic American you know.[36]

With the repetition of expressions such as 'fighting the battle of our lives against Islam', 'chase them back to their caves', 'Muslim attacks' and 'those whom this stamp honors', one can only assume that public perceptions were swayed towards linking Islam and Muslims with the September 11th attackers as enemies of the US.

During the past few years, a number of politicians and public figures had to offer apologies and/or resign from important positions because of the outcry at some remarks they made which were racist in nature. One notable example is the humiliation suffered by Senator Trent Lott and his subsequent apologies and resignation from his powerful position as Republican majority leader in December 2002. This was caused by Senator Lott's praise of Senator Strom Thurmond on his 100th birthday, a speech that was considered an endorsement of Thurmond's past as a segregationist.

Another example is the humiliation of Don Imus and the cancellation of his popular radio program *Imus in the Morning* over his racist reference to the Rutgers University women's basketball team in April 2007. In January 2007, the grandson of Mahatma Ghandi, Arun Ghandi, had to resign from his post of Resident and Founder of the M. K. Ghandi Institute for Nonviolence attached to Rochester University. His resignation came because of objections to a piece he wrote in the *Washington Post* criticizing Israel's treatment of Palestinians in the Occupied Territories. Finally, former President Carter was subjected to sharp attacks and criticism over his characterization of Israel's policy of confiscation of Palestinian land and the slicing of Palestinian territories into separate cantons as a policy similar to South African Apartheid.

Offensive and racially loaded remarks against Arabs and Muslims, unfortunately, do not elicit such response; Senator Schumer's comparison of Arabs with skinheads in the case of the official American contract with the Dubai Ports Company did not cause a stir, nor did Schumer have to apologize or retract the statement. In November 2006, Representative John Murtha told Chris Matthews on *Hardball* that he thought the undercover FBI agents were legitimate Arab businessmen because "They were the slimiest guys I've ever seen."[37]

Michael Savage is not known for courtesy and finesse, but the vile language he has used against Islam and Muslims defies description. On the 27 October 2007 edition of *The Savage Nation*, (aired on 300 radio stations) Michael Savage had this to say:

> I'm not gonna put my wife in a hijab. And I'm not gonna put my daughter in a burqa. And I'm not getting on my all-fours and braying to Mecca. And you could drop dead if you don't like it. You can shove it up your pipe. I don't wanna hear anymore about Islam. I don't wanna hear one more word about Islam. Take your religion and shove it up your behind. I'm sick of you … What kind of religion is this? What kind of world are you living in when you let them in here with that throwback document in their hand, which is a book of hate? Don't tell me I need reeducation. They need deportation. I don't need reeducation. Deportation, not reeducation.[38]

Savage added his characterization of Muslims: "I think [Muslims] need to be forcibly converted to Christianity … It's the only thing that can probably turn them into human beings."[39] In 2006, he called for a ban on Muslim immigration and recommended making "the construction of mosques illegal in America".[40]

The list of racist remarks and abuses against Muslim and Arabs is long. It includes statements by Sean Hannity, Bill O'Reiley, Randall Terry, Jerry Falwell, Pat Robertson, Benny Hinn, Franklin Graham, Gary Bauer, James Dobson and Ann Coulter, to name only a few prominent influential persons.

Linking Islam and Muslims with terrorisms and the 'enemy' prompted those (who did not particularly care for Islam or thought positively of it) like Michael Medved, to warn that declaring war on Islam and the Muslim world is dangerous for American security and "destroys our tradition of religious pluralism". Medved stated that

> If we proclaim Islam (or any other religion) as an "enemy of the state," then we've clearly abandoned our cherished First Amendment tradition of neutrality among religious faiths. Studies suggest that American Muslims represent a mostly prosperous and assimilated segment of the population, but public hostility to Islam would encourage a disturbing trend toward radicalization already apparent among some young Muslims. If Islam is our enemy, should Homeland Security start closing down mosques? The very idea represents an obvious violation of the First Amendment's "free exercise" clause.[41]

This debate during the presidential campaign over the Islam 'smear' and the place of Islam in the American system escalated from a purely religious-political question to become at times an essentially constitutional issue. The question became: "Is America ready for a Muslim President?" Answers to this question will shed a great deal of light on the 'contemporary scene of Islam in America' as well as on the historical position of Islam in America, and the answers come from many sources, old and new.

One recent answer came from an American war hero, one-time prisoner of war, a long-time member of the Legislature, and candidate for the presidency; responding to the question, Senator John McCain openly stated in a recent interview: "Since this nation was founded primarily on Christian principles ... personally, I prefer someone who I know has a solid grounding in my faith." McCain was careful not to appear as anti-Islam in any way. He made sure to pay the usual courtesy to Islam: "I admire Islam", he said.

> There're a lot of good principles in it ... an honorable religion. But no, I just have to say in all candor that since this nation was founded primarily on Christian principles ... personally, I prefer someone who I know has a solid grounding in my faith ... I just feel that that's an important part of our qualifications to lead.[42]

According to McCain, "The number one issue people should make [in the] selection of President of the US is 'will this person carry on in the Judeo-Christian principled tradition that has made this nation the greatest experiment in the history of mankind?'."

Curiously enough, Senator McCain had a different view when it came to Governor Romney's qualifications as a Mormon; he emphatically said, "I think that Governor Romney's religion should not, absolutely not, be a disqualifying factor ... [for] his candidacy for President of the United States, absolutely not."[43]

And one can safely assume that the Senator would not consider Senator Joe Lieberman's religion a disqualifying factor, not only because it falls under the rubric 'Judeo-Christian' but also by the evidence that Lieberman became a constant companion of McCain on his campaign appearances.

Obviously, then (and in spite of the respect McCain shows to Islam), Islam does not qualify a person to be President of the US. A number of points are indirectly raised by McCain's statement. First, the fact that a reporter should ask the question to begin with is an indication of how important this issue became in the contest against Obama in particular, and not against other candidates. Second, one is forced to ask if McCain seriously bases his opinion on the Founding Fathers' intentions or statements on the issue of religion when they wrote the Constitution, and whether or not they had in mind the Judeo-Christian tradition. Third, where does McCain place the separation of church and State in the American system if he thinks the Judeo-Christian tradition is a must qualification? One is left to wonder if McCain is aware of the presence in America of not only Muslims but scores of others who do not belong to the Judeo-Christian tradition, and who just might be offended by this. But fourth, and more importantly, where does the Constitution really stand on this issue?

McCain cited the Constitution as the document on which he based his answers about religion; he said: "The Constitution established the United States of America as a Christian nation."

Now, as a prominent long-time member of the Legislature, we have to assume that McCain here speaks as an authority on the Constitution. What does the Constitution actually say about this particular point?

The First Amendment to the Constitution states:

> Congress shall make no law respecting an establishment of religion, or prohibiting the free exercise thereof; or abridging the freedom of speech, or of the press; or the right of the people peaceably to assemble, and to petition the government for a redress of grievances.

But this brief text, succinct as it is, gave rise to heated debates and controversies over the years in the legislative bodies and courts of many states, and it still does to this day.

With remarkable foresight, one of the framers of the Constitution, Thomas Jefferson, argued, with reference to the "Virginia Act for Religious Freedom", that:

> where the preamble declares, that coercion is a departure from the plan of the holy author of our religion, an amendment was proposed by inserting "Jesus Christ", so that it would read "A departure from the plan of Jesus Christ, the holy author of our religion"; the insertion was rejected by the great majority, in proof that they meant to comprehend, within the mantle of its protection, the Jew and the Gentile, the Christian and the Mohammedan, the Hindoo and the Infidel of every denomination.[44]

Indeed, one reads the following inscription on the Jefferson Memorial in Washington, DC:

> No man shall be compelled to frequent or support any religious worship or ministry or shall otherwise suffer on account of his religious opinions or belief, but all men shall be free to profess and by argument to maintain, their opinions in matters of religion.

A very recent case in point in this debate is that of Keith Ellison. Ellison was the first Muslim ever to be elected to Congress, and in November 2006 he decided to use the Quran in the House swearing-in ceremony. The outcry that resulted was not only because somebody should dare to suggest the use of the Quran, but by the mere fact that a Muslim should be elected to Congress. In a letter written by Representative Virgil H. Goode to his constituents, he said in reference to 'the Muslim Representative from Minnesota':

> I fear that in the next century we will have many more Muslims in the United States if we don't adopt the strict immigration policies that I believe are necessary to preserve the values and beliefs traditional to the United States of America.[45]

With only one Muslim in the 535-member Congress, it was one too many for Representative Goode. Goode also made sure to throw in, for good measure, the fear of Muslim immigration in his argument knowing, no doubt, that Ellison was not a Muslim immigrant.

And commenting on the same subject on November 28, 2006, Dennis Prager decided in a piece on America Family Association, Action Alert that "America, not Keith Ellison, decided what book a congressman takes his oath on". Prager (a member of the Jewish faith, host of a radio talk show and member of the US Holocaust Memorial Council) proposed that his edict was not based on "any American hostility to the Koran, but because the act undermines American civilization". He added:

> Forgive me, but America should not give a hoot what Keith Ellison's favorite book is. Insofar as a member of Congress taking an oath to serve America and uphold its values is concerned, America is interested in only one book, the Bible. If you are incapable of taking an oath on that book, don't serve in Congress.[46]

The Founder and Chairman of America Family Association added his endorsement to Prager's opinion, and suggested that his readers "Send an email asking [their] US Representatives and Senators to pass a law making the Bible the book used in the swearing-in ceremony of Representatives and Senators."[47]

Evidently, for McCain, Goode, Prager and a host of other pundits, the First Amendment as well as Jefferson's statement that no man must be made to "suffer on account of his opinions and beliefs" must not have included Muslims and those whom McCain declared disqualified because they do not belong to the Judeo-Christian tradition. In the current climate of public opinion, what would happen if such statements of disqualification were made of members of the Jewish faith or of declared atheists or any other group that falls beyond the pale?

Yet all of this is not entirely new to the American tradition of political debate. The question of a Muslim possibly becoming president of the United States, was debated as far back as the eighteenth century, in fact very soon after Independence and the drafting of the Constitution. The First Amendment to the Constitution had actually come on the heel of questions which were raised about the religion of the new republic. The debates that took place for the adoption of the First Amendment were prophetic of things to come. Even one of the writers of the Constitution, no other than Thomas Jefferson, voiced the fear of bigots coming later to subvert the religious pluralism which he and his eminent colleagues sought for America. On 12 June 1779, Jefferson warned:

> [A]ll attempts to influence [man's mind] by temporal punishments or burdens, or by civil incapacitations, tend only to beget habits of hypocrisy and meanness, and are a departure from the plan of the holy author of our religion, who being Lord both of body and mind, yet chose not to propagate it by coercions on either, as was in his Almighty power to do, but to extend it by its influence on reason alone: That the impious presumption of legislators and rulers, civil as well as ecclesiastical, who, being themselves but fallible and uninspired men, have assumed dominion over the faith of others, setting up their own opinions and modes of thinking, as the only true and infallible, and as such, endeavouring to impose them on others, hath established and maintained false religions over the greatest part of the world, and through all time.[48]

Jefferson's firm stand on religious freedom and pluralism came at the time when Americans were debating the exact intention of the Constitution and the First Amendment. The central point of the debate seems to have been whether the First Amendment intended a total separation of religion and state or an attempt to prevent the domination over the state by one Christian Church to the exclusion of the others.

Almost ten years after Jefferson's statement, William Lancaster, debating in the North Carolina Legislature the adoption of the Constitution by the State of North Carolina, considered the possibility of a Muslim serving as president of the US. He said:

> As to a religious test, had the article which excludes it provided none but what had been in the states heretofore, I would not have objected to it. It would secure religion. Religious liberty ought to be provided for. I acquiesce with the gentleman, who spoke, on this point, my sentiments better than

I could have done myself. For my part, in reviewing the qualifications necessary for a President, I did not suppose that the pope could occupy the President's chair. But let us remember that we form a government for millions not yet in existence. I have not the art of divination. In the course of four or five hundred years, I do not know how it will work. This is most certain, that Papists may occupy that chair, and Mahometans may take it.[49]

Clearer and more definitive statements on the issue were made by Justice Joseph Story (Supreme Court Justice, 1812–1845, US Congressman, 1808–1809, and Harvard Law School professor, 1821–1845) who said in 1833:

The real object of the amendment was, not to countenance, must less to advance Mahometanism, or Judaism, or infidelity, by prostrating Christianity; but to exclude all rivalry among Christ sects, and to prevent any national ecclesiastical establishment, which should give to an hierarchy the exclusive patronage of the national government.[50]

For Justice Story, as he had explained in a speech at Harvard,

I verily believe Christianity [is] necessary to the support of civil society. One of the beautiful boasts of our municipal jurisprudence is that Christianity is a part of the Common Law ... There never has been a period in which the Common Law did not recognize Christianity as lying at its foundations.[51]

And in commenting on the relationship between Christianity and the government when the First Amendment was being debated, Justice Story made the point very clear:

We are not to attribute this prohibition of a national religious establishment [in the First Amendment] to an indifference to religion in general, and especially to Christianity (which none could hold in more reverence than the framers of the Constitution).[52]

Justice Story explained:

At the time of the adoption of the Constitution, and of the amendment to it, now under consideration [i.e., the First Amendment], the general, if not the universal, sentiment in America was that Christianity ought to receive encouragement from the states, so far as was not incompatible with the private rights of conscience, and the freedom of religious worship. Any attempt to level all religions, and to make it a matter of state policy to hold all in utter indifference, would have created universal disapprobation, if not universal indignation.[53]

The arguments over the Constitution and the First Amendment took on a number of dimensions which resonate today in the presidential campaign debates. Two examples of such arguments are especially predictions of things to come: first is the question whether the Founding Fathers meant for America to be established on Christian principles, and the second is the possibility of a non-Christian becoming president.

That some state legislatures considered America a Christian nation is seen in state constitutions. The North Carolina Constitution of 1776 is an appropriate example of the contemporary debate. Article 32 of this Constitution says:

> that no person, who shall deny the being of God or the truth of the Protestant religion, or the divine authority either of the Old or New Testaments, or who shall hold religious principles incompatible with the freedom and safety of the State, shall be capable of holding any office or place of trust or profit in the civil department within this State.[54]

And Article 34 gives evidence that the notion of separation of church and state, although high on the agenda of legislatures at the time, was meant to prevent the domination of one Christian denomination over the others and not to exclude Christianity from government. The article states "That there shall be no establishment of any one religious church or denomination in this State, in preference to any other."[55]

The possibility of a Jew or Muslim becoming president was also in the minds of those who debated the First Amendment. The debate in North Carolina Legislature on 30 July 1788, for example, focused in part on this possibility. At one point, Governor Samuel Johnston advocated leaving the matter of religion out of the debate. Johnston "expressed great astonishment that the people were alarmed on the subject of religion". This, he said, "must have arisen from the great pains which had been taken to prejudice men's minds against the Constitution". Governor Johnston said that:

> [He] read the Constitution over and over, but could not see one cause of apprehension or jealousy on this subject. When I heard there were apprehensions that the pope of Rome could be the President of the United States, I was greatly astonished. It might as well be said that the king of England or France, or the Grand Turk, could be chosen to that office. It would have been as good an argument. It appears to me that it would have been dangerous, if Congress could intermeddle with the subject of religion. True religion is derived from a much higher source than human laws. When any attempt is made, by any government, to restrain men's consciences, no good consequence can possibly follow. It is apprehended that Jews, Mahometans, pagans, &c., may be elected to high offices under the government of the United States. Those who are Mahometans, or any others who are not professors of the Christian religion, can never be elected to the office of President, or other high office, but in one of two cases. First, if the people of

America lay aside the Christian religion altogether, it may happen. Should this unfortunately take place, the people will choose such men as think as they do themselves. Another case is, if any persons of such descriptions should, notwithstanding their religion, acquire the confidence and esteem of the people of America by their good conduct and practice of virtue, they may be chosen. I leave it to gentlemen's candor to judge what probability there is of the people's choosing men of different sentiments from themselves.[56]

The debate over the First Amendment also included fear of immigration to the US of non-Christians and the possibility that America would lose its Christian character. One extreme example of this fear was expressed by Rep. Joseph Caldwell who

thought that some danger might arise. He imagined it might be objected to in a political as well as in a religious view. In the first place, he said, there was an invitation for Jews and pagans of every kind to come among us. At some future period, said he, this might endanger the character of the United States. Moreover, even those who do not regard religion, acknowledge that the Christian religion is best calculated, of all religions, to make good members of society, on account of its morality. I think, then, added he, that, in a political view, those gentlemen who formed this Constitution should not have given this invitation to Jews and heathens. All those who have any religion are against the emigration of those people from the eastern hemisphere.[57]

And the issue of the oath of office to be taken by the President or other elected representative came up in the debates over the First Amendment. An interesting view came from Rep. James Iredell who said:

It was long held that no oath could be administered but upon the New Testament, except to a Jew, who was allowed to swear upon the Old. According to this notion, none but Jews and Christians could take an oath; and heathens were altogether excluded. At length, by the operation of principles of toleration, these narrow notions were done away. Men at length considered that there were many virtuous men in the world who had not had an opportunity of being instructed either in the Old or New Testament, who yet very sincerely believed in a Supreme Being, and in a future state of rewards and punishments. It is well known that many nations entertain this belief who do not believe either in the Jewish or Christian religion. Indeed, there are few people so grossly ignorant or barbarous as to have no religion at all. And if none but Christians or Jews could be examined upon oath, many innocent persons might suffer for want of the testimony of others. In regard to the form of an oath, that ought to be governed by the religion of the person taking it.[58]

Mr. Iredell concluded: "We may, I think, very safely leave religion to itself; and as to the form of the oath, I think this may well be trusted to the general government, to be applied on the principles I have mentioned."[59]

These early debates and opinions regarding the intentions of the framers of the Constitution and the Founding Fathers show that the current debates are not new. What is interesting here and relevant to the status of Islam in America is an apparent intolerance of most candidates and of their aids of the notion of a Muslim becoming president. Despite the genuine tradition of democratic principles of government and of equality regardless of race, religion, gender and ethnic background, there still lingers this exclusionist tendency towards Islam and Muslims in America in the twenty-first century.

One cannot help noticing that none of the presidential candidates (with the exception of Cuccinic) made any serious attempt to court the support of Muslim and Arab Americans. This is a recent development, in contrast to previous practice. When she was First Lady, Hillary Clinton told the Muslim Women's League in Los Angeles that the US must work to understand and respect Islam. She said:

> The President and I are committed to doing everything we can to make sure that Muslim children, just like Jewish and Christian children in America, will be able to look at the White House and know there is recognition of the importance of their religious beliefs.[60]

During the 2000 Presidential Campaign, Mrs. Gore went to Detroit and met with representatives of the Arab community and sampled Arab sweets.[61] During the same campaign George W. Bush spoke to American Muslims and promised to do his best to repeal the Secret Evidence Act.[62]

In contrast, not only have candidates in the recent elections avoided Muslims and Arabs, the Muslim 'smear' has been strengthened indirectly by most candidates' unusual emphasis on their religious faith and on the Bible as the guiding light for their lives and policies. The *Huffington Post's* William Fisher noticed in an editorial entitled "The 2008 Campaign: Candidates Compete To Be 'More Christian'", that major candidates "are running as fast as they can from one potentially influential constituency … the seven-million-strong American Muslim constituency".[63] Most candidates – Clinton, Obama, McCain, Guilani, Huckabee – went out of their way to prove that they were Christian. On many occasions this argument went hand in hand with a process of striking fear of Islamic terrorism and the Islamic threat in general.

Mike Huckabee claimed that he understood the true nature of the struggle against Muslim extremists more than any other candidate because he was the only one with a degree in theology. Speaking on one of the Christian Right networks, CBN, Huckabee said:

> People look at my record and say that I'm as strong on immigration, strong on terror as anybody. In fact I think I'm stronger than most people because

I truly understand the nature of the war that we are in with Islamo fascism. These are people that want to kill us. It's a theocratic [*sic*] war. And I don't know if anybody fully understands that. I'm the only guy on that stage with a theology degree. I think I understand it really well. And know the threat of it is absolutely overwhelming to us.[64]

Although the former Arkansas Governor recognized that the enemy is a perversion of Islam, he nonetheless considered the war on Jihadist terrorism the core of the presidential election. Huckabee told a Daniel Webster College audience: "We need to understand that this is, in fact, World War III ... and this one we cannot afford to lose." On his first trip to New Hampshire as a candidate, Huckabee insisted that anything short of a total victory would bring about an end of American culture. This was "the goal of the Jihadists".[65] Huckabee's message during the campaign was punctuated with the fear of the Islamic Jihadist threat and the need for a genuinely Christian president.

Mike Huckabee participated with Kenneth Copeland – who makes no secret of his hatred of Islam – in a six-day religious program in a bid to attract Religious Right voters. Following the terrorist attacks of September 11th, Copeland prophesied:

There's going to be close to a billion people that have been trapped in that religion [Islam] that over the next few months are gonna come into the kingdom of God. That's gonna happen, you watch and see what I'm telling you ... I can tell you this, that this thing has come to an end, it's over. I'm talking about Islam and all that that stands for.[66]

The Clinton campaign 3 a.m. ad has been interpreted as a suggestion that Obama was not experienced enough to make the right decision in times of crisis. Yet, the language of the ad and the period just preceding it point more to the allegations over his lack of patriotism and his perceived religious affiliation. The security of American families in the context of the fear of an Islamic threat was highlighted by the constant fear tactics used mainly by the Republican administration.

Fear-mongering has been a constant factor in American political and religious life ever since September 11, 2001. The drums for vigilance during the presidential campaign were often, in a subtle way, coupled with a warning against electing Obama. The warning came from public representatives like Steve King who warned that "the radical Islamists, the al-Qaida ... would be dancing in the streets in greater numbers than they did on September 11th because they would declare victory in this war on terror".[67]

Although McCain chided Bill Cunningham for his emphasis on the 'Hussein' factor, he has accepted the support of Rev. Rod Parsley and called him at a Cincinnati rally his 'spiritual guide'. And Parsley has consistently urged for a war against 'the false religion of Islam' with the aim of destroying it. His book, *Silent No More* contains warnings against "Islam: the Deception

of Allah", and advocates a "war between Islam and Christian civilization".
He said:

> I cannot tell you how important it is that we understand the true nature of
> Islam, that we see it for what it really is. In fact, I will tell you this: I do not
> believe our country can truly fulfill its divine purpose until we understand
> our historical conflict with Islam. I know that this statement sounds extreme,
> but I do not shrink from its implications. The fact is that America was
> founded, in part, with the intention of seeing this false religion destroyed,
> and I believe September 11, 2001, was a generational call to arms that we
> can no longer ignore.[68]

Parsley has no doubt that the fight is with Muslims, and not only extremists:

> There are some, of course, who will say that the violence I cite is the excep-
> tion and not the rule. I beg to differ. I will counter, respectfully, that what
> some call "extremists" are instead mainstream believers who are drawing
> from the well at the very heart of Islam.[69]

No effort was made by McCain to distance himself from Parsley, much less
repudiate the inflammatory statements.

Mayor Guiliani was by far the candidate who made more use of fear of
terrorism and of his September 11th performance as his qualification for the
presidency. Guiliani's ardent supporter, Daniel Pipes, warned his countrymen that
"Islam intends to replace the Constitution with the Quran" in the US. Pipes agreed
with Bernard Lewis that "Europe will be Islamic by the end of the century."[70]

Another Guiliani supporter, Congressman Peter King, a ranking Republican on
the House Homeland Security Committee, has warned that there are too many
mosques in the US and that they should be put under surveillance.[71] Guiliani did
not asked King to retract the statement, nor did he disapprove of Pipes' vicious
attacks on Islam.

But the most influential supporter of Guiliani's, Pat Robertson, has long been
such a vocal enemy of Islam, Mohammad, Muslims and the Quran that no words
can describe the venom he has spread against the religion, and his incitement of
millions of his followers to bring about Armageddon in the Middle East.

Judging from the differences between Robertson's views on domestic social
issues and those of Guiliani, it is easy to see that the war on terror and Islam can
be a strong motive of his support. His advocacy of Israel's right to the 'Promised
Land' is similar to Guiliani's unconditional support for Israel.

The Democratic tradition in America allows for a diversity of opinions and
the freedom of expression for all. This freedom is also protected by the
Constitution and the First Amendment. Americans take pride in this tradition, and
rightly so, and exercise those freedoms without fear of repression or persecution.
Americans also take pride in the 'melting pot' metaphor which truly represents
the way the American nation has developed from its beginnings until today.

In this democratic environment there has also been a system of checks and balances whenever the exercise of these freedoms steps over a red line and becomes a slanderous or racially motivated action. Racial sensitivity, in particular, has characterized the behaviour of Americans from the 1960s when the process of equality for African-Americans began to take shape. Since then, racial, ethnic and religious intolerance has gradually been reduced to a minimum in American public discourse.

This is why it becomes painfully surprising to see exceptions to these rules in the case of Islam, Muslims and Arabs. The instances mentioned here are some examples of the insensitivity towards racial and religious prejudice that still exists unchecked in public forums in the United States. In an environment of fear of terrorist attacks and wars with predominantly Muslim countries one can understand, though not justify, this prejudice.

It is all the more admirable for persons like Presidents George W. Bush and Jimmy Carter to stand firm in what they see as objective views despite a barrage of criticism and attacks in this environment of fear and warnings of terror threats.

The story of Islam in America cannot be complete without mention of the equally objective and heroic efforts of mainstream churches, religious leaders, academics and fair-minded ordinary Americans to balance the views of extremists – political and religious – against Muslim and Arabs. The works of Alfred Lilienthan, Norton Mezvinsky, Charles Kimball, Robert Bellah, John Esposito, Michael Sells, Raymond Baker and Karen Armstrong and the efforts of the National Council of Churches (with all its extensive membership of churches) and Churches for Middle East Peace are only few examples of this group.

Where do we go from here?

What does the future hold for Islam and Muslims in the US?

The answer lies in the remote possibility that moderate voices in America get a public hearing. Hundreds of Christian churches and many Jewish organizations have publicly condemned this prevailing tendency to demonize Islam and present it as the enemy. Many individuals have risked their safety and sometimes careers because they opposed this tendency.

It remains to be seen if politicians, public figures and decision-makers who work hand-in-hand with bigoted individuals and organizations on both sides of the ideological conflict will realize the danger of their alliances and step back a little, not only for the sake of Islam and Muslims, but to preserve and repair the ideals of democracy, equality and plurality in America. It is only appropriate to end on the optimistic note struck by Madeline Albright in her book. *The Mighty and the Almighty*. She says:

As a practical matter, however, a nation (or group) that believes its success or failure is a direct consequence of the wishes of God is likely either to invite or create trouble … I was not qualified to deliver a sermon, but I did want to capture as precisely as I could what 9/11 did and did not mean: I see no sign of God's hand in these crimes, not any trace of religious faith or social conscience in their motivation. The perpetrators could not be loyal to Islam, for, by their acts, they have betrayed the teachings of that benevolent faith. The perpetrators of these outrages do not care about the Palestinians, whose leaders have expressed anger and sorrow at the attacks. They do not care about the poor, for they use their resources not to teach skills but to install hate. They are not crazy, for they acted with frozen-hearted calculation. These were crimes of purest evil, wholly unjustified by any reason of politics, culture, or faith.[72]

Notes

1 President George W. Bush, *Al-Arabia Television* interview, World Net Daily, posted 7 October 2007, www.worldnetdaily.com.
2 Ibid.
3 Ibid.
4 President George W. Bush, Television interview with MBCTV (Middle East Broadcasting Center), 5 December 2008. These balanced statements by President Bush, however, have not been matched by his foreign policy, especially in the Arab world. The Bush administration's behavior and actions have caused more devastation, tragedy and pain in Arab and Muslim countries than those of any previous administration. President Bush and his lieutenants have done everything to encourage and to give legitimacy to Israel's violations of every international convention and human rights principles, from building settlements to ethic cleansing to the use of illegal weapons and invading and destroying civilian communities, and to committing mass murders and devastation. The Gaza holocaust taking place at this writing is still being blatantly called 'defensive action' by Bush and his officials, with no regard to the hundreds of innocent civilians murdered and maimed and the tens of thousands made refugees for the third time in one lifetime.
5 Pat Robertson, ABC's *This Week*, posted 2 December 2002. Available at: www.slate.com/id/2074749.
6 Jen Shroder, *Blessed Cause*, posted 26 June 2004. Available at: www.blessedcause.org/forums.
7 Daniel Pipes, 'Shoeless George Bush [Discusses Islam]', *New York Sun*, 3 July 2007.
8 Randall Mikkelsen, "Bush Takes on Christian Right Over Anti-Islam Words", *Reuters*, 13 November 2002.
9 Ibid.
10 "Testing the Faith", *WorldNetDaily* Exclusive, posted 7 October 2007. Available at: www.worldnetdaily.com.
11 Ibid.
12 President George Bush W., White House Release, 26 November 2001.
13 Barack Obama, *Associated Press*, posted 27 February 2007. Available at: www.timesonline.com.
14 Debbie Schlussel, cited by *Media Matters for America*, posted 20 December 2006. Available at: www.mediamatters.org.
15 *Time Magazine*, 28 February 2008.
16 Mike Allen, "Hillary Gets Last-Minute Hope", Barack Obama response to question by Steve Kroft during *60 Minutes*, 22 September 2008.
17 Barack Obama, "Obama Hits the Web to 'Fight the Smears'", *ABC News*, posted 13 June 2008. Available at: www.abc.net.au.
18 Daniel Pipes, "Was Barack Obama a Muslim?", *Front Page Magazine*, 24 December 2007.
19 Ibid.

20 Ibid.
21 Ibid.
22 Gary Sillett, "Don't Betray Your Heritage for Obama's 'Change'", *Community Viewpoint*, 1 February 2008.
23 Andrea Elliot, *The New York Times*, 23 June 2008.
24 Ibid.
25 Hillary Clinton, "As Far As I Know", in an interview on *60 Minutes* with Steve Croft, 2 March 2008.
26 Eric Zorn, cited by *Change of Subject*, posted 10 October 2008. Available at: www.chicagotribune.com.
27 Daniel Pipes, "The Islamic States of America?", FrontPageMagazine.com, 23 September 2004. Available at: www.danielpipes.org.
28 Ibid.
29 Ibid.
30 John Deady, "Giuliani Surrogate: Rudy Will 'Chase Muslims Back To Their Caves'", *The Huffington Post*, 29 December 2007.
31 Lewis Loflin, "Muslim Immigration Must Be Halted", posted 2 May 2005. Available at: www.sullivan-county.com/wcva/index0.htm.
32 Ann Coulter, *NRO* editorial, 13 September 2001.
33 Ibid.
34 Peter King, *Politico*, posted 19 September 2007. Available at: www.politico.com.
35 Paul Weyrich, "Stamping Out Islam", *Christianity Today*, 4 September 2007.
36 Leonard Cyr, "US New Stamp", posted 23 November 2004. Available at: www.christianitytoday.com/ct/2001.
37 John Murtha, *Hardball*, 15 November 2006.
38 Michael Savage, *The Savage Nation*, 27 October 2007.
39 Ibid.
40 Ibid.
41 Michael Medved, "Is Islam Itself the Enemy?", *Townhall.com*, posted 27 February 2008. Available at: www.townhall.com.
42 John McCain, "John McCain: Constitution Established a 'Christian Nation'", interviewed by Dan Gilgoff, *Beliefnet*, 20 September 2007.
43 Ibid.
44 Thomas Jefferson, "Thomas Jefferson, Autobiography", Amendment I (Religion), Document 45, Works 1:71, 1821.
45 Virgil H. Goode Jr., "A Bigot in Congress", posted 22 December 2006. Available at: www.washingtonpost.com/wpdyn/content/article/2006/12/21/AR2006122101612.html.
46 Dennis Prager, "America, Not Keith Ellison, Decides What Book a Congressman Takes His Oath On", *Action Alert*, posted 28 November 2006. Available at: www.Townhall.com/Columnists/DennisPrager/2006/11/28.
47 Ibid.
48 Thomas Jefferson, "Thomas Jefferson, A Bill for Establishing Religious Freedom", Amendment I (Religion), Document 37, 12 June 1779.
49 William Lancaster, "William Lancaster, North Carolina Ratifying Convention", Article 6, Clause 3, Document 26, Elliot 4:215, 30 July 1788. In Jonathan Elliot (ed.) *The Debates in the Several State Conventions on the Adoption of the Federal Constitution as Recommended by the General Convention at Philadelphia.*
50 Joseph Story, "Joseph Story, Commentaries on the Constitution", Amendment I (Religion), Document 69, 1833.
51 Joseph Story, "On Christianity and Laws in America", *Eads Home Ministries*, 5 February 2007.
52 Ibid.
53 Ibid.

54 Francis Newton Thorpe (ed.) "North Carolina Constitution of 1776", Article 32, in *The Federal and State Constitutions, Colonial Charters, and Other Organic Laws of the States, Territories, and Colonies Now or Heretofore Forming the United States of America*, 7 vols., Washington, DC: Government Printing Office, 1909.

55 Francis Newton Thorpe (ed.) "North Carolina Constitution of 1776", Article 34, in *The Federal and State Constitutions, Colonial Charters, and Other Organic Laws of the States, Territories, and Colonies Now or Heretofore Forming the United States of America*, 7 vols., Washington, DC: Government Printing Office, 1909.

56 Jonathan Elliot (ed.) "Debate in North Carolina Ratifying Convention", Amendment I (Religion), Document 52, 30 July 1788, in *The Debates in the Several State Conventions on the Adoption of the Federal Constitution as Recommended by the General Convention at Philadelphia in 1785*, 5 vols., 2nd edn, 1888.

57 Ibid.

58 Ibid.

59 Ibid.

60 Hillary Clinton, quoted in *The Washington Report on Middle Eastern Affairs*, 21 March 2000, Richard H. Curtiss.

61 Tipper Gore, quoted in *Democracy in Action*, 16 October, 2000.

62 Richard S. Dunham, "Washington Outlook: Muslims Are Angry – And They Matter", *Business Week*, 1 December 2003.

63 William Fisher, "The 2008 Campaign: Candidates Compete to be 'More Christian'", *The Huffington Post*, posted 16 January 2008. Available at: www.huffingtonpost.com.

64 Mike Huckabee, "Huckabee: Nominate Me, I'm the Only One with a Theology Degree", posted by Steve Crickmore, 9 November 2007. Available at: www.bluetips@wizbangblog.com.

65 Mike Huckabee, "Huckabee Warns of Wars with Islam, Unhealthy Behavior", *Associated Press*, 9 February 2007.

66 Earnest Dumas, "Scary Evangelists", *Arkansas Times*, posted 22 November 2007. Available at: www.arktimes.com.

67 Steve King, Iowa Representative, "Iowa Rep. Steve King: Terrorists 'Would Be Dancing in the Streets' If Obama Wins Presidency; Middle Name Matters", Looking In At Iowa, posted by John in *Political, Terrorism, War*, 8 March 2008. Available at: www.iowaindependent.com/2057/steve-king-warns-terrorists-will-declare-victory-if-obama-wins.

68 Rob Parsley, quoted by David Corn on *MotherJones.com*, "McCain's Spiritual Guide: Destroy Islam", 12 March 2008. Available at: www.motherjones.com.

69 Ibid.

70 Pipes, op. cit.

71 King, op. cit.

72 Madeline Albright, *The Mighty and the Almighty*, New York: HarperCollins, 2006, pp. 147–148.

6 'Jihadiology' and the problem of reaching a contemporary understanding of Jihad

Abdel Salam Sidahmed

The tremendous interest in Islam and Islamism generated by September 11, 2001 is best illustrated by the mushrooming in writings on jihad, or what I would here call *Jihadiology*. The literature dealing with jihad in Western sources today ranges from academic writings and mainstream media to popular and scaremongering internet blogs such as Jihad Watch. Most debated in this diverse literature are questions associated with the meaning of the word 'jihad', what the concept of jihad entails in the Islamic history, and what it entails for contemporary Muslims. In the years following September 11th these questions have been posed with some urgency because of the apparent security implications attached to the concept of jihad. Within this context, a majority of specialists in Islamic studies in Western academic institutions – both Muslim and non-Muslim – have been painstakingly working to divorce the concept of jihad from its inherent association with violence that came to be the hallmark of 'terror analysts' and media reporters. Yet, for several media, academic, policy contributors and specialists, the word 'jihad' became, more or less, synonymous with terrorism, hatred and destruction. As far as the latter are concerned all attempts by Muslim and non-Muslim scholars to present multiple meanings of jihad are nonsensical apologetic views, if not plain lies deliberately aimed at deception.

This chapter's aim is to give a critical assessment of samples of populist, legal and academic writings that dealt with the question of jihad in its contemporary and historical manifestations. Common among the samples of these works is that all of them appear to have settled for a definition of jihad that associates the word primarily with violence and aggression, invariably giving the message that there is a profound reason to be worried whenever the word jihad is deployed in political or ideological discourse. That said, the three categories of writing are indeed divergent in their focus and orientation, the message they endeavour to communicate, and the target audience.

The blogs examined here seek to communicate an ideologically-driven message directed to the public at large by using an increasingly popular medium, the internet. The material posted on these blogs is meant to advocate a particular message mostly revolving around the danger that Islamism – and, by extension, Islam and Muslims at large – pose to the West, Western lifestyle and civilization. Their rationale apparently is that if there is a war of ideas within the Muslim world, this war has already been won by the radicals and jihadis. As such, all Muslims effectively become suspects until proven otherwise.

The legal documents, for their part, are significant in the sense that they are rather technical and designed to serve a particular purpose, namely administration of justice. However, being technical in the legal sense does not necessarily mean that the documents were addressing the subject of jihad from a position of expert knowledge. Therefore, it is rather curious to find that these documents contain definitions of jihad which equate the term with violence and terrorism. The implication of jihad being defined in criminal terminology is profound in its own right, but it is also significant as far as our discussion of the security implications of the term is concerned.

The academic material, though maybe limited in scope and audience, is quite significant particularly in a debate about concepts. When the matter involves 'other' people's culture, as in the case of Islam and jihad, then academic knowledge or expertise is all the more important. It provides other forums such as the media, policy-makers, and other interested parties (e.g. the legal profession, or security institutions) with an insight into those cultures, or as in this case, an explanation of how best to understand jihad in its historical and contemporary connotations. For these considerations, and particularly the fact that academic literature is meant to provide an expert, in-depth exploration of the subject at hand, we have devoted most of this chapter's attention to dealing with a scholarly book on jihad: David Cook's *Understanding Jihad*.

The concluding section of the chapter will briefly present an alternative view of a contemporary understanding of jihad.

Populist Jihadiology

I will examine here two samples of writings concerned with jihad and dedicated to alerting and 'educating' the public about the dangers associated with jihad, if not Islam and Muslims at large. The samples are taken from the Jihad Watch and Daniel Pipes websites.

Jihad Watch sets its mission as "correcting popular misconceptions about the role of jihad and religion in modern-day conflicts". The blog goes on to argue confidently that

> Modern Muslim theologians have spoken of many things as jihads: the struggle within the soul, defending the faith from critics, supporting its growth and defence financially, even migrating to non-Muslim lands for the purpose of spreading Islam. *But violent jihad is a constant of Islamic history.*[1]

Jihad Watch argues further that:

> No major Muslim group has ever repudiated the doctrines of armed jihad. The theology of jihad, with all its assumptions about unbelievers, lack of

human rights and dignity, is available today as a justification for anyone with the will and the means to bring it to life.[2]

The main thrust of the site is that there is visible and rather imminent danger threatening the Western world and beyond in the form of "Islamic terrorism". In fact, Jihad Watch argues that it exists in the first place:

> Because non-Muslims in the West, as well as in India, China, Russia, and the world over, are facing a concerted effort by Islamic jihadists ... to destroy their societies and bring them forcibly into the Islamic world – and to commit violence to that end ... That effort goes under the general rubric of *jihad*.[3]

As far as Jihad Watch is concerned, there is a sense of urgency in informing the public about the new enemy, its true nature, its goals, and the danger it poses, not just to the West, but the world at large.

On 21 January 2009, the blog, commenting on the news that the UN Special Rapporteur on torture had requested that former US President Bush and his Defense Secretary Rumsfeld should be prosecuted for torture, said the following: "If the Obama Administration allows this to happen, then U.S. sovereignty will be gone, in the air, never to be captured again, and the door will be wide open to the Islamization of the West."[4] It is rather difficult to treat the material posted on Jihad Watch with the necessary degree of seriousness and provide a rational critique of the arguments involved. Yet, it is a discourse that is directed to and readily accessible to the layperson and popular mind. The message operates not just as the backdrop of accumulated histories of perceptions, and prejudices and the strong sense of insecurity brought home by the September 11th attacks, but rather perpetuates all these in a wholesale manner and insists that the danger is pounding at the door. This danger is not just the threat to safety of person and property, but nothing less than the destruction of Western societies and their forcible integration into the Islamic world.

If Jihad Watch is too crude to be taken seriously in a solemn discussion, what about scholarly voices such as Daniel Pipes? In "What is Jihad?", Pipes says, "Jihad is 'holy war'. Or, more precisely: It means the legal, compulsory, communal effort to expand the territories ruled by Muslims at the expense of territories ruled by non-Muslims." He goes on to emphatically confirm that, "Jihad is thus unabashedly offensive in nature, with the eventual goal of achieving Muslim dominion over the entire globe."[5] As do the editors of Jihad Watch, Pipes also argues that jihad is "a central aspect of Muslim life". As regards the status of jihad today, "jihad is the world's foremost source of terrorism, inspiring a worldwide campaign of violence by self-proclaimed jihadist groups".[6] Clearly, the concept of jihad advanced by Pipes seems almost identical with the reasoning adopted by Jihad Watch; simply put, jihad is violence and expansionism legitimized by religion.

Daniel Pipes is alarmed that several scholars in the field of Islamic studies are bent on finding definitions of jihad that take it away from its "real meaning". He states, "It is an intellectual scandal that, since September 11, 2001, scholars at American universities have repeatedly and all but unanimously issued public statements that avoid or whitewash the primary meaning of jihad in Islamic law and Muslim history." He went on to affirm that, "For usage of the term in its plain meaning, we have to turn to Islamists not so engaged. Such Islamists [like Osama bin Laden and Mullah Muhammad Omar] speak openly of jihad in its *proper, martial sense*."[7]

According to Pipes and like-minded 'Jihadiologists', there is no evidence to substantiate the opinions expressed by the majority of scholars and Muslim specialists that there are multiple meanings of jihad, and that the term should not be reduced to warfare only. Pipes *et al.* also argue that in accordance with Islamic history and jurisprudence, jihad is invariably offensive, and any attempt to define – or explain it away – in defensive or spiritual terms is deceptive. As regards modern and contemporary Muslims, Pipes discusses two groups of them: the Islamists and reformists. The Islamists promoted jihad against infidels, as well as "against putatively Muslim rulers who failed to live up to or apply the laws of Islam". As for the reformists – who emerged in the nineteenth century, Pipes characterizes their approach as owing "more to Western than Islamic thinking". He went on to argue that the reformists of today have gone as far as "to deny that jihad has any martial component whatsoever".[8]

Pipes was careful to state that the majority of Muslims side with neither Islamists or reformists. However, he quickly adds that "the classic notion of jihad continues to resonate with vast numbers of [Muslims]". Furthermore, and crucially, he sums up his discussion with the statement that: "jihad in the raw remains a powerful force in the Muslim world, and this goes far to explain the immense appeal of a figure like Osama bin Laden in the immediate aftermath of September 11, 2001".[9] The writer affirms in a matter-of-fact manner that Bin Laden cultivated an "immense appeal" in the Muslim world on the morrow of September 11th. What is more, this alleged appeal is to be explained not so much by the intricacies of today's international and regional politics, but rather by the religious conviction of the majority of Muslims and their jihad belief.

One of the major problems of the logic advanced by the above-mentioned polemicists is their denial of intellectual pluralism among Muslims and Muslim scholars, and their contemptuous attitude towards any endeavour to come up with other interpretations of the concept of jihad that are more in tune with the contemporary international relations. Furthermore, their attestation that the concept of jihad espoused by the radical Islamists is the only authentic and *proper* meaning of jihad gives immense credence to claims by those radicals that they are the true representatives of Islam and Muslims. If such logic becomes acceptable, then Islamophobia becomes an equally acceptable approach towards Muslims at large. Islamophobia is exactly what groups like Jihad Watch are tirelessly promoting.

For his part, Pipes ends his "What is Jihad?" article on a belligerent note,

> Violent jihad will probably continue until it is crushed by a superior military force (Defense Secretary Donald Rumsfeld, please take note). Only when

jihad is defeated will moderate Muslims finally find their voice and truly begin the hard work of modernizing Islam.[10]

Well, Rumsfeld and subsequently the administration of George W. Bush, departed without completing that 'crushing defeat' on jihad, so obviously moderate Muslims have to wait a little longer; now that the chance is apparently gone, who knows for how long?

Jihadiology in US legal documents

Perhaps nothing better represents the security connotations of jihad than the occurrence of the word jihad in legal documents prepared by the US legal authorities against individuals accused of terrorism and terrorism-related offences. In this section I will examine two such documents: United States of America vs Adham Amin Hassoun aka Abu Sayaf *et al.*; and United States of America vs Hamid Hayat & Umer Hayat.

The two cases came to light in 2005 when the two indictments were publicized, though some of the defendants were in custody for about three years without charge. Both cases deal with alleged conspiracies by the individuals in question to carry out violent actions against people and property in the USA. The first case – USA vs Hassoun *et al.* (known in the US media as the Jose Padilla case) accused five individuals who were US citizens and permanent residents – of being part of a North American "Jihad support cell". This cell was allegedly providing support and assistance to *jihadi* groups across the world. According to the indictment in this case, members of the cell were either involved in providing assistance – financial or otherwise – or through recruitment of new members to join global jihad (one of such alleged recruits was apparently a US citizen of Costa Rican origin and Muslim convert Jose Padilla).[11] The second case – USA vs Hamid & Umer Hayat – accuses a young man, Hamid Hayat, of allegedly travelling to Pakistan to enrol in a "jihadi training camp" and returned to the USA in June 2005 with the intention of "waging jihad" on US soil. His father, Umer Hayat, was accused of making a fraudulent statement to the Federal Bureau of Investigation (FBI), when questioned about his son's activities.[12]

In both cases, the indictment included a definition by the US Federal Attorney of what is meant by the word jihad and some of its derivatives like Jihadist and mujahideen. In USA vs Hamid Hayat and Umer Hayat, the indictment released on September 22, 2005 defines jihad as follows:

As used in this First Superseding Indictment, "jihad" is the Arabic word for "holy war." In this context, jihad refers to the use of violence, including paramilitary action against persons, property or governments deemed to be enemies of a fundamentalist version of Islam. "Jihadist training" is paramilitary training received by individuals in preparation to wage jihad.[13]

Likewise, in the case of Adham A. Hassoun et al., the indictment released on November 22, 2005, defines jihad as follows:

> As used in this Superseding Indictment, the terms "violent jihad" or "jihad" include planning, preparing for, and engaging in, acts of physical violence, including murder, maiming, kidnapping, and hostage-taking. The term "mujahideen" means warriors engaged in violent jihad.[14]

Both definitions basically mean one thing, violence or "terrorism". These definitions raise two important questions of relevance to our discussion: (1) Why did the US prosecutors felt the need to adopt an *official* definition of the term jihad in their indictments? and (2) Why did they opt for these particular definitions? One possible answer to the first question may be that in a legal document of that sort, language should be explicit and precise, and so the meaning of words used should be clearly explained to remove any potential ambiguity or multiple interpretations.

Let us take a closer look at the text of these indictments to see whether the purpose of clarity has been served by the US prosecutors adopting a categorical definition of jihad. To start with, there is no explanation as to why the same institution, the US Department of Justice, has adopted two different definitions for the same word of jihad in cases that revolve – more or less – around the same offences and involve like-minded individuals. In one of the definitions we even encounter the now fairly outdated phrase of "holy war", and there are further ambiguities. In USA vs Hassoun *et al.*, the indictment speaks interchangeably of jihad and violent jihad, both of which are defined as involving acts of physical violence. Yet, the reference to "violent jihad", which occurs in various passages of the document, may give the impression that there is *non-violent* jihad. That is, however, not possible because the indictment was categorical in stating that violent jihad or *any* jihad, for that matter, refers to one and the same thing: physical violence, which makes the adjective in violent jihad redundant.

When it comes to the case of Hamid Hayat (USA vs Hamid Hayat & Umer Hayat), the word 'jihad' and its derivative 'jihadist' occur 21 times in a six-page document. Again there is the ambiguity with regard to usage of the word 'jihad' – which as defined refers to violence and terrorism – together with words with identical. meaning. For instance, the following passage from the indictment relates that defendant Hamid Hayat made a fraudulent statement denying that

> [He never] attended any type of *terrorist training* camp, that he never attended a *jihadist training* camp, that he never attended a *terrorist training* camp in Pakistan, ... when in truth and fact, ... he had attended one or more *jihadist terrorist training* camps.[15]

As far as the US prosecutors' definitions cited above go, the word 'jihad' is indeed synonymous with terrorism. As such, the phrases' terrorist' and 'jihadist' training camps' should be understood as one and the same thing. If that was the case, then what does the charge *jihadist* [read terrorist] *terrorist training* precisely mean?

Therefore, if the intention of the US prosecutors, in adopting a definition of jihad, was to provide the jury and US public at large with clearly defined charges, the indictments at hand do not serve that purpose. This is compounded by making references to particular Islamic institutions or terminology without proper explanation. In USA vs Hassoun *et al.*, the first paragraph of the indictments reads as follows:

> There existed a radical Islamic fundamentalist movement dedicated to the establishment of a pure Islamic state ("Caliphate") governed by strict Islamic law ("Sharia"). Followers and supporters of this movement adhered to a radical Salfist ideology that encouraged and promoted "violent jihad" to be waged by "mujahideen" using physical force and violence to oppose governments, institutions and individuals that did not share their view of Islam.[16]

The paragraph – quoted here in full – does not attempt to adequately define the unique terminology it uses such as "Caliphate", "Sharia" (both of which were casually and inaccurately explained) or Salafist ideology, which was not explained at all. Furthermore, the paragraph makes reference to one "radical Islamic fundamentalist movement", and in its last sentence refers to this movement using force against those who "did not share their view of Islam" implying that the force is mainly directed against other Muslims who do not share the view of the radical Salfists. However, the third paragraph of the indictment make reference to actual groups "espousing this radical Salafist ideology" and goes on to name such organizations as the Islamic Group of Egypt, the Egyptian Islamic Jihad, al-Qaeda, and "violent jihad groups in other countries, including Afghanistan, Algeria, Bosnia, Chechnya, Lebanon, Libya, and Somalia".[17]

It is not clear whether the authors of the indictment are indicating that there is one Islamic fundamentalist movement scattered over all these countries and composed of multiple organizations, all of which share the same goals and ideology. Furthermore, the countries outlined above are characterized by divergent socio-political conditions ranging from failed states such as Afghanistan and Somalia, to regions battling non-Muslim adversaries as in the cases of Bosnia and Chechnya. Moreover, in addition to the fact that most of these countries harbour at least more than one Islamist group, there are clear differences between the transnational al-Qaeda, and the other organizations listed above. These considerations seemed to have mattered little to the authors of the indictment whose attention soon shifted – in the fourth paragraph – to the jihad support cells in North America. "The physical violence committed by these jihad groups was supported and facilitated by a network of smaller groups or cells operating within the United States and in other countries."[18] This is understandable given the likely focus of the indictment and its concern with US citizens and residents accused of being part of these support cells. The questions posed above, however, remain valid with a few additional ones pertaining to whether those support cells were designed to provide assistance to a particular organization from those mentioned above, to a network linking these organizations, or to the ill-defined "radical Islamic fundamentalist movement".

Turning now to the other question: what has been the rationale of the respective authors of the two indictments to define jihad as a synonymous with violence and terrorism? As far as the indictments and related media coverage of the two cases are concerned, no acts of violence were carried out in the USA under the name of jihad by the defendants in question. There were also no statements from the groups in question threatening jihad, or violent/terrorist acts in the name of jihad. The only ground of the respective indictments appear to be the prosecutors' claims that the individuals in question have trained in terrorist or jihadist camps in Pakistan and Afghanistan for the purposes of "waging jihad" in the United States. There were heated debates – among lawyers, human rights activists and other observers – with regard to the nature of evidence provided in support of the prosecutors' claims in both cases.

It is not the place of this chapter to pass a judgement as to whether the US prosecutors had solid evidence to accuse the concerned individuals of a terrorist plot or not. But let us assume that the prosecutors did have a case substantiated with evidence that could (and in these cases they may argue that it did) stand in court, why couldn't they just confine themselves to outlining the criminal offences punishable under US law such as conspiracy to commit acts of murder, kidnapping, ... etc.? If need be, and since this is a political case, they can refer to the organizational or ideological affiliation of the defendants as appropriate. Instead, we read the following in the indictment of the Hassoun case:

It was a purpose and object of the conspiracy [of the defendants] to advance *violent jihad*, including supporting, and participating in, armed confrontations in specific locations outside the United States, and committing acts of murder, kidnapping, and maiming, for the purpose of opposing existing governments and civilian factions and *establishing Islamic states under the Sharia*.[19]

In the Hayat case, the indictment stated that:

Hamid Hayat intended to return to the United States and intended, upon receipt of orders from other individuals, to *wage jihad* in the United States against persons within the United States and against real and personal property within the United States.[20]

Though the document did not elaborate on how exactly Hayat was planning to carry out his "jihadi tasks", the implications were clear as far as the authors of the indictment were concerned.

One is tempted to think that had the US prosecutors opted for our suggestion of outlining criminal charges under US law and in *normal* legal terminology, they would have perhaps found it very difficult to gather the necessary evidence and present it in court. Rather it was more dramatic to present the case as part of a global conspiracy to wage jihad in various parts of the world with the perpetrators being part of a global network, individuals – possibly part of a sleeping cell – who attended jihadist training camps abroad in places like Afghanistan and Pakistan, and returned to wage jihad in the United States "upon receipt of orders". As such, the two cases become something reminiscent of September 11; they become almost trial by analogy.

Regardless of whether the men in the two cases were indeed guilty as charged and convicted by their respective juries, or not (as their lawyers had argued), their conviction should have been on account of recognizable criminal charges punishable under US law. If the defendants in question were accused of plotting 'terrorism' (a consensual legal definition of terrorism in its political context, is yet to be provided), then they should be tried as such; not on account of vaguely formulated charges revolving around 'waging jihad' and subscription to a 'jihadi' ideology or group. Thus, the word jihad penetrated the US justice system as nothing else than a criminal offence.[21]

Jihadiolgy in academia: *Understanding Jihad*

David Cook's book *Understanding Jihad*[22] has been hailed as a most helpful and important contribution to the subject since the events of September 11th.[23] To his credit, Cook does provide a succinct overview of the subject of jihad in both historical and contemporary Muslim sources and mainly worked with primary source material in Arabic. His work is generally well documented and reasonably argued, and his tone is on the whole scholarly. Yet, one cannot escape the conclusion that his thesis is basically similar if not identical to that of Pipes *et al.* Cook's position is that on the grounds of the evidence collected by his research, "one can say that during the first several centuries of Islam the interpretation of jihad was *unabashedly aggressive and expansive*".[24] Despite the rather sharp tone, this conclusion would have been perfectly fine as an objective understanding of jihad in Muslim's early history. Cook, however, effectively spends the rest of the book discounting and dismissing attempts by Muslims – in both historical and contemporary times – to conceptualize of jihad in any way other than the *aggressive and expansive* role he had accorded it. Furthermore, he also argued that "the importance of classical jihad is latent and can be brought to the fore in Islam *at any time*".[25] In what follows, I will try to give a critical examination of Cook's views with regard to: (1) Islamic primary legal sources and the early Muslim conquests; (2) greater and lesser jihad; and (3) contemporary Muslim theories of jihad.

Muslim conquests and Jihad

As is customary in these sort of studies, Cook turned to the Islamic primary sources (the Qur'an, Prophetic traditions, and works of the scholars) to search for jihad's rationale and regulations. Starting with the Qur'an, Cook, commenting on *sura* [Chapter] No. 9, indeed referred to the famous verse known as the verse of the sword [9.5] "But when the forbidden months are past, then fight and slay the pagans wherever you find them … etc."[26] He argued that although early commentaries on the Qur'an understood this verse as applicable to the pagan Arabs only, "later Muslim jurists will use this verse to proclaim a universal jihad against all non-Muslims". Cook goes on to state that one of the goals, or perhaps the main goal of jihad, was to conquer and dominate non-Muslims. Accordingly, Cook maintained, on the basis of his understanding of *sura 9* that the revelation represented "*a declaration of war*", and "explains the aggressiveness of the early Muslims".[27] Finally, Cook says that the Qur'anic text "provides the religious basis for the doctrine of jihad that would result in the great Muslim conquests of the seventh and eighth centuries".[28]

Elsewhere, he stated that "the Qur'an was a powerful exponent of an aggressive jihad doctrine".[29]

As regards the Prophetic tradition (also known as Prophetic sayings or exemplary deeds or *hadith* literature), Cook once again draws a direct link between the Prophetic traditions and conquests, noting that the early traditions reflected "a belief system capable of inspiring the conquest of so much territory and achieving what the early Muslims achieved".[30] After a brief review of some relevant Prophetic traditions, Cook remarks:

> [From] the *hadith* material, [it is clear] that the subject of militant jihad was of critical concern to Muslims during the formative first three centuries of Islam, and there is no indication from any of this material that the jihad is anything but military.[31]

Clearly Cook appears to understand the actions of early Muslims as primarily driven by doctrines, in this case the doctrine of jihad as formulated in the Qur'an and Prophetic tradition and subsequently codified by Muslim jurists. Despite his repeated assertions about the martial and aggressive mandates of the Qur'an and prophetic traditions, Cook does not provide a careful study to substantiate his claim that the Qur'an was indeed a universal "declaration of war", and that the early Muslims were following this declaration in practice when they embarked on the conquests. Rather than treating them as a response to a jihad doctrine, Muslim conquests should be first placed in their historical context as political and military events in the first place.

Though one may not discount the religious dimension in inspiring the early Muslim conquests, historians who studied the period emphasized political, economic or strategic considerations. Hugh Kennedy outlined several reasons for the conquests such as: extending the authority of the emerging Islamic state in Medina over the Arab inhabitants of Syria and Iraq; directing the energies of Arab tribesmen from internal raids (which was a way of life in pre-Islamic Arabia) to external conquests; and the power of patronage given to the Muslim leadership as a result of these conquests.[32] Other historians such as M. A. Shaban have argued that after a decade of wars in Arabia following the rise of Islam, trade had all but stopped, and the conquests provided the new regime in Medina with compensation in the form of booty.[33] Though many Muslims may not agree with these assessments, the readings of those scholars appear sounder historically than Cook's speculative logic that Muslim armies were marching under a "declaration of war" made by the Qur'an. Indeed, Cook himself conceded that conversion was not necessarily the purpose of conquests. "Islam was not in fact 'spread by the sword' – conversion was not forced on the occupants of conquered territories – but the conquests created the necessary conditions for the spread of Islam."[34] This is a sound observation, but it does not sit well with Cook's assertion that the Qur'an was a "powerful exponent of an aggressive jihad" premised on religious grounds. It is a fact that conquests created an Islamic polity that allowed Islam to gradually strike roots and eventually produced what is currently known as the world of Islam. It is also a known fact that the process of Islamization took generations to mature (over three centuries in Egypt, for example), an indication that the dynamics through which the inhabitants of the conquered territories were quite complex.

A related issue is Cook's belief that the early Muslim conquests represented a practical exercise in the theory or doctrine of jihad (indeed he called that particular section: "The Early Muslim conquests: Theory to practice").[35] Naturally, Cook is aware of the fact that there was no jihad theory in place, neither had the body of Islamic jurisprudence been produced, at the time of the conquests and throughout the first century of the Muslim empire. Apparently, what Cook had in mind was the relevant jihad teachings in the Qur'an and *hadith* literature. These too, however, had their limitations at the time in question. The Qura'n was collected, classified into chapters and written down during the time of the third Caliph Uthman b. 'Affan (644–656 CE) after the first wave of conquests had mostly been completed. Therefore, at the time of the conquest, though several of the Prophet Muhammad's companions may have memorized the Qur'an, one cannot say the same about the majority of fighters who joined the campaigns (some of whom had even fought against the Muslims during the apostasy wars after the Prophet's death, 632–634CE). Even for those who knew the Qur'an, there was the question of exegesis that had not yet developed into the sophisticated science it did later on during the height of Islamic civilization. When the Qur'anic commentaries developed and proliferated, scholars differed in the interpretation of some aspects of the much quoted verse 9.5 between those who say the verse abrogated all other verses that regulated relations between Muslims and polytheists, and those who say that the verse itself is abrogated by another one.[36] In any event, most of the commentaries dealt with this verse within the context of Arabia, as an instruction for Muslims to use force against the polytheists of Arabia after the expiry of any peace treaty that hitherto existed between them and Muslims.

The question of the Prophetic traditions is even more complicated, given the fact that traditions were compiled much later, in the ninth century CE (third century of the Muslim calendar), with the earliest among them – such as Malik's (d. c. 795CE) and Awza'i's (d. 773CE) compiled during the second century of the Muslim calendar. In the absence of those collections, it becomes extremely difficult, if not impossible, to measure the magnitude of the spread of this tradition or that among the Muslim communities in various locations. Hence, it is equally difficult to ascertain that the traditions quoted by Cook – assuming their authenticity – were sufficiently in circulation to be considered "capable of inspiring the conquest of so much territory".[37]

This is not to argue that the religious motive and inspiration were completely absent from the Muslim conquests. Yet, to say that the conquests were essentially a response to a clearly formulated jihad doctrine at the time is both speculative and problematic. Rather, a jihad doctrine and theory appeared to have been formulated by the jurists several generations after the Muslim conquests were completed. In this regard, rather than being manuals for conquests, the numerous books on jihad were in fact a rationalization of the practice of jihad, or more precisely Muslim warfare.

Evidently, a jihad theory evolved in Islamic classical jurisprudence, formulated by scholars primarily during the second and third centuries of the Islamic calendar. According to the majority of classical scholars, jihad is an obligation incumbent upon Muslims as a collective, not individual, duty for defence of the community and propagation of Islam. As a legal doctrine, the jihad theory revolved around warfare – offensive or defensive. As such, jihad became a component of Muslim's external relations, as is clear from the jurists' classification of the world into *Dar al-Islam* (the abode of Islam) – where Muslims are presumably secure and free to observe their religious obligations – and *Dar al-Harb* (the abode of war) – where Muslims will not be secure, nor would they likely be free to observe their religion, with intermediary zones regulated by peace treaties. From the perspective of classical jurists, peace can only be achieved or sustained through the establishment and supremacy of a Muslim polity – a *Pax Islamica*. The other body of legislation that classical jihad theorists dealt with was what is known as *jus in bello* – or regulation of warfare. In this body of legislation, classical scholars went to great lengths detailing what is permissible or prohibited during wars. In these Muslims' 'laws of war' the jurists paid special attention to the necessity of distinguishing between combatants and non-combatants, mostly arguing that only combatants or those who are able to fight should be targeted by Muslim armies.

In formulating a jihad theory, the classical scholars had indeed devised their own methodology of interpreting the Qur'an, Prophetic Tradition, and the relevant precedents set by the Prophet himself, and his immediate successors who oversaw the early Muslim conquests. As such, they were responding to the historical circumstances of their time and applying the knowledge and sciences at their disposal. Whether their laws of war were accurately followed by generals and fighters of Muslim armies or not is difficult to ascertain one way or the other. One approach of viewing the classical jihad theory in its both components – *jus ad bellum* and *jus in bello* – is to treat it as primarily an *academic* exercise by the jurists. In other words, the jurists – having taken war as a reality – went on to rationalize the justification of warfare and its conduct on religious grounds. This is how warfare was converted into jihad and formulated into a doctrine of a 'just war' that is distinct from other types of wars that are waged for 'worldly' purposes or gains. That may also explain why the concept of jihad – despite its multiple meanings – became so intricately intertwined with warfare. That having been the case, it should not be used to dismiss attempts by Muslims in history and modern times to find other conceptualization of jihad, as Cook tried in his discussion of *greater* and *lesser* jihads.

Greater and lesser jihad

Cook devotes a chapter in *Understanding Jihad* to discuss the issue of the multiple meanings of jihad: greater jihad which is regarded as fighting against one's passions; and lesser jihad, which refers to conventional warfare, the meaning with which the concept is usually associated. In his chapter, Cook seeks evidence of greater jihad in the Qur'an, the Prophetic tradition, the works of scholars and mystics; he also devotes a section to dealing with contemporary scholars who dealt with the subject. Cook contends that there is no solid historical evidence to support the concept of spiritual jihad (i.e. what is commonly known as greater jihad), no details on how it should be pursued in practice, and that if it ever existed, it was complementary to, not a substitute for, militant jihad. He further argued that greater jihad was primarily promoted by leaders of mystical or *Sufi* Islam; even they, however, understood the concept as an addition to, rather than instead of, lesser jihad.[38] Cook finally sums up his position as follows:

> [Emphasis on greater jihad] seems to the outside observer a patently apologetic device to promote a doctrine that has little historical depth in Islam, is not well attested in *hadith* literature, has few practical examples to illustrate precisely how it is practiced, and was adduced in order to overcome a resistance to the acceptance and legitimacy of jihad. The name [*greater* jihad] is nothing more than false advertisement designed to pull the wool over the eyes of the audience.[39]

In his study of this issue, Cook makes a well-argued point that greater jihad is not as straightforward as it seems. His approach, however, appears rather lop-sided. Having settled for his central thesis that jihad has been essentially "aggressive and expansive", Cook seems intent on removing any other interpretation that may interfere or blur his vision of jihad, which he apparently holds to be more *authentic*. Thus, Cook reviews a number of relevant Qur'anic verses and Prophetic traditions in a way that would either question the interpretation or authenticity of the source in question. I will take just a couple of examples by way of illustration:

Cook says that a number of passages in the Qur'an present jihad in a "nonviolent or not exclusively violent" interpretation and quotes verse 25.52 as an example, which says, "Therefore, do not listen to the unbelievers, but strive (*jahiduhum*) against them with utmost strenuousness, with the [Qur'an]."[40] Commenting on this verse, Cook argues that although the word 'jihad' has generally been translated as *strive*, a better translation would be *combat*. His rationale is that the general meaning of the verse deals with proclamation of the Islamic message, which may also be an objective of jihad in its 'militant interpretation', and that several traditions refer to jihad as combining the 'sword and tongue'. So even when jihad appears in the Qur'an in a clearly non-violent context, Cook is determined to bring it back to what he regards as its original meaning. Leaving aside the author's confidence which induced him to pose as an exegete in his own right, his is a rather puzzling logic. First, this particular *sura* – known as the Criterion in reference to the Qur'an – is devoted to speaking about the Holy Book, its merits and significance as drawing a dividing line between right and wrong, and generally warns unbelievers and praises those who believe. There is no context of war or direct conflict in either the verse in question or the verse before or after to warrant the usage of combat, or understanding of jihad as warfare in this instance. Second – and perhaps unbeknown to Cook – this *sura* was revealed in Mecca at a time when Muslims were not 'permitted' to fight or fight back even when they were subjected to systematic persecution.

The second example is from Cook's review of the Prophetic traditions. In this regard, he discusses the famous tradition of greater jihad:

> A number of fighters came to the Messenger of Allah, and he said: "You have done well in coming from the 'lesser jihad' to the 'greater jihad'." They said: "What is the 'greater jihad'?" He said: "For the servant [of God] to fight his passions."

According to Cook, this tradition is an attempt to radically reinterpret "the *aggressive* intent of the Qur'an and the *hadith* literature [in terms] of *spiritual* warfare".[41] Cook believes that the tradition in question perhaps dates to the first half of the ninth century, "when the ascetic movement in Islam was beginning to coalesce into Sufism". Furthermore, he casts doubts on the validity of this tradition and others as they are almost completely absent from the official canonical collections of *hadith*. His rationalization in this regard is that the *hadith* collectors did not include these traditions in their compilations because they "construed as illegitimate the entire line of thought leading to the conclusion that spiritual warfare is part of or equivalent to aggressive jihad".[42]

It is noticeable that Cook did not show the same level of robust scrutiny when he was relating traditions inciting jihad in its martial sense, gave no discussion about their authenticity or otherwise, or the possibility they might have not been widely in circulation during the early conquests (as we have pointed out above). Furthermore, the methodology he employed to argue that certain *hadith* may have not been regarded as sound because they violate an established understanding of jihad – as an aggressive military action – is not consistent with the criteria the *hadith* collectors adopted in their compilations. In fact, a major criticism that can be directed at those compilers, and classical Islamic historiography in general would be their over-emphasis on the chain of transmission with very little regard to the substance of the narrative itself. Hence their criterion as to whether a particular *hadith* is sound or not, was not the subject matter of that *hadith*, but rather the credibility of transmitters.

Another problem associated with Cook's discussion of the question of greater jihad is that he addresses his subject in an either/or manner. If one is to believe in greater – spiritual – jihad, they have to forsake militant jihad. This led him to discount any tradition or source that combines the two jihads together. Furthermore, he goes on to argue that even the Sufis, who were the most important advocates of the concept of spiritual jihad continued to *believe* in the traditional military jihad. Therefore, Cook concluded that greater jihad was nowhere to be found in the classical literature of Islam, and if it existed at all, it did so only in association with the other and better-known form of jihad, that of warfare. That the concept of greater jihad may exist in tandem with lesser jihad is not enough reason to discount the concept altogether. Nobody has suggested, including the Muslim apologetics, that jihad is completely devoid of any war dimension, but rather there is more to the concept of jihad than war and violence. There are enough references in the Qur'an to jihad as a non-violent activity.

Finally, Cook contends that there was a lack of clarity on how the spiritual jihad may be pursued in practice. One way to better appreciate the distinction between spiritual jihad and militant jihad is to view the former as an *individual* activity and the latter as a *communal* activity.

Contemporary theory of jihad

David Cook examines the contemporary theory of jihad, which emerged during the nineteenth and early twentieth centuries when most of the Muslim world was under direct or indirect European control. As with his discussion of spiritual or greater jihad, Cook sets for himself the task of deconstructing all attempts by Muslim reformists to devise a new interpretation of jihad doctrine as mere apologetics with no foundation in the authentic Muslim tradition. In contrast to his contemptuous approach to the reformists, Cook treats radical Islamists with deference, apparently on the assumption that their views are more *consistent* with the nature of Islam and its *aggressive* theory of jihad.

Commenting on the efforts of Muslim reformists Muhammad Abduh (1849–1905) and Rashid Rida (1865–1935), Cook states that they "do not achieve deeper intellectual clarity in their commentary on the Qur'an". He argues that Abduh and Rida are "confronted with the unambiguously aggressive character of several verses in the holy book and their lack of congruence with the picture of Islam they wish to paint".[43] He goes on to discuss Abduh's and Rida's attempts to advance a unique interpretation of the Qur'anic verse 9.5, the verse of the sword, in ways that would render it less universal in its applicability. Abduh and Rida rationalized their interpretations of the verse in that way by making reference to certain prophetic traditions that instruct Muslims to avoid certain groups such as Ethiopians and Turks. Such an interpretation was unacceptable to Cook who argues that it is "unprecedented, as are many of Abduh and Rida's other interpretations".[44] Cook goes on to argue against Abduh and Rida from a *true Islamic perspective*: "From a Muslim point of view, it is a bit of a stretch to say that a comparatively obscure *hadiths* on Turks and Ethiopians nullify a major Qur'anic doctrine."[45]

There are at least two contentious points about Cook's critique of Abduh and Rida. First, there are many precedents in classical jurisprudence where Muslim scholars gave more weight to a Prophetic practice and tradition that contradicted a formal or literal meaning of a Qur'anic verse. Ibn Rushd, the medieval scholar and philosopher, said that there was controversy among the jurists about the lawful and unlawful damages to the enemy particularly with regard to the combatants and non-combatants. Ibn Rushd then goes on to state that, "the source of this controversy is to be found in the fact that in a number of Traditions, rules are given which are at variance with the general rule from the Book [i.e. the Koran]".[46] Likewise, the exegete Ibn al-Arabi, commenting on the famous Qur'anic verse 9.5, stated that the *Sunna* – the Prophetic tradition – exempted the categories of women, minors, the elderly, monks, etc., from those who may lawfully be killed, significantly adding that the injunction of the verse should be understood as, "kill the polytheists who fight you".[47] Second, what if Abduh and Rida's modernist interpretation of the Qur'an is unprecedented in classical jurisprudence? Isn't it natural that Muslim scholars of the nineteenth and twentieth centuries should find ways of interpretation that are different from, and in some cases opposite to, the understanding of classical jurists of a millennium ago?

Cook then goes on to explore the views of Hasan al-Banna (1906–1949) and Abu al-A'la al-Mawdudi (1903–1979), the two champions of contemporary Islamism. Here, Cook exhibits some disappointment with their – unexpectedly – apologetic views on jihad:

> Al-Banna wrote his twenty-page pamphlet in the spirit of apologetics that were common during the second quarter of the twentieth century … Mawdudi's most evident apologetics are expressed in his radical re-definition of what constitutes jihad in Islam. According to him, jihad has nothing whatsoever to do with fighting.[48]

Cook finds comfort only with Sayyid Qutb (1906–1966), the patron of radical Islamism, who, Cook states, "is not apologist for jihad, nor is he uncomfortable with its implications or with the historical material that demonstrates the offensive use of war".[49] Indeed, Cook treats the works of Qutb with a degree of admiration that is only matched by his contempt of the reformists Abduh and Rida: "In all his works Qutb demonstrates himself to be a highly original and courageous thinker. Virtually the only works he cites are the Qura'n and the Prophet Muhammad biography."[50]

Well, as a matter of fact, Qutb does cite the medieval jurist Ibn al-Qayyim in his *Milestones* chapter on jihad and adopts the assessment of the latter that Islam progressed from peaceful propagation to total warfare.[51] Furthermore, Qutb – as he himself acknowledges – borrowed the idea of sovereignty of God from al-Mawdudi. But originality aside, Qutb who joined the Islamist movement in his forties and was not known to have been a trained scholar in Islamic jurisprudence, is regarded by Cook as more authentic in his understanding of Islam than a towering figure like Muhammad Abduh.

As long as Qutb's writing serves Cook's purpose of emphasizing the aggressive nature of jihad – and Islam for that matter – Qutb is given red carpet treatment, even when his logic doesn't make sense. For example, Cook relates that Qutb argued that only under Muslim rule will humanity be free to choose between Islam and infidelity. He goes on to comment:

> Thus Qutb interprets the important verse, "there is no compulsion in religion (2:256) to redefine the issue of compulsion, as well as defensive and offensive war, to the point where these concepts no longer mean what they do in the West."[52]

Fair enough, but Cook doesn't seem that troubled with Qutb's strange logic the way he was with Rida when the latter dealt with the same subject of offensive and defensive jihad. After accusing Rida of glossing over Islamic history, Cook quotes Rida as saying, "our defence of our religion is the proclamation of truth and the removal of the distortion and misinterpretation of it". To this statement, Cook comments as follows: "This definition of defence blurs the lines between 'defence' and 'offence' to the point where there is no real distinction between the terms and reduces the question to a semantic game."[53] The explanation is simple. While Rida was painstakingly trying to emphasize the defensive nature of jihad to the extent of trying a different reading of the Muslims' conquests, Qutb was bent on emphasizing the aggressive nature of jihad even to the extent of re-interpreting a Qur'anic verse that clearly speaks about freedom of religion in a belligerent manner; naturally Qutb would have Cook's vote.

In this framework, Cook's conclusion with regard to the place of radical Islamist groups and their jihadi agenda is not surprising. He argues:

> From an outsider's point of view, after surveying the evidence from classical until contemporary times, one must conclude that today's jihad movements are as legitimate as any that have ever existed in classical Islam, with the exception of the fact they disregard the necessity of established authority – that a legitimate authority such as a caliph and *imam* could declare jihad. Other than this one major difference, contemporary jihad groups fall within the confines of classical definition of jihad. That this is true can be seen by their careful regard for classical and contemporary law, their heavy emphasis on the spiritual rewards of jihad, and their frequently voiced claim to be fighting for the sake of Islam.[54]

Cook's assessment, in my opinion, misses the target on a number of accounts. In the first place, the views of radical Islamists are generally at variance with the views of the majority of contemporary Muslim opinion which acknowledges – directly or indirectly – that warfare is not the primary form of interaction between

Muslims and non-Muslims in today's world. Second, the radicals are out of tune with the core of classical jurisprudence which did not consider rebellion against a Muslim ruler, even a bad one, as a form of jihad. Rather classical jurists refrained from excommunication of rulers no matter how unjust or lax in their religious observation as long as they continue to profess Islam, and generally disapproved of rebellion as a greater evil than living under an unjust ruler.[55] Furthermore, though Cook recognized the radicals' disregard of the rule, devised by classical jurists, that only a legitimate authority could declare jihad, he in effect downplayed this important divergence by contemporary jihadis. Classical jurisprudence had not just accorded the prerogative of declaration of jihad solely to the Imam (which is important enough as it distinguishes between legitimate jihad and unlawful rebellion), but gave the imam wide discretionary power with regard to the strategy of fighting, treatment of prisoners of war, and more importantly the sole right of contracting or nullifying a truce. The responsibility of declaration of war or jihad, in this case, is not a mere technicality, but rather an essential prerogative that underwrites the legitimacy of jihad itself. Otherwise, who should be entrusted with this important responsibility and its associated tasks in the absence of a legitimate authority, the *Emir* of a jihadi group?

Another point that was also acknowledged but quickly downplayed by Cook is his concession that:

> Both anti-governmental and globalist radical groups are guilty of taking exceptions listed in the classical texts and making them the rule – for example with killing innocents … [yet] as far as their conduct of jihad, they fall within the limits set by classical and contemporary Muslim law.

As pointed out above, the thrust of the laws of war elaborated by the classical jurists rested on the principle that fighting should, as a rule, be confined to combatants, which means women, children, the elderly, peasants, religious devotees (such as monks), the wounded, in short, all non-combatants must be spared by Muslim armies. In this context it is rather puzzling how one can classify the actions of contemporary radical groups who frequently, and in most cases, deliberately attack civilians as falling "within the limits set by classical and contemporary Muslim law".[56]

Jihad and jihadism

In summary, the examples of academic and journalistic works outlined above (Cook, Pipes, and Jihad Watch) emphasize a concept of jihad that is aggressive and expansive and closely associated with violence and warfare. They essentially argue that the jihad espoused by the radical Islamist groups is the proper or authentic meaning of jihad as it developed in Islamic history, not the spiritualized jihad advocated by Muslim apologists. Finally, they contend that the classical concept of militant or martial jihad resonates with the majority of Muslims.

To place the question of a contemporary understanding of the concept of jihad in its proper perspective, it is important to distinguish between *jihad as a religious doctrine*, and *jihadism as a political ideology*.

In search of a modern doctrine of jihad

As a religious doctrine, jihad is indeed a central concept in Islamic history and teaching, but should the terms of reference of our understanding of jihad and its applicability in today's world be the classical Islamic jurisprudence? The simple answer to this question is that it should not. The classical jurists were essentially responding to an international context that is significantly different from today's international relations. They were operating in a world where warfare was the dominant norm of international relations, and peaceful co-existence the exception; a world dominated by imperial borders and expansion, and competing religious creeds and communities; and a world where plunder of the vanquished and enslavement of captives were common practices. Islamic classical jurisprudence was a product of this international climate, and as such it has a questionable applicability to the current international relations, which has been built, at least since the Second World War, around the idea of peaceful co-existence as the norm between *nation states*, and where war is widely regarded as the exception. The majority of Muslims in today's world are aware of this contextual discrepancy, and in effect treat the theme of jihad – particularly in its warfare connotations – as something of the past, unless in situations of foreign occupation. Should a particular Muslim country or territory falls under foreign occupation, as is the case with Iraq and Palestinian territories, then the question of jihad props up to debates around strategies of resistance, and may be pursued in practice by Islamist, or Islamic nationalist groups.

This is not an argument to the effect that history is no longer relevant for today's Muslims, because it is. Indeed, the majority of Muslims continue to accord primacy of place for their history and 'glorious past'. However, Muslims continue to differ in how they read their history and what lessons they take from it in the same way they differ in how to interpret the foundational texts of Islam: the Qur'an, Prophetic traditions and rulings of classical jurists. Invariably (as in other religious traditions) there are those who adopt a literalist-fundamentalist understanding, as well as those who take a moderate, liberal or apologetic approach. These divergent approaches may be informed by ideological or epistemological positions, or influenced by the prevailing socio-political conditions at a given moment in history.

Therefore, a concept of jihad derived from the works of classical jurists cannot be easily deployed in the contemporary national and international realities of Muslim societies. Likewise, if the concept of jihad espoused by the militant Islamist groups is in fact just an extremist version of the classical jihad doctrine, then it is all the more incompatible with the contemporary world, particularly when it had rid itself of most of the standards and restraints elaborated by classical jurists. On the other hand, the works of Muslim modernists and liberals have often been dismissed as apologetics but they contain two useful ideas: the first relates to a concept of jihad which is mainly defensive, that should be pursued at times of aggression or occupation; and the second treats most of the jihad literature, including the relevant Qur'anic injunctions as historically bound, or primarily spiritual in direction. Such a creative approach should be encouraged as a paradigm of peaceful co-existence and tolerance, rather than discounted as inauthentic or blatantly deceptive. Observers or outside scholars may try to deconstruct or reconstruct the conditions and influences that inform a particular position or class of opinions, but on what grounds will they be able to pass a value judgement that such a position represents true Islam, while the other does not?

The politics of Jihadism

As a political ideology, Jihadism, on the other hand, may be traced, first, to the decline of secular ideologies in Middle Eastern and Muslim societies (particularly during the 1980s and 1990s) and the rise of Islamism; and, second, to the rise of the militant or radical tendencies on the fringe of Islamism. There are three broad categories of Islamist groups that use force to reach their political goals, hence the label: Jihadists, or Jihadi Islamists. These categories include: (1) Islamic nationalism; (2) militant Islamist opposition; and (3) global Jihadism.

First, *Islamic nationalism* refers to these Islamist organizations whose main political objective is resistance to foreign occupation and 'national' liberation of their countries or occupied territories. Examples include organizations like the main Palestinian Islamic Resistance Movement, better known by its Arabic acronym HAMAS, the Palestinian Islamic Jihad, the Lebanese Hizbullah (Party of God), and most recently several Iraqi insurgent groups that have emerged on the Iraqi political and military scene after the US-led invasion of Iraq. As is clear from these examples, organizations under this category operate under conditions of occupation such as the Occupied Palestinian Territories (occupied by Israel in 1967), South Lebanon (also occupied by Israel from 1978 to 2000), and recently Iraq since the US-led invasion of 2003.

Second, the term *militant Islamist opposition* groups refers to the radical Islamist groups whose main objective is to eventually overthrow the regimes of their respective countries by force. This category include groups such as the Egyptian Islamic Jihad, the Egyptian Islamic Group (al-Jama'a al-Islamiyya), the Algerian armed Islamic Group (GIA), and the Algerian Islamic Salvation Army, among others. These groups were particularly active during the first half of the 1990s when they became locked in a violent confrontation with the regimes of their respective countries: Egypt and Algeria.

Finally, the *global Jihadist* category includes groups such as al-Qaeda which perpetrated the September 11th attacks on the United States and similar actions in other countries. The main target of these groups appears to be the United States and other Western nations, and the scope of their activities is the world at large. After September 11th, many groups appeared with al-Qaeda label in various regions of the world, such as al-Qaeda in the Arabian Peninsula that carried out a number of violent actions in Saudi Arabia between 2003 and 2005, al-Qaeda in Mesopotamia which has been engaged in acts of violence against the US troops in Iraq as well as Iraqi civilian and military targets, and al-Qaeda in Europe which was apparently behind the Madrid and London bombings in March 2004, and July 2005 respectively. Whether these groups are somehow linked to an al-Qaeda global network under the leadership of Osama bin Laden and Ayman al-Zawahiri, or act independently but use the label of al-Qaeda is beside the point as far as this discussion is concerned. What matters is that they use similar tactics and raise similar slogans, and appear to be sharing the same objectives. They target Western nations, their interests and allies across the world, and they all claim that they are fighting to liberate Muslims worldwide from the 'hegemony and tyranny' of Western powers.

Common to all these three categories of militant Islamist groups is the fact that they all employ religious sentiment and ideology to recruit and mobilize followers and supporters. Indeed, they all share a passion about Islam and a desire to see it ruling supreme in the Muslim world and beyond. In historical terms, all three categories can trace their origins to the rise of the modern Islamist movements or what came to be known as the phenomenon of political Islam, which grew out of the transnational Muslim Brotherhood in the Middle East and the Jamati Islami (the Islamic Group) of Pakistan, and was subsequently influenced – in various ways – by the Iranian Revolution in 1979 that replaced the secularizing monarchy of the Iranian Shah with an 'Islamic' republic.

Despite their commonalities, the three Jihadi categories may be differentiated on account of their respective strategies, constituencies, and discourse. As can be seen from the categorization outlined above, the three groups have divergent goals as far as their political and military actions are concerned: national liberation in the case of Islamic nationalists; toppling secular national regimes in the case of militant Islamists; and fighting/destabilizing Western powers in the case of global Jihadis. These divergent strategies influence their respective discourses, and the constituencies they hope to appeal to. In broad terms, the respective goals of the three Jihadi categories define the 'enemy' against which their jihad is being waged: occupying powers for the Islamic Nationalists; national regimes for the militant Islamists; and Western powers for the global Jihadis. In this broad categorization, the three Jihadi groups adopt divergent strategies and approaches to warfare with regard to the geographical limitations of their operations, deference or indifference to international humanitarian laws, and, most significantly, the ultimate political objectives of their military operations.

Herein lies the major difference between the Islamic nationalists, on the one hand, and the militant Islamists and global Jihadis, on the other. Whereas the Islamic nationalists virtually represent a mainstream tendency engaged – through their military wings – in a violent resistance against an occupying power, the militant Islamists and global Jihadis represent the extreme tendency on the fringe of the mainstream Islamist movement.

At first sight, there appear clear differences between the global Jihadis and the militant Islamist opposition. While the latter are nationally bound in their objectives and activities, the former operate globally with a rather elusive religio-political objectives. A closer examination, however, reveals significant similarities between the two tendencies in terms of ideology, emphasis on the use of force or political violence as their central activity, and their *modus operandi* in carrying out indiscriminate attacks without distinction between civilian and military targets. At the level of political objectives, although the militant Islamists are generally committed to overthrowing the secular-leaning regimes in their respective countries, they are equally elusive with regard to their concept of an Islamic state, which is supposedly their ultimate goal. The main distinction therefore between militant Islamists and global Jihadis is the context of their operations as national and international respectively. In this regard, one can argue that we are essentially dealing with one Jihadi movement or tendency, a faction of which is operating globally, while the other operates nationally.

The September 11th attacks represented the culmination of al-Qaeda's violent activism and so far the deadliest and largest in scope and implications. These attacks, however, proved not to be the last activities of the transnational jihad and its violent bid to engage the US and its Western allies in multiple fronts of confrontation across the world. Despite the apparent destruction of the logistical and military base of al-Qaeda in Afghanistan in 2001, globalist Jihad showed no signs of eclipse in the face of the "war on terrorism" that has been declared and actively pursued by the US administration in the aftermath of September 11th. The difference is that the organizational and tactical dynamics of globalist Jihad changed as a result of changing circumstances.

The resilience of the globalist trend may be explained in view of the negative developments that characterized the political scene of the Middle East during the last decade or so: the deteriorating situation in the Occupied Palestinian Territories; the occupation of Iraq and the outbreak of violence there; the incessant absence of meaningful participatory politics and outlets of peaceful protest throughout the region; and the continuing infringement of human rights by authoritarian regimes in the region under the pretext of "war on terror" with the apparent acquiescence of the US, and other Western powers. Such a situation generated further resentment and fuelled the anti-Americanism sentiment that had become a conspicuous feature of Middle Eastern politics since the Gulf War of 1990/1991. This wide range of grievances and anti-American resentment does not mean that people in the Middle East and other Muslim societies will be converted *en masse* to the cause of global Jihadists, but it creates a climate that is conducive for the latter to legitimize their cause and facilitate their drive for new recruits.

Within this framework, Jihadism figures as a component of the *Salafist* ideology[57] of global radical Islamism. Despite their selective and de-contextualized employment of Islamic jurisprudence and the equally selective quotes from the Qur'an and the Prophetic traditions, radical Islamist groups are essentially living in, and responding to, contemporary domestic and international socio-political situations. It is this contextual framework – *not* the mirror of Islamic history and its corresponding jurisprudence – that essentially determines the place or legitimacy of radical Islamist groups within the political map of Muslim-majority countries.

Notes

1 Jihad Watch website. Available at: www.jihadwatch.org/, accessed at various times between 10 December 2008 and 22 January 2009.
2 Ibid.
3 Ibid.
4 Ibid.
5 Daniel Pipes, "What is Jihad?", 31 December 2002. Available at: www.danielpipes.org/, accessed at various times between 15 December 2005 and 30 January 2009.
6 Ibid.
7 Daniel Pipes, "Jihad and the Professors", November 2002, in ibid.
8 Ibid.
9 Ibid.
10 Pipes, December 2002, op. cit.
11 United States District Court: Southern District of Florida, Case No. 04–60001: United States of America vs. Adham Amin Hassoun; Mohamed Hesham Youssef; Kifah Wael Jayyousi; Kassem Daher; Jose Padilla [hereafter referred to as USA vs. Hassoun *et al.*].
12 United States District Court, Eastern District of California, Case No. 05–240 GEB: United States of America vs. Hamid Hayat, and Umer Hayat [hereafter referred to as USA vs. Hamid & Umer Hayat].
13 Ibid.
14 USA vs. Hassoun *et al.*
15 USA vs. Hamid & Umer Hayat, pp. 4–5.
16 USA vs. Hassoun *et al.*, p. 2.
17 Ibid., p. 2.
18 Ibid.
19 Ibid., p. 5; emphasis added.
20 USA vs Hamid & Umer Hayat, p. 3, emphasis added.
21 See, for example, the press statement by the US Department of Justice on the conviction of Hamid Hayat, dated 10 September 2007. Available at: www.usdoj.gov, accessed 24 January 2009.
22 David Cook, *Understanding Jihad*, Berkeley, CA: University of California Press, 2005.
23 One of the reviewers, Reuven Firestone, says, "This book increases our understanding of the seemingly odd behaviors we observe through the media", found on the back cover of the book.
24 Cook, op. cit., p. 30, emphasis added.
25 Ibid., p. 31, emphasis added.
26 The Holy Qur'an, trans. Abdullah Yusuf Ali, New Delhi: Goodword Books, 2005, p. 114.
27 Cook, op. cit., p. 10.
28 Ibid., p. 11.
29 Ibid., p. 19.
30 Ibid., p. 15.
31 Ibid., p. 19.
32 Hugh Kennedy, *The Prophet and the Age of the Caliphates: The Islamic Near East from the Sixth to the Eleventh Century*, 9th edn, London: Longman Group, 1999, p. 59.
33 M.A. Shaban, *Islamic History AD 600–750 (A.H.132): A New Interpretation*, Cambridge: Cambridge University Press, 1971, pp. 24–25.
34 Cook, op. cit., p. 13.

35 Ibid., p. 11.
36 See, for example, Ibn Kathir, *Tafsir al-Qur'an al-'Azim* [Exegesis of the Glorious Qur'an], vol. 2, 6th edn, Beirut: Dar al-Ma'rifah, 1993, p. 350; *al-Shawkani, M, al-Jami'bayn fannay al-riwayah wal-dirayah min 'Ilm al-tafsir* [Combining Narrative and Interpretative Knowledge in Exegesis], vol. 1, Beirut: Aalm al-Kutub, 2002, pp. 574–576.
37 Cook, op. cit., p. 15.
38 Ibid., pp. 32–39.
39 Ibid., p. 47.
40 *The Qur'an*, A. Y. Ali's translation, p. 235.
41 Cook, op. cit., p. 35, emphasis added.
42 Ibid., p. 35.
43 Ibid., p. 96.
44 Ibid., p. 97.
45 Ibid.
46 Ibn Rushd, *Bedayat al-mujtahid*, chapter on Jihad, Beirut, n.d, vol. 1, pp. 384–385; trans. and annotated by Rudolph Peters, in *Jihad in Medieval and Modern Islam*, Leiden: E. J. Brill, 1977, p. 15.
47 Ibn al-Arabi, Abu Bakr, *Ahkam al-Qur'an* [Regulation of the Qur'an], vol. 2, Beirut: Dar al-Fiker, n.d, p. 456.
48 Cook, op. cit., pp. 98–99.
49 Ibid., p. 105.
50 Ibid., p. 106.
51 Ibid., pp. 103–104; Sayyid Qutb, *Ma'alim fil Tariq* [i], 6th edn, Beirut: Dar al-Shuruq, 1979, pp. 55–56.
52 Cook, op. cit., p. 105.
53 Ibid., p. 97.
54 Ibid., p. 164.
55 A maxim of classical jurists was that it is better to live for forty years under an unjust or impious ruler, that to live one night without one, or under conditions of rebellion (commonly known as *fitnah*).
56 Cook, op. cit., p. 164.
57 Slafism [Arabic *Salafiyya*] refers to an Islamic school of thought that proclaims affinity with the ways of the venerated ancestors in Islam [Arabic *al-Salf al-Salih*], namely the Prophet Muhammad and his companions and immediate successors, and the first two generations of Muslims who continued and preserved the Qur'an and the Prophetic traditions. The Salafist School is regarded as an ultra-conservative, literalist in its approach to the religious scriptures and on the whole "fundamentalist" in its outlook.

7 Islam, Muslims, neighbors in Asia?

The transformation of Japan's perceptions of Islam as shown in its media

Keiko Sakai

> The draft constitution [of Iraq] rejects the personal dictatorship of the Saddam era and establishes a federal system, a parliament and democracy as the main pillars [for the building of the state]. We can say that, *for an Islamic society, this is relatively progressive.*
>
> (emphasis added)[1]

> Arab countries do not perceive this situation as a fight between terrorists and anti-terrorism. They understand it as "resistance movements against the invasion of the kafirs". *In the eyes of the Japanese, this seems a much too simplified, Islamic approach*, but Arab newspapers use the term "resistance" for the group that killed Mr. Oku and others.
>
> (emphasis added)[2]

These excerpts, appearing in newspaper articles, are typical examples of how the Japanese media have perceived Islam in recent times. Everything that happens in the area where a Muslim lives is "Islamic", and everything regarded as backwards is described as being related to Islam. In this discourse, what the media don't understand is ascribed to Islam, which is alien to the Japanese. Therefore it is considered natural that Japanese people do not understand it.

It is true that the media seldom focused on Islam before September 11, 2001. During the quarter century between 1975 and 2001, 51,539 articles about Islam appeared in the four major daily newspapers,[3] and almost the same number of articles (51,735) referred to Islam in the mere six years following September 11th until the end of 2007. If we only select editorials, those referring to Islam numbered 937 before September 11th, but increased to 1,084 after September 11th.

With such an increase in the use of the word 'Islam', it seems very likely that the media naively imported Western perceptions of Islam from Western media and followed them by generalizing about Muslim society as an 'other' that may cause a 'clash of civilizations' with the West. If we look at the number of editorials in major newspapers that referred to Islam using the word 'terrorism' before and after September 11th, this increased from 252 to 803. This means that only 26.9 per cent of the editorials referring to Islam mentioned terrorism before

September 11th, but the percentage increased to 74.1 per cent after the attacks. It is clear that the word 'Islam' has been likened to terrorism after September 11th. As for the articles on Islam, the share of those using the word 'terrorism' before September 11th was 16.5 per cent, and this increased to 50 per cent after September 11th.

Does this mean that the negative perception of Islam in the Japanese media was influenced by Western Orientalism only after September 11th? Can Japan's misperception of Islam be understood as part of a Western epistemology that is based on the dichotomy of "the West versus Islam"? If so, part of the explanation might lie in the fact that there is only a small Muslim community in Japan. The number of Muslims who reside in Japan from the member countries of OIC is slightly more than 40,000.[4, 5] Most of the Muslims living in Japan are non-Japanese, except those who have married Muslims. Non-Japanese Muslims who came to work in Japan rather recently, after the 1980s, are mainly from Indonesia, Pakistan, and Bangladesh, and work as traders of second-hand cars and construction workers or in the service sector.[6]

This does not mean, however, that Japan did not know about Islam before September 11th. On the contrary, Japan's military tried to use the Pan-Islamic movement against European imperialism in Asia before and during WWII in the context of the Asianism that Japan was using to implement its own imperialist ideology.

The perception of Islam/Muslim societies in modern Japan faced a dilemma during the country's modernization before World War II. Intellectuals in Meiji Japan feared that Japan might follow the same fate as Muslim societies in the Middle East and South Asia by being the target of European colonialism. At the same time, however, Japan focused on these communities in Asia with the imperialist goal of colonizing them. On the eve of WWII, some nationalists combined these two understandings into a theory of justification for Japan's colonial policy, saying that Japan's leadership was necessary in order to de-colonize Asia and rid it of Western control.

The question is, what happened to Japan's perception of Islam/Muslim society before WWII? Did it disappear completely, and was it only recently that a replica of the West's stance on Islam/Muslims was introduced? Or does the current perception in Japan of Islam/Muslims bear some of the traits present in Japan before WWII?

In this chapter, I will briefly summarize Japan's policy on Islam/Muslims before WWII. Then I will analyze the discourse in the editorials and commentaries of the major newspapers published in Japan in order to see how their perceptions of Islam/Muslim society have changed.

Japanese intellectuals' perceptions of Muslims/Islam in the pre-war period

The early encounter between Japan and Islam can be seen in the literature of the Heian era (794–1192). Islamic culture and philosophy flowed into Japan through China and Southeast Asia in the medieval period. Japanese literature in the tenth century contains the story of a *kento-shi* (an official envoy from Japan to China) who drifted by mistake to Persia.[7] Relations were established in an exchange of images between the Islamic Middle East and Japan without any direct communication, but through China, the main power in the region and one of Japan's main sources of civilization at that time. This pattern continued until after the arrival of Western merchants in Japan in the seventeenth century, among whom were, on occasion, Muslim merchants. The activities of these merchants were limited, however, as Japanese authorities in the Edo era strictly regulated trade with foreign countries. Thus, information on Islam and Muslims came mainly through China. This is very clear if we look at the description of Islam by Hakuseki Arai, the most famous intellectual of the mid-eighteenth century, as he refers to a history of Islam that is based on the Chinese version of the legend of Waqqas.[8] His work was based on a Chinese translation of Western geography texts by Italian Christian missionaries.

The Chinese influence on Japan's notions of Islam is clearly shown in the Japanese translation of the word 'Islam' itself, 'Kaikyo'. The term *Kaikyo* (*Huízú* in Mandarin) was originally used by the Han people, the main linguistic group in China, for the religion of the Hui tribes, the main Muslim group in China.[9] Japan borrowed this term to describe Islam until the 1979 Islamic Revolution in Iran.[10] Interpreting Islam through the name of an ethnic group may have affected Japan's understanding of Islam, as I shall discuss later in this chapter.

Japan's knowledge of the Islamic Middle East greatly increased after Japanese intellectuals started to import and translate Western works during the Edo era. At the end of the Edo era and at the beginning of the Meiji period, scholars started to translate Western texts on Islam/Muslim societies. *Konkou Zushiki*, written in 1830–1843 by Shogo Mitsukuri, was based on information given in Dutch publications. *Chikyu Setsuryaku*, a translation of the work of the American missionary, Richard Quarterman Way, was widely used as a textbook in the early Meiji period. While importing correct and updated information on Muslim societies in the Middle East, Japan also imported Western Orientalists' views on Islam. Arabs were described as people living on plunder, and as being brutal (*Konkou Zushiki*), stupid, less intelligent, and illiterate (*Chikyu Setsuryaku*).[11]

These images were constructed without any direct experience of Muslims, but they were strengthened when Japan opened its borders to the outside world at the end of the Edo era and Japanese elites visited Egypt for the first time on their way to Europe. A government delegation to Europe, headed by Tomomi Iwakura, briefly visited Cairo and left with the impression of "poverty and laziness" among the local people. The main concern of intellectuals and politicians in the Meiji era was to introduce Westernization and maintain Japan's independence, which was under threat from Western imperialism.[12] In their eyes, Muslim societies, not only in the Middle East but also in Africa, were the negative result of Western colonialism, and they provided a cautionary lesson for the future of Japan in its relations with the West. In his book *Sekai Kuni Zukushi* (1869), which was widely used as a school textbook for a long time, Yukichi Fukuzawa, the founder of the modern education system in Meiji Japan, categorically labeled Africa as a "world of chaos and barbarians" that was inhabited by "the lowest strata" in the world.[13]

In contrast to these intellectuals who pursued Westernization and considered the colonized countries in Asia and Africa as negative examples, there were others who sympathized with the fate of these societies and felt a sense of solidarity with them. Sanshi Toukai, a novelist at the end of the nineteenth century, wrote a best-selling novel in which he insisted that Japan should challenge the Western imperial powers. In his novel, he praised Urabi Pasha, and expressed his support for the Mahdi movement.[14]

We can therefore see that Japan's intellectuals were divided into two camps in the late nineteenth century and the beginning of the twentieth century. The mainstream pursued a policy of "getting out of Asia and joining the West", and they looked down on Muslim societies in Asia and Africa, whose fate was sealed by the failure of Westernization. The other group reflected Japan's frustration through their sympathy with colonial Asia and Africa, and they took the path of anti-Westernization. The latter group developed the idea of Asianism in the late nineteenth century and insisted that Japan should liberate colonial Asia from the West and be a leader in Asia. Islam was judged to be a very important factor in colonial Asia and Africa. One famous ideologue, Shumei Okawa (1886–1957) vociferously expressed his compassion for Muslims in Algeria under French occupation and urged Japan to support them.[15] He gradually increased his interest in Islam, translated the Qur'an and wrote *Kaikyo Gairon* which covered the history of Islam and presented basic information about it.[16]

The study of Islam started to be promoted when the Japanese military discovered that they could use Muslim communities in China and Southeast Asia to make it easier to control them, their land and their natural resources. After the Manchurian Incident of 1931, Japan started to employ a strategy of mobilizing the Muslim minorities in Inner Mongolia and northwest China and manipulating the anti-communist sentiment among them to prevent the expansion of Soviet communism.[17] Japan also established the Greater Japan Islamic League (*Dai Nippon Kaikyo Kyokai*), which incorporated Muslims living in Japan. The intention behind promoting these ties with Muslims in Japan was to combine "The Far East with the Near East, and Imperial Japan with Pan-Islamism".[18] Dundar points out that Japan's military planned to establish an East Turkistan state in the Hsinchiang Uighur area and invited Abd al-Karim, a member of the Ottoman ruling family, who was in exile in India at the time, to be the emperor there.[19] In Indonesia and Malaysia, Japan's military also mobilized local ulama by stimulating their hatred toward the Christian West.[20]

Under the totalitarian regime, study of Islam/Muslim societies was mobilized to help carry out this imperialist strategy. Research institutes were established on the eve of WWII. An example is the Institute of the Islamic Studies (*Kaikyoken Kenkyujo*), which was founded one year after Japan launched its war against China. Usuki points out that scholars of Islam seriously addressed the issue of the close networks within the *umma* at that time. Then the idea emerged of combining basic academic studies with policy-oriented studies. Yukiji Okubo, the head of the Institute of the Islamic Studies, explained the purpose behind the founding of the Institute as follows:

> If we want to obtain the trust of the Kaikyo-to [Muslim], we need to conduct precise research and studies, obtain a deep and thorough knowledge of their situation ... European powers, such as the British and Soviet Russia, where there are many Muslims, have been studying Muslim issues. They have wide experience of how to deal with Muslims, so they are well informed.[21]

In short, Japan started to introduce its policy of mobilizing Muslim societies to its advantage in WWII, and the study of Islam was promoted with strong support from the state. Given such a history, it was natural that intellectuals after WWII would omit this past and end their study of Islam. Both the Institute of the Islamic Studies and the Greater Japan Islamic League were abolished after WWII. Islamic/Muslim studies in Japan were then almost suspended until the 1970s.

Japanese media's perceptions of Muslims/Islam after WWII

Post-war perceptions in the newspapers during the age of nationalism

After WWII, Japan abandoned its pre-war policy of Asianism and its intention to mobilize Muslim societies to aid its expansion. Not only did this cause a total neglect of Islamic studies after the war until the oil crisis in the 1970s, which compelled the government to promote the study of the Middle East once again, it also ended Japan's expressions of solidarity and compassion with Muslim peoples in the Middle East and Asia in the context of Islam. Japan's perception of Muslim communities through the eyes of the West became dominant once more.

Lack of interest in Islam/Muslim societies can clearly be seen in how often the word 'Islam' was used in the newspapers. It is only rather recently that the major Japanese newspapers have started to mention Islam as a key word in their editorials. Figure 7.1 shows the number of editorials whose headlines contain the terms 'Islam', the 'Middle East', or the names of the major countries in the region. We find that the word 'Islam' was used in headlines only after 2001, except for a few cases in the late 1970s and late 1980s. Even after 2001, 'Islam' only appears in the headlines of a few editorials, except for eight editorials in 2001. Instead, the phrase 'Middle East' is more often used as a key term. Also, the word 'Arab' was frequently used in the headlines of the 1960s and 1970s.

In articles concerning Muslim countries, references to Islam are not very common. Among the op-eds referring to certain countries or areas where Muslims are living, the percentage of op-eds that referred to Islam is smaller than half, except with respect to Central Asia during 1991–2001 (Figure 7.2).

Concerning the Middle East, only 49 op-eds mention Islam/Muslims among the 452 that touched on the Middle East before the Gulf War. The number of

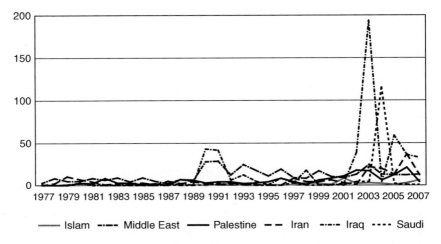

Figure 7.1 Number of op-eds referring in their headline to Islam or to the names of major countries in the Middle East.

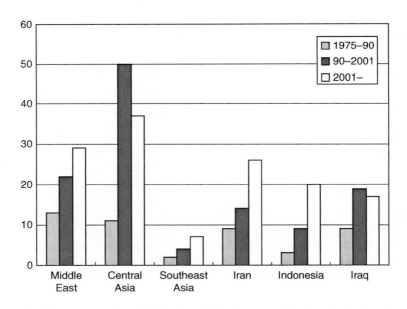

Figure 7.2 Share of op-eds using the word 'Islam' among those that deal with the area/ countries concerned.

op-eds that referred to the Middle East increased to 1348 during the period between 1991 and 2001, which means that concern about the Middle East increased in the media, but only one-fifth referred to Islam. This means that this concern with the Middle East was principally expressed through other factors, i.e. nationalism, oil, and international politics.

*Disappearance of the feeling of solidarity with Muslims in the 1950s
and 1960s with some remnants of sympathy on the basis of a shared
non-European-ness*

After WWII, almost none of the articles on the Middle East/Islam showed any
signs of Japan's pre-war work on Islam. Only in a few cases were some journalists
reminded of the war when they visited Palestine:

> Civilians in Jerusalem live with the sound of guns. Even the boy selling
> cheese carries a gun from his shoulder. A young guy who is wondering
> whether or not to buy the cheese looks very firm, different from the Arabs
> we usually see. The scene reminded me of the days when Tokyo was fire-
> bombed [during WWII].[22]

Although Japan abandoned its willingness to support Muslim societies against
the West, we can still find a sympathy toward colonized Muslim societies in some
articles. The following editorial shows some sympathy for nationalism, especially in Algeria, with signs of compassion for the Arabs as victims of European
colonialism:

> The diabolical attitude of the OAS in Algeria is not that of human beings at
> all. ... Bleeding Arabs who bear the challenge of the OAS are nothing but
> martyrs. It is quite natural for Allah to dominate a land where there is no
> Christ [to save the people].[23]

This compassion never led the Japanese media to justify Japan's policy before
WWII. On the contrary, some editorials show Japan's regret for its imperial past.
The following comment shows a clear and striking difference from Okawa's
sympathy for the Algerian revolution against French colonialism:

> French nationals were brave and sensible when, in the face of a storm of
> organized terrorism, they expressed support for the ceasefire and for Algerian
> independence. This is thought-provoking when we compare it with our past
> when we were dragged into war, although we were fed up with the arrogance
> of the military and the rightists [in WWII].[24]

Sympathy toward the Middle East and Africa under Western control was,
however, expressed through praise for their nationalism. Considering nationalism
as secular modernization, many editorials understood Islam as an obstacle to
modernization. Admitting that religious zeal is a source of nationalism in the
developing world, the following editorial points out the negative effects of Islam
when it came to nation-building by regarding it as supportive of feudalism:

> In this area [from Morocco to Indonesia] where many states have been left in
> a pre-modern stage, religious zeal rather than patriotism has been the driving

force behind the unification of the nation. In that sense, we cannot ignore trends in Kaikyo-to.

... It was also natural that, as time passed, the anger of the layman, who shares the same fate as other people, should spread to all of Kaikyo. ... Thus the Kaikyo belief became a spiritual pillar for the national independence movement ... But the principles and tradition of Kaikyo itself contain contradictions, because Kaikyo preserves feudalism.[25]

The separation of men from women in the train is also perceived as a sign of backwardness:

6 years ago, the British and French occupiers were the first race in Egypt ... At the bottom of the society, there were Kaikyo-to. It was a purely class society. This was overturned by the last revolution ... I feel that the real Egyptian revolution will be accomplished if they can abolish the women-only cars and second class coaches on the trams.[26]

As in the Meiji era, Islam was considered not only as a hindrance to development but also as a source of laziness and lack of productivity:

What made the nomadic people ... build a big empire and a great culture? It was the inspiration of Kaikyo.

Then what made the Arabs, a people with a glorious history and tradition, apathetic, inefficient, impractical and watered-down?

Many answer that this is also because of Kaikyo [Islam]. (Some say, however, that it is the result of a long period of foreign control, especially Western imperial rule.) ...

It is true that its [Kaikyo's] daily discipline and customs generally clash with what is required for modern production and modern life, that is to say, industriousness, morale, and efficiency.[27]

In contrast to the above stance, which seems to approve of nationalism as opposed to Islam, some writers find Islam at the center of the "militant nationalism" that emerged in the 1950s. This perception easily turned into the idea of connecting Islam and nationalism in the Middle East with terrorism, as we can see in the following editorial, which describes the assassination of King Abdullah of Jordan and the nationalist movement in Iran as 'terrorist':

In the Kaikyo area now, there are serious problems, such as Morocco's independence movement, Egypt's rejection of its treaty with Britain, Iraq's request for an amendment of its treaty with the British, Iran's attempt to regain its oil concession, and conflicts between Israel and the Arab countries. What is especially striking is that some radical elements among Kaikyo-to are trying to attain their political ends immediately by using the terrorist method of assassination.

.... [because] some elements or a country pursue their ambitions under the name of national liberation or freedom for Kaikyo-to.[28]

This critical discourse might be considered as being influenced by European perceptions of nationalism in the Middle East, but it also reflects Japan's sensitivity about her pre-war "ambitions (for Muslims) under the name of liberation".

The 1960s and 1970s: solidarity or images of violence within 'nationalism', not in Islam/Muslim societies

Even after 1973, when the Japanese government had to change its policy toward the Arab oil-producing countries, any understanding of Islam was left in the shadows. After Japan came to be seen as an "unfriendly country" by Arab governments, the Japanese government issued the Nikaido Statement, which emphasized guidelines for future Japanese diplomatic policy toward the Middle East.[29] This focused on the need for an Israeli withdrawal from the territories occupied during the 1967 War, and on respect for the right of Palestinians to self-determination. It also activated Japan's diplomatic and economic efforts to improve relationships with the oil-producing countries in the Middle East. The government dispatched Takeo Miki, who would become prime minister the following year, on a special mission to Saudi Arabia, Egypt and other major Arab countries. As a result, the volume of Japanese imports from the Middle East (except North Africa), as well as exports to the Middle East increased tremendously. This sudden flurry of diplomatic efforts was called, rather disdainfully, "oil-begging diplomacy". Here the oil factor was added to the question of whether or not to sympathize with the national independence movements in the Middle East against the West.

The following editorial proposes a reconsideration of Japan's excessively pro-U.S. policy:

> Basically we can find the reason in the traditional Japanese approach to diplomacy, which lacks a policy on the Arabs. Japan didn't depart from the parameters, established after World War II, of following the U.S. ... More fundamentally, we have to locate our diplomatic relations with the Arabs inside our foreign policy as a whole.[30]

On the other hand, the following editorials warn that Japan would be acting too selfishly if it bowed its head to the Arabs at the expense of its relations with the West:

> We should learn a lesson from the fact that the OPEC resolution offered to limit oil production in an equal way that may affect not only the U.S. but also the EC and Japan. This issue prevents us from thinking that Japan should go ahead and be a good boy for the oil producing countries.[31]

> Do not get the impression that Japan chose the unreasonable option and abandoned its reason just to get oil, thereby incurring the displeasure of the world.[32]

Both those for this policy and those against it accepted the need for some change in Japan's policy toward the Arab countries. It was, however, the importance of the "Arab nation" that the media emphasized, not Islam. Here Islam was mentioned rather mockingly:

> Ironically, we may thank Allah, if we understand that we have learnt a lesson from this reduction in our oil supplies, and that we have therefore been given a chance to reconsider our foreign policy and base it on our own decisions.[33]

> [After recommending an energy-saving lifestyle in Japan] We don't know whether Almighty Allah is generous enough to encourage us to regain our healthy state of mind by depriving us of oil![34]

During these days of Arab nationalism, the media seldom understood political developments in the Middle East as being related to Islam. In the 1960s and 1970s, religion was not an important factor in their analysis and did not provide a suitable explanation for the conflicts with Western colonialism or with Israel.

1979: The impact of the Iranian Revolution: Islam seen as a "backward religion" or as a protest against Western civilization

It was the Iranian Revolution and the actions of Shiite activists that made the Japanese media focus on Islam as a driving force behind political events.

When the Japanese media witnessed the Iranian Revolution in 1979, reaction was divided. One camp once again saw backwardness in the Islam of the Iranian revolution and considered Islam a source of militancy and totalitarianism in the Middle East:

> It [Kaikyo] has no idea of a division between church and state, thus politics can reflect very strong Kaikyo ethics ... There is a tendency not to understand a difference of opinion as a sign of rivalry between different interests and then to coordinate those interests, like we do in a Western democracy. Instead, this is understood as being a conflict between good and evil, so one is required to destroy the evil.
>
> This is backed by a strong and idealistic ethical tradition that was built up over centuries through conflicts and rivalries with the Sunnis, the mainstream of Kaikyo.
>
> If Iran becomes a Kaikyo republic, it might be a militant republic that is different from a Sunni republic such as Pakistan.
>
> We can summarize the real voice of the nationalists in the Middle East as follows: "First, give us independence and freedom. Then we will decide which way our homeland should go." But if a Kaikyo republic is established in Iran with no basis in a Western type of democracy, it may very well develop into a dictatorship, ... understanding criticism and resistance as "evil" from the strict ethical view which is specific to the Shiites.[35]

The main tendency in the media regarding the Islam represented by the Iranian revolution was to see it as fanatical, violent and backward. This tendency continued into the 1980s. It was reinforced by the suicide attacks in Beirut against the U.S. Marines. It ascribed the violence of the Shiite activists to a primordial element in Shiite belief:

> Terrorism in the Middle East has spread to the oil producing Gulf countries, as we feared. The bombings at the French and U.S. Embassies and at other institutions in Kuwait were obviously cases of terrorism carried out by those seeking martyrdom, backed by political and religious beliefs ... there is no doubt that the most peculiar nature of Shiite martyrdom encourages a "Kamikaze" spirit among the terrorists.
>
> ... The sect of Ali, whose sons were killed, considers such a death as noble, and it promises enduring pleasures for the martyrs in another world. Radicals with such a religious background can draw support for their political beliefs from the strong leadership of Khomeini, the leader of the Shiite revolution, who opposes the U.S. and, on occasion, existing international customary law, also.[36]

Another writer went further by hinting that Shiite Islamists belonged to an uncivilized world:

> Earlier this month, three French citizens, who had been kidnapped by an Islamic radical group in Lebanon, were released ... Frankly, we would like to bless the fact that the three were freed from the terrorists and returned to the civilized world.[37]

It was after 1983 that the Japanese media started to use the term 'terrorists' or 'fundamentalist' for the activists. In the 1960s and 1970s, nationalist activists were called Arab guerrillas, not terrorists. The term 'fundamentalism', borrowed from the Western media, started to be used frequently mainly for Iran after the Iranian Revolution. Figure 7.3 shows the percentage of editorials that referred to 'fundamentalism' among those that used the word 'Islam'.

It is the same with the use of the word 'terrorism'. The word 'terrorism' mainly appeared in the media after September 11th, but Iran is the exception in that 'terrorism' was often used, even before September 11th (Figure 7.4).

In addition, it seems that some editorials hint at a similarity regarding the role of religion between, on the one hand, the Iranian Revolution and Shiite militancy, and, on the other, Japan's religiously oriented totalitarianism before the war. This made their comments about Islamism more sensitive and emotional:

> I felt a chill of fear when I saw Mr. Bazargan as he accepted his nomination as prime minister, thanking God and showing profound respect, as if he was a student in front of a schoolmaster.

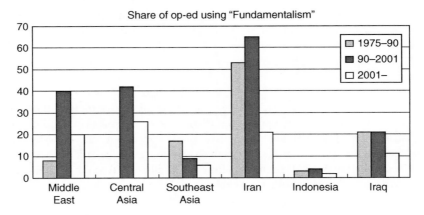

Figure 7.3 Percentage of op-eds using the word 'fundamentalism' among those that used the word 'Islam'.

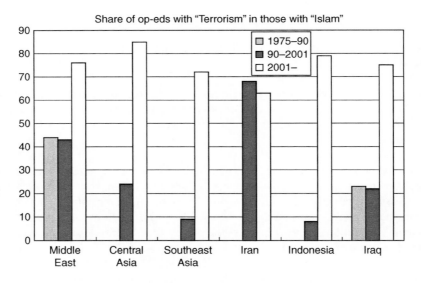

Figure 7.4 Percentage of editorials that used the word 'terrorism' among those that used the word 'Islam'.

Whether we should regard this as an ideal similar to that of the politics of the Platonic philosophers or we should see the dark shadow of totalitarianism here … It seems that the perplexity felt by Iranian people is becoming more profound.[38]

At the same time, we can find some editorials that tried to show an appreciation of the revolutionary regime by understanding it within an ideological framework of the developing world. These showed compassion for the feelings of people "who were disappointed by modernization" and they show a rather progressive image of Shiite Islam:

> To some extent, he [Khomeini] reminds us of Mahatma Gandhi. Some may say that the idea of a Republic of Kaikyo is old-fashioned, but we cannot deny that a deep frustration with modern society lies behind the reason why people have started to rely on religion again.
>
> ... Shiites, compared to Kaikyo-to in general, have been fighting against oppression for a long time. Thus, it is a progressive sect and is said to contain the idea of social reform.
>
> Now is not the time to think that increasing work efficiency is the only virtue. The slow life of Kaikyo-to can still find a way to pursue modernization.
>
> We need to think about this issue from a rather wider point of view: that of the coordination between religion and modernization.[39]

Some also perceived the Iranian Revolution in the framework of anti-colonialism, the non-aligned movement in Asia and Africa, and the North–South problem. For them, this was a new trend of anti-Westernization. The argument by the liberal columnist Katsuichi Honda is a good example. He understands that Iran's revolutionary movement is a kind of Cultural Revolution, as was seen in China, and he adopts a positive stance on its de-Westernization. He points to the nature of the Iranian Revolution as being a "cultural revolution", then he moves on to criticize the situation in Japan, which in his eyes has become too Westernized and had lost its standpoint. The Iranian Revolution attracted some anti-US intellectuals in Japan:

> An important goal that Ayatollah Khomeini has pursued in the Islamic revolution is, simply, de-Westernization. This is part of a Cultural Revolution searching for a traditional culture. In this case, Westernization is often confused with Modernization, but it should be clearly differentiated ... If he [Khomeini] accepts TV as one aspect of modernization, he says its content should not be "Westernized."
>
> Don't you think that cultural colonialism [which we can read as Westernization] is much too prevalent [in the current Japan]?[40]

After the Gulf War: not a matter of Japan but a matter of "Islam vs. the West"

The Gulf War had a tremendous impact on Japan's policy toward the Middle East, but this did not mean that the war greatly changed Japan's perception of Islam. What is very noticeable is that Islam was referred to more in the context of criticizing the U.S. that had introduced the framework of "Christianity versus Islam". Interestingly enough, the Japanese media insisted that they did not believe in the concept of "The Christian West versus the Islamic Middle East" but they did believe that the U.S. believed in it:

> There will never be a successful framework for establishing the basis of a Western and Christian civilization [in Saudi Arabia], when people can witness this attitude of sending troops into the land of Islamic civilization and of never hesitating to start a war.[41]

> We wonder whether the attack without compunction against an Islamic/Arab land by the U.S., where many of the population are Christians, may not provoke the deep and historic enmity of the Arab world, as the attack is considered not only as a punishment for [Iraq's] invasion [of Kuwait] but also as being closely related to an oil strategy that is rooted in Western interests.[42]

In other words, the Japanese media tended to use Islam when they criticized the U.S. as the sole superpower, and many perceived Islam as an alternative to nationalism, or at least as part of the resistance movement against colonialism, and an expression of people's dissatisfaction at being discriminated against by the West. This is clearly shown in the following editorial:

> Prayer, pilgrimage, fasting … the actions and logic of Muslims are sometimes unimaginable for those who are in the non-Muslim world. It seems that we often label this "Islamic fundamentalism" without any deeper consideration … We can say that there are two reasons why Islamic fundamentalism is attractive. One is the collapse of the Cold War system. Ideological rivalries have disappeared. There then emerged conflicts based on ethnicity and religion. People pursue their identity through their ethnicity and religion, and now especially we are witnessing many conflicts where Muslims are the main actors. The other reason is the current, overwhelming globalisation. There is a tendency for people to search for a base in Islam to challenge this new type of internationalisation, which is led by the U.S. People, departing from the idea that profit in the market constitutes the sole value system, are trying to resort to traditional Islamic values.[43]

The shift of perception from nationalism to Islam that was considered a source of anti-Western feeling in the Middle East affected the framework for understanding the Palestinian conflict. In the 1960s and 1970s, Palestinian issues were never described in the context of Islam, as I mentioned. Rather they were understood as a core issue of Arab nationalism. The first Intifada in Palestine in the late 1980s was not called 'Islamic' either. In the 1980s, Islam was referred to only in the context of the Lebanese civil war. On the other hand, in the 1990s, editorials started to explain the Palestinian conflict as "Islam vs. Israel" or "Islam as a common resort for the people."

> This is because Islam is not only a religious act. This religion is in some ways similar to social movements that embrace dissatisfaction because of

various problems in the Islamic world, and the religion works to support people mentally. Now that Arab nationalism has lost its power to unite people, and even the Palestinian liberation movements have lost their energy, Islam has become a common resort for the people.[44]

[Japanese tourists were victims in an Islamist attack in Luxor.] The terrorist attacks that happened recently are deeply related to the historical problems of the Middle East/Islamic World. In addition, political and economic instability delays a solution to the problem ... We seriously feel that the terrorism in the Middle East is rooted in the long rivalry between Israel and Islamic countries.[45]

It is worth noting that the argument here was mainly between Islam and the West, not between Islam and Japan:

It is nothing but a double standard to say, from fear of Islamic fundamentalism, that it is impossible to do the same thing in Algeria as was done in Haiti.

Is it impossible to accomplish either conciliation or co-existence between democracy and religious fundamentalism? Before we ask such a question, we should do a number of things.[46]

Things are deeply related to the political relationship between the West and the Islamic countries. We should get rid of the tendency to see each other as "plagues" and "locusts."[47]

Muslims as regional neighbors of Japan

A different perception of Muslim societies in Central Asia. Are they the same as the "radical" Islam in the Middle East? Asia or Islam?

Japan's view of Islam started to become broader and more varied after the independence of the Central Asian states following the collapse of the USSR. If we look at the frequency of the use of the word 'Islam' in editorials during the 1990s, half of the editorials concerning Central Asia referred to Islam in their argument. This is far more than the number appearing in those on the Middle East.

Before the Gulf Crisis, a little more than one-tenth of the editorials concerning the Middle East referred to Islam, compared to about one-fifth before September 11th. These figures are less than those for the editorials on Central Asia after independence. This means that Central Asia in the 1990s and 2000s is described as being related to Islam/Muslims more frequently than the Middle East. In this section, I will pick up on the typical view of Islam in the context of the argument concerning Central Asia and contrast it with the context of the Middle East to see whether there is any difference in the perception of Islam/Muslims in the two regions.

In most cases, the editorials used the word 'Islam' not only to provide basic information about Central Asia but also to use it as a way to distinguish some countries in the CIS from others. It is interesting to see, however, that Islam is referred to when the editorials show concern both about the possibility of an influx of Islamism from the Middle East and about the future expansion of the Islamic world, including in Hsinchiang Uighur. The editorials emphasize the fact that the people living there are Muslim more than the religion of Islam itself and they consider being Muslim a factor which may create a link between Central Asia and the Middle East, which may lead Central Asia to adopt radical, anti-Western militancy:

> We wonder whether they [people in Central Asia] can smoothly apply the framework of dialogue, a notion born in Europe, to Asian countries with Muslim residents.[48]

> The West expresses its concern about the direction of the ECO (Economic Cooperation Organization). This is because Iran, who used to insist on "the export of Islamic revolution," is taking a leadership role. The fact that Iran holds onto a theocratic system that is based on Islam appears to have the potential of posing a great threat to the West. In contrast, Turkey, another Muslim country, also aims to strengthen its political and economic relations with Central Asia ... Turkey, together with the West, is now clearly intending to be at the core of future regional economic cooperation.
> We should not disrupt Central Asia with a political and religious ax.[49]

This means that Japan's media perceived the newly independent Muslim countries in Central Asia as possible objects, not proactive actors, of 'radicalism' in Islam. In other words, being a Muslim in Central Asia does not necessarily mean that the individual automatically believes in radical Islam but it may mean that they might easily be exposed to 'radical Islam' from the Middle East:

> It seems that both Turkey and Iran are trying to lead [the ECO]. In Turkey's case, this is being done through its relationship with the U.S. Iran, on the other hand, is using Islam for the same purpose. The U.S. is afraid that Islamic fundamentalism may cross the border from Iran and become a regional power, and it is trying very hard to establish Turkey at the helm of the ECO.[50]

Such discourse assumes that different standards apply when it comes to an appreciation of Muslim societies in Central Asia and the Middle East with one set of standards being used for Westernized and democratic countries, which happen to consist of Muslims, and another for the Islamic fundamentalism in the Middle East.

Notwithstanding this categorization of Muslim countries, it seems that the media assume that it is very probable that communication among Muslim countries will naturally promote a radicalization of policy. We can guess this from the following comment:

> There was no radical expression in the final communiqué that was announced at the end of the two-day conference, contrary to what was expected

at the beginning. The only Islamic expression was the introductory term of "In the name of God". Even religious solidarity was not mentioned ... It is too early to think that Iran is planning to use the ECO to "export revolution".[51]

We can see that concern about Muslim societies in Southeast Asia focused on the same point: whether or not 'radical Islam' from the Middle East might affect Muslim societies in Asia. As we can see in Figure 7.2, Islam was seldom mentioned in editorials concerning Southeast Asia. The Japanese media started to pay attention to the expansion of fellow feeling among Muslims in Asia as early as the end of the 1980s, and it was the Gulf War that reminded the media that the presence of these Muslim communities meant that they might be objects of attention for those seeking to spread Islamism:

> It is the ASEAN countries with whom Japan feels some intimacy through our notion of Asia ... In ASEAN, in total, there are more than 150 million Muslims.
>
> The regimes in these countries supported both the UN resolutions and the multinational forces in the Gulf War, but they feel agony when they find that their Muslim populations are sympathetic to Iraq. This might lead to destabilization in their domestic politics.
>
> We should understand trends among Asian Muslims in the context of an increase both in their assertiveness and in the conflicts based on ethnicity and religion after the end of the Cold War, in addition to the current revival of the Islamic world.[52]

The media understand that Muslims in the Southeast Asia are subject to an Islamic fundamentalism that partly originated in the Middle East. This means they assume that the Islam there is different from that in the Middle East; that is to say that in Southeast Asia Islam is more tolerant and acceptable for Japan, although Islam in the Middle East, especially in Iran, is categorically considered as being related to radicalism, a fundamentalism that causes political instability. On the other hand, Islam in Southeast and Central Asia is simply a characteristic of the local community.

When the editorials say that a Muslim in Southeast Asia is different from a Muslim in the Middle East, they often make the judgment on the basis of a difference in customs or manners:

> In Indonesia, Malaysia, and Brunei, people generally tolerate the drinking of alcohol if you behave properly. This is true even though they are part of the Islamic world, where such drinking is forbidden. Thus these countries are far removed from Islamic fundamentalism, and Japan can be on good terms with these countries – despite the fact that the concentration of Muslims is equal to that in the Middle East – without being particularly conscious of the difference in religion.[53]

Differences in the political ideologies and movements that are based on Islam are reduced to a matter of customs or manners caused by regional differences arising out of how Islam is applied in each region. They focus less on the ideological and political factor of Islamism, and the difference between political Islam and being a Muslim within the geographical area of the Middle East is neglected.

The difference between Islam and being a Muslim: perceived as a regional difference

Japan's media have a milder image of Islam in Southeast and Central Asia, partly because of their wishful thinking that Muslim societies near Japan should not, in essence, be 'radical' or based on 'fundamentalism'. This means that Japan's perception of Islam is different according to the region, with Islam in Asia being considered tolerant and acceptable to Japan.

Here we are reminded of the inconsistency in Japan's two perceptions of Islam since the nineteenth century. One perspective is used for Muslim communities who are seen as part of the same region: Asia. Another is used for those in the Middle East who are regarded through Western eyes. Just as Japanese intellectuals in the Meiji era were torn between adoration for the West and sympathy for a colonized Asia, contemporary Japanese media also show two types of reaction to Islam.

From such an understanding, which depends on a particular view of the nature of the geographical reach of Islam, there occasionally appears the opinion that Japan can play a role in mediating between Islamic countries in Asia and the West. This is attended by an emphasis on the fact that Japan belongs to both parts of the world: "Central Asia is part of the Islamic Area, and strengthening relationships with it will result in the spread of Japanese diplomacy as this may act as a wedge in the Islamic world ... as a whole."[54]

Here it is often pointed out that Japan has no "dirty past of imperialism" in the Middle East:

> For Japan, it is nothing but a treasure that the Middle East and the Islamic world feel close to Japan. There is no religious conflict between Japan and the Middle East, and people there pay us respect as the nation that accomplished modernization in our own way ... In the Islamic world, there is a strong tendency for people to pursue their own model for development, different from so-called "Westernization." ... So, it's your turn, Japan![55]

> [Rafsanjani visited Japan.] This is the first time since the Iranian Islamic revolution that relations between Japan and Iran have deepened to this extent. The U.S. and Europe were rejected as they were allies of the former Shah regime, and the revolutionary regime approached Japan, which "does not have a dirty hand." As a result, Japan has become Iran's number one friend. More than this, they appreciate Japan's efforts to facilitate an atmosphere conducive to neutral peace negotiations in the Iran-Iraq War.[56]

Moreover, the image of Japan as a victim of U.S. atomic bombings is often used as a source of solidarity with Muslim countries:

> Japan can be a bridge between the U.S. and Europe and the Islamic world. Japan is one of the few developed countries that, historically, did not experience relations of rivalry with the Islamic World. We have not inflamed conflicts by exporting weapons. The Islamic World also feels sympathy for Japan as it suffered from a nuclear attack, and they have also paid respect to the fact that Japan, overcoming the tragedy of war, has become an economic superpower. This is a treasure for Japanese diplomacy. Japan should persuade Islamic countries to join in solidarity with international anti-terrorism efforts, and should request the U.S. and Europe to pay sufficient consideration to the dignity of Islam. Islamic countries will listen to the word of Japan seriously.[57]

Such perceptions, however, contain the following serious misunderstandings.

First, it is not true that Japan has "no dirty past of imperialism" in Muslim societies, as I have shown in the previous section. It is true that Japan has had no colonial experience in the Middle East, but it has had in Southeast Asia. Thus the media use the notion "Islamic world" in a very vague way. Sometimes they categorize Southeast Asia as part of the "Islamic world" when they want to shed light on the presence of Muslim societies there, and sometimes they regard the area as less Islamic when compared to the Islam practiced in the Middle East, if they prefer to highlight the difference in the nature of Islam between Asia and the Middle East.

Second, the idea that Japan can be a mediator between Islam and the West takes account of the notion of "a clash of civilizations" and is based on the Orientalist idea of considering Islam as being opposed, in its essence, to the West.

Third, Japan uses a double standard when it comes to understanding Islam. Islam is confused as a religion with a Muslim as a human being. One of the reasons for this confusion might be linguistic. There is no specific term in Japanese for a Muslim. "A Muslim" is translated as *Isuramu-kyoto*, that is, "a believer of Islam", so journalists often use the term 'Islam' as shorthand for *Isuramu-kyoto*, i.e. "a Muslim". There is therefore no clear distinction between Islam and a Muslim. This causes confusion when it comes to differentiating Islam as a creed from the daily life of Muslims or Muslim societies. That is the reason why the media see a difference in 'Islam' between the Islam of Asia and that of the Middle East. They describe different things with a single term, 'Islam'.

This does not mean, however, that the confusion only comes from the language. The most serious issue is that Japan's media have no clear idea about where Japan should place itself: in Asia, in the West, or somewhere else? Also, how does Japan consider the area where Muslim communities exist? Is this Asia, the Middle East, or is it an area opposed to the West? The issue of Islam is thus the issue of how Japan places itself in the world, geographically as well as historically. The transformation of the Japanese perception of Islam and the Middle East reflects the transformation of the perception of Japan's own position in Asia.

Conclusion

Information and knowledge about Islam/Muslim communities abroad came to Japan through two routes: first, through China, and then later through the West. This means that Japan sees the outside world either according to its regional and geographical relationships, or as a process of Westernization. While epistemology in modern Japan was formed on the basis of an imported Western philosophy, Japan's regional interests developed and created the idea of Asianism. The former brought an Orientalist understanding of Islam and a prejudice against it, while the latter was transformed into something that Japanese imperialism could use to manipulate Muslim communities. When Asianism was negated and buried, together with the memory of the war, sympathy was shown for the anti-colonial and independence movements of Asia in the context of nationalism, not Islam. As Usuki clearly states, Japan's policy concerns over Islam started as a strategic "issue about Muslims, not as an issue about Islam".[58] The issue of Muslims for Japan changed and became the issue of nationalism in Asia, while the issue of Islam died out after WWII.

It is not too much to assume that European Orientalism again compensated for the absence of an epistemological framework concerning Islam after WWII. This may explain the two different perceptions regarding, first, Muslim societies in Southeast and Central Asia, and, second, the same societies in the Middle East. The former is based on a regional relationship, and it concerns the Muslims living in the area. The latter perception, however, is mainly based on concerns about political thought in Islam which is believed to be 'fundamentalist', 'radical' and mostly related to 'terrorism'.

When the Japanese media decided not to continue to use the term Kaikyo in the late 1970s, they accepted the term 'Islam' for this world religion. When the media and intellectuals in general naively jump at the idea that Japan can be a mediator between Muslim societies and the West, they consider Muslim countries as regional neighborhoods, where Japan has a strategic interest. As Usuki warns:

> The task facing Japanese scholars in Islamic studies is serious indeed. How can we overcome the negative heritage of pre-war Islamic/Muslim studies, which could not move beyond thinking of these studies as an issue about Muslims, and so make the leap forward to Islamic studies?[59]

Japanese scholars of Islam/Muslims should share his awareness, not ascribing all the misperceptions of Islam to an imported Western view.

Notes

1 "Editorial: On the Draft Constitution in Post-war Iraq", *Chunichi Shimbun*, 31 August, 2005.
2 "Editorial: On the Dispatch of SDF: Necessary to See it from the Iraqi Point of View", *Asahi Shimbun*, 7 December, 2003.

3 Data were derived from the Nikkei Telecom database, selecting four major daily newspapers in Japan (*Asahi Shimbun, Yomiuri Shimbun, Nikkei Shimbun,* and *Mainichi Shimbun*). I used the database of Nikkei Telecom, which contains the news articles published in Nikkei Shimbun from 17 April 1976, in *Asahi Shimbun* from 1 January 1985, in *Yomiuri* from 1 September 1986 and in Tokyo, *Mainichi* from 17 November 1987.

4 Keiko Sakurai, *Nippon no Musurimu shakai* [Japanese Muslim Communities], Tokyo: Chikuma Shobou, 2003.

5 A recent report on Muslims in urban areas in Kanto region (Waseda University, Faculty of Human Sciences, Office of Study on Asian Societies 2006, *Zainichi Musurimu Chousa: Kanto Daitoshiken Chosa Dai-ichiji Houkoku-sho* [Research on Muslims in Japan: First Report on Muslims in Urban Areas in Kanto Region], Tokyo: Waseda University: 2006) gives a different figure, estimating it as 90,000. This gap comes from the lack of statistics gathered on individual religion.

6 Naoto Higuchi, Inaba Nanako, Tanno Kiyoto, Fukuda Yuko, and Okai Hirofumi (eds) *Kokkyo wo Koeru: tainichi musurimu imin no shakai-gaku* [Crossing the Border: Sociology on Muslim Migrants in Japan], Tokyo: Seikyu-sha, 2007.

7 Hideaki Sugita, Nihon-jin no Chuto Hakken [Japanese Discovery of the Middle East] (Chuto Isuramu Sekai 2) Tokyo: Tokyo Daigaku Shuppankai, 1995, p. 23.

8 In China at that time it was widely believed that Sad bin Abi Waqqas had come to China to introduce Islam, before his death there in Guangdong (Sugita op. cit.).

9 According to Tomomi Hamada, the term Hui-hui was used for the Uyghur people in the eleventh century, and it became the general term for ethnic groups and areas west of Uyghur. In the Yuan dynasty it meant Muslim in general (see Ohtsuka, Kazuo, Kosugi Yasushi, Komatsu Hisao, Tounaga Yasushi, Haneda Tadashi, and Yamauchi Masayuki (eds) *Iwanami Isuramu Jiten* [Iwanami Encyclopedia on Islam], Tokyo: Iwanami, 2001, p. 238).

10 Sekihei Saito, "'Isuramu' ka 'Kaikyo' ka: shinzen no tamenimo tadashii koshou wo" [Islam, or Kaikyo? Use the Correct Name for a Better Relationship], *Asahi Shimbun* (Rondan) 15 March 1979.

11 Sugita, op. cit., p. 97.

12 It is well known that, among those who wanted to abolish Japan's unequal treaties with the West, there were many who were keen to research Egypt's Mixed Court because they saw it as a way to gradually abolish the treaties.

13 Midori Fujita, *Afurika Hakken: nihon ni oekru afurika zou no hensen* [Discovering Africa: Transformation of Images of Africa in Japan], Tokyo: Iwanami Shoten, pp. 114–118).

14 Ibid., pp. 133–134.

15 Cemil Aydin, "Overcoming Eurocentrism?: Japan's Islamic Studies during the Era of the Greater East Asia War (1937–45)", in Renee Worringer (ed.) *The Islamic Middle East and Japan: Perceptions, Aspirations, and the Birth of Intra-Asian Modernity*, Princeton, NJ: Markus Wienner Publishers, 2007, pp. 137–162.

16 Shumei Okawa, *Kaikyo Gairon* [Introduction to Islam], Tokyo: Keiko Shobo, 1942.

17 Akira Usuki, "Senzen Nihon no 'Kaikyo-to Mondai' Kenkyu" [Study on the "Issue of Islam" in Pre-war Japan], Mio in Kishimoto Mio, *Teikoku Nihon no Gakuchi*, vol. 3: *Touyougaku no Jiba* [Academism in Imperial Japan: Sphere of Oriental Studies], Tokyo: Iwanami Shoten, 2006, p. 225.

18 For details on how Pan-Islamists such as Abdul Resht Ibrahim were invited to Japan as a head of this association and his relation with Asianists, see Tsutomu Sakamoto (ed.) *Nicchu Sensou to Isuram: Manmou Asia chiiki ni okeru Touchi Kaiju Seisaku* [The Japan-China War and Islam: Policy for Rule and Manipulation in Manchuria, Mongolia and Asia], Tokyo: Tokyo University Press, 2008; Hisao Komatsu, *Iburahimu, Nihon he no Tabi (Sekaishi no Kagami: Roshia "Osuman Teikoku" Nihon)* [Ibrahim's Trip to Japan: Mirror of World History: Russia, Ottoman Empire, and Japan],

Tokyo: Tosui Shobo, 2008; and Dai Nippon Kaikyo Kyokai, *Higashi Hankyu ni okeru Boukyo Teppeki Kousei to Kaikyo-to* [Construction of the Iron Shield against Communism in the Eastern Hemisphere and Muslims], Tokyo: Dai Nippon Kaikyo Kyokai, 1939.

19 Merthan Dundar, 2008, "Osuman Koutei Abudyuru Kerimu no Rainichi" [Visit of Abdul Karim, Ottoman Emperor to Japan], in Tsutomu Sakamoto (ed.) *Nicchu Sensou to Isuram: Manmou Asia chiiki ni okeru Touchi Kaiju Seisaku* [The Japan-China War and Islam: Policy for Rule and Manipulation in Manchuria, Mongolia and Asia], Tokyo: Tokyo University Press, 2008, pp. 135–164.

20 Aiko Kurasawa, "Dai-touwa Sensou ki no Tai-Isuramu Seisaku" [Policy on Islam during the Period of the "Greater Asia (Dai Toa)" War], in Tsutomu Sakamoto (ed.) *Nicchu Sensou to Isuram: Manmou Asia chiiki ni okeru Touchi Kaiju Seisaku* [The Japan-China War and Islam: Policy for Rule and Manipulation in Manchuria, Mongolia and Asia], Tokyo: Tokyo University Press, 2008, pp. 233–293; Yasuko Kobayashi, "Isuramu Seisaku to Shokuminchi/Senryouchi Shihai" [Policy on Islam and Colonial/Occupation Control], in Aiko Kurasawa (ed.) *Iwanami Kouza Ajia/ Taiheiyou Sensou (7) Shihai to Bouryoku* [Iwanami Series on Asia/Pacific War (7): Occupation and Violence], Tokyo; Iwanami Shoten, 2006; Komatsu, op. cit.

21 Usuki op. cit., p. 232.

22 "Menuki Doori no Kokkyousen" [Border in the Main Street], Yomiuri Shimbun, 22 January 1959.

23 "Yomiuri Sunpyou" [Yomiuri's Snapshot], *Yomiuri Shimbun*, 6 April 1962.

24 "Henshu Techou" [Editor's Diary], *Yomiuri Shimbun*, 13 April 1962.

25 "Mokuhyou wa Houkensei Datou: Mujun suru kyougi to dentou" [Aiming at Defeat of Feudalism: Contradiction between Creed and Tradition], in Special Issue, "Kaikyo-to to Minzoku Undo" [Muslims and the Nationalist Movement], *Asahi Shimbun*, 9 July 1958.

26 "Norinomo ni Miru Kakumei" [Revolution Seen in the Vehicles], *Yomiuri Shimbun*, 19 January, 1959.

27 "Eikou to Hi-Genjitsu to: Seikatsu no Furusa ni Tomadou" [Being Glorious and Unrealistic: Perplexed by Old-fashioned Way of Life], *Asahi Shimbun*, 12 September 1967.

28 "Kaikyo-to no tero koui" [Terrrorist Acts of Muslims], *Asahi Shimbun*, 18 October 1951.

29 Yukiko Miyagi, *Japan's Security Policy toward the Middle East: Theory and Cases*, London: Routledge, 2008.

30 "Editorial: EC Muke Sekiyu Seigen Kanwa to Nihon" [Japan and Relaxation of Limitation of Oil Supply to EC], *Yomiuri Shimbun*, 20 November 1973.

31 "Editorial: Chuto no Shin Sekiyu Jousei he no Taiou wo" [Tackling the New Situation on Oil Supply], *Yomiuri Shimbun*, 19 October 1973.

32 "Henshu Techou" [Editor's Diary], *Yomiuri Shimbun*, 21 November 1973.

33 Ibid.

34 "Yomiuri Sunpyou" [Yomiuri's Snapshot], *Yomiuri Shimbun*, 19 November 1973.

35 Masahiro Sasagawa, "Iran Kakumei-ha ga Mezasu 'Kaikyou Kyouwa-koku towa Nanika" [What Is the 'Islamic Republic' that Iranian Revolutionaries Are Searching For?], *Asahi Shimbun*, 13 February 1979 .

36 "Editorial: Chuto no Kyoushin Tero no Haikei ni Arumono" [What Is the Background of Fanatical Terrorism?], *Nihon Keizai Shimbun*, 14 December 1983.

37 "Editorial: Hitogoto de nai Chuto no Hitojichi" [Concerning the Hostages in Lebanon], *Yomiuri Shimbun*, 17 May 1988.

38 "Junkyo heno Ijouna Keisha: Shukyo to fukabun no seiji" [Extraordinary Inclination to Martyrdom: Politics Indivisible from Religion], *Asahi Shimbun*, 12 February 1979.

39 "Homeini-shi wa Kyuseishu ni Nareruka?" [Can Khomeini Be a Messiah?], *Yomiuri Shimbun*, 3 February 1979.

40 Katsuichi Honda, "Minzokuteki Hokori Ushinau Osore" [Fear of Losing National Dignity], *Asahi Shimbun*, 25 February 1980.

41 "Editorial: Beigun Zouha no Imi wo Tou" [Questioning the Meaning of the Increase in U.S. Military Dispatches], *Asahi Shimbun*, 11 November 1990.

42 "Editorial: Wangan Sensou no Souki Shuketsu wo" [Requesting an Early End to the Gulf War], *Asahi Shimbun*, 18 January 1991.

43 "Editorial: Isuramu Genrishugi: Ishitsu-sa wo rikaisuru doryoku wo" [Islamic Fundamentalism: Efforts are Needed to Understand the Difference], *Mainichi Shimbun*, 24 December 1999.

44 "Editorial: Bei-Isuramu Sen: Aratana Tero no Rensa Soshi wo" [War between the U.S. and Islam: Avoid the Chain Reaction of Terrorism], *Mainichi Shimbun*, 24 August 1998.

45 "Editorial: Tero Giseisha ni Chikau Beki Koto" [What We Should Promise the Victims of Terrorism], *Asahi Shimbun*, 19 November 1997.

46 "Editorial: Kyouzon Dekinuka 'Minshu' to 'Genri'" [Isn't It Possible for 'Democracy' to Live with 'Fundamentalism'?], *Asahi Shimbun*, 28 November 1995.

47 "Editorial: Shuukyou-tou no Yakushin ni Urotae Muyou" [No Need to Panic at the Rise of Religious Parties], *Asahi Shimbun*, 27 December 1995.

48 "Editorial: Aratani Tanemaku CSCE" [Conference of Security and Cooperation in Europe Sow a New Seed], *Asahi Shimbun*, 30 March 1992.

49 "Editorial: Isuramu Keizaiken no Fuan Youin", Factors Creating Instability in the 'Islamic Economic Area'], *Yomiuri Shimbun*, 18 February 1992.

50 "Editorial: Isuramu Keizaieken no Yukue wa" [What Direction for the Islamic Economic Area?], *Asahi Shimbun*, 19 February 1992.

51 "Editorial: Yomigaerasetai 'Bunmei no Jyuujiro: ECO Shunou Kaigi'" [Let's Revive 'The Crossroads of Civilizations': ECO Summit], *Mainichi Shimbun*, 24 February 1992.

52 "Editorial: Wangan Sensou no Ajia ni Nani wo Miruka?" [What Shall We See in Asia after the Gulf War?], *Nihon Keizai Shimbun*, 4 March 1991.

53 "Editorial: Iraku Sensou Me wo Yureru Ajia ni" [Iraq War: Look toward Trembling Asia], *Chunichi Shimbun*, 28 March 2003.

54 "Editorial: Gaikou 'Kinu no Michi' ni Atarashii Ibuki wo" [Diplomacy: Need to Bring a New Spirit to 'the Silk Road'], *Mainichi Shimbun*, 16 May 1994.

55 "Teigen: Nihon no Shin Senryaku Gurobaru-ka to Ajia Isuramu 13, Isuramu to no Tsukiai [Recommendation for Japan's New Strategy: Globalisation and Asia, Islam 13, How to Deal with Islam], *Asahi Shimbun*, 3 May 2007.

56 "Editorial: Iran karano Hinkyaku" [VIP from Iran], *Asahi Shimbun*, 29 June 1985.

57 "Editorial: Isuramu Shakai: Nihon wa Oubei to no Hashiwatashi wo" [Islamic World: Japan Should Bridge it with the West], *Mainichi Shimbun*, 25 September 2001.

58 Usuki, op. cit., p. 218.

59 Ibid., p. 248.

8   U.S. politics, media and Muslims in the post-9/11 era

Janice J. Terry

In the years following the September 11, 2001 attacks, Muslims and Arabs in the United States have become increasingly vulnerable to stereotyping by the media, pro-Zionist lobbyists and interest groups as well as by politicians. Anti-terrorism legislation has contributed to this stereotyping and vulnerability, but the inter-relationships between hostile lobbyist forces and special interests groups, particularly the Zionist lobby that often operates under the cloak of anti-terrorist campaigns and the Patriot Act, have also been major contributors to the current animosity toward Muslims and Arabs in the United States. Stereotypes were deeply embedded in popular culture long before the September 11, 2001 attacks but given the current antagonism between the United States and many predomi-nately Muslim states, these negative images have been even more difficult to refute.

Polls indicate that a significant number of Americans hold negative images of Islam and Muslims. In a 2003 Pew Research Center survey, 44 per cent thought Islam encouraged violence; this was an increase from 23 per cent in the 2002 poll.[1] Given their general hostility to non-Christians, it is perhaps not surprising that Evangelicals were more likely to hold negative attitudes toward Muslims than secular, mainstream Protestant or Catholic Americans. On the positive side, young Americans were less likely to have negative opinions and seemed much more tolerant toward religious differences and diversity.[2] In a similar poll conducted by the Council on American-Islamic Relations (CAIR) in 2004, over one quarter of the respondents had negative stereotypical attitudes toward Muslims, believing, for example, that Muslims valued life less than others.[3]

There is a large literature on the distortion of media coverage regarding the Arab and Muslim worlds.[4] Hence only a few examples here will suffice to under-score the pervasive distortions and stereotypes commonly found in the popular media throughout the United States. In *Israel-Palestine on Record: How the New York Times Misreports Conflict in the Middle East*, Richard Falk and Howard Friel detailed the many distortions of the *Times'* coverage of Israeli policies and actions toward the Palestinians and the slant in its coverage toward more positive stories about Israel while downplaying or ignoring Israeli actions that contravene international law.[5] Using over two dozen electronic outlets and news publications, Marda Dunsky expanded on the media bias in *Pens and Swords: How the American*

Mainstream Media Report the Israeli-Palestinian Conflict.[6] Even National Public Radio (NPR), commonly believed to be a liberal voice in the U.S. media, was found to be lacking balance. For example, very few spokespersons of people of color, particularly those from the Middle East, appeared on broadcasts. Experts supporting the continuation of U.S. military presence in Iraq outnumbered the sole peace activist 5 to 1.[7] NPR also described the September 2007 attacks by Blackwater employees on Iraqi civilians as a 'shoot out' and an attack by U.S. army personnel on Iraqi civilians as a 'fire fight,' not as massacres.

Stereotypes in the popular media are even more blatant. Bookstores in shopping malls to airports showcase novels and biographical accounts, real or imagined, that portray Muslims, especially women, in negative terms.[8] However, experts and translators of more balanced and objective accounts have great difficulty in finding publishers. Films such as the *The Kingdom*, a thriller in which U.S. personnel in Saudi Arabia are attacked by Arab terrorists, also perpetuate negative stereotypes on the big screen. The film is rife with negative images, with few positive images to balance the pictures that demonized Arabs and Muslims in general.[9]

Both the media and government perpetuate distortions and stereotypes about Muslims and Middle Eastern peoples. The media communicates these negative images to the general public that, in turn, unconsciously assimilate these images and then frequently uses them as the basis for negative attitudes toward specific peoples, leaders, and religions. As long as the media continues to popularize false images of Muslims and Islam while using distorted language to describe and explain current events in the Middle East and the rest of the Muslim world the negative attitudes evidenced by large segments of the U.S. public toward Arabs and Muslims is unlikely to change.

Politicians have further contributed to the perpetuation of these stereotypes and hostile attitudes. Some acted out of ignorance and bigotry while others were motivated by political agendas. For example, in a 2007 public interview, Congressman Peter King (R-NY), an advisor to Republican former presidential hopeful Rudy Giuliani, stated that there were too many mosques in the U.S. In earlier statements, King supported racial profiling of Arabs and Muslims.[10] Other Members of Congress have publicly criticized the Justice Department for sending representatives to the 2007 CAIR convention, labeling the organization a group of "radical jihadists".[11] In response to King's racist comments, Keith Ellison (D-MN), the sole Muslim in Congress, responded that such comments undermined U.S. security and that "Just as we don't want to be judged by the actions of a small minority, I ask the Muslim world not to judge Congress by the remarks of one congressman."[12] Ellison also called the criticisms of CAIR "ill informed".[13]

Racial profiling, especially by airlines, also continued to be a major problem.[14] The American-Arab Anti-Discrimination Committee (ADC), in particular, kept track of instances of racial profiling on airlines and elsewhere and responded to them on a case-by-case basis. In other instances, police used racial profiling to pull over drivers who appeared to be Muslim or of Middle Eastern descent. Wiretapping of Arab American and Islamic organizations were other infringements on freedom of expression that were too numerous to enumerate here but that were well documented and fairly well publicized.[15]

Predictably the overwhelming negative attitudes have resulted in an increase in civil rights infringements and hate crimes against Arabs and Muslims or those perceived to be Muslims. Crimes reported to CAIR from 2004 to 2005 increased almost 30 per cent with most complaints coming from states with large Arab/Muslim populations such as California, Illinois and New York.[16] Interestingly Michigan, with a large and highly visible Muslim population, was notably absent from this list. The reasons for the relative low number of civil rights infringements and hate crimes against Arabs and Muslims in Michigan will be discussed later in this chapter.

The case of the Hussein family in Gaithersburg Maryland is illustrative of the problems faced by Muslims and people of Middle Eastern descent. The family's car was vandalized six times from 1999 to 2007 with "Go Home" and "Pig" scratched in the side. Their home was also attacked. Disturbingly, the Montgomery County police showed a marked reluctance to pursue this case and refused to visit the home. Ultimately the Gaithersburg City police followed up on the case as did CAIR and, encouragingly, members of the community offered support.[17]

The reactions, or lack thereof, by law enforcement agencies raised "red flags" regarding the objectivity of the police, many of whom hold the same negative stereotypes as the general public. The Los Angeles Police Department's plan to develop a "mapping plan" that targeted individuals for surveillance based on religion was particularly worrisome. Although this form of religious profiling violates constitutional rights, the LA Commander Michael Downing opined that if the plan succeeded it could be adopted by other large U.S. cities.[18]

The attacks and campaigns to brand Muslims and Arabs as un-American or in negative terms did not go unnoticed or appear in a vacuum. Since September 11, 2001, Arab American and Muslim organizations have responded vigorously.[19] CAIR conferences have been well attended and speakers urged American citizens and government agencies to eradicate stereotypes of Arabs and Muslims. To some extent government agencies have taken notice. At least eight federal departments attended the 2007 CAIR convention. Attempting to attract new markets from the sizeable Muslim community, numerous private businesses also had booths at the convention.

At a large CAIR-sponsored event in California in 2007, Representative Ellison urged Muslim Americans to "make demands" like other lobby groups and recommended that they "Litigate, legislate, educate our case in a righteous manner."[20] At its annual banquet in the Washington, D.C. area, CAIR's National Board Chairperson bemoaned the hijacking of "the image of our faith ... by extremists and fear-mongers" and urged the audience to be proactive in their struggles to counteract stereotyping.[21]

Similarly, ADC monitored attacks, issued position papers, action alerts and press releases, initiated law suits, and responded to stereotyping in the media. It also took proactive steps to challenge stereotyping and government legislation perceived as unlawful or prejudicial. The National Association of Arab Americans (NAAA) and the Arab American Institute (AAI), among others, spoke out against attacks and stereotyping of Muslims and Arabs. In Michigan, Arab Americans announced plans to establish an Arab-American Center for Civil Rights (ACCHR) in Dearborn, Michigan, in 2007. Once completed, the center will serve as an educational and resource center, not only for Arab Americans, but for the larger community as well. At least in part these proactive approaches encouraged Congress to modify its hard-line stances against Muslims. On the positive side, in 2007, Congress unanimously passed the Ramadan Bill wherein for the first time in U.S. history the month of Ramadan was recognized as the Islamic holy month.

A 2004 Study by the Institute for Social Research at the University of Michigan found that although a number of Arab Americans in the area had experienced some harassment based on ethnic or religious identity after September 11, 2001, at least one-third had received support from the larger community.[22] At least in part, these positive responses may be attributed to the long-term educational outreach programs for teachers, community activists, and law enforcement and media professionals that the Arab Community Center for Economic and Social Services (ACCESS) has conducted for over 20 years.

Special interest groups, pro-Zionist lobbyists, neo-conservatives, and Evangelicals, with sometimes overlapping agendas, have actively worked to perpetuate negative images and stereotypes of Muslims and Arabs. More insidiously, they have attempted to prevent the truth about Muslims, Arabs, and Islam as a religion and culture from reaching the U.S. public. They have made considerable efforts to impede open and objective debates, especially in universities and other academic forums.

Experts agree that knowledge and education are the best defenses against stereotyping of all peoples, including Muslims and Arabs. Ignorance is the best friend of bigots. The concerted attacks on speakers and authors who provided informed and objective information about Arabs, Muslims, Palestine, Iraq, and other Arab states since September 2001 have added to the climate of fear and lessened the prospects for open discussion of critical issues. The so-called "war on terror" as exemplified in the 2001 USA Patriot Act created a favorable climate of opinion for pro-Zionist lobbyists and political special interest groups to attack writers, speakers, scholars, and academic programs that criticized Israel, U.S. support for Israel, the war in Iraq, or those who depicted Muslims and Arabs in a positive light. A 2006 Middle East Academic Survey of 2,300 academics with specialties in Middle East studies found that almost half (49 per cent) believed that the academic community was hostile to critical studies of Israel. Some 65 per cent believed that charges of anti-Semitism were the most powerful tools used by pro-Israeli forces to intimidate opponents. An astounding 91 per cent believed that pro-Israeli lobbyists and organizations caused hostility toward the United States in the Middle East.[23]

Campaigns to limit or stop freedom of thought within the academy have intensified in recent years. No one who spoke out against Israeli policies regarding the

Palestinians or U.S. policies in the Middle East, especially the war in Iraq, was immune, including a former U.S. president and Nobel Prize winner, noted scholars, religious leaders, and Middle East area studies programs at major universities.

The 2006 publication of *Palestine: Peace Not Apartheid* by Jimmy Carter precipitated angry outcries from many Jewish Americans and pro-Israeli forces. The furor was largely based, not on the book's content, as on the use of the word 'Apartheid' to characterize the Israeli occupation of the West Bank and control over the Gaza Strip and by its author's status as a former president of the United States. Following the book's publication, Kenneth W. Stein, a professor at Emory University who had served as an advisor to Carter in the early years of the Carter Center, resigned from his position as a fellow of the Center. Although Stein offered no specific details, he accused Carter of factual errors and even plagiarism.[24] Predictably, Alan Dershowitz, well known for his hostility to all critics of Israel, railed against the book.

In part owing to this public opposition, the book became a best seller. Carter appeared on major talk shows and had a successful book tour even as leading Democrats, including Nancy Pelosi, the new Speaker of the House, hastened to disavow the book. They too failed to offer any specific refutations of the book's contents or conclusions. These instantaneous knee-jerk reactions indicated that many of the critics had not read the book nor could they find fault with its content, rather they objected to the title and the fact that Carter called for an end to the Israeli occupation and the creation of a meaningful independent Palestinian state. In response, Carter pointed out that, "My most troubling experience has been the rejection of my offers to speak, for free, about the book on university campuses with high Jewish enrollment and to answer questions from students and professors."[25] He went on to emphasize that his purpose in writing the book had been:

> [To] present facts about the Middle East that are largely unknown in America, to precipitate discussion and to help restart peace talks (now absent for six years) that can lead to permanent peace for Israel and its neighbors. Another hope is that Jews and other Americans who share this same goal might be motivated to express their views, even publicly, and perhaps in concert. I would be glad to help with that effort.[26]

However, Carter's pleas for balance and objectivity went unheeded by those determined to silence open debate or discussion of the issues facing Israel and Palestine. Subsequently, Joel Kovel's *Overcoming Zionism: Creating a Single Democratic State in Israel/Palestine*, published by Pluto Press in the UK with distribution by the University of Michigan Press, was similarly attacked. Founded by Daniel Pipes, the pro-Israeli StandWithUs organization launched a campaign against the University of Michigan Press, demanding that it halt distribution of the book. The U of M Press quickly announced that it was suspending distribution not only of Kovel's book but all other Pluto Press books. Within weeks the university reconsidered its hasty decision and resumed distribution of all Pluto publications including the Kovel book. In reaction to the controversy, Roger van Zwanenberg, Pluto Press chairman, commented:

> Many presses in the United States are frightened of the pressures the Lobby can place on them ...We get authors from the United States precisely because they can't obtain adequate representation elsewhere ... We probably have the best collections of any university press in the area.[27]

Interviewed on Pacifica Radio, Kovel, who is Jewish, noted that he had written the book about a single state in Palestine, an idea that had "very small support",[28] precisely in order to open up debate on the subject. The fact that most of the critics did not address the book's contents, but instead called for the press to stop distribution indicated that they found any discussion about Israel's treatment of the Palestinians and the occupation threatening, if not wholly unacceptable.

New regulations under the Patriot Act also made it more difficult for visiting scholars from the Middle East, let alone for students, to obtain visas to enter the United States. Audiences in the U.S. were thereby deprived of hearing from those who have first-hand personal knowledge of the region. In 2004, the State Department suddenly revoked the visa for the Swiss citizen and respected Muslim scholar, Tariq Ramadan. Ramadan was scheduled to teach at the University of Notre Dame and had previously toured the U.S. Following pressure from pro-Israeli groups regarding his alleged anti-Semitic remarks, Bishop Desmond Tutu, the highly esteemed Nobel Peace Prize recipient from South Africa, was banned from speaking at the St. Thomas Justice and Peace Studies program in St. Paul in 2007. The very public uproar over Iranian President Mahmoud Ahmadinejad's appearance at Columbia University in late September 2007 was yet another example of attempts to stifle free speech on issues pertaining to the Middle East; however, in this instance, Ahmadinejad appeared as scheduled.[29]

The cancellation of historian and author Tony Judt's talk on "The Israel Lobby and US Foreign Policy" to Network 20/20 (a group of business leaders, academics, and non-governmental organizations) in New York City in 2006 demonstrated that not only speakers from overseas were prevented from stating their views. Network 20/20 meets at the Polish Consulate in NYC but following threats from the ADL that were Judt to speak the ADL would publicly discredit the Polish Consul, the talk was cancelled and later rescheduled.[30]

In a compilation of incidents since 2001, the American Association of University Professors (AAUP) found a "pattern of coordinated actions, organized through networks that tie to, if not directly emanate from, the pro-Sharon, pro-occupation lobby" against critics of Israeli policies.[31] Invited guest speakers on the Arab Israeli Conflict and the war in Iraq in universities as diverse as Harvard, the University of Colorado, the College of the Holy Cross in Worcester, Massachusetts, and Rockford College in Illinois were publicly criticized or harassed by students, faculty, and lawmakers. In some instances, the universities stood up to the public criticism and the events went on as scheduled; in others, faculty, student or outside pressure caused administrations to cancel the events or to withdraw invitations.[32]

More disturbing in terms of the long-term integrity of Middle East area studies programs and classes, as well as for the freedom of the academy, has been the coordinated action against specific teaching or administrative appointments and the granting of tenure. Perhaps the most well-publicized case involved Yale University and Juan Cole of the University of Michigan. Although he has a widely-read blog "Informed Comment", Cole's scholarly publications focus, not on the contemporary era, but on the Middle East during the eighteenth and nineteenth centuries. His most recent book is on the Napoleonic Expedition to Egypt in 1798. On the basis of this scholarship, 13 faculty members in the history department, with three abstaining, and the majority in the sociology department voted in the spring of 2006 to appoint Cole to teach the modern Middle East at the Yale Center for International and Area Studies, a joint position of the history and sociology departments. The announcement of Cole's nomination elicited a public outcry from Michael Rubin at the conservative pro-Zionist American Enterprise Institute, Joel Mowbray, a columnist at the conservative *Washington Times*, and from other public forums. Some faculty at Yale also campaigned within the university against Cole. Mowbray widened the attack by sending a personal letter to a number of the major financial donors to Yale. Although it is not known how many, if any, of these contributors pressured the university, the Yale tenure committee – in a rare reversal of departmental recommendations – rejected Cole's nomination.

Similar attacks were launched against Joseph Massad's promotion at the University of Columbia and Wadie Said's appointment to the law school at Wayne State University in Detroit. Writing about outside influences on faculty hires, columnist Daniel Pipes, director of the Middle East Forum in Philadelphia, audaciously argued that organizations like Campus Watch (which he, not coincidently, founded) and others had every right to interfere and to "track university developments, including personnel decisions".[33]

Campus Watch and the David Project are two of the most active groups monitoring classes, professors, and programs dealing with the Middle East on college campuses across the United States. Campus Watch was formed by Daniel Pipes, who has advocated the total Israeli military victory over the Palestinians as the means of securing peace.[34] Pipes, known for his support of Israel, the war in Iraq, and for attacks on Iran, was nominated by President Bush to the board of the U.S. Institute of Peace in 2003. The Institute is a government-sponsored think tank and Congress must approve nominations to its board. When Pipes' nomination was delayed, Bush did not resubmit his name. Were it not an indication of the support enjoyed by hard-line supporters in the U.S. for the political right in Israel and for military adventurism in the Middle East, the nomination of the hawkish Pipes to a position in an institute allegedly fostering and studying peace would be laughable.

Initially, Campus Watch maintained a highly controversial website that listed, by name, scholars who had publicly written or spoken in favorable terms about the Palestinians or who had criticized Israel. Many on the original list were then barraged with hate mail and, in some instances, death threats. In response to criticism the list was dropped from the website. However, the site continues to track Middle East studies programs and academic institutions with Middle East programs. Students are also encouraged to inform on professors presenting negative critiques of U.S. policies in the Middle East.

Similarly, the David Project was founded in 2002 to train pro-activist students and Jewish community members about Israel. Its film on the professors of Middle East studies at Columbia University led to a series of sensationalized articles in the *New York Sun* and a barrage of complaints about specific professors from the New York community.[35]

Islamo-Fascism Awareness Week (IFAW) was yet another attempt to vilify Muslims and Arabs. Initiated by David Horowitz of Campus Watch and Students for Academic Freedom, IFAW was a so-called educational campaign about Islam to be held on campuses around the country in the fall of 2007. Virulently anti-Islamic and Arab speakers were listed on websites advertising the week of events; sites also listed universities where events were to be held. IFAW was a nation-wide attempt to link Islam and Fascism and Arabs with Nazism and to popularize, under the guise of education, these notions on university campuses. Both ADC and *The Washington Report* reacted to IFAW by sending letters of concern and protest to universities about the potentially racist and prejudiced nature of the campaign.[36] A number of universities responded that they had no such events listed on their schedules and objected to their inclusion on the website lists. In an unexpected backlash for Horowitz and his supporters, student organizations and others started their own counter-campaigns to provide and distribute objective information about Islam and the Arab world. At least partially owing to the proactive measures by ADC and others, IFAW events were cancelled or sparsely attended and clearly failed to have the impact Horowitz had anticipated.

Under the guise of increasing national security and promoting "diversity",[37] the same lobbyists and groups that attempted to stifle free speech and the independence of academic programs, sought to secure legislation to oversee and monitor Middle East programs. In 2003, Representative Peter Hoekstra, a conservative Republican from Michigan, sponsored bill H.R. 3077, as part of the reauthorization of the Higher Education Act. The bill mandated the creation of an advisory board (International Higher Education Advisory Board) to oversee and make recommendations regarding funding for university area studies and outreach programs that received Title VI funding. The board was to be composed of seven members, two of which were to come from national security agencies. Two of the board members were to be appointed by the Speaker of the House, two by the president pro tem of the Senate and three by the Secretary of Education. The board had the responsibility for drawing up criteria for fellowships and national resource centers, to oversee outreach programs, and to make recommendations about funding for programs receiving Title VI monies – a major source of finance for university area studies and language programs.

Supporters for the bill included the ADL, the American Jewish Congress, Empower America, the neo-conservative group founded by William Kristol, and interestingly the relatively new U.S. India Political Action Committee that has cooperated with pro-Israeli lobbyists. Martin Kramer, professor of Arab Studies at Moshe Dayan Center at Tel Aviv University, Stanley Kurtz, and Daniel Pipes also supported Bill 3077. Kurtz also testified in favor of the bill in Congress. In an unrecorded voice vote, thereby making it impossible to identify which members, or how many voted, the Bill easily passed the House in September 2003 and was sent on to the Committee of Health, Education, Labor and Pensions in the Senate for deliberations in 2004.

By this time, a wide array of civil rights and academic organizations had become alarmed at the Bill's potential to hobble the independence of area studies programs and, in some instances, to imperil the safety of U.S. academic researchers and their informants working in the Middle East and elsewhere. Anthropologists, and other academics, voiced their concerns that the Bill might well contribute to the perception or belief that "U.S. researchers and students are an arm of the intelligence community. This is problematic on an ethical level, and could put both U.S. researchers, and their informants, in danger."[38] The American Civil Liberties Union (ACLU), the AAUP, the Middle East Studies Association (MESA) and others issued Action Alerts, sent letters to appropriate Senators, and rallied their memberships to oppose Bill 3077.[39] The Bill died in the Senate and Title VI funding was renewed for five years. Given the determination of neo-conservative and Zionist forces to curtail the free exchange of ideas and study of the Middle East in the United State, it would not be surprising were it to be resubmitted, in one form or another, in the future.

Neo-conservative and pro-Zionist David Horowitz, who was involved in a number of the campaigns detailed above, also initiated the academic bill of rights for students (ABOR). The Students for Academic Freedom and Campus Watch joined the campaign in support of ABOR. The website for Students for Academic Freedom lists unverified complains against university professors, specific courses, and universities by conservative students. Again masquerading as means of promoting diversity, ABOR, in fact, was a blatant attempt to shift the academy to the right. It also sought to influence course offerings, contents of class syllabi and lectures, as well as professorial appointments, promotions, and tenure. History Professor at the Institute for Advanced Study and a member of the Special Committee on academic freedom and national security in a time of crisis formed by AAUP after the September 11th attacks, Joan W. Scott detailed the dangers posed by ABOR in a lengthy essay. She noted that ABOR had:

> created an atmosphere of concern on university campuses. I'd even call it fear, and this has led to a great deal of self-policing by many faculty and administrators … it substitutes political criteria (the numbers of conservatives or liberals measured by Republic or Democratic party affiliation) for social criteria (how many women, African-Americans, etc. are employed) and so changes the terms of what counts as a measure of discrimination.[40]

In "A Philosopher Looks at the 'Academic Bill of Rights'", published in the AAUP journal *Academe*, Professor Kurt Smith effectively demolished the sophistry upon which Horowitz's claims to promote diversity was based.[41] Emphasizing the inherent dangers posed by ABOR, Smith noted that "ABOR will provide a legal basis for students to sue their professors if they teach evolution and ignore creationism."[42] Given this slippery slope, it is not difficult to image lawsuits being filed by disgruntled students against faculty who teach proven historical facts that contradict the conventional Israeli mythology in courses on the Arab Israeli Conflict.

In spite of vigorous lobbying by the AAUP and concerned university administrations and professors, ABOR gained some support on the local level, especially in state legislatures that in the past have demonstrated a marked eagerness to further direct control over universities. In 2005, the Pennsylvania House of Representatives essentially signed on to ABOR by forming a committee to investigate how faculty members were hired and promoted in state universities. The committee was also to study whether or not students had the freedom to express their own viewpoints. How the committee was to research these issues was not made clear.

ABOR and similar campaigns indicate a pattern of concerted, long-term efforts by pro-Zionists and neo-conservatives to limit debate, free speech and thought, and to crush opposing viewpoints regarding Israel, the war in Iraq and prevailing hostile attitudes toward Islam and Arabs. These campaigns create the same type of political fear many believe exists in Congress where individuals fear criticizing Israel. In the words of former Senator James Abourezk, the aim is "to suppress any congressional dissent from the policy of complete support for Israel … Even one voice is attacked."[43] It has been said that "Truth is strong." Some say that it "will prevail," but it can only prevail through the concerted organized efforts by those who want objectivity and balance in matters pertaining to the Middle East and the Muslim world.

Notes

1 Scott Keeter and Andrew Kohut, "American Public Opinion about Muslims in the U.S. and Abroad", in Philippa Strum and Danielle Tarantolo (eds) *Muslims in the United States*, Washington, DC: Woodrow Wilson International Center for Scholars, 2003, p. 189.
2 Ibid.
3 CAIR Poll: "Poll: 1-in-4 Americans Holds Anti-Muslim Views", 4 October 2004. Available at: www.cair-net.org/downloads/pollresults.ppt, accessed 5 October 2004.
4 See among others: Michael Suleiman, *The Arabs in the Mind of America*, Brattleboro, VT: Amana Books, 1988; Jack G. Shaheen, *The TV Arab*, Bowling Green, OH: Bowling Green State University Popular Press, 1984 and *Reel Bad Arabs: How Hollywood Vilifies a People*, Northampton, MA: Interlink Publishing Group, Inc., 2001; Janice J. Terry, *Mistaken Identity: Arab Stereotypes in Popular Writing*, Washington, DC: American-Arab Affairs Council, 1985; Kathleen Christison, *Perceptions of Palestine: Their Influence on U.S. Middle East Policy*, Berkeley, CA: University of California Press, 1999; Michael C. Hudson and Ronald A. Wolfe (eds) *The American Media and the Arabs*, Washington, DC: Center for Contemporary Arab Studies, Georgetown University, 1980.

5 Richard Falk and Howard Friel, *Israel-Palestine on Record: How the New York Times Misreports Conflict in the Middle East*, London: Verso, 2007. See also ADC response to the January 24, 2008 *Washington Post* editorial that claimed "no one is starving in Gaza", in spite of the Israeli closure of the entire strip and UN calls for immediate humanitarian aid. ADC Action Alert; 25 January 2008. Available at: www.adc.org.

6 Marda Dunsky, *Pens and Swords: How the American Mainstream Media Report the Israeli-Palestinian Conflict*, New York: Columbia University Press, 2008.

7 Fairness & Accuracy in Reporting (FAIR): "Study Finds Lack of Balance, Diversity, Public at PBS NewsHour Public TV's Flagship News Program Offers Standard Corporate Fare". Available at: www.fair.org, 4 October 2006; accessed 10 October 2006.

8 Lorraine Adams: "Beyond the Burka", *The New York Times Book Review Section*, 6 January 2008, is one of the most recent writers to bemoan the problem of finding publishers for balanced accounts of Muslims and the Middle East.

9 Jack G. Shaheen, "Stereotypes Reign in 'The Kingdom'", *The Washington Report on Middle East Affairs*, December 2007, p. 71.

10 See www.youtube.com/watch for the full King interview with *The Politico*. See also: ADC Press Release: "ADC Condemns Recent Racist and Islamophobic Remarks from Rep. Peter King (R-NY)", 20 September 2007. Available at: www.adc.org.

11 Neil MacFarquhar, "Abandon Stereotypes, Muslims in America Say", *The New York Times*, 4 September 2007. The criticism was delivered in the form of an open letter by Peter Hoekstra (R-Mich) and Sue Myrick (R-NC).

12 Arab American Institute Countdown, September 25, 2007. Available at: www. AAIUSA.ORG, accessed 29 September 2007.

13 *The New York Times*, op. cit., 4 September 2007.

14 Juan Cole, "Islamophobia as a Social Problem: 2006 Presidential Address", *Middle East Studies Association Bulletin*, June 2007, p. 5; Janice J. Terry "Arab-American Political Activism and Civil Liberties in the Post 9/11 Era", in Philippa Strum (ed.) *American Arabs and Political Participation*, Washington, DC: Woodrow Wilson International Center for Scholars, 2006, pp. 120–121; Anton Hajjar, "Appendix: Selected Legal Issues Affecting Arab-Americans", in *American Arabs: History, Identity, Assimilation, Participation*, Special Report 2.1, Washington, DC: Woodrow Wilson International Center for Scholars, 2001, pp. 37–43.

15 Terry, 2006, op. cit.

16 Cole, op. cit., p. 5.

17 "Muslim Family Endures Hate Crime – Again", *The Washington Report on Middle East Affairs*, November 2007, p. 53.

18 ADC Press Release, "ADC Deeply Troubled by LAPD Plan to 'Map' LA-Area Muslims", 10 November 2007. Available at: www.adc.org.

19 Terry, 2006, op. cit., pp. 117–129.

20 "Rep. Ellison Addresses 2,000 at CAIR Event", *The Washington Report on Middle East Affairs*, January/February 2008, p. 45.

21 Speech by Dr. Parvez Ahmed, "CAIR Hosts Fund-raiser in DC", *The Washington Report on Middle East Affairs*, January/February 2008, p. 59.

22 Ronald R. Stockton, "Arab-American Political Participation: Findings from the Detroit Arab American Study", in Philippa Strum (ed.) *American Arabs and Political Participation*, Washington, DC: Woodrow Wilson International Center for Scholars, 2006, pp. 53–78.

23 The Middle East Academic Survey Research Exposition. Available at: www.Irmep. org/measure5.htim and www.Irmep.org/PDF/measure5.pdf, accessed 11 April 2006.

24 Karen DeYoung, "Carter Book on Israel 'Apartheid' Sparks Bitter Debate", *The Washington Post*, 7 December 2006.

25 Jimmy Carter, "Speaking Frankly about Israel and Palestine". Available at: www.latimes. com/news/opinion/commentary/la-oe-carter8dec08, accessed 11 December 2006.

26 Ibid.
27 Ron David, "Israel Lobby Unrelenting in Efforts to Stifle Speech It Doesn't Want Americans to Hear", *The Washington Report on Middle East Affairs*, December 2007, p. 23.
28 Ibid.
29 Jonathan D. Glater, "Between Free Speech and a Hard Place", *The New York Times*, September 30, 2007, p. 3; Julian Border and Ewen MacAskill, "Crowd Jeers Ahmadinejad at US College", *The Guardian Weekly*, 30 September 2007, p. 4.
30 See www.antiwar.com/blog/2006/10/04/tony-judt-speech-shut-down-by-adl, accessed 12 October 2006.
31 Joan W. Scott, "Middle East Studies Under Siege", *The Link*, 39(1) (January–March 2006). Available at: www.ameu.org/page.asp, accessed 2 February 2006.
32 "Academic Freedom and National Security in a Time of Crisis: A Report of the AAUP's Special Committee", *Academe*, 89(6) (November–December 2003).
33 Daniel Pipes, "Outsiders Should Influence Faculty Hires". Available at: www. detnews.com/apps/pbcs.dll/aricle?AID=/20061206/OPINION01/61206030, accessed 12 December 2006.
34 Scott, op. cit.
35 Ibid.
36 "Islamo-Fascism Week Backfires", *The Washington Report on Middle East Affairs*, December 2007, p. 82; "Regarding The Action Alert 'Alternative to Islamo-Fascism Week'", *The Washington Report on Middle East Affairs*, December 2007, p. 6.
37 Martin Kramer and Stanley Kurtz on HR 3077, 9 December 2003. Available at: www. washingtoninstitute.org/distribution/POL813.doc, accessed 31 January 2008.
38 Action Alert: HR 3077 Talking Points, Task Force on Middle East Anthropology, December 2003. Available at: www.ga.berkeley.edu/academics/hr3077.html.
39 Action Alert: HR 3077 Talking Points, Task Force on Middle East Anthropology, December 2003. Available at: www.ga.berkeley.edu/academics/hr3077.html; www.aaup. org/govrel/hea/2033/9-23alart.htm (AAUP Alert on HR 3077); www.international studies.uchicago.edu/titleVI.shtml.
40 Scott, op. cit.
41 Kurt Smith, "A Philosopher Looks at the 'Academic Bill of Rights'", *Academe*, September–October 2006, pp. 29–32.
42 Ibid., p. 31.
43 Letter from U.S. Senator James Abourezk to Jeff Blankfort, 4 December 2006, on Israeli Lobby. Available at: www.signs-of-the-times.org/signs/chains/signs2006 1204_TheLobbythatdoesn27texist.php, Accessed 7 December 2006.

9 Self and Other in a time of terror

Myth, media and Muslims

Karim H. Karim

Violence is, sadly, a perpetual and ever-present characteristic of human society. Yet it is shrouded in mystery. Society teaches its inhabitants to understand violence in particular ways that accomplish specific functions relating to the shaping of power. Arrangements that specify who is permitted to use force legitimately and who is not determine the structures of hierarchies. Those who are allowed to use violence are provided a key means to maintain control over people and institutions. Propagandists employ deep myth to present arguments that support the legitimacy or illegitimacy of the violence perpetrated by specific kinds of persons. The fundamental myths centred on the notions of Self and Other are made the frameworks for interpreting who carries out 'good' and 'bad' violence. Our era's dominant discourses have used this binary scheme to pit the Western Self against the Muslim Other. The mainstream media, largely adhering to the interpretations of events offered by societal elites, are drawing on the polarizing tendencies of myth to shape the public understanding of terrorism. They seem to disregard completely another aspect of the myths of Self and Other that present them as fundamentally interconnected with each other.

Competing discourses on the meanings of violence

As a recurring feature of human history, violence appears in myth, scripture, folk tales, classics, and contemporary media. The acts of violence conducted by the heroes of a community are commemorated ritually; and they are honoured as martyrs when they fall. Those who have killed them are reviled as villains, or terrorists. Violence occurs at the level of the individuals, groups, and nations, and is conducted to obtain status as well as control over people, property, and territory. It is also carried out with a view to overcome the violence of others, to right a wrong, or to pursue vengeance. The *meanings* attached to the uses of violence by specific persons against others serve to attain legitimacy for such actions and the gains that they provide. Therefore it is not only violence itself but the explanations for it that are crucial in achieving its objectives.

Similarly, terrorism cannot be separated from the struggle to attach specific meanings to it. The battles to attach a particular kind of reasoning to a terrorist act are more significant than the act itself. Perceptions of victory and defeat are significantly influenced by the result of the war over public opinion. A non-state group fighting against a state cannot match the latter's military resources; it therefore seeks targets or carries out actions that have a high symbolic value. The mere act of eluding the state's surveillance network and conducting violence in a dramatic, public fashion carries a potent statement about the failure of the government's ability to provide security – thus bringing into question the right of the ruling elites to remain in power. In response, the state seeks to ensure that the group does not obtain any credibility by attacking the legitimacy of the group's violence and, by extension, its existence.

The ideological war over the meaning of terrorism is conducted publicly through the media. Non-state groups carrying out violence do so in manners which ensure maximum coverage. They then issue statements providing explanations for their actions. Al-Qaeda's audio and video 'press releases' to Al Jazeera have become familiar to audiences far beyond the reach of the Arabic-language channel because they are re-played frequently by almost every other TV outlet. These statements seek to give meaning to the terrorist acts within the group's world-view. Governments of course disagree and usually respond through the media by presenting the group as acting criminally.

This competition of discourses[1] unfolds in public as the real war between state and non-state actors. Each claims legitimacy and insists that the other's use of violence is terroristic. They draw on forms of argument and presentations that have profound resonance for their audiences. Perennial conflicts between Self and Other, the nature of violence and its proper uses, and the cultural images that each have of the other all underlie the media portrayals of the struggle between the two. Therefore, in order to understand the contemporary 'war on terror' it is important to examine the ways in which human beings conceptualize Self, Other, and violence. An historical inquiry into Northern[2] imagery of Muslims assists in better comprehending media's[3] particular framing of the perceived struggle between 'Islamic terrorism' and global interests.

Self and Other

Human beings inherently divide the world into the Self and the Other. This form of thinking takes place at a fundamental, unconscious level. It derives from the source of deep myth.[4] The ideas of Self and Other operate in the mind as primary organizing concepts which give shape to frameworks of thought. These are held commonly by human beings, but the particular narratives of each culture shape the specific identity of the Self and the Other. These two cognitive frameworks provide room for a range of images that range from the microcosmic to the macrocosmic: the Self can be thought of as the first person subject or as the entire universe and, similarly, the Other as another person or as transcendent divinity.

At the beginnings of individual consciousness, a baby begins to realize that it is distinct from its mother. The infant becomes aware of its own characteristics in relation to others, and in this develops the conception of a separate identity. Its gender and age become pertinent features in relationships with members of its family. As it grows, there emerge individual and collective notions of the Self. It sees the uniqueness of its own facial and bodily features and is taught that it belongs to an extended Self based on gender, culture, ethnicity, religion, class, nation – distinct social groupings that may or may not overlap with each other. It learns to deal with the contradictions in which certain people may be considered part of the extended Self in certain contexts but not in others. Although it is common to think of the Other as a rival or even an enemy, in many cases it is the foil that enhances the existence of the Self. Whether hostile or not, the Other is usually the entity in relation to which the Self defines itself wholly or partially, depending on the context of interaction. Human existence is filled with the tension of differences. But this tension is often a creative force that is a vital source of life's dynamism. The Self, in some cases, may seek to unite with the Other, seeing its destiny as the fulfilment of such union. Unions of the male with the female and of the human worshipper with the divine are among the primary themes in art, music, and literature.

Conflict is integral to the human condition. Every relationship holds a possibility for it. The resolution of a dispute provides a movement forwards. But conflict in society can also lead to the deterioration of relations. When the Other is viewed in a hostile manner, the Self tends to take up an aggressive stance towards it. Cultures and nations usually adopt belligerent positions against the Others whom they view as a threat to their own existence. The goal becomes the reduction or the destruction of the threat, which sometimes can mean elimination of the people who are seen as posing the danger. In many cases, the opposing parties who view the Other as a menace to the respective Self continually feed on each other's fears, giving rise to a growing spiral of aggression. In this zero sum game, the Self views itself as necessarily losing out when the Other enjoys a benefit – it becomes inconceivable within such a zero-sum game for both to have gains through cooperation. This is why it is usually very difficult to bring two warring parties to the negotiating table.

Rival groups, usually prompted by their leaders, develop "mirror images" of each other,[5] as happened during the Cold War between the West and the Soviet Bloc. Both sides come to view the other in the same manner – as untrustworthy and ill-meaning. On the other hand, the Self is viewed in positive terms as seeking to do good. The actions of the Other, no matter how benign, are usually interpreted through negative perspectives. Each side launches parallel propaganda attacks against the Other. Despite these similarities in behaviour, both ironically see each other as being at the polar opposite. The Self's media and other channels of public discourse are key elements in disseminating the images that often mirror those produced by the Other.

Hostile tendencies between Self and Other tend to disregard the multiplicity of hybrid fusions that take place through contact between different social groups. However, there is a deliberate effort, frequently on the part of societal elites, to emphasize distinctions with the Other in order to enhance the unity of the Self. Every single person in the extended Self is expected to conform in his or her personal identification against the Other. Communal identity is maintained in categories of essentialized (ethnic, racial, ideological) purity; great lengths are taken to avoid 'contamination' from contact with the Other. Some examples are the historical restrictions placed on North American aboriginal peoples, the separation of 'racial' groups under apartheid, the traditional caste-based practices in India, as well as the extreme suspicion during the Cold War of communist values in the West and capitalist ones in the Eastern Bloc. Such thinking suppresses the subtle and overt linkages that people of varying backgrounds develop with each other over time.

A key motivation on the part of certain leaders is to "divide and rule". In fabricating or exaggerating a threat from another group, some elites seek to convince their community about their own indispensability by promoting the belief that it is only they who will be able to protect the population. This serves to reinforce their positions of power. A common tactic is to present the Self as good and the Other as evil. Such essentialization helps set up a situation in which the faults of the Self, particularly the elites, tend to be hidden under the veil of goodness as those of the Other are magnified. In this absolute scenario, the Self can do no evil and the Other can do no good. Indeed, in the most extreme cases, they become personifications of good and evil. When this happens, it becomes easier to carry out and justify massive harm to the Other. With the effective use of the mass media by the elites, large sections of the nation are brought to acquiesce to genocide (as in Nazi Germany, the former Yugoslavia, and Rwanda). Notions of 'the evil empire' and 'the axis of evil' have also helped leaders rally populations against other countries. Once a country has been labelled a 'rogue' state or 'terrorist' group, fewer justifications have had to be made when brutal military action is taken against it.[6]

It would be incorrect to suggest that societal leaders are always bent on fomenting discord. Contemporary governments are often engaged in sustaining harmony between the people of diverse characteristics who are part of society. This was not necessarily the case until the mid-twentieth century due to the entrenched concept of the nation-state as consisting primarily, if not solely, of a population that was similar in language, culture, ethnicity and religion. A number of factors have brought about the willingness to deal positively with various aspects of pluralism within a country. Current patterns of migration have given rise to populations which have an unprecedented level of diversity. Whereas newcomers would usually in the past be absorbed culturally into host societies, the scale of human relocations as well as the ability to maintain one's social and cultural characteristics has grown due to factors such as the availability of media (film, video, satellite television, the Internet, telephony) that provide continual links with the land of origin and its diaspora.[7] People are also able to travel frequently to interact with their transnational communities. Additionally, the human rights movement that emerged in the mid-twentieth century has helped to assert the legitimacy of minority groups within states and has led to the emergence of policies such as multiculturalism, which provide enabling mechanisms for migrants to maintain and cultivate their cultural institutions. It has also encouraged the recognition of multi-layered identities that many individuals hold as well as of the evolution of hybrid cultures.[8] Nevertheless, the polarizing tendencies of othering have not disappeared and continue often to divide groups. As with most other public debates, it is in media content where the competition of these discourses unfold.

The naming of violence

The actions that are considered violent and those that are not are determined in every culture according to societal consensus. This consensus is usually not a formal one, but is based on the myths to which the extended Self subscribes.[9] Joseph Gusfield[10] identifies three steps through which societal consensus on specific issues is engineered:

1   Naming the problem.
2   Giving it public status by assigning responsibility to deal with it.
3   Legitimating a particular way of viewing the problem.

Various discourses compete in the naming of violence, a phenomenon which has been an integral yet enigmatic feature of human history. George Gerbner, who has carried out extensive studies of violence in television programming, states: "Violence is a legitimate and necessary cultural expression. It is a dramatic balancing of deadly conflicts against tragic costs."[11] Since there is an integral link between power and violence, those who hold power have a major stake in ensuring that their preferred meanings remain dominant. They attempt to promote in their propaganda that their interests are the same as those of the extended Self.

But whereas violence is often used to repress people, it is also a means to oppose and develop checks against excessive power. Symbolic violence has long been used in rituals to bind communities and stave off real, destructive violence.[12] It is sublimated in a variety of contemporary socio-cultural institutions that have adversarial structures, for example, courts of justice where lawyers 'fight' cases (harking back to the times when knights jousted to determine the justness of particular causes), parliamentary houses of assembly where members of rival political parties debate and hurl ritual insults at each other, and sports arenas in which opposing teams endeavour to 'beat' each other. Being a primary feature of our myths, violence in symbolic forms emerges as a functional imperative that structures relationships within communities and underlies the manners in which societies are organized. Who belongs to the Self and to the Other is often determined according to the person's positioning with respect to certain kinds of violence. Its public display and narration are present in all cultures, and its use is often intimately related to the constructions of respective moral and socio-political orders. Physical and psychological violence is used by societies to penalize non-conformity to their particular rules and laws. Power is based to a significant extent on the demonstrated or potential capability for violence: hierarchies within the extended Self, from the smallest to the global community, are created and maintained through its symbolic or actual uses.

Actual physical violence is endowed with high symbolic value when it is depicted in forms that ideologically support one or another view of political and social reality. Narratives that dramatize deadly struggles involving heroes, villains and victims give meaning to the conflicts that exist in human society. Media portrayals of particular uses of violence by specific kinds of people ideologically construct which social role they are playing. Those who control the production and dissemination of these dramaturges can thus engender public consensus on which types of people are to be considered as the heroes, the villains, and the victims in society, according to their interpretations of the uses of violence. The hero and the victim are usually identified with the Self, who carries out good violence, and the villain with the Other, who conducts terrorism.

Due to their very nature, incidents of terrorism allow very dramatic renderings, especially for television. Since dominant discourses will have already established the proper and improper uses of violence, the integration propagandist does not have to expend much ideological labour in constructing scenarios of struggles between the 'right' and the 'wrong' sides and can almost perfunctorily endow specific actors in these incidents the roles of hero, villain, and victim. Philip Elliot tells us that in "the human interest accounts of incidents and their aftermath people are portrayed acting out their roles with the appropriate emotions as prescribed by the norms and traditions of their culture".[13] Mainstream media generally sustain consensus on the moral order that supports the status quo by portraying state agents as heroes who apply force in the cause of national security, terrorists as villains who use it to destroy life and property, and citizens as victims whose security is threatened by terrorists. Such dramaturgical enactments are among the potent rites through which the legitimacy of the incumbent structures of power is continually validated: they provide opportunities for the public depiction of dramaturgically 'correct' actions by the agents of the state, their opponents, and the citizenry. (They also serve to reinforce further the goodness of the Self and the evil nature of the Other.)

Dominant discourses support the actions of existing hegemonic powers to preserve themselves from threats that they themselves name as violent and terroristic. Robert Fisk, the Middle East correspondent for the London-based *Independent* whose reporting usually goes beyond the standard clichés about the region, notes in his book *Pity the Nation: Lebanon at War*:

> "[T]errorism" no longer means terrorism. It is not a definition; it is a political contrivance. "Terrorists" are those who use violence against the side that is using the word. The only terrorists whom Israel acknowledges are those who oppose Israel. The only terrorists the United States acknowledges are those who oppose the United States or their allies. The only terrorists Palestinians acknowledge – for they too use the word – are those opposed to the Palestinians.[14]

The word is manipulated to serve the ideological purposes of the political source that is using it.

Johan Galtung, a renowned scholar of peace studies, provides useful analytical concepts of violence. He offers the notion of 'structural violence', manifested in the denial of basic material needs (poverty), human rights (repression) and 'higher needs' (alienation) as distinct from direct or 'classical' violence,[15] thus allowing for the placing of violent actions within a larger framework that takes into account historical, political, and socio-economic conditions from which they arise. The consequences of systemic institutional behaviour that does not involve direct, physical force but that, nevertheless, leads to alienation, deprival, disability or death, as under poor working conditions, is also not usually described as violent in dominant political discourses. However, direct, forceful reactions to structural violence by the Other are invariably called violent. As no immediate violent causes can be uncovered for such (re)actions within dominant conceptualizations of violence, they are often described as being irrational and barbaric – normative characteristics of the Other.

Whereas violence is integral to the operative dynamics of society, it is also a social problem since it continually threatens to disrupt social order. In a utopian state, where absolute order is conceived to be the norm, violence would be an anomaly. However, in practice, the state and the socio-economic elite continually use various kinds of structural and direct violence to exercise and maintain power, especially against those who challenge the status quo. According to Max Weber, the modern state claims monopoly over legitimate violence:

> Today the relation between the state and violence is an especially intimate one. In the past, the most varied institutions – beginning with the sib – have known the use of physical force as quite normal. Today, however, we have to say that a state is a human community that (successfully) claims the *monopoly of the legitimate use of physical force* within a given territory ... Specifically, at the present time, the right to use physical force is ascribed to other institutions or to individuals only to the extent to which the state permits it. The state is considered the sole source of the "right" to use violence.[16]

Those who carry out violence without authorization from the state are punished by the state's "bureaucracy of violence (police, army, jails)".[17] However, the modern state tends to downplay its own massive and systemic use of violence as it simultaneously emphasizes its opponents' uses of violence. In this, the state's propaganda presents itself as the political embodiment of the peaceful Self and its opponents as that of the brutal Other.

Historical applications of direct violence to establish the ruling elite and the structural violence used in sustaining the elite's dominance are generally made invisible through processes of dehistoricization. The hegemonic structure is depicted as being part of a natural and rational social order of the collective Self for whom violence is an anomaly. Thus, ignoring the blood-soaked American past and present, a US judge could declare: "Violence in pursuit of any goal is an aberration in American society and simply cannot be tolerated."[18] Yet, when there emerges a threat to the status quo, the state immediately marshals its own massive means of violence to stem it. This often occurs when demonstrators mount large protests against government policies or actions, and are met with large contingents of riot police. Some examples are the Ohio National Guard's shooting and bayoneting of Kent State University students demonstrating against the US bombing of Cambodia in 1970, the RCMP's pepper spraying of protestors at the 1997 APEC Summit in Vancouver, the 1999 WTO "Battle of Seattle", and the arrests of hundreds of student demonstrators in Paris in the winter of 2006. In democratic regimes, where public opinion needs to be assured of the benevolence of the state, the latter has to strive harder than autocratic ones to veil the force that it itself applies against its citizens. This violence against elements of the collective Self is presented by state propagandists and the mainstream media as being in the interests of maintaining order and security. The applications of force that sustain the hegemonic structure are thus put outside the dominant discourses on violence, which instead revolve around criminality, irrationality, and deviance. The term "violence" is generally reserved for the use of force of the Other; and when it is used to upset the established political order it is characterized as terrorism. "More violent than the violent – such is terrorism", notes Jean Baudrillard.[19]

The state's use of force is usually portrayed as being carried out within a rational and moral framework. While structural violence by the state remains almost completely invisible in dominant political discourses, even direct violence by its agents – when publicly uncovered – is usually left unpunished or dismissed with a mere slap on the wrist. The Israeli government's Landau Commission found in 1987 that "abusive interrogation methods" were being systematically used by Shin Bet, the security police, which had been lying to military courts in the West Bank and Gaza for seventeen years. Nevertheless, the commission's report recommended that none of the Shin Bet agents should be prosecuted or even disciplined either for abusing detainees or for perjury. At the same time, it also endorsed "non-violent psychological pressure" in the interrogation of security detainees and, if this did not suffice, "a moderate measure of physical pressure".[20] This ruling has provided the "legal" basis of perpetrating torture against Palestinian and Lebanese prisoners in the democratic state of Israel.[21]

Whereas the Self is permitted to brutalize the Other, even the latter's *nonviolent* resistance to the former's violence is sometimes highlighted as "terrorism". Thomas Friedman, a former *New York Times* correspondent in the Middle East, wrote in his book *From Beirut to Jerusalem* about the Israeli military's failure to respond to the slaughter of Palestinian refugees and others in the Sabra and Shatila refugee camps in 1982:

> The Israeli soldiers did not see innocent civilians being massacred and they did not hear the screams of innocent children going to their graves. What they saw was a "terrorist infestation" being "mopped up" and "terrorist nurses" scurrying about and "terrorist teenagers" trying to defend them, and what they heard was "terrorist women" screaming.[22]

The essential identification with terrorism of all Palestinians (as the embodiment of the Other) was so complete in their minds that they could not seem to bring themselves to think of them as victims of violence even in such circumstances. Very high casualty rates over the last few decades among Palestinian and Lebanese children resulting from Israeli military actions ostensibly aimed at terrorists appear to be a result of such thinking. On the other side, the indiscriminate killing of Israeli civilians by the suicide bombers of Hamas and Islamic Jihad as well as by Hizbullah appear to have been prompted by the similar conceptualization of the Israeli Other.

A wide range of legitimate violence, from surveillance to execution, is available to the state and is administered by its bureaucratic structures. Governmental retribution for use of direct violence by non-state actors generally takes the form of the violence involved in incarceration or death. The state's harshest punishments are reserved for actions against itself, such as treason and terrorism. Those who are judged guilty of these offences are either executed or given very long sentences in maximum security prisons. Some may not even be given a proper trial and are jailed under very harsh conditions, such as those suspected of terrorism by the US Government and incarcerated in Guantanamo Bay. Naming of the government's Other is carried out according to the strength of the threats posed to the Self. Whereas 'activist' is used to denote those opponents who remain within what is considered legitimate opposition to the state, the term 'terrorist' is often attached to someone who violently rejects the premises of the prevailing socio-political order. If the medium of reporting sympathizes with the latter's cause they are called 'freedom fighters' or 'resistance members' – a more neutral approach may use 'insurgents' or 'guerrillas'. Elements of the Self who carry out state-sanctioned violence are 'secret service operatives', 'soldiers', 'commandos', 'tactical squads', 'SWAT teams', 'riots corps', 'police', and 'prison guards'.

The second in Gusfield's three steps of consensus-construction is to assign responsibility to specific persons within the collective Self for dealing with the social problem. There is general acceptance that certain issues are to be handled by those playing particular public roles or holding specific offices that can command public attention, trust, and influence.[23] 'Experts' from government, the military, academia, and the media have emerged as the owners of dominant discourses on terrorism, making themselves readily available to the public through the mass media to define and describe the problem as well as to respond to alternative discourses on the issue. This does not mean that they are engaged in a conscious, coordinated conspiracy to produce a monolithic view, but that they subscribe to a general common purpose and to a common field of meanings that favours the Self. Such "authorized knowers"[24] have a privileged say in the two other aspects of assigning responsibility for the problem of terrorism: who and what causes it and who and what will deal with it. Specific issues involving political violence are generally shorn of their structural causes and are placed under general rubrics such as 'narco-terrorism', 'nuclear terrorism', 'Islamic terrorism'. Lack of security is often pinpointed as a key reason for the occurrence of terrorist incidents and the solutions are seen in technological and legislative improvements by the state to better detect, prevent, and punish terrorism. Persons who are not agents of the state and who use violence for political reasons are portrayed as criminals – they are to be dealt within the judicial structures that normally process violent criminals. Public attention is thus kept focused on the *violence* rather than the *politics* of political violence. The Other is generally portrayed as not acting in good faith and as conducting violence for unjust and often evil reasons.

The last step in consensus-engineering is legitimating a particular way of viewing the problem. As with the first two steps, this one is also largely achieved with the broad co-operation of mainstream media. Once the status quo has been determined as a just arrangement for all within the collective Self, there can be no logical or legitimate reason for rebellion. If the modern state is considered to be the most rational model for organizing political community and represents the cultural and intellectual achievements of civilization, then militant opposition to its power structures is irrational. When the structural and direct violence of the state is rendered non-existent, the violence against it can be seen as being terrorism on the part of the Other. Once the massive violence of the colonial era and its continuing effects have been glossed over, the contemporary world order comes to be perceived as a natural consequence of a benign history of the global Self. Since international structures and the global activities of powerful Northern states are viewed as beneficial for all humankind, the atrocities by certain Muslims acting in the name of Islam against symbols of Northern hegemony can be attributed solely to the barbarism of 'Islamic terrorism'. Thus, the dehistoricized dominant discourses help create moral consensus about the nature of political violence by influencing how public opinion perceives correct and incorrect modes of political behaviour in modern states and in international relations.

The Muslim as violent Other

The dominant Northern image of the global Other has roots in age-old European notions about Islam.[25] Certain basic views about the characteristics of Muslims, having survived hundreds of years, feed the dominant discourses of contemporary media just as the primary stereotypes that Muslims have about Northerners inform their current constructions of Europe and North America. However, Muslim societies have not institutionalized their imaginaries[26] about Northern societies to the extent that the latter have done of Islam, especially over the past two centuries.[27] The view of the Muslim East as the source of danger to the West has old origins in European discourses. Even in the Middle Ages, narratives about the alliances linking Muslim and Christian rulers were overshadowed by the polarized construction of the relationship between Islam and Christianity. Polemical discourses produced in the centuries when Europeans fought long wars with 'Saracens', 'Moors' and Turks are embedded in the classic works produced by the likes of Dante, Shakespeare, Voltaire, Beethoven, Mozart, and Delacroix. Their continued consumption by post-Enlightenment generations sustains a world-view in which

'Mohammedans' are essentially gripped by violence, lust, greed, and barbarism. These core images are reproduced with remarkable regularity in contemporary cultural productions, like film, television programs, and websites, as well as in press accounts.[28] Depictions of Middle Eastern terrorists by Hollywood and transnational wire services seem to bear a striking resemblance to the Muslim characters in European polemics penned a thousand years ago. Whereas Muslims also produced negative imagery about Europeans, they did not develop an over-arching discourse about the West comparable to Europe's institutionalized study of the East (Orientalism) that grew in tandem with the imperialist venture.

The idea of Islam constituting a primary threat to the West was eclipsed in the latter part of the nineteenth century by the military defeat of Muslim powers. Many Muslim lands were brought under European colonial control and the Ottoman Empire was in retreat. The First World War resulted in the triumph of the Allies over the remnants of the Muslim Caliphate, which had been in exist-ence since the early period of Islam. Indeed, as British troops marched into Jerusalem, General Allenby remarked that the Crusades were finally over. But the Red Army proved victorious in Russia, and the communist East replaced the Muslim East as the primary enemy of the West. Dominant discourses presented the entire world as a red and blue checkerboard in this global struggle between communism and capitalism during the Cold War.

Development theory propounded by the likes of Daniel Lerner (who carried out a study of the use of media in several Middle Eastern countries in the 1950s[29]) assumed that the gradual replacement of religion by westernization was inevita-ble and irreversible. Islam's influence on public life was seen as being on the wane. The secularly-oriented policies of twentieth-century leaders such as Atatürk, Jinnah, Nasser, Suharto, and the Shah of Iran were viewed as evidence that Muslim states were "modernizing" (i.e. westernizing). However, the mid-1970s saw a growing movement to revive the role of religion in the public sphere in various Middle Eastern societies, partly due to the failure of the Eurocentric model of development. The overthrow of Shah Reza Pahlevi of Iran in 1979 and the assassination of President Anwar Sadat of Egypt in 1981 (both major allies of the US) by separate elements of Muslim revivalism signalled "the return of Islam" to Western opinion leaders.

This 'return' in many ways is a continuation of the attempt by Muslims since the eighteenth century to understand the contingencies of contemporary life from traditional Islamic perspectives. Its manifestations range from the profound intel-lectual debates with Enlightenment philosophy to the fashioning of practical strat-egies for development within Muslim frameworks to the militant rejection of all Western influences. Many variants of this broad 'revival' have emerged in Muslim countries from western Africa to South-East Asia, leading to differing responses from their governments. Several insurgencies have threatened governments in Muslim-majority countries and have launched terrorist attacks against Northern targets. As the Muslim resurgence was gaining ground in the 1980s, European communism was steadily declining. The fall of the Berlin Wall in 1989 and the subsequent collapse of the Soviet Union marked the end of the Cold War.

These significant historical developments have led to the reordering of the ways in which global conflict is constructed. For most of the twentieth century, the West had been pitted against the Soviet Union. As state-based communism expanded its locus after the Second World War, Eastern Europe had come to be conceived as the primary ideological and military Other, and, in some quarters, "the evil empire". Vast institutional and economic infrastructures were built in the West and in Eastern Europe to wage the Cold War. NATO, the Warsaw Pact, national military machines, military industrial complexes, and foreign intelligence services furthered innumerable careers and created enormous wealth for armaments producers. Weapons manufacturers in the North sold billions of dollars worth of arms to Southern countries to fight many proxy wars between the two superpowers.

Even before the collapse of the USSR, the confrontations of Western powers with state and non-state Muslim actors seemed to prepare the way for Islam to become a post-Cold War Other. Over the last few decades, reportage of various Middle Eastern wars, 'the OPEC crisis', the Iranian and Lebanese hostage situations, 'the Rushdie Affair', the conflicts in Afghanistan, Algeria, Azerbaijan, Bosnia-Herzegovina, Chechnya, East Timor, Egypt, Iran, Iraq, Kashmir, Lebanon, Mindanao, and Sudan, as well as of the terrorist acts committed by Muslims often tended to attribute blame explicitly or implicitly to Islam, regardless of these separate events' specific historical, economic, and political factors. Since the age-old images of the religion embedded over the centuries in European lore are of discord, the credibility of current media accounts about Muslims as being inherently disruptive do not tend to be contested. Even though contemporary Northern discourses are secular, the memory of a medieval Christendom in military conflict with Muslim societies seems latent in present-day attitudes. Referring to the conflict in Bosnia-Herzegovina, Susan Sontag notes:

> Not to be underestimated ... is the pervasiveness of anti-Muslim prejudice, a reflex reaction to a people the majority of whom are as secular, and as imbued with contemporary consumer-society culture, as their other Southern European neighbours. To bolster the fiction that this is, at its deepest source, a religious war, the label "Muslim" is invariably used to describe the victims, their army and their government – though no one would think of describing the [Serbian and Croat] invaders as the Orthodox and the Catholics. Do many secular Western intellectuals who might be expected to have raised their voices to defend Bosnia share these prejudices? Of course they do.[30]

Despite the veneer of secularism in public Northern discourses, the age-old conceptualization of the Christian Self pitted against the Muslim Other appears to colour contemporary thinking.

While there remain other forces opposed to the hegemony of Northern elites, such as the governments of North Korea and Cuba, 'narco-terrorists' in Colombia and South-East Asia, as well as popularly-based movements in the industrialized and non-industrialized societies like the environmentalist and the women's movements, Islam, with its world-wide body of adherents, is often constructed as presenting the most dangerous threat. It is variously linked to communism, fascism, Nazism, and anti-Semitism.[31] These propagandic themes capitalize on traditional Northern images of Muslims as violent and as irrational barbarians intent on destroying Judeo-Christian culture. Even though relatively few individuals have made common cause with violent groups like al-Qaeda, the constant use of 'Islamic' and 'Muslim' to describe terrorism links entire Muslims societies with their violence and world-views. A monolithic and static 'Islam' is presented as the antithesis of the Western liberal values developed over the past 300 years.

In the aftermath of the Cold War, the 'Islamic peril' has become a convenient common enemy of the West and Eastern Europe since it can be presented as a fundamental threat to the global Self. However, since Northern powers frequently seek allies in Muslim states, the conflict with 'Islam' cannot be portrayed as a clear-cut struggle such as that which was perceived to exist between NATO and the Warsaw Pact. Nevertheless, when required, it can be used effectively to demonize certain enemies: the use of terms such as 'Islamic', 'Sunni', 'Shia', '*jihad*' frequently serve in dominant Northern discourses to discredit Muslim groups. This was done with great effectiveness to sway public opinion in the US to support the wars against Iraq in 1991 and 2003.

Several Muslim groups and individuals have attempted to respond in non-violent manners to the long-standing hegemonic status of the North that has existed since the colonial era and has come to be part of the 'natural' scheme of things in dominant international discourses. However, this resistance is usually portrayed by Northern propagandists as being irrational and unwarranted, and as stemming from what is perceived as the regressive nature of Islam. The broad range of alternative discourses seeking to counter the present dominance of the North over Muslim cultures is often lumped together with violent opposition as 'Muslim extremism'.

Keeping the Self pure

The discovery and the arrest in June 2006 of Muslim Canadian suspects planning a series of attacks in Toronto and Ottawa saw the use in media narratives of the term 'homegrown terrorist'.[32] It seemed astonishing to observers that young men who grew up in the West would contemplate terrorism against it: the 'Islamic terrorist' was supposed to be a foreign Other. Most commentators appeared to be disregarding the long history of the conflicts in Northern Ireland, Sri Lanka, India, Egypt, the US, Japan, Germany and many other countries where the state had engaged with the political violence of local groups. Indeed, the Canadian government had itself contended with the Front de Libération du Québec (FLQ) during the October 1970 crisis.

Since Islam in dominant discourses is an alien religion, journalists seemed to be surprised that Canadians were taking up arms for an ideological cause that supposedly did not have anything to do with the Self or its constituent parts.

They were forgetting that in the 1990s the Canadian children of some Serbian and Croatian immigrants had travelled back to the former Yugoslavia to fight on the respective sides of their ethnic/national groups. Nicholas Ribich, born in Canada and of Serbian heritage, was tried in Edmonton in 2002 for taking UN peacekeeping soldiers, including a Canadian captain, hostage in the former Yugoslavia.[33] It is also not rare for Jews from Canada and other countries to serve in the Israeli military forces. Thom Farkas, an Israeli air force pilot born in Canada, died in the 2006 war with Hizbullah.[34] This conflict also saw a Canadian UN observer and 11 members of a Lebanese-Canadian family killed by Israeli aerial bombing.

The Self and Other are not as polarized in reality as their dominant conceptions make them out to be. As mentioned earlier in this chapter, they are also presented in cultural narratives as seeking union with each other in romantic and spiritual contexts. Despite the resistance of dominant political discourses to the possibility of the joining of Self and Other, the traditional conception of the nation-state as composed of a monolithic population with a consistently singular loyalty is becoming increasingly untenable. Lateral links of diasporas and other transnational connections of a country's citizens are straining the vertical adherence to exclusivist national ideologies. The national Self is not insular, and most likely never was.

Nevertheless, dominant discourses, including those of the media, hold on to the fiction of a consistently binary positioning of Self and Other. By endowing the "homegrown terrorists" with the primary identity of the Other, the Self does not have to deal with the uncomfortable thoughts about how 'Islamic' violence against the nation could be engendered from within. As with so much in current global relations, the centuries-old imagery of the Muslim as the violent Other serves culturally to underpin the public explanations for this as well. Through emphasis on the Muslim rather than the Canadian identity of the malcontents, it becomes possible to avoid consideration of even the remotest likelihood that some of the causes of deviance may find their sources in the Self. The Self is kept pure by disregarding the hybrid nature of young Canadians of various origins who contemplate political violence – the blame is placed on what are viewed as the inherently violent characteristics of their alien heritage. The polarizing aspects of myth, which serve best the primary interests of societal elites, are put into service; those that raise difficult questions about current realities are not given prominence by the mainstream media or other channels of public discourse.

Conclusion

Conflict usually leads people to favour the demonization of the Other. Society's dominant discourses spout streams of invective against those who are seen as embodying the enemy. They usually overwhelm the discourses that seek to present alternative views about the relationship between Self and Other. These two are more often inter-related than societal elites would admit. The powers that be frequently exaggerate the threat posed by the Other in order to fortify their own position. These views are often echoed by the mainstream media, which are usually owned by the state or elites.

Violence is present in society in varying manners. Structural violence is imperceptible, but it has an extensive reach. The state also strives to make its own use of force invisible. However, that employed by its opponents is magnified in dominant discourses. Mass media play an integral role in attaching specific meanings to particular acts of violence. The Other's use of violence is usually presented as evil and terroristic; that of the Self is rendered benign. More than the act of violence itself, the effective dissemination of its interpretations determines whether it succeeds in attaining its aims.

The Muslim has emerged as the primary Other of the West in contemporary times. His use of violence is essential in his demonization. Its continual portrayal in the media is vital to enhancing his image as the enemy. It even serves to justify invasions by the Self of Muslim-majority countries and harsh measures against individual Muslims suspected as security threats. The twin myths of Self and Other are pressed into service in this way by propagandists to promote the interests of those who seek to benefit from creating fear among the public. By sustaining a polarized framework, the Self and Other are presented as being completely different from each other and always antagonistic.

In reality, the multicultural mix that exists in the populations of many countries is making it increasingly untenable to depict people of varying ethnicities and religions in binary manners. Yet, dominant discourses persist in carrying out rearguard action that strives to present the Self as monolithically pure. Violence is used as a way to mark out the domestic Other as a 'home-grown terrorist', even though violence is carried out by elements of the Self as well. A healthier society would attempt to come to terms with all forms of conflict in its midst. Whereas some violence by its citizens may be inspired by foreign sources, it is vital to acknowledge the inter-relationships that exist between Self and Other. The myth-based roots of Self and Other hold out the possibility for recognizing the fundamental tendency for them to coalesce in multiple ways. It is by transcending the binary framework that presents the two as completely alien from each other that we can begin to lift the veil that we have placed on violence.

Notes

1 Karim H. Karim, *Islamic Peril: Media and Global Violence*, 2nd edn, Montreal: Black Rose Books, 2003, pp. 5–6.
2 In the aftermath of the Cold War, a common Northern front has developed between the governments of NATO countries and the Russian Federation against what is largely viewed as "Islamic terrorism".
3 Despite the inroads made by regional, non-Western broadcasters like Al-Jazeera and the growth of Internet-based media, the Western-based mass media remain globally dominant.
4 The operative concept of myth in this chapter is not that of false story but that of a universally shared cognitive grammar. In the words of Carl Jung, myth is "what is believed always, everywhere, by everybody". Carl J. Jung, *The Basic Writings of C.J. Jung*, ed. Violet Staub de Lazlo, New York: The Modern Library, 1993, p. 5.

5   Robert L. Ivie, "Images of Savagery in American Justifications for War", *Communication Monographs*, 47, November 1980.
6   Karim, op. cit., pp. 139–157.
7   See Karim H. Karim, "Mapping Diasporic Mediascapes", in Karim H. Karim (ed.) *The Media of Diaspora*, London: Routledge, 2003, pp. 1–17.
8   Homi Bhabha, *The Location of Culture*, London: Routledge, 1994.
9   Barbara Whitner, *The Violence Mythos*, Albany, NY: SUNY, 1997.
10 Joseph R. Gusfield, *The Culture of Public Problems: Drinking-Driving and the Symbolic Order*, Chicago: University of Chicago Press, 1981.
11 George Gerbner, "Violence and Terror in and by the Media", in Marc Raboy and Bernard Dagenais (eds), *Media, Crisis and Democracy*, London: Sage, 1992, p. 97.
12 René Girard, *Violence and the Sacred*, trans. Patrick Gregory, Baltimore, MD: Johns Hopkins University, 1979.
13 Philip Elliot, "Press Performance as Political Ritual", in Harry Christian (ed.) *The Sociology of Journalism and the Press*, London: Constable, 1979, p. 161.
14 Robert Fisk, *Pity the Nation: Lebanon at War*, Oxford: Oxford University Press, 1990, p. 441.
15 Johan Galtung, "The Specific Contribution of Peace Research to the Study of Violence", in UNESCO, *Violence and its Causes*, Paris: UNESCO, 1981, pp. 3–4.
16 Max Weber, *From Max Weber: Essays in Sociology*, trans. H.H. Gerth and C. Wright Mills, New York: Oxford University Press, 1946, p. 78.
17 David I. Kertzer, *Ritual, Politics, and Power*, New Haven, CT: Yale University Press, 1988, p. 132.
18 United Press International, "3 Montrealers Jailed in U.S. Bomb Case", *The Ottawa Citizen*, 23 June 1988, p. A23.
19 Jean Baudrillard, *Fatal Strategies*, trans. Philip Beitchman and W. G. J. Niesluchowski, New York: Semiotext[e], 1990, p. 34.
20 Aryeh Neier, "Watching Rights", *The Nation*, 24 June 1991, p. 841.
21 In cases where the law does not permit the state to torture prisoners, it sometimes seeks to by-pass such rules. The George W. Bush administration has both "off-shored" torture to states which do permit such practices and has conducted its own torture at its prison complex in Guantanamo Bay by developing ambiguity about the status of this location and of its prisoners.
22 Thomas Friedman, *From Beirut to Jerusalem*, New York: Anchor Books, 1990, p. 163.
23 Gusfield, op. cit., p. 10.
24 James Winter, *Common Cents: Media Portrayal of the Gulf War and Other Events*, Montreal: Black Rose Books, 1992, p. 40.
25 See Norman Daniel, *Islam and the West: The Making of an Image*, Edinburgh: Edinburgh University Press, 1960.
26 According to Castoriadis:

> [W]e speak of the "imaginary" when we want to talk about something "invented" whether this refers to a "sheer" invention ("a story entirely dreamed up"), or a slippage, a shift of meaning in which available symbols are invested with other significations than their "normal" or canonical significations.
>
> (Cornelius Castoriadis, *The Imaginary Institution of Society*, Cambridge, MA: MIT Press, 1998, p. 127)

27 Edward Said, *Orientalism*, New York: Pantheon, 1978.
28 See Karim, *Islamic Peril*, op. cit.; Elizabeth Poole, *Reporting Islam: Media Representations of British Muslims*, London: IB Tauriis, 2002; Kai Hafez (ed.) *Islam and the West in the Mass Media: Fragmented Images in a Globalizing World*. Cresskill, NJ: Hampton Press, 2000.

29 Daniel Lerner, *The Passing of Traditional Society: Modernizing the Middle East*, Glencoe, IL: World Publishing Co, 1958.
30 Susan Sontag, " 'There' and 'Here': A Lament for Bosnia", *The Nation*, 25 December 1995, pp. 818–819.
31 Karim, *Islamic Peril*, op. cit.
32 For example, see Michael Friscolanti, Jonathon Gatehouse and Charlie Gillis, "Homegrown Terror: It's Not Over", *Maclean's*, 19 June 2006, pp. 18–25.
33 Alban Mitrushi, "UN Abduction Trial Adjourned: Prosecution Winds up Evidence in Trial of Canadian Serb Charged with Abduction of UN Soldiers", *Institute for War and Peace Reporting*, No. 287, 28 October–November 2002. Available at: www.iwpr. net/?p=tri&s=f&o=163597&apc_state=henitri2002.
34 The Canadian Press, "Canadian-born Pilot Killed in Israeli Helicopter Crash", CBC, 25 July 2006. Available at: www.cbc.ca/canada/toronto/story/2006/07/25/ canadianpilot.html.

10 Understanding the Muslim world

We *can* do better

Raymond W. Baker and
Alexander Henry

Introduction

The world is in the grips not only of a deep economic crisis, but an intellectual one as well. More and more, the problems of our day call for cooperation across diverse cultural groups. Yet while the need for cross-cultural understanding has never been greater, its prospects have never been more in doubt. In public and academic discourse alike, one hears the same story: people who have not been acculturated like us cannot share the beliefs and values we take for granted in understanding and evaluating one another. The analysis of Islamism has not been immune to this skepticism about cross-cultural understanding. An all-too-familiar symptom is the tendency to rely on external causes in explaining Islamist practices where we would use reasons in explaining our own. If not for certain causes, such explanations seem to imply, the practices in question would have turned out more like ours. Liberal intellectuals like Bruce Lawrence and conservative ones like Bernard Lewis differ on precisely what these causes are, for example, the pressures of global political economy or the imprint of a static religious tradition. Ultimately, however, they all wear the same interpretive blinders. If we want to bring Islamists into view as *people*, we must find a way to always interpret them as expressing beliefs and values we can understand, even in the difficult cases in which we object to the practices we are interpreting.

Cultural relativism is the purest form of this skepticism about understanding across cultures. Much as Descartes posited privileged access to one's own mind, at the cost of access to the minds of others, cultural relativism posits privileged access to one's own culture, at the cost of access to the cultures of others. Co-culturalists are supposed to understand one another in ways that people from other cultures simply cannot. Acculturation has caused them to share a unique set of beliefs, claims, intentions, norms, values, and concepts—'commitments' as we use this blanket term hereafter.[1] Having all of the *same* commitments grants them access to each other's reasons, enabling interpretation and critique. The *uniqueness* of what they share denies such access to outsiders. To share a culture, on this account, is thus to share a perspective on the world, to see things in the same way. Relativism, simply put, is the view that cultural boundaries circumscribe the space of reasons—the normative realm where people make sense of, and justify themselves to, one another. *Rational access* to other people must then be constrained by contingent facts about the way we are brought up.

Translation as a problem for relativism

There are, however, interpretive abilities that we clearly possess which do not fit comfortably into this relativist picture. Languages, for example, are social practices: they are context-dependent, norm-governed activities into which practitioners are educated over time. To speak a language is to be responsible to those norms, to be sensitive to reasons for speaking one way rather than another. If relativism is right, linguistic translation should be impossible, since to translate a sentence from one language into another is to say that moves made in two separate social practices (utterances made in each language) can express one and the same commitment (whatever commitment the sentence expresses, e.g. the belief that it is hot today). Of course, linguistic translation is often imperfect, but the basic fact of translations among languages spoken in very different cultures proves that at least some commitments can be shared cross-culturally in the way understanding and evaluation require.

The fact of translation undermines the 'uniqueness' premise in the relativist account of rational access to others. There simply cannot be a set of commitments unique to a culture. Equally problematic is the 'sameness' premise: the notion that each member of a culture has the same set of commitments. While it is certainly true that people must share a lot of commitments to make sense to each other at all, it cannot be a requirement of their rational access to one another that they share *all* of their commitments. It simply does not follow that they must be on the same page about everything in order to be on the same page about anything. If it did, the only people who *could* talk to each other would never have anything to say. They would already intend and believe all of the same things.[2] On the contrary, even where language and culture are shared, communication must constantly navigate differences between interlocutors' repertoires of commitments. No two people share *exactly* the same perspective on the world.

Our strategy in this chapter is to model cultural interpretation on linguistic translation. To that end, we employ a 'social practice' theory of language, one that approaches language as an aspect of culture rather than of nature.[3] Traditional philosophical theories of language treat semantic concepts like meaning, truth, and reference as basic and then explain the normative dimensions of linguistic practice in terms of them. Social practice theories stand this traditional approach on its head, explaining semantic concepts in terms of the norms implicit in linguistic practice.[4] The social practice theory we have found most useful in our empirical work comes from Robert Brandom, perhaps the most prominent living heir of the great pragmatist tradition. His work embodies the spirit of Dewey in a new age, extending its dominion to issues concerning interpretation in the philosophy of language that Dewey never had to deal with. By making our interpretive practice explicit to us, this kind of work can help us find our way in less familiar settings. It becomes possible to rigorously specify the commitments Islamists share with us. The point is not just better understanding, but highlighting opportunities for cooperation on shared projects as well as developing strategies for more constructive engagement over contested practices, such as female circumcision.

The aim of this chapter, however, is not limited to developing guidelines for cross-cultural interpretation. The guidelines we offer are to be understood as the explicit formulation of commitments that are already implicit in the practice of interpretation. Once articulated, the explicit model of interpretation becomes a powerful analytical tool. It enables us, for example, to analyze the emergence of an integrated Islamist political culture through the interactions of diverse actors with differing sets of commitments. A social practice theory of cultural interpretation can thus *improve* our practice of interpreting other cultures by making that practice explicit to us, and at the same time, *explain* the process by which cultures change, so critical to understanding contemporary Islamism, in terms of interpretive interactions across cultures and within them.

Interpreting other cultures

Commitment and entitlement

The social practice theory of language we employ assumes from the outset that no sentence means in my mouth quite what it does in yours. Communication, then, cannot be a matter of *conveying* things from one person to another, the way I might hand you a glass of water, which is the same glass of water whether in my hand or in yours. Instead, we should think of communication more as a kind of joint endeavor, in which interlocutors enable one another to extract information from their performances through the practice of keeping normative score.[5]

Score is kept through the attribution of commitments and entitlements, understood as normative social statuses. Commitments are things we take to be true in judgment, and try to make true in action. To undertake a commitment is to render oneself liable to assessment in view of its content—whatever it entails, permits, or rules out. If I commit myself to 'being a good Muslim', I thereby undertake a whole host of responsibilities. At the same time, I *entitle* myself to a myriad of further, optional commitments, such as 'pursuing studies in Islamic law' or 'building a mosque for my community'. For every commitment there is the responsibility to do what it requires counterbalanced by the authority to engage in performances it permits, so long as they are not already ruled out by one's other commitments. The circumstances in which one is entitled to undertake a given commitment, and the consequences that follow from undertaking it, are both a function of the other commitments that one has already undertaken, or in other words, a function of one's *context*. Funds saved for the pilgrimage might, for example, quite properly be diverted to the care of a sick child for whom one has assumed responsibility. Grasp of a commitment's content is thus practical mastery of the pattern of inferences linking contexts to consequences as premises and conclusions in this way (a "practical pattern" hereafter).

Acknowledgment and consequence

Which commitments apply to us is a matter of our authority. We are responsible only for the ones that we acknowledge. But the content we have bound ourselves to cannot be up to us in the same way. Otherwise, as Wittgenstein says, "whatever is going to seem right to me is right. And that only means that here we can't talk about 'right'."[6] As Brandom sums up this crucial point: "One must bind *oneself*, but one must also *bind* oneself."[7]

To acknowledge a commitment is to entitle others to keep your score in relation to it. This acknowledgement may be made explicitly with words, or implicitly with actions. In acknowledging a commitment we may sign on to far more than we realize.[8] Signaling your intention to join a group of fellow Muslims praying entails an obligation to perform the ablutions in an acceptable way. Members of the group with whom you intend to pray will feel entitled to comment should you, for example, simply wet your hand and wipe your foot with it rather than putting your foot under the water in the sink.

This critical disjuncture between what one thinks one is responsible for and what one has actually committed oneself to is rooted in the way score is kept on one's behavior. Each scorekeeping perspective is double-barreled: it tracks both the actor's *conception* of a given commitment and the *actual content* of that commitment according to that scorekeeper. The actor's *conception* of the commitment, rather than the commitment itself, is what will causally influence her dispositions to judge and to act in different circumstances. Those she recognizes as scorekeepers—other good Muslims, Islamic scholars, leaders or simply other members of her particular Islamic community—specify the actual, *consequential* content of what she has committed herself to from their distinctive perspectives, i.e. in context of the facts[9] they are committed to.[10] In order for that consequential content to have any bearing on what she actually is responsible for, of course, the commitment they attribute to her must be the right one (e.g. she must indeed be committed to 'being a good Muslim').

Anaphora

However, if what we have said so far about communication and content is correct, how can they attribute commitments to her at all? No two people have the same conception of any commitment. No two people express the practical pattern of 'tying one's shoes' with exactly the same behavior, let alone 'being a good Muslim' or 'defending human rights'. To consider a mundane example, if you make me a cup of coffee, there will be a whole host of descriptions, specifications, and ways of indicating the coffee that each of us could substitute for "the coffee" in inferences but the other could not ("the thing in my hands", "the last place I saw that fly", from your standpoint; "the thing I'm looking at", "the fifth and final cup I'll have today", from mine). How, then, can we count as talking about the *same* cup of coffee?

The answer is what linguists call "anaphora", the ability of one term to inherit the substitutions appropriate for another.[11] When you say "Here's some coffee", and I say "Thanks! Is *it* decaf?" my "it" picks up all of the correct substitutions for "coffee", whatever the correct substitutions may turn out to be.[12] In recognizing my use of "it" as being about the same thing as your use of "coffee", you are regarding both uses as subject to the same responsibilities. Taking one another to be 'playing the same game' becomes our basis for understanding our differences as differences in how we each play it. Anaphora allows us to stipulate that we are talking about one and the same thing, grasping the same content at different places. It is then up to us to see how much sense we can make of each other on that basis. By wielding the thing we are grasping, making judgments that lead to other judgments and to actions with results, we will both come away with a firmer grasp than we started with, no matter on how little we may ultimately agree.[13] To grasp this important concept, it may be helpful to consider one-sided cases, situations in which one picks up an 'anaphoric chain' without knowing anything about the thing that anchors it. Brandom uses the example of walking in on a conversation in which a stranger is being denounced and saying "If *he* did that, he deserves whatever he gets." Even though you may know nothing about the "*he*" you are talking about, you will have made yourself responsible to the facts about him and a debate can ensue if the other people disagree with your assertion.[14]

Noura, from Egypt, may disagree with Iman, from Morocco, about how to calculate what one owes for the *zakat* [obligatory alms], but through anaphora she can still attribute a commitment to 'paying the *zakat*' to Iman, securing common ground for their discussion. Her attribution will reflect the double-barreled structure of her scorekeeping perspective, specifying the commitment in the context of her own other commitments in the first barrel, and in the context of the other commitments she attributes to Iman in the second: "Iman believes <u>of</u> the *zakat* <u>that</u> **it** is unnecessary to include the value of one's jewelry in calculating what one should pay." The *of*-clause in this sentence specifies the content from Noura's point of view, establishing what Iman's belief is *about*, what standard it is responsible to as a representation (according to Noura). The *that*-clause specifies the same content from (what Noura takes to be) Iman's point of view—it is the representation to be assessed.[15]

Anaphora is the lifeblood of interpretation. It puts other people on our map, situating their words and deeds in a geography of possible topics and purposes (i.e. possible *commitments*). Nearly effortless in familiar settings, anaphora can be exhausting and frustrating when we are interpreting far from home.

Grasping the unfamiliar

Living in a culture quite different from one's own often involves a passage from a sense of certainty about what is going on to a state of despair in which that initial certainty is understood to have been an illusion. Rabinow described this process in his classic *Reflections on Fieldwork in Morocco*:

> In the early stages of fieldwork, the anthropologist operates with his own version of 'naive consciousness'. The reality 'out there' seems so concrete, so easy to gather in. My exhilaration during the initial months in the village was tied to this sureness. There was not much to interpret; the facts seemed to speak for themselves ... Actually, what the 'facts' demonstrated was far from obvious.[16]

To say that we observe *behavior* when we interpret may be somewhat misleading. In familiar contexts, we simply observe commitments—we see actions, hear claims.[17] When we enter unfamiliar contexts, however, the commitments we are initially disposed to attribute will very often be the wrong ones. Part of what one must acquire in order to interpret other cultures properly is the ability to *pause* these initial dispositions, so that we can step back and recontextualize what we observe in a more appropriate practical pattern. The pattern one conjectures for this purpose can of course then be revised and reshaped in light of subsequent observations. The price of failing to take the first step, pressing the normative pause button and putting one's interpretive dispositions temporarily on hold, is all too familiar. Failure to take the second step, recontextualizing the behavior in a practical pattern, however, leads to problems just as serious.

We can consider each step ('pause' and 'recontextualize') as it applies to interpretations of linguistic practice in order to shed light on the interpretation of other kinds of social practice. If we hear an Arabic speaker utter "*ana asif*" and interpret her noises as though she were trying to speak English, we might conclude she was saying something like "Anna as if". Falling into this first trap, regarding our familiar contexts as all of the contexts that there are, is characteristic of moral absolutism. Falling into this trap not just in moral cases, but in general, would be 'normative absolutism'. Neither is helpful in understanding others.

To perform the first step successfully would be to realize that she was not speaking English. To stop there, though, would leave us only with a noise ('ah-nah ah-siff'). We would have gone from interpreting her as a very odd person who seems to think our name is Anna to not interpreting her at all. This second trap, pausing but not recontextualizing, is what we would do if we took the advice of relativism seriously. The scope of the resulting paralysis would depend on the type of relativism we bought into (cultural, moral, conceptual, etc.).

Rabinow avoids both traps, endorsing a *via media* between them:

> Taking the external world as it appears is an essential first step; it is gratifying, easy to hold onto, but inadequate ... The passage from broad assertions ... to individual cases must be mediated by particular determinations, because otherwise there is no way to differentiate one village from the next, one country from another.[18]

These 'particular determinations' are how interpretation alters our conceptions of our commitments. It turns out that under certain circumstances *"ana asif"* can be the right way to apologize. Interpreting people from other cultures is at least initially interpreting them just as though they were members of our own, projecting our commitments into their practices. What legitimates such projection is the open texture of the content of commitments, the possibility of always specifying that content in greater detail, and in doing so discovering new branches of the practical patterns it contains. The content of a commitment is whatever it *ought* to be, and thus can always turn out to be somewhat different than we had imagined.

When interlocutors anaphorically stipulate that they are holding one and the same commitment at different places, they are treating what they are holding—two separate chunks of content—as conceptions of a single content that contains both, as appearances of a single thing from different points of view. Taking it that a commitment is held in common but expressed differently thus involves *undertaking* an additional interpretive commitment. Under the aegis of the common commitment, differences in expression may be further interpreted either as genuine disagreements or as reflecting mere differences in context (i.e. as entitled by other things we attribute to them). Thus there is a certain degree of art involved in our decision to interpret someone either as sharing a commitment of ours but differing in how she expresses it, or as doing something else entirely. There can be no guidelines to determine such decisions for us in advance. Going one direction rather than the other in our interpretation decides the normative orientation we adopt towards their behavior. When they adopt this same normative orientation towards our behavior as well, a scorekeeping relationship will have been founded, enabling disagreements over the expression of shared commitments to be ironed out over time through the process of giving and asking for reasons.

Translation between languages exemplifies this practice. Translating a foreign expression into one's native tongue equates a commitment from one's home practice with a commitment in the linguistic practice being interpreted (e.g. 'saying "I'm sorry"' = 'saying *"ana asif"*'). The purport of the translation is that both expressions belong to a single practical pattern, that both are included in the content of a single commitment ('apologizing when appropriate'). The circumstances in which one would speak Arabic figure in the pattern as dictating when it is appropriate to say *"ana asif"* rather than "I'm sorry". Performing such a translation, we endorse the unfamiliar activity by assimilating it to the practical pattern entailed by the shared commitment, a pattern now revealed through the accommodation of the new material to be slightly different than we had conceived it. The translation remains a valid one even if it turns out that there are differences in when it is appropriate to apologize in each cultural context. These additional differences are incorporated as yet new wrinkles in the overall pattern of 'apologizing when appropriate'. If such differences continue to pile up, however, our translation may be called into question. And so it is with attributions in general.

Translations between our own commitments and those we are trying to under-stand may be suggested directly by the people we are interpreting. When the centrist Islamist Fahmy Huwaidy claims that commitment to *Shari'a* already is commit-ment to a constitutional separation of powers, he is saying that a commitment he shares with his Islamist audience ('implementing *Shari'a*', a sub-commitment of 'being a good Muslim') already entails a commitment that most Westerners acknowledge ('judicially restraining executive power', a sub-commitment of 'being a good Western liberal').[19] In other words, he is attributing to himself (and thereby acknowledging) a commitment we also acknowledge. Whether or not we should interpret him as entitled to this attribution depends on how it squares with the evidence. It is characteristic of New Islamist intellectuals in particular that they do a certain amount of the hermeneutic heavy lifting for us, self-attributing a variety of democratic, humanitarian, and liberal commitments. Of course, the propriety of these self-attributions cannot be taken on faith, a point the New Islamists certainly realize and articulate clearly in their uncompromising criti-cisms, for example, of the deeply flawed Islamic regimes that have ruled in the Sudan and Afghanistan.[20]

Anaphora is our cross-cultural passport. If we can make sense of others, and they of us, by regarding certain commitments as shared, we will have achieved through the difficult work of interpretation, commitment by commitment, the same entitlements members of that culture enjoy by default. Over the course of such a relationship, conceptions on both sides of the equation will change to vari-ous degrees as new chunks of content are integrated into the familiar practical patterns. For as long as it lasts, a scorekeeping relationship entitles each party to require reasons from the other for judgments and actions. It also obligates both to change their behavior whenever it cannot be justified. In this way, scorekeeping tends to iron out problematic discrepancies over time.

There is nothing about this process that necessarily involves the imposition of one's own values on the culture of another. The content of the commitment to *istikhlaf* ['acting as God's regent on earth'] as understood by an Islamic centrist may turn out to include a number of behaviors that belong also to the content of the commitment to 'promoting human dignity and liberty' as conceived by a Western liberal. When Fahmy Huwaidy indeed says that "[economic] backward-ness is a sin because it means a neglect of the duty of *istikhlaf*", he is not submit-ting to a foreign culture, but simply confirming that one and the same commitment ('overcoming economic backwardness') can have its score kept in more than one jurisdiction.[21]

Critics of our approach may point to the mistaken idea that Islam is implicitly socialist, propounded by the Soviets in their proxy rule of Afghanistan, or to the mistaken idea of the American government, in its effort to break that rule, that the mujahideen were implicitly Jeffersonian democrats. Our position though is *not* that Islam and other non-Western cultures can be whatever we want them to be. The point is rather that cross-cultural attributions of commitments are indeed correct some of the time, and that a better understanding of their mechanics will allow us to get them right more often. The lesson to draw from the failed

Brezhnevian and Reaganite interpretations of Islamism is that you cannot immediately infer that broader commitments are shared from the fact that more concrete, particular commitments are shared. A commitment of theirs that we acknowledge may well fit into a broader pattern of theirs that we do not. For most of the mujahideen, 'opposing Soviet rule' was a sub-commitment of 'opposing foreign rule', not of 'opposing authoritarian rule', as some Reagan-era officials seem to have hoped.

In addition, we have to be able to tell the difference between a commitment to solving a problem in one's own case and a commitment to solving that *type* of problem whenever it occurs. Haddad's commitment to having a beautiful view of the Nile may find expression in violence to the Nile-views of others. This distinction should not obscure, however, the tendency of personal commitments to elide into more universal ones. If a woman in Cairo is committed to 'leaving the country without a man's permission', a lot of the normative infrastructure is already in place for her to become committed to 'getting Egyptian women the right to leave the country without a man's permission'. In all cases, we must be ready to revise our attributions in the face of new evidence.

Interpreting behavior we object to

The same interpretive strategy should be followed even when we object to the behavior we are interpreting. In objecting to behavior, we are in effect denying that it satisfies the commitment it is classified under, that it defeats its purpose.[22] To do so, it is necessary to specify the commitment it defeats. Clearly the commitment must be one that the actor herself has undertaken, either by acknowledging it directly or by acquiring it consequentially. The more subtle point here is that the commitment must also be one—or be contextualized in one—that we acknowledge too.

This follows from what we have already shown about interpretation. It is only by attributing commitments that we can locate observed behavior in a practical pattern that suggests, however fallibly and prospectively, what the actor will go on to do in subsequent contexts or would have done in counterfactual ones. However, no amount of behavioral evidence can settle exactly what set of commitments it is appropriate to attribute.[23] The only commitments we can use to classify the observed behavior are those that would govern our own behavior in the same *type* of context. Properly classifying the context at hand under a general type can involve translation and the assimilation of novel contexts to already-specified practical patterns in the way that we have seen. The point of such translations and assimilations is, however, to bring what we observe under commitments we acknowledge as governing our behavior in contexts of that type. It is only by contextualizing the observed behavior in our own commitments that we gain rational access to its actor.

Attributions of commitments we object to, like 'robbing the bank', draw their content from attributions of commitments that we acknowledge. The more abstract the shared commitments, the weaker our understanding of the behavior in question. We will better understand a commitment to 'robbing the bank' that we can contextualize in 'preventing one's family from starving' than we will a commitment to 'robbing the bank' that we can contextualize only in 'improving one's lot'. But there will always be some attributable commitment we acknowledge in relation to which behavior we object to can be critiqued.

To take a more controversial example, we could attempt to gain rational access to Muslims who practice female circumcision by understanding it as a way of trying to prepare young women for a healthy adult life. In other words, we could classify instances of this practice under a commitment to 'preparing [a young Muslim woman] for a healthy and balanced adult life', and ascribe the belief "of female circumcision <u>that</u> it prepares young Muslim women for a healthy and balanced adult life". Certainly there will be a tremendous amount of difference between the substitutions we as opponents and they as supporters of the practice would make ("female circumcision" = "female genital mutilation" = "a practice that does irreparable damage to the adolescent psyche", etc.), but by formulating the ascription in this way, we have undertaken to regard ourselves and them as grasping a single commitment, and thus securing in principle a common topic for discussion and debate.

In arguing against female genital mutilation (FGM), there are then at least two tacks we could legitimately take. We could, as just rehearsed, attempt to found a scorekeeping relationship on mutual commitment to 'raising healthy and well-adjusted young women', and then, using arguments from medicine or developmental psychology, demonstrate the incompatibility of 'practicing female genital mutilation' with 'raising healthy and well-adjusted young women'. If this attempt failed, it would not be because cross-cultural argument is inherently illicit. Insofar as the commitment to 'raising healthy and well-adjusted young women' is indeed shared, arguments against FGM from medicine and developmental psychology are mutually pertinent. A more rhetorically effective route might be to support centrist Islamists like Selim al-Awa in their efforts to demonstrate that 'practicing female circumcision' is incompatible with 'being a good Muslim', insofar as it is not Islamic in origin and puts the woman's health at risk.[24] These Islamist exegetical efforts are to be classified under the commitment 'putting a stop to female genital circumcision'. Whatever route we take, our decision would be driven by considerations about practical efficacy, not the theoretical possibility of cross-cultural understanding.

Interpreting terrorism

To fail to supply this broader background is to pause without recontextualizing. We will then be left with only the noise and motion of the behavior we observe. This may be enough if the observed behavior is all we care about (say, if someone is coming at us with a knife). Whenever prediction and counterfactual reasoning are involved, however, rational access is a must. It might seem that an alternative solution would be to locate observed behavior in mere regularities of behavior that extend beyond what we can see. However, this just adds to the mess, increasing complexity without adding clarity. Regularities, after all, can only be extrapolated over observed types of context, observed sets of causal conditions. To say of someone smoking a cigarette on her balcony at 4 o'clock in the afternoon that she will smoke a cigarette on her balcony every day at 4 o'clock in the afternoon is not yet to suggest anything about the other types of context in which she might smoke, or about what she would do if her balcony collapsed during the night, or if she ran out of cigarettes. Western views of terrorism, especially those expressed in political discourse, exemplify this alternative solution and reveal its limitations.

An objection at this point might be that terrorist behaviors are not rational. To treat them as though they were, on this view, is at least to misunderstand them and at worst to attempt to cast them in a favorable light. However, to characterize an actor as rational in the sense that rational access requires is merely to regard that actor as sensitive to reasons. It is not to say that the reasons they are sensitive to are the right ones, or that the outcome they lead to is a good one. In gaining rational access, we are using the behavioral evidence to gain insight into an agent's commitments by asking what commitments could lead one to produce that behavior. We are not saying that the behavior is correct according to our own commitments, or in other words, that it squares with the facts as we take them to be. The consequence of an ungrounded aversion to interpreting terrorists as rational agents is to deny ourselves a counterfactual supporting analytical framework, one that allows us to extrapolate practical patterns, rather than mere regularities, from the available evidence, and to revise those extrapolations as new evidence comes in. Another route to the same impoverished, non-normative framework is to explain terrorism as the necessary result of some set of causal antecedents.[25] We might label this approach 'polite ethnocentrism'. The politeness of this ethnocentrism consists in the implication that acts of terrorism are not even the *kind* of event on which it is appropriate to keep normative score, in that they result inevitably from the influences to which the terrorists have been subject. If any way of analyzing terrorism can be accused of implicitly defending it, it is this one, insofar as those who commit acts of terror end up effectively exculpated for what they have done. The exculpating causal influences differ from analyst to analyst, some pointing to fundamentalist brainwashing, others to the traumas the West has inflicted. To be clear, our complaint with such analyses is not that they paper over terrorists' free will, but that they impede the genuine insight rational access allows. Human beings are normative creatures, producers and consumers of reasons, actors that take themselves to be bound by their commitments as they conceive them. Any analysis of human behavior that obscures this normative dimension by restricting itself to non-normative vocabulary is a nonstarter.

Another variant of this same non-normative approach attributes commitments only to the very behavior observed. As we have seen, commitments become intelligible to us as such only if contextualized in commitments we acknowledge. If 'blowing up a bus' is interpreted through the context of 'deriving satisfaction from murdering innocent civilians, destroying property, exulting in a culture of death', and so forth, no actual interpretation has been accomplished, no commitments actually attributed. For the second term is just 'blowing up a bus' spelled out in greater detail and stapled onto a tendency to do just that—a *virtus dormitiva*, if there ever was one. When this kind of pseudo-interpretation is put forward in political discourse, the analyst will often attach a disparaging adjective like 'sick' or 'deranged' to the contextualizing commitment they are attempting to employ. However, when we are justified in calling people sick or deranged, as we sometimes are, it is not because we have hit upon a proper interpretation of them. Rather, it is because we are justified in *refusing to try* to interpret them, which is what we are doing when we make such pronouncements.

More sophisticated cases of this error feature contextualizing commitments like 'being in a rage', or 'having a mystical experience'. The latter, invoked by Olivier Roy and Faisal Devji among others, has an air of plausibility when the terrorists are Islamist extremists—these are, after all, fairly religious people.[26,27] Devji even goes so far as to link extremist violence to "Sufism, which has been enjoying a global revival of late."[28] We need to be clear what is going on in such cases. What we have here are not interpretations, but refusals or failures to interpret masquerading as interpretations.

The risk is not simply that we might miss opportunities to get a handle on things, but that we will think that terrorism really is how it seems to be in these interpretive misfires. Devji, for example, concludes that acts of terrorism are "not … political", but rather "complete in themselves", that they "do not represent anything beyond themselves", and are thus "act[s] shorn of all teleology".[29] If this were true, it would be bad news for anyone who thinks more intelligent policy might curb the incidence of terrorism worldwide by reducing the recruitment rate of terrorist groups.

Fortunately, these non- and pseudo-interpretive strategies are not the only ones in play. Scholars such as Robert Pape have shown the power of the genuine interpretive strategy that we have endorsed here, rendering terrorist behaviors intelligible by contextualizing them in shared commitments, enabling predictions and counterfactual reasoning.[30] To be sure, we are not saying human behavior should always be interpreted. Interpretation, however, has uses other than setting us up for dialogue, and refusals and failures to interpret should be acknowledged and recognized as such.

Explaining culture in terms of interpretation

Scorekeeping and cultural integrity

It may seem only natural to say that co-culturalists share a culture by being similar to one another, by behaving in the same way in certain key situations. This, however, cannot be quite right. As the philosopher Michelle Moody-Adams has emphasized,[31] every culture exhibits diversity, inconsistency, and disagreement. Even in a practice as public and as regulated as a language, no two people string their words together in exactly the same way. The differences in question are not simply a matter of behavioral dispositions misfiring, as when one accidentally writes 'its' instead of 'it's'. They are exhibited systematically. If someone mispronounces Freud as '*Frood*', we have to interpret her utterances of this noise as attempts to do what we would do by saying 'Freud', not just this once, but in general (until someone corrects her). Once we have classified her mispronunciation in this way under a commitment to 'saying "Freud"', we keep score on her claims in relation to what we take the facts about Freud to be. In other words, despite the systematic divergence in her dispositions, she still falls under the relevant norms, is still to be regarded as responsible to a commitment to 'speaking accurately about Freud'. The same goes for malapropisms, odd nicknames, misidentifications, and more.[32] This means that acculturation does not result in shared dispositions to behave and assess behaviors. People can diverge in their dispositions systematically and fairly dramatically and nonetheless count as co-culturalists. If cultures are demarcated by some set of commonalities, the story of demarcation cannot be a purely causal or naturalistic one. The sense in which something is shared must be a normative one.

Co-culturalists share in a culture not by sharing behaviors but by sharing commitments. Though they may differ in their actual concrete expressions of the commitments that constitute their culture, in acknowledging those commitments (perhaps only implicitly) they have made themselves responsible for expressing one and the same normative content. The different conceptions they express are understood in each case to be conceptions of one and the same commitment. And insofar as they recognize one another as members of the same culture, they recognize also a default entitlement to keep each other's score on those commitments, to demand reasons for specific differences between conceptions when those differences show up in practice as problems. The boundaries of the default entitlement to keep score for a particular commitment mark out that commitment's scorekeeping jurisdiction. Members of a culture possessing sufficient authority[33] enjoy a standing entitlement to keep score on other members over a range of sayings and doings that might otherwise seem unrelated. This is what keeps the conversation going, inclining them to reconcile differences in how they carry out the constituent commitments.

A culture on this account is demarcated in much the same way as a language.[34] It is obviously not the case that all Arabs speak Arabic in just the same way, but it is the case that none of them is trying to speak, say, Farsi. The following criticism could thus never get off the ground: "Don't say *min fadlak* because 'saying *min fadlak*' is incompatible with 'speaking Farsi properly'." A criticism of this sort with a fighting chance would be: "Don't say *kebeereen* because 'saying *kebeereen*' is incompatible with 'speaking Arabic properly'; that's not how you pluralize *kebeer*."

It is the jurisdiction of exhortations of this latter type that defines the group "Arabic speakers". What ties this group together is a default entitlement to keep one another's score on 'speaking Arabic properly', rectifying incompatibilities between that commitment and the various conceptions of it they express, through the game of giving and asking for reasons. The practical pattern of 'speaking Arabic properly' does not have to be spelled out explicitly so long as speakers of the language can acknowledge their responsibility to it, and so long as there are ways of deciding in most cases whether or not a given utterance counts as proper Arabic ("See, Naguib Mahfuz uses the same word right here").[35]

Of course, grammar books help to make the pattern explicit (and in practice affect how it is conceived at a given time), but they do not establish it. Grammar books are in principle subject to revision if it can be shown that they fail to capture the pattern—if, say, exemplary contemporary Arabic speakers regularly ignore one of the commitments such books enjoin, or if there are additional commitments they fail to delineate. Though cultural boundaries are on this account determinable, they are at the same time relatively permeable, as we have seen, and can always in principle be redrawn.

Determining the future by arguing about the past

Every expression of a commitment is both determining and determined. No one has ever expressed the commitment you express now in *this* precise context before, and so no one has ever given the commitment *this* precise expression. For the newness of what one does to be justified by the novelty of the context, it cannot really be new at all, but simply the commitment's implicit content brought out "into the explicit light of day".[36] Now that it has been brought out, however, it will form a part of what subsequent expressions will be responsible to. One's authority to extrapolate is bounded by responsibility to past expressions that one recognizes as authoritative—the precedents for what one does now. This responsibility is administered by future users who must evaluate whether one's extrapolation was actually entitled by the commitment. Deciding that it was entitled means treating it as a precedent in their own extrapolations. The basis for this decision is whether the new content one expresses can be seen as implicit in all earlier precedents, read back into past expressions in a recollection of the commitment's history.[37]

This process of recollection legitimates anaphora, enabling interlocutors to classify themselves under one and the same commitment by reading unfamiliar content back into the history of the commitment. The interpersonal process of keeping normative score, whether within a single culture or between different cultures, *determines* the content a commitment will be treated in practice as having. The determination arrived at is the content the commitment must be conceived as having in order for it to count as shared. Though this process is understood retrospectively as the *discovery* of what the commitment had entailed all along, it is nonetheless the case that its occurrence *alters* the content that each party acknowledges, putting each on a path different from the one they otherwise would have taken. This is how cultures change.

This theoretical backdrop is helpful for interpreting Islamist disputes over *ijtihad* [Qur'anically sanctioned interpretation of sacred texts]. What distinguishes authoritative interpretation (*fiqh*) from illicit innovation (*bid'a*) is the propriety of the retrospective integration offered as rationale. Properly interpreting the Qur'an and *hadith* [sayings of the Prophet] is not a matter of simply saying in Islamic language whatever one would like other Muslims to believe.

Properly interpreting the Qur'an and *hadith* requires "a huge effort of the mind", explains the centrist Muhammad al-Ghazali, so much so that interpreters regard themselves as "deficient explorers" using "limited abilities" in the hopes of making it possible for "others to go further in serving the Qur'an and uncovering its greatness and glories".[38]

The centrist stance on *ijtihad* is to insist that proper extrapolation of prior content to new contexts requires the hard work of *translation* at the level of what one acknowledges as entailed in a particular case. As Kamal Abul Magd explains, "Everything else is open to question so that *Shari'a* can respond to changing conditions."[39] Recall how the extrapolation of 'apologizing when appropriate' from Anglophone to Egyptian contexts entails a translation between the commitments to 'saying "I'm sorry"' and 'saying "*ana asif*."' Likewise, through *ijtihad*, Islamist commitments turn out to entail translations between the sub-commitments acknowledged in prior contexts and those acknowledged in new ones. The argument in such cases, as in constitutional scholarship in the US, is that the only way to preserve the integrity of a commitment is to counterbalance changes in context with changes in our behavior.

The conservative stance, by contrast, is to maintain old behaviors in the face of contextual change. The same sub-commitments are to be acknowledged even though the consequences they entail in new contexts are different. What typically underlies this stance is a distrust of translation because of the authority it accords the translators. Conservatism and anti-intellectualism thus go hand in hand. However, reluctance to recognize translators as authoritative does not save one from the need to translate. 'Riding a horse to work' has different consequences in New York in 2009 than it had in 1809. Asserting 'Taking the train to work' as the appropriate translation of the 1809 New York commitment to the 2009 New York context involves integrating both into a retrospective narrative of the content that 'getting to work in a reasonable fashion' has turned out to entail. Asserting instead that 'riding a horse to work' is what 'getting to work in a reasonable fashion' entails in *both* contexts still involves translation because the *consequences* of 'riding a horse to work' in New York have changed from 1809 to 2009. Recall that in acknowledging a commitment, one undertakes not only what one acknowledges but its consequences as well. Conservative and centrist interpreters are thus equally saddled with new content to integrate into the old.

In engaging in *ijtihad*, a *faqih* [Islamic scholar trained in *fiqh*] is responsible both to the past and to the future. The decisions of past *fuqaha* that he cites as instructive exercise authority over his interpretation by displaying content that must be integrated in recollection. Future *fuqaha*, in turn, exercise authority over his interpretation insofar as they can decide whether or not to employ his interpretation in justifying interpretations of their own. It is only insofar as they integrate his applications of commitments into the recollections that underwrite their own applications of them that he exercises any actual authority at all:[40]

> Despite all of this constraint, there is genuine room for choice ... depending on which prior commitments are taken as precedential and which respects of

similarity and difference are emphasized. After all ... all there is to the content ... in question is what has been put into it by the applications of it that have actually been endorsed or rejected.[41]

In this way, the authority to determine the future is fought for on the battlefield of the past.

Contingency and cultural change

Recollection makes merely strategic and parochial moves available as precedents to subsequent scorekeepers by giving them a normative shape. What a *faqih* is authorized to do is circumscribed by the entitlements that go with the commitments attributed to him. Even if his interpretation of an important concept, such as martyrdom or jihad, was motivated by irrelevant facts, such as rivalry with a peer, its scorekeeping significance will depend on the justifications he is able to provide for it, the collateral commitments he is able to marshal in its defense, and the evolution of the conceptions of those commitments in the period subsequent to his decision.[42]

All commitments, no matter how mundane, are subject to a process of retrospective rationalizing, attaining normative content through their use over time. The dynamics determining how interlocutors specify the content of 'a fair price for fish' in a given case are probably better described in the language of game theory than that of disinterested conceptual investigation. But although the moves each player makes in the game of giving and asking for reasons may just be the ones with the highest payoffs under prevailing conditions, responsibility to the concepts of fairness, price, and fish determines the moves available to each player, since it will be in the interest of each player not to let the others exceed their entitled authority (just as it is in the interest of chess players not to let opponents move the rook diagonally). The content of players' acknowledged commitments thus determines the landscape of possible outcomes of the game available at any given time. It does this, moreover, not only through the players' conceptions of those commitments, but through the conceptions of other scorekeepers not involved in the original game who may assess its outcome. This holds even if a player regards the moves she makes as insincere—as concessions made only to push things along or as attempts to sway the other player through effective rhetoric. The form her moves take in the retrospective integrations of subsequent players is the contribution they make to the determination of the contents they involve. It is their legacy to later rounds of the game. Understanding this process allows us to grasp the proper significance of observations like the following quotation from Roy:

> Islam is recast as a strategic factor only *post hoc*, when there is a coincidence between ethnic and religious affiliations; for example Muslim Chechens versus orthodox Russians, or Christian Molucans against Muslim immigrants from Borneo.[43]

And again: "The reference to Islam is everywhere and nowhere; it is diluted, pragmatically put forward for any purpose, ostensibly expressed in dress and speech and instrumentalised in courts."[44] Observations such as these need not entail the conclusion that Islam is on the decline. As Brandom explains:

> Genealogical explanations ... are always in principle available. That is, one can find causal explanations that do not cite norms, rules, or principles, appealing instead to ... factors such as collateral political concerns, contingencies of class background or training in one school rather than another, and so on. But if [subsequent scorekeepers] can find a principle implicit in prior [moves] that is brought out into the light of day in further refinement by the [move in question], that [move] can nonetheless be seen as governed by that authoritative norm.[45]

The importance of Islam as a global culture is not that it settles in advance what all Muslims will say and do by motivating their behavior, but that it enables particular Muslims to settle what they are responsible for saying and doing by keeping score on one another. Cultures cannot be specified in purely non-normative terms. What co-culturalists share is not a matter of their having been programmed through upbringing to all behave in the same way. The kind of determination that pertains to culture, therefore, is not causal but normative. It is neither static nor given all at once but rather both dynamic and ongoing.

What we are describing, in however cursory a fashion, are the dynamics of cultural change. To offer a rough analogy to biological evolution, conceptions of commitments: dispositions to express them as genotypes: phenotypes. The analogue of sexual reproduction, with its standing possibility of mutation, is the interface between distinct scorekeeping perspectives (distinct repertoires of commitments), with the acknowledgment of content as the analogue of birth. The fidelity of conceptions to the commitments they are conceptions of is like the fitness of an organism to its environment. The game of giving and asking for reasons, in specifying the content of the commitments in play, causes each side's conception to develop in a somewhat different direction than it otherwise would, which in turn alters the practical dispositions to express the repertoires of resultant conceptions in behavior. The comparative degree to which each side revises its conceptions will be a function of the balance of authority and responsibility between them.

There are of course many ways such interfaces can play out, redrawing the boundaries of the scorekeeping jurisdictions that give each culture its distinctive shape. If the resultant conceptions are maintained and nurtured, but limited in jurisdiction more or less to the original parties to the interface, we have what linguists call Creolization. At the other end of the spectrum would be full integration of the two cultures, with the jurisdictions of the new, mutually endorsed conceptions encompassing all of the normative terrain formerly possessed separately by each. (*Something* along these lines happened in late antiquity with the integration of classical and Hebraic cultures—the blending of Athens and

Jerusalem—though the case is far too complex to be done justice here.) In between these two extremes lie various forms of partial integration of one group to the other's jurisdictions or of both to each.

Islam as a culture

It has become a commonplace in books about Islam and Islamic societies to warn against the tendency to gloss over variety, to generalize "processes that are flexible, always changing, and contested"[46] into a unitary, transnational Islam. This talk of 'many Islams' is salutary as far as it goes, providing a much-needed corrective to the images of a homogeneous Muslim world we find all throughout the Western media and political discourse. It is critical, however, that in our effort to properly represent the heterogeneity of the Islamic world, the diversity of commitments different Muslims actually acknowledge, that we do not lose track of the unity that's there as well, the way that Islam ties the whole vast terrain together.

The account of culture on offer here allows us to accommodate heterogeneity without obscuring unity. The overlapping scorekeeping jurisdictions that constitute Islam as a culture are explicitly integrated in the normative status of 'being a good Muslim'. The unified jurisdiction of this overarching commitment entitles diverse Muslims across the world to keep each other's score in all areas of life, to object to behaviors not merely because they are displeasing, but because they are incompatible with commitments regarded as shared. That an Egyptian Muslim may be unable to persuade a Moroccan Muslim how much to pay for the *zakat* is beside the point. What matters is that the Moroccan, insofar as she sees herself and the Egyptian both as Muslims, will treat the other as entitled in principle to keep her score, and regard herself responsible for justifying her behavior in the terms of their shared Islamic jurisdiction.

This default entitlement to keep score is what gives the Islamic world the degree of cultural integrity that it exhibits, rendering events at any location potentially relevant to every other, and encouraging Muslims to reach across borders and engage one another on their differences, whether it be Ibn Battuta administering *Shari'a* in the Maldives in the fourteenth century, or the Egyptian Islamist journalist Fahmy Huwaidy writing about Iran today, or centrist Islamists around the world condemning the attacks of September 11th on Islamic grounds.

The concept of scorekeeping jurisdiction makes it much easier to understand the power wielded by centrist Islamists in particular, and the threat they pose in the eyes of authoritarian regimes.[47] It is not of course that they have raw numbers or firepower or even necessarily mass support. Rather, it is their authority to specify a local scorekeeping jurisdiction within the broader jurisdiction of Islam that covers much more ground than an authoritarian state ever could. Huwaidy, discussing the Mubarak regime's response to extremist violence in Egypt, points to this difference in scorekeeping authority when he says: "The security authorities addressed the problem according to their jurisdiction only ... because the underlying social crises are the responsibility of political and civil institutions which were absent."[48] The Egyptian government, in its arbitrary brutality, cannot convincingly acknowledge many of the commitments on which it would like to keep its citizens' score. Though it can imprison and execute, it cannot bring about changes in the violent extremists' commitments. Brute force alone will not disabuse the extremists of their extremism. What you need to do that is scorekeeping on commitments that they themselves acknowledge.

For some terrorists at least, and much more so for the Muslim publics they appeal to for support, the commitment to extremist violence hinges on the belief that it is entailed by commitment to 'being a good Muslim'. Where this is so, extremism will tend to be rejected if the relevant incompatibilities can be demonstrated. Extremist sub-commitments are read into the content of 'being a good Muslim' through recollections that systematically fail to integrate *hadith*, Qur'anic passages, and interpretations of them that the Muslim publics they appeal to are at least implicitly committed to recognizing as authoritative. Extremist interpretations of the Qur'an can thus be revealed as incompatible with the acknowledged interpretive commitments of their proponents, in that their recollections fail to integrate text and interpretations that they are not entitled to exclude. If an extremist group ignores or rejects the interpretive authorities recognized by its audience, it weakens its power to recruit. In an article comparing extremist groups in Egypt, David Zeidan notes that *Takfir wal-Hijra* "repudiated both *fiqh* and *hadith*, accepting only the Qur'an from traditional Islam ... This ... ensured that Takfir would remain more of a cult than a revolutionary organization."[49] To avoid Takfir's fate, *Jama'at al-Jihad* "had to argue, using specific incidents and some commentators from Islamic history, that killing Muslims and overthrowing a Muslim-led government was the correct interpretation of Islam".[50] But to make such arguments is necessarily to acknowledge interpretive commitments on which score may be kept. Thus extremist groups must purport to recollect their tradition correctly if they want to have any sway at all, but in so doing they open themselves up to interpretive challenges.

To have the authority necessary to challenge these recollections, however, the people you are trying to persuade must be entitled to attribute the relevant commitments to you. Though it might be possible to imagine very circumscribed scenarios in which non-Muslims would be entitled to keep score on commitments to interpreting the Qur'an on the basis, say, of broader exegetical commitments, for practical argumentative purposes it is just too long a walk to get from the attribution of those broader commitments to their acknowledgment and then to the demonstration of their incompatibility with the extremist interpretive commitments in question.

Centrist Islamists are better positioned to make such arguments, and so in this context supporting their important work may be one way to express the commitments against extremism we share with them.[51] Centrists like Muhammad al-Ghazali have indeed succeeded at just this kind of argument. In a 1994 interview on Egyptian television, Abdul Baqi, the so-called repentant terrorist, described how Ghazali's critique of the recollections offered by extremist thinkers like Qutb and Maududi led him to break with the militant group he had joined:

> I knew the Quraish as unbelievers who had done such great harm to the Prophet that he had been forced to flee. Yet [as Ghazali pointed out] he still returned their wealth. I went through other books and confirmed that the incident really happened in this way. At that point, I was certain that we were doing the wrong thing.[52]

The Egyptian government had arranged the interview in the hopes that Abdul Baqi's testimony would support their portrayal of the extremists as lawless and corrupt, which it did. What was unintentionally revealed, however, was that the remedy for these ills was something the regime itself could not provide.

Thirty or forty years ago, before the statist secular project in the Middle East had been discredited, it might have been possible for the Egyptian state to keep score on 'doing what's best for Egypt' or 'improving the lives of the country's least well off'. However, the regime has long since lost the authority to attribute these commitments to itself. Today, few believe that the Egyptian state even knows how to deliver on them (let alone that it is attempting to do so). The weakness of the Egyptian state shows itself in the extent to which it controls and manipulates official Islamic institutions, hoping to gain Islamic legitimacy. These propagandizing efforts are, however, transparent and ineffective, as for example the claims of establishment Islamic figures like Shaikh Tantawi, Grand Mufti of al-Azhar that "Egypt has an Islamic state;" though it may "not have a religious party or a political religion ... [it] does not accept the separation of religion from politics".[53] The domesticated Islam of the state has no chance of stealing the thunder of independent or movement Islamists. The regime will never be able to out-Islamize the Islamists.

The centrist Islamist discourse of the New Islamists easily trumps the authority of statist rhetoric through its moral and intellectual capacity to integrate more types of content, keep score authoritatively on more commitments, and hence, potentially regulate a larger portion of Egyptian life than can the state. When centrists call for inclusiveness, recognizing a greater variety of commitments as compatible with Islam and urging tolerance of a greater variety of perspectives, they are expanding their scorekeeping jurisdiction and weakening those around it. When Qaradawi says, "All actions of increasing productivity are acts of worshiping God",[54] or when Kamal Abul Magd says, "God protects the expression of opinion from any aggression",[55] or when Ghazali says "Islam is defeated in the area of pharmaceuticals",[56] we should understand this as centrist Islamists holding Egyptians responsible in ways the state cannot. For an authoritarian regime facing a crisis of legitimacy the long-run threat of terrorism pales in comparison. The outcome of these games of giving and asking for reasons will be codified as the content to which future Muslims will regard themselves responsible. In this way, conversations going on around the world right now are normatively determining the future of Islam.

Conclusion

Interpretation is keeping normative score. Its aim is rational access to others. By employing a social practice theory of language, we can use translation between languages as a paradigm for cross-cultural interpretation. Specifying the mechanics of interpretation along these lines shows how we can make sense of other people in terms of commitments we share with them. Interlocutors regard one another as sharing commitments by *stipulating that* they are talking about, or acting towards, one and the same thing, and then seeing how much sense they can make of each other on that basis. What allows them to do this is the *open texture* of what commitments entail in practice, the standing possibility of discovering new normative content as having been implicit in a commitment all along.

Keeping normative score provides a powerful framework for extrapolating predictions and counterfactuals from observed behavior. We have argued that the only way to apply this framework to behavior we consider objectionable is to contextualize it in commitments we acknowledge. The fallibility and revisability of this framework save it from paternalism, and the only alternative to using it is to regard the behaviors in question as mere natural phenomena. With this conclusion in place, we applied it to the analysis of terrorism, contrasting non- and pseudo-interpretive strategies with the sort of genuine normative scorekeeping deployed by analysts like Robert Pape.

We then transformed this model of interpretation into a tool for the analysis of what cultures are and how they change. Cultures cannot be analyzed into shared behavioral dispositions or regularities. Specifying what co-culturalists share in sharing a culture requires a vocabulary that fundamentally involves normative terms. Distinguishing separate cultures can in certain respects be modeled on distinguishing separate linguistic communities. Scorekeeping can be for theories of cultural change what sexual reproduction is for theories of biological evolution. Instead of genotypes and phenotypes we have conceptions of commitments and dispositions to express those conceptions in practice. The outcome of "the game of giving and asking for reasons" is often to change players' conceptions of what their commitments entail. Players articulate these changes as the explicit revelation of content that had been implicit in their commitments all along. They do this by reading the new content back into a privileged set of prior expressions of the commitment in question, treating those prior expressions as *precedents* for the behavior they are justifying now. In this way, whatever contingent causes and strategic motivations may influence each player's moves in the game, what gets passed down to subsequent games is the rational form those moves exhibit as precedents in the reasons put forward by subsequent players to justify moves of their own. The Islamic scholarly practice of *ijtihad* exemplifies this process. This model of cultural integrity and change provides a unique perspective on Islam as a culture, one that recognizes that there are 'many Islams' without losing sight of their unity, and that appreciates the *post hoc* character of Islamic rationalizations of actions in politics and social life without seeing this as a symptom of decline.

***

When it comes to interpreting people from other cultures, we are on the same justificatory footing as we are in interpreting people from our own. It is an interpretive endeavor (masked though it may be by habit, coercion, and authority) to say ever that *any* commitment is shared. No two people do anything in precisely the same way. Scorekeeping allows them to manage and negotiate the areas in which they differ and build upon the areas in which they do not. If it is unjustified to mix it up morally with conversation partners from other cultures, it is unjustified to mix it up over any kind of conduct with anyone else at all, or even, to be really puritanical about it, to turn our attention to our own behavior, since the self judging is no longer precisely the same as the self being judged. What makes scorekeeping justified is that it is consensual.[57] This is how norms mate.

Notes

1 Following Robert Brandom's use of this term. See Robert Brandom, *Making It Explicit: Reasoning, Representing, and Discursive Commitment*, Cambridge, MA: Harvard University Press, 1994.
2 Ibid, p. 480.
3 The term "social practice theory of language" comes from Richard Rorty, and is used to cover John Dewey, Robert Brandom, the later work of Ludwig Wittgenstein, the early work of Martin Heidegger, Wilfrid Sellars, Donald Davidson and others. See Richard Rorty, "Representation, Social Practice, and Truth", *Philosophical Studies*, 54 (1988): 215–228.
4 Brandom, op. cit., p. xvi.
5 Ibid., p. 479.
6 Ludwig Wittgenstein, *Philosophical Investigations*, Oxford: Blackwell Publishing, 1953, 2001, §258.
7 Robert Brandom, *Animating Ideas of Idealism: A Semantic Sonata in Kant and Hegel*, The 2007 Woodbrige Lectures, 2007. Available at: www.pitt.edu/~Brandom/index.html, Lecture II, p.14. Publication forthcoming as Robert Brandom, *Reason in Philosophy: Animating Ideas*, Cambridge, MA: Harvard University Press, 2009.
8 Brandom, 1994, p. 488.
9 Where facts are just true claims, and so include not only naturalistic facts, but normative facts, aesthetic facts, and so forth too. See Brandom. 1994, pp. 327–330.
10 Ibid., p. 646.
11 See ibid., Chapter 7, *passim*, for a much richer discussion of this topic than we can provide here.
12 Ibid., p. 455.
13 The most important point to recognize is that the anaphoric inheritance of substitution is stipulative and prospective: we do not need to work out just what the correct substitutions are in order to treat the anaphorically dependent "**it**" in "Is **it** decaf?" as being governed by them. Each of us regards the other as responsible to whatever the facts actually are, but each of us can only assess the other in relation the facts as we take them to be. You will assess my use of "**it**" in the context of your own substitutional commitments and I will likewise assess your use of subsequent dependents in the anaphoric chain in the context of mine. Many of the differences in the substitutions we would make can be justified by differences in our respective contexts (e.g. a sensitivity to caffeine, an intention to take a nap). Sometimes, in more complicated situations, we may end up concluding that we were not actually talking about the same thing at all ("No, I was talking about *Gamal* Mubarak, not Hosni"). In between these two scenarios are cases in which we still take ourselves to be talking about the same thing, despite

genuine friction between our respective substitutional commitments. The game of giving and asking for reasons can then be played to try to smooth over our differences.

14 As Brandom writes about this example:

> The speaker may under such circumstances have no idea at all of who it is that is being talked about. The form in which the later claims are expressed nonetheless commits the speaker anaphorically to their being about whoever it is the others were already talking about. That is, a scorekeeper will assess the doxastic commitment [i.e., belief] the latecomer has undertaken according to whatever substitutional commitments that scorekeeper takes to govern the antecedent of the anaphoric tokening 'he'. Anaphora is a mechanism that permits undertaking and attributing commitments concerning objects that one need not be able to specify (nonanaphorically) if challenged. Thus one is not obliged to know or accept the descriptions by means of which the utterer of the anaphoric initiator might pick out the subject with respect to which both are undertaking and attributing commitments ... The anaphoric antecedent is what determines the substitutional commitments relevant to the assessment of the significance of its dependents. But in using a pronoun that is anaphorically dependent on a tokening uttered by another, one is not thereby bound by whatever substitutional commitments the other happens to acknowledge as governing the tokening.
>
> (Brandom, 1994, pp. 486–487)

15 See ibid., Chapter 8, *passim*, which is about this kind of attribution.
16 Paul Rabinow, *Reflections on Fieldwork in Morocco*, Berkeley, CA: University of California Press, 1977, p. 121.
17 Ibid., p. 648. To be clear, we are not endorsing the behaviorist notion that mere behavior (motions of limbs, etc.) is logically or ontologically prior to the actions and claims it is taken to be. The fact that certain of our practices may involve isolating an action's merely behavioral component does not mean that mere behavior is really all there is. Indeed, it is only against the backdrop of a practice of hearing claims, seeing actions, and so forth that a practice of describing mere behavior could so much as be intelligible. The relation between "mere behavior" and "actions/claims/etc." is analogous to the relation between "orphan" and "son/daughter". The analogue of a behaviorist would then be someone who claimed: "We are all orphans fundamentally, it's just that some of us were adopted by our biological parents."
18 Ibid., pp. 121–122.
19 Huwaidy argues that this claim follows from the distinction between *Shari'a* (injunctions from the Qur'an and *Sunna*), which is understood as divinely given, and the *fiqh* (applications of *Shari'a* to cases), which are understood as the product of human ingenuity. (Note the parallel to the distinction between the commitment itself and fallible conceptions of it.)
20 See also E. Sivan, "Why Radical Muslims Aren't Taking Over Governments", in B. Rubin (ed.) *Revolutionaries and Reformers: Contemporary Islamist Movements in the Middle East.* Albany, NY: SUNY Press, 2003.
21 Huwaidy, in *al Ahram*, 26 January 1999.
22 "Objecting to" should in this regard be distinguished from simply disliking or trying to get rid of. The latter attitude does not require bringing people into view as such, instead treating what it targets as in effect mere natural phenomena, whereas "objecting to" makes sense only in application to actions and judgments. If an asteroid were heading towards the earth, one would not *object* to it, but simply try to destroy it.
23 As Brandom points out:

> No matter what a candidate performance whose correctness is at issue is like, and no matter what the history to which it must answer is like, there is *some* way of

specifying the pattern exhibited by those prior performances so as to include the candidate as just what is required to continue the pattern "in the same way".

(Brandom, 1994, p. 208)

24 See al Awa's article in *al-Ahram*, 3 November 1994.
25 Robert Pape traces this strategy for analyzing terrorism to three articles published in a 1990 volume entitled *Origins of Terrorism* (Walter Reich, ed., New York: Cambridge University Press): Jerrold M. Post, "Terrorist Psycho-Logic: Terrorist Behavior as a Product of Psychological Forces"; Martin Kramer, "The Moral Logic of Hizballah"; and Ariel Merari, "The Readiness to Kill and Die: Suicidal Terrorism in the Middle East". As cited by R. Pape (2005), pp. 281–282.
26 Olivier Roy, *Globalized Islam: The Search for a New Umma*, New York: Columbia University Press, 2004, p. 246.
27 Faisal Devji, *Landscapes of the Jihad: Militancy, Morality, Modernity*, Ithaca, NY: Cornell University Press, 2005, pp. 41–49 and 118–130.
28 Ibid.
29 Ibid., p. 120.
30 Robert Pape, *Dying to Win: The Strategic Logic of Suicide Terrorism*, New York: Random House, 2005.
31 M. Moody-Adams, *Fieldwork in Familiar Places: Morality, Culture, & Philosophy*, Cambridge, MA: Harvard University Press, 1997.
32 D. Davidson, 'A Nice Derangement of Epitaphs', 1986, reprinted in D. Davidson, *The Essential Davidson*, ed. E. Lepore and K. Ludwig, Oxford: Oxford University Press, 2001, pp. 251–265.
33 This qualification about sufficient authority serves simply to acknowledge the fact that asymmetries in the balance of authority and responsibility accorded to, for example, adults and children, men and women, masters and slaves, and so forth, limit the franchise of this default entitlement.
34 Or, more strictly put, a dialect.
35 Arguments against the possibility of valid cross-cultural scorekeeping often point to linguistic practice to back up their claims, and it will be worth pausing a moment to distinguish the role linguistic practice plays in our argument from the one it does in theirs. In the work of philosophers such as Lyotard and Rorty, what we have is a *reduction* of normative evaluations in general to evaluations of verbal behavior within linguistic communities (see J-F. Lyotard and J-L. Thebaud, *Just Gaming*, Minneapolis: University of Minnesota Press, 1985, and R. Rorty, *Contingency, Irony, and Solidarity*, Cambridge: Cambridge University Press, 1989). Only people who are trying to speak English can be evaluated in relation to "speaking English properly". Likewise, such theorists argue, the jurisdiction of moral evaluation is limited to those who use our "moral vocabulary", who are committed to playing our language game of moral right and wrong. On this view, we can attribute a commitment to, say, "renouncing torture" only to people who use the phrase "renouncing torture" in the same way as us. But this is obviously incorrect. Using the phrase "renouncing torture" as we do is not a necessary element of the pattern of practical reasoning of "renouncing torture". Wherever the symptoms of that pattern occur we have grounds to attribute the commitment and, if we can elicit its endorsement, keep score on that basis.
36 R. Brandom, "From Irony to Trust: Modernity and Beyond", in *A Spirit of Trust*, rough draft available at www.pitt.edu/~Brandom/hegel/index.html, forthcoming, p. 174.
37 R. Brandom, Lecture III, 2007, *passim*. It is worth pointing out in passing that nothing about the process of recollection entails and endorsement of the prevailing status quo. Brandom recollects the history of voting rights to demonstrate this point:

Consider the lessons we might draw from looking retrospectively at the history of the extension of the voting franchise in modern times. A progressive trajectory can be discerned, in which various supposedly essential qualifications are gradually shed: noble birth, property-ownership, being the male head of a household, not being a member of a despised minority ... We might construe this tradition as the gradual emergence into explicitness of the principle that those who are *subject* (responsible) to laws should exercise some authority in determining their content. But if *that* is the norm implicit in this development, then it seems our current practices are still only distorted expressions of it. Are we sure that excluding teenagers, resident aliens, or ex-felons aren't restrictions that belong in a box with excluding women, blacks, or those who do not own property? Reconstructing the tradition around an expressively progressive trajectory and trying to formulate a principle that makes explicit the norm that is implicit in it gives us a *critical* grip on where we are now. It opens up the possibility of seeing ourselves as still making versions of old mistakes.

> (R. Brandom, "Towards Reconciling Two Heroes: Habermas and Hegel", presented May 18, 2009 at the Hungarian Academy of Sciences, publication forthcoming, available at www.pitt.edu/~Brandom/index.html, p. 13)

38 M. al Ghazali, *Towards a Substantive Interpretation of the Surahs of the Holy Qur'an* (in Arabic), Cairo: Dar al Shuruq, 2005.
39 See Abul Magd, in *al Ahram*, 11 December 1998.
40 Brandom, 2007, Lecture III, pp. 8–15.
41 Ibid., p. 15.
42 Ibid., p. 21.
43 Roy, op. cit., p. 71.
44 Ibid., p. 99.
45 Brandom, 2009, pp. 11–12.
46 Asef Bayat, *Making Islam Democratic: Social Movements and the Post-Islamist Turn*, Stanford, CT: Stanford University Press, 2007, p. 2.
47 This may be what leads Bayat to underestimate the New Islamists in Egypt. See Bayat, op. cit., pp. 250–201.
48 Huwaidy, *Weghat Nazar*, no. 13, February 2000.
49 D. Zeidan, "Radical Islam in Egypt: A Comparison of Two Groups", in B. Rubin (ed.) *Revolutionaries and Reformers: Contemporary Islamist Movements in the Middle East.* Albany, NY: SUNY Press, 2003, p. 15.
50 Ibid, p.17
51 It is worth pointing out in passing that at times the best way to support these allies may be to keep our distance, for fear of undermining their authority in the eyes of other Islamists.
52 Raymond Baker, *Islam Without Fear: Egypt and the New Islamists*, Cambridge, MA: Harvard University Press, 2003, p. 21.
53 *Sawt al-Azhar*, 7 December 2001, as cited in Bayat, op. cit., p. 247.
54 Y. Qaradawi, *The Islamic Awakening: The Concerns of the Arab and Islamic Homeland* (in Arabic), Cairo: Dar al Sahwa, 1988, p. 13.
55 Abul Magd in *Weghat Nazar*, September 1999.
56 As cited by Huwaidy in *al Ahram*, 19 January 1999.
57 Though of course this consensuality may be merely implicit. See the "Acknowledgment and Consequence" section above.

11 Applying "the McCarthy Test" to Canadian and American security legislation

A 10-year retrospective on the impact of September 11, 2001 on privacy rights

Patrick Smith

On 15 October 2001, just thirty-four days after the September 11, 2001 terrorist attacks in the United States, the Government of Canada introduced Bill C-36 – *An Act to amend the Criminal Code, the Official Secrets Act, the Canada Evidence Act, the Proceeds of Crime (Money Laundering) Act and other Acts, and to enact measures respecting the registration of charities, in order to combat terrorism* or (The Anti-Terrorism Act).

There were four central objectives of *Bill C-36*:

- stop terrorists from getting into Canada and protect Canadians from terrorist acts;
- bring forward tools to identify, prosecute, convict and punish terrorists;
- prevent the Canada-US border from being held hostage by terrorists and impacting on the Canadian economy; and
- work with the international community to bring terrorists to justice and address the root causes of such hatred.[1]

Safety and security, rather than the more careful concerns of a balance between security and rights evident when Canada's Security Intelligence Service was created in the early 1980s, was the order of the day. As noted by Ministers responsible, the bill was intended to "give law enforcement and national security agencies new investigative tools to gather knowledge about and prosecute terrorists and terrorist groups, as well as protect Canadians from terrorist attacks", including:

- making it easier to use electronic surveillance against terrorist groups;
- creating new offences targeting unlawful disclosure of certain information of national interest;
- amending the *Canada Evidence Act* to guard certain information of national interest from disclosure during courtroom or other judicial proceedings;

- amending the *National Defence Act* to continue and clarify the mandate of the Communications Security Establishment (CSE) to collect foreign communications;
- within carefully defined limits, allowing the arrest, detention and imposition of conditions of release of suspected terrorists to prevent terrorist acts and save lives;
- requiring individuals who have information related to a terrorist group or offence to appear before a judge to provide that information; and
- extending the DNA warrant scheme and data bank to include terrorist crimes.[2]

Despite assurances from the Minister of Justice – that "the measures we are introducing strike the right balance between civil liberties and national security, and signal our resolve to ensure Canadians will not be paralyzed by acts of terrorism" – Canada's new Anti-Terrorism Act clearly tipped the delicate balance between rights and security toward security. Despite the undertaking that "the proposed Anti-terrorism Act includes rigorous checks and balances in order to uphold the rights and freedoms of Canadians", the only recognition on the rights side were to amend the Criminal Code to add 'on-line hate' and 'mischief against places of religious worship/religious property' and to amend the Canadian Human Rights Act to prohibit 'spreading repeated hate messages' by any method of communication. To counter anticipated criticisms "the scope of the Criminal Code provisions [were] clearly defined to ensure they only apply to terrorists and terrorist groups".[3] A 'three year Parliamentary review' of the legislation was also added.[4]

Even before the introduction of Bill C-36 – and related legislative efforts C-35 and C-42 – civil libertarians anticipated a "trampling of civil rights" in the post-September 11th 'war on terrorism'. For example, British Columbia Civil Liberties Association President John Dixon reminded Canadians of the McCarthy-era attack on "civil rights – presumptions of innocence, privacy, and freedoms of conscience, association and speech". For Dixon, there was the likelihood that intelligence gathering through the over-riding of privacy rights would alter "the balance to be struck between principle and need … That depends both upon the importance of the principle and the likelihood that some sacrifice of it will yield significant results." His conclusion: "trampling on civil rights will not lead to a genuine victory against terrorism".[5] Editorial writers came to the same conclusion: the *Vancouver Sun*'s David Beers bemoaned attacks on free speech following September 11th, arguing that the "you're either with us or you're against us" strategy made one wonder "whether any of it served to bring us closer to defeating the enemy out there, or whether it really was about manufacturing an enemy within".[6] It was a caution posed by Osama Bin Laden himself, just weeks after the September 11, 2001 attacks: In a televised statement in October 2001. Bin Laden stated the most likely outcome from September 11th: "Freedom and human rights in America are doomed. The US government will lead the American people – *and the West in general* – into an unbearable hell and a choking life".[7]

The concerns around human rights continued following introduction of Bill C-36 in Canada: within days, there were widespread calls for amendments to the speedily drafted legislation. One of the biggest issues was the definition of terrorism which seemed to include both illegal strikes and civil disobedience, ("an act or omission ... intended to endanger a person's life ... [and] to cause serious interference with or serious disruption of an essential service" and an unlawful act committed for "ideological purpose" that causes "serious disruption of an essential service, facility or system").[8] This was far more than the US definition of terrorism: "premeditated, politically motivated violence perpetrated against non-combatant targets by sub-national groups or clandestine agents".

Beyond this, critics objected to other powers and controls: these included: (1) the power of detention (to allow holding a suspect without charge, with judicial approval, for 72 hours); (2) the power to detain, without charge, with judicial approval (for up to one year, if the person does not agree to reasonable restrictions on their behaviour as a condition of release); (3) the possibility of up to ten years imprisonment for "legally" 'participating or contributing' to activities of a known terrorist group; and (4) the requirement to testify at 'investigative hearings'. Essentially allowing the Solicitor-General the power to create a "List of Terrorists" on "reasonable grounds" only – and then not require the government to even notify individuals or groups that they are on the list.

As one editorial noted:

> Balancing freedom and security is always complex ... We've seen legitimate dissent suppressed in the name of public safety ... Some revision [to C-36] is needed before the law is passed. It's a free and democratic society we seek to protect and those values aren't adequately served by this draft of the law.[9]

After much pressure, the government agreed to consider amendments in early November 2001. The discourse during this period was in both directions – on human rights *and* security – though mostly the calls were for major changes to favour the security side of the equation: the Canadian Police Association called for even greater investigative tools to wiretap, guard the borders and catch people with fake ID, and rejected a call for a five-year sunset clause, claiming that sensitive work on ongoing terrorist investigations could be "put on hold in the months leading up to a vote on the sunset clause"; civil rights groups countered that the bill gave far to much power to authorities and threatened basic rights and freedoms.[10]

A positive governmental response on some of the rights concerns was largely predicated on the recommendation of Canada's Senate that a five-year sunset clause be included. In a unanimous bi-partisan Senate committee report, the senators noted that "Bill C-36 gives powers that, if abused by the executive or security establishments of this country, could have severe implications for democracy in Canada." As a result, the Senate committee recommended that "new police powers of detention, investigation and surveillance be rescinded in five years unless specifically extended by Parliament".[11] This view was supported by civil libertarians and groups like the Canadian Bar Association.[12]

Confronting dissent from the Senate and even within his own Cabinet, as well as a "national backlash", Prime Minister Jean Chrétien indicated he was 'flexible' in terms of considering several amendments to the "hastily-conceived and ill-defined act", C-36.[13] One British Columbia lawyer, constitutional law expert James Aldridge, in appearing before the House Justice Committee, argued that people and groups could have all their assets stripped away "without there even having been a charge, a trial or a finding of guilt". For Aldridge, Bill C-36 was simply "a law that strips away basic legal protections" because of fear, and "as surely as night followed day, will be misused".[14] Amnesty International Canada felt that while it "recognizes the right, indeed the obligation, of governments to provide to their citizens meaningful protection in the face of potential human rights abuses, including attacks of the nature of those that took place on September 11th". However,

> peaceful forms of dissent, widely recognized as legitimate and supported and defended by groups such as Amnesty International, could conceivably fall under the unacceptably broad definition of "terrorism" found in Bill C-36. The proposed legislation applies not only to acts motivated by political belief, ideology or religion that cause or lead to deaths or serious threats to public safety – human rights abuses that clearly must be addressed with utmost seriousness – but also to acts motivated by political belief, ideology or religion that disrupt an essential service, facility or system whether or not this disruption is intended or is likely to endanger lives and public safety.[15]

For Amnesty International Canada, "the only protection that the Bill provides for peaceful protest is that it excludes 'lawful' acts of dissent that don't endanger lives or cause a serious risk to public health or safety". Yet, "even 'unlawful' forms of dissent should not be characterized as 'terrorism' unless they endanger lives or public safety. Alex Neve, Secretary General of the English-speaking branch of Amnesty International Canada noted that the line between 'lawful' and 'unlawful' is too fine and often too arbitrary to say that one is acceptable, perhaps even commendable, and the other is 'terrorism':

> Protesters often stray beyond the bounds of what is strictly lawful through acts of trespass or civil disobedience. Should Canada respond to such acts as "terrorism"? Absolutely not ... By asserting that acts of political protest can be considered "terrorist" acts, even when lives and public safety are not endangered, the Canadian government plays into the hands of governments that ruthlessly suppress human rights ... Not only does Bill C-36 have the potential to stigmatize legitimate human rights defenders in other countries, it could create a chill on Canadian organizations trying to assist these defenders when they most need our help.[16]

In their brief to the Commons Committee, Amnesty International Canada presented five case histories of human rights defenders abroad who could conceivably be considered terrorists under Bill C-36 because they led disruptive strikes, anti-logging blockages and civil disobedience campaigns declared to be unlawful by their respective governments. These activists included recipients of international human rights prizes and prisoners of conscience currently being defended by Amnesty International. The group's recommendation to the government was that "Bill C-36 be amended to cover only acts that result in or are likely to lead to deaths, serious bodily harm or grave threats to public health and safety."[17]

The human rights organization also noted some positive elements in Bill C-36 such as "the commitment to launch judicial proceedings against individuals accused of serious human rights abuses such as attacks on civilians" and "the provisions ... which would strengthen Canada's laws dealing with hate crimes and propaganda".[18]

Bill C-36 was amended and passed by the House of Commons on 28 November 2001; Justice Minister Anne McLellan's Edmonton constituency office was the subject of a protest sit-in during parliamentary consideration of C-36.[19] The Anti-Terrorism Act was passed by Senate and received Royal Assent on 18 December 2001. The key amendments introduced on 20 November 2001, included the following 'responses' to rights criticisms:

- *a sunset clause* – in addition to a three-year Parliamentary review, the government agreed to add a sunset provision to both preventive arrest and investigative hearing provisions. These would expire after five years unless renewed by Parliament;
- *an Annual Report to Parliament* – a new provision which would require the Federal Attorney and Solicitor-General, and their provincial equivalents, to report annually to Parliament on any use of either preventive arrest or investigative hearings;
- *a new definition of terrorist activity* – 'to ensure that protest activity, whether lawful or unlawful, would not be considered a terrorist activity unless it was intended to cause death, serious bodily harm, endangerment of life or serious risk to public health or safety'; a separate interpretive clause was added for greater clarity regarding the protection of political, religious or ideological beliefs/expression;
- *a review mechanism for A.G. Certificates* – rather than being issued 'at any time', these could only be issued after an order by the Federal Court in a proceeding; they were to be published in the *Canadian Gazette* and could last for no more than 15 years. FOI provisions were to be the rule v. the exception;
- *a re-definition of facilitation* – offences related to facilitating terrorism were to be clarified by an interpretive section on such activity;
- *technical amendments* – to clarify the intent of the Act and some technical changes.[20]

Bill C-36 had garnered substantial criticism from trade unions such as the Canadian Labour Congress (CLC) and the Canadian Auto Workers (CAW), civil liberties organizations such as the Canadian Human Rights Commission, Amnesty International and the British Columbia Civil Liberties Association, ethnic organizations such as the Canadian Arab Federation, the National Association of Japanese Canadians and the Canadian Race Relations Foundation, privacy advocates and freedom of information officials from federal and provincial jurisdictions, religious groups such as the Mennonite Central Committee, university associations such as the Canadian Association of University Teachers, peace activists, environmentalists, anti-globalization entities, pro choice advocates and Canadian nationalists.[21] All commented on the incorrectness of the Government's tilt away from a balance between rights protection on the one hand and perceived security needs after September 11th on the other. The only real shift from the early 1980s debate was that the later focus was no longer on necessity. Despite the fact that the 1980s debate about the creation of the Canadian Security Intelligence Service (CSIS) had simply been on the creation of a civilian security and intelligence agency, all other areas of the 1980s policy discourse continued in 2001–2002: (1) on security of the collectivity versus individual rights; (2) mandate and functions for various authorities; (3) powers; (4) structure and location of this emergency authority; and centrally, (5) accountability. All of these concerns from the early 1980s had reappeared. The only difference was that the new anti-terrorism plan's legislative framework in the twenty-first century was across most departments and a broad cross-section of amended legislation.

Overlapping with the initial Canadian anti-terrorism legislation, C-36, was another important piece of the government's Anti-Terrorism Plan: Bill C-42 – the Public Security Act. If the Chrétien Government tipped its original C-36 legislative proposals too far in the direction of security over rights, then C-42 represented a complete unbalancing. C-42, the second Anti-Terrorism Bill, was introduced in November 2001 – before final approval of C-36. From the government's perspective, this second Bill, the Public Security Act, was "an appropriate continuation of the legislative amendments tabled in Bill C-36 and introduces new amendments to the National Defence Act (NDA), etc." Some of the highlights of the Bill were:

- measures to ensure the Canadian Forces have the authority to protect their computer systems networks and the information they contain from attack or manipulation. The unique role of the Canadian Forces and their ability to operate with their allies requires that they have the authority to protect their networks.
- Modernization of the definition of 'emergency' to reflect the new security environment that would include clear reference to circumstances of armed conflict short of formally declared war. A number of important powers under the National Defence Act, such as the authority to generate forces to deal with terrorist threats, are tied to the existence of an emergency.

- The authority to establish temporary "military security zones" to protect Canadian Forces and visiting forces personnel and equipment that are located off Defence establishments. Military security zones may also be established to protect property, places and things that the Canadian Forces have been directed to protect.
- The establishment of a panel of military reserve judges to increase the flexibility of the Military Justice System to respond to increased demands for judicial services flowing from sudden changes in the operational tempo of the CF.
- The Bill includes job protection measures for reservists in the event that they must be called out compulsorily by the government in an emergency such as armed conflict or war. At the conclusion of a period of compulsory call-up, employers would be required to reinstate reservists in equivalent employment. This amendment ensures that reservists do not have to choose between possibly losing their livelihoods and breaking the law that requires them to serve when called. The new legislation will also amend the procedures that are followed when Provinces request military assistance and align it with existing mechanisms that permit the Canadian Forces to provide assistance to civilian law enforcement, which involve Federal Government input. Requests for aid of the civil power will continue to be made directly to the Chief of Defence Staff (CDS). However, the NDA amendments would allow the Minister of National Defence to provide direction to the CDS to ensure that the Government of Canada is able to manage simultaneous or multiple requests for assistance during an emergency.[22]

According to the Minister of National Defence:

> Proper security measures are necessary to safeguard our freedom and democracy. This legislation is an appropriate response to the security threat facing Canada. The Bill introduces legislation that will help the Government of Canada, the Department of National Defence and the Canadian Forces improve their ability to protect Canadians from terrorism and its effect.[23]

If Bill C-36 garnered criticism for the range of its provisions, C-42 was seen as insupportable on narrower grounds – though one seen as just as fundamental regarding rights v. security. Backbench governmental criticisms, opposition questioning and the same array of rights-centred entities all suggested that one of its central intents was to allow the Minister of National Defence to declare the June 2002, G-8 summit site at Kananaskis, Alberta, 'a military zone' to prevent protests. This, despite the fact that C-42 involved amendments to the following Acts:

> Aeronautics Act, Canadian Environmental Protection Act, 1999, Criminal Code, Department of Health Act, Explosives Act, Export and Import Permits Act, Food and Drugs Act, Hazardous Products Act, Immigration Act, National Defence Act, National Energy Board Act, Navigable Waters Protection Act,

Office of the Superintendent of Financial Institutions Act, Pest Control Products Act, Proceeds of Crime (Money Laundering) Act, Quarantine Act, Radiation Emitting Devices Act, Canada Shipping Acts, Biological and Toxin Weapons Convention and the Proceeds of Crime (Money Financing Act.[24]

Due to internal dissent and extensive external criticism, Bill C-42, intended to deal with the 'emergency' situation perceived after the events of September 2001, was allowed to languish in Parliamentary limbo. On 24 April 2002, it was formally withdrawn. Within a week a replacement bill – Bill C-55 – the Public Safety Act, was put before Parliament by the government. As one media columnist noted: "Bill C-42 replacement is less offensive than the original", but C-42 was mostly "yanked due to concerns about its capacity to withstand a legal challenge":

Don't for a moment believe federal government claims that the decision to dilute blatantly anti-democratic security legislation is the result of a deliberative consultation. ... Much to the embarrassment of the ruling Liberals, Bill C-42 was yanked last week and replaced yesterday with a modest sibling for the more pressing reason that it was, and may still prove to be, lousy legislation. In its political wisdom, the government reached the inescapable conclusion that the original bill would fail the first, inevitable, legal challenge. So Liberals today are deep in damage control ... Bill C-42 was bad law and the Liberals knew it was bad law. They were told that by a Who's Who of non-partisan critics whose concerns ranged across the original bill's four main provisions before settling on egregious, potentially dangerous infringements of personal privacy and plans to give cabinet ministers extraordinary, unnecessary, powers. Some of those concerns were sidelined when the government split and amended legislation primarily dealing with air safety. Still, the queue of critics remained long and impressive ... [for] a bill that had already raised the hackles of lawyers, academics and activists. C-42 badly failed critical tests. If that legislation became law, Canadian ministers would have gained powers that would raise eyebrows and howls of protest in places with a more suspect grasp of democratic principles. Grabbing powers that more properly belong to Parliament and the people, the legislation would have given some ministers unprecedented authority to impose interim orders in secret. Loaded with the baggage of martial law and free of the necessary constraints imposed on the similar but more open Emergencies Act, the orders could have only required cabinet approval within 90 days of being imposed. More remarkable than the powers themselves is the singular absence of any justification. No minister or government background papers ever convincingly explained why such obvious infringements of the federal Charter of Rights and Freedoms were necessary or how the legislation would make Canadians safer. Still, the government hoped to slide this law past a public grown unwary in the aftermath of other security legislation hurriedly amended with sunset clauses. That intention is now the most worrisome aspect of this sorry adventure in law making. It is reassuring the original bill is dead. What isn't comforting is that this government would once have willingly given it life.[25]

C-55: The Public Safety Act

On 29 April 2002, five days after the withdrawal of Bill C-42, the Chrétien Government introduced what they termed "an improved package of public safety initiatives in support of its Anti-Terrorism Plan". This single integrated Bill (Bill C-55 amended 21 Acts of Canada) kept key elements of the tarnished C-42. For the Minister of Transportation, David Collenette, "this legislation … responds to the need for enhanced security while respecting the rights of Canadians".[26] Not everyone agreed. However, the new C-55 legislation responded to some of the concerns raised with respect to Bill C-42, by, for example:

- further defining and circumscribing the power of the Minister of National Defence to establish Controlled Access Military Zones, and of other ministers to use interim orders in emergency situations;
- providing comprehensive parameters for the new terrorist hoax offences; and,
- providing strong measures to ensure accountability and transparency.

The Public Safety Act of 2002 still contains key measures that will increase the Government of Canada's capacity to prevent terrorist attacks, protect Canadians, and respond swiftly should a significant threat arise. Notably, it will:

- clarify and update existing aviation security authorities to maximize the effectiveness of Canada's aviation security system and enhance the ability of the Government of Canada to provide a safe and secure environment for air travel;
- facilitate the sharing of law enforcement and national security information between federal departments and agencies;
- deter hoaxes that endanger the public or heighten public anxiety;
- establish tighter controls over explosives and hazardous substances, activities related to other dangerous substances such as pathogens, and the export and transfer of technology;
- help identify and prevent harmful unauthorized use or interference with Department of National Defence computer systems;
- deter the proliferation of biological weapons; and,
- respect the privacy rights of Canadians.

In addition, the legislation includes new provisions to do the following:

- improve the capacity of federal departments and agencies involved in anti-terrorism and national security activities to share critical information and coordinate their work;

- provide for the smooth flow of information between Canada and its partners internationally, particularly the United States, in order to prevent terrorist activity and protect public safety; and,
- provide a mechanism by which the Government of Canada can provide financial assistance, where necessary, to enhance marine security.

It continued to garner mostly negative response. The Public Safety Act, C-55, was seen by the Government as the next step in its broad-based anti-terrorism plan, which began with the Anti-terrorism Act (Bill C-36) and was bolstered by a \$7.7 billion investment in Budget 2001.[27] "Where the Anti-terrorism Act focused mainly on the criminal law aspects of combating terrorism, C-55 addressed gaps in the federal legislative framework for public safety and protection."[28]

One of the measures that continued to cause concern was the powers given to the new Canadian Air Transport Security Authority, funded with \$2.2 billion for air security in the December 2001 federal Budget, and responsible for aviation security services in Canada, including:

- pre-board screening of passengers and their belongings;
- certification of screening officers;
- purchase, deployment, maintenance and operation of explosives detection systems;
- federal contributions toward airport policing related to civil aviation security; and
- contracting with the RCMP for armed officers on board aircraft.[29]

Under C-55 changes to the Aeronautics Act, passenger data that may be required in the interest of transportation security are:

> The amendments would enable the Government of Canada to require air carriers and operators of aviation reservation systems (systems that provide the capability to make air reservations or issue tickets for air services) to provide information on passengers while balancing the privacy rights of passengers. Specifically, the new provisions would require that an air carrier must, upon request, provide a designated RCMP or CSIS officer with passenger information for the Air Carrier Protective Program (RCMP officers on board aircraft), for reasons related to: immediate threats to life, health, safety or transportation security; execution of warrants for serious offences, such as murder or kidnapping, as well as warrants under the Immigration Act; compliance with subpoenas or court orders; and counter-terrorism investigations by CSIS. The proposed scheme would include strict controls on access, use, and disclosure, and strong privacy safeguards.
>
> Another section of the Aeronautics Act is being amended to clarify that air carriers may only provide information to a foreign country on passengers on board an aircraft departing from Canada, or on a Canadian airlines'

aircraft departing from somewhere else, if that flight is scheduled to land in that country.[30]

Canada's Privacy Commissioner, among others, considered this an unnecessary intrusion on the privacy rights of Canadians. George Radwanski expressed 'serious concerns' about C-55, noting it "raised very, very serious privacy issues".[31] He was supported by Privacy Commissioners in several provinces. These concerns were expressed even within the Liberal caucus – Montreal MP Irwin Cotler criticized C-55;[32] and Amnesty International also raised concerns about the capacity of Ministers to designate 'controlled military zones' in ways which would not infringe on free speech and assembly rights. Here the June, 2002 Kananaskis, Alberta, G-8 Summit was front and centre.[33]

These concerns were reflected in editorials and columns across the country: *The Ottawa Citizen*, for example, asked:

> Why should police be allowed to see the private data Canadians give airlines? It's not enough to cite, as Solicitor General Lawrence McCauley did last week, the "changed security environment" … It [the government] should amend the bill [C-55] to remove this unwarranted intrusion into our privacy.[34]

Federal Privacy Commissioner George Radwanski called C-55 provisions, simply, "a power grab by the police".[35]

With the September 2002 Throne Speech and a new session of Parliament, C-55 died on the old Order Paper. Its successor – C-17, the Public Safety Act – seems to have learned few lessons from the protests over its intrusiveness and impingement on rights of Canadians. The government sought to continue surfing airline manifests for information on travelers. Some small concessions appear likely here but the thrust of the most recent Canadian responses to post September 11 appears significantly dictated by our closest North American neighbour.[36]

Even here that does not appear enough. American responses such as racial profiling led to an October 2002 Canadian Government travel advisory to Canadians of Arab origin.[37] Even when Canadian pressure and possible constitutional challenges produced an alteration to this US policy, photographing and fingerprinting will only 'no longer be automatic by place of birth' – but will continue as deemed useful by INS officials.[38]

Conclusions: Lessons for and from Canada

The vernacular of the policy discourse of 2001/2002 around anti-terrorism (C-36) and public safety (C-42 and C-55 -and its autumn 2002 C-17 successor) turns out not to be dramatically different than that posed in the early 1980s debates over (C-157 and C-9) the creation of CSIS.

The governmental side in both eras tended to exaggerate threats and over-emphasize security needs. In both cases, the critics were able to force withdrawal of legislation (C-157 and C-42 or to wring small concessions from the new

Public Safety Act) – but, that success aside, to lose ground on the rights vs. security balance. More importantly, the content of the criticisms were remarkably similar and forced each government of the day to recognize a need to move toward a closer balance between security needs and rights protections.

The fact that C-55 was not passed/proclaimed before the summer 2002 recess of the Canadian Parliament[39] – and died on the order paper until reintroduced as C-17 in late October 2002 after a new Throne Speech – does not diminish the fact that the more recent legislation continue to generate vigorous opposition based on the same rights-concerns as in the early 1980s. The main difference between the policy discourse of the two eras may be that the Canadian Government of today is able to generate more concerns on the security side of the equation to bolster their fundamental re-balancing of security over rights.[40] In response to the new Public Safety legislation, Canada's Privacy Commissioner George Radwanski suggested it "effectively expanded police powers in the guise of fighting terrorism; and 'raises the spectre' of a 'police state'".[41] As the Privacy Commissioner has stated:

In Canada, it is well established that we are not required to identify ourselves to police unless we are being arrested or we are carrying out a licensed activity such as driving. The right to anonymity with regard to the state is a crucial privacy right. Since we are required to identify ourselves to airlines as a condition of air travel and since section 4.82 would give the RCMP unrestricted access to the passenger information obtained by airlines, this would set the extraordinarily privacy-invasive precedent of effectively requiring compulsory self-identification to the police.

I am prepared, with some reluctance, to accept this as an exceptional measure that can be justified, in the wake of September 11, for the limited and specific purposes of aviation security and national security against terrorism. But I can find no reason why the use of this de facto self-identification to the police should be extended to searching for individuals who are of interest to the state because they are the subject of warrants for Criminal Code offences unrelated to terrorism. That has the same effect as requiring us to notify the police every time we travel, so that they can check whether we are wanted for something.

If the police were able to carry out their regular Criminal Code law enforcement duties without this new power before September 11, they should likewise be able to do so now. The events of September 11 were a great tragedy and a great crime; they should not be manipulated into becoming an opportunity – an opportunity to expand privacy-invasive police powers for purposes that have nothing to do with anti-terrorism ...

The place to draw the line in protecting the fundamental human right of privacy is at the very outset, at the first unjustifiable intrusion. In this instance, that means amending the bill to remove all reference to warrants and thus limit the police to matching passenger information against anti-terrorism and national security databases.

The concerns that I have raised in this matter since last spring have been publicly endorsed by the Information and Privacy Commissioner of British Columbia and the Information and Privacy Commissioner of Ontario; by members of every party in the House of Commons, notably including a member of the government's own Liberal caucus who is an internationally recognized expert on human rights, Irwin Cotler; and by editorials in newspapers including the *Toronto Star*, the *Globe and Mail*, the *Vancouver Sun*, the *Vancouver Province*, the *Calgary Herald* and the *Edmonton Journal*.

These concerns have now been ignored by the Government.

The changes that have been made in this provision in the new bill do nothing to address the fundamental issues of principle that are at stake.

The Government now proposes to have regulations limiting the Criminal Code offence warrants for which the RCMP will be searching. But this does nothing to address the fundamental point of principle that the police have no business using this extraordinary access to personal information to search for people wanted on warrants for any offences unrelated to terrorism.[42]

The concerns of Canada's former Privacy Commissioner about C-17, Canada's Public Safety Act – supported by most provincial privacy commissioners, civil liberties associations, the Canadian Bar Association and many national media editorials – is the same today: "we must guard against falling prey to the illusion that wholesale erosion of privacy is a reasonable, necessary or effective way to enhance security".[43] On the matter of a possible national identity card as one way to ensure greater security:

The creation of a national identity card is … an idea totally without merit. [It] would radically change Canadian society by drastically infringing on the right to anonymity that is part of our fundamental right of privacy. [It] is unthinkably invasive.

C-17 and ideas like a national identity card that remain pending in Canada show the trend line is clear: in Canada – as in the United States with the Patriot and Homeland Security Acts, and in many other western democracies – September 11, 2001 did alter the 'delicate balance' between security and rights; a real re-balancing may be some time in coming.

Anti-terrorism legislation: US lessons and questions

The American experience on finding the delicate balance between human rights and security needs is not a lot different than that in Canada. The significance of constitutionally protected rights is an important feature in America.

But despite the significance of a rights culture in the United States, examples of rights-security/public order imbalance exist. Notwithstanding a strong Bill of Rights from its beginning, it took the 13th through 15th Amendments around the

Civil War, and a Warren Court almost a century later for some achievement of rights such as real 'equal protection'.

The excesses of the McCarthy-era House Un-American Activities Committee continue to animate Americans. It took some time for Americans to find a re-balance of their rights over perceived security-dominated needs in the country during the early Cold War. But some balance was achieved.

On 24 October 2001, just five weeks after the September 11th terrorist attacks on the US, Congress passed the 'Uniting and Strengthening America by Providing Appropriate Tools Required to Intercept and Obstruct Terrorism – USA PATRIOT ACT of 2001'. The Patriot Act involved changes to 15 different legislative acts; the changes varied from minor to more broad. The Patriot Act itself ran to 342 pages and

> [gave] sweeping new powers to both domestic law enforcement and international intelligence agencies and ... eliminated the checks and balances that previously gave courts the opportunity to ensure that these powers were not abused. Most of these checks and balances were put into place after previous misuse of surveillance powers by these agencies, including the revelation in 1974 that the FBI and foreign intelligence agencies had spied on over 10,000 U.S. citizens, including Martin Luther King.[44]

According to one Humans Rights organization, the USAPA was a 'rush job':

> even just considering the surveillance and online provisions of the USAPA, it is a large and complex law that had over four different names and several versions in the five weeks between the introduction of its first predecessor and its final passage into law. While containing some sections that seem appropriate – providing for victims of the September 11 attacks, increasing translation facilities and increasing forensic cybercrime capabilities – it seems clear that the vast majority of the sections included have not been carefully studied by Congress, nor was sufficient time taken to debate it or to hear testimony from experts outside of law enforcement in the fields where it makes major changes. This concern is amplified because several of the key procedural processes applicable to any other proposed laws, including inter-agency review, the normal committee and hearing processes and thorough voting, were suspended for this bill.[45]

The response of Americans was mixed. For many traumatized by the events of September 11th, the Act contained measures which were prudent and deliberate. But the Electronic Frontier Foundation (EFF– a non-profit group re: digital rights) asked, simply "Were our Freedoms the Problem?" Their answer was that the Patriot Act provisions represented a victory for those who would alter the American way of life:

> The civil liberties of ordinary Americans have taken a tremendous blow with this law, especially the right to privacy in our online communications

and activities. Yet there is no evidence that our previous civil liberties posed a barrier to the effective tracking or prosecution of terrorists. In fact, in asking for these broad new powers, the government made no showing that the previous powers of law enforcement and intelligence agencies to spy on US citizens were insufficient to allow them to investigate and prosecute acts of terrorism. The process leading to the passage of the bill did little to ease these concerns. To the contrary, they are amplified by the inclusion of so many provisions that, instead of aimed at terrorism, are aimed at nonviolent, domestic computer crime. In addition, although many of the provisions facially appear aimed at terrorism, the Government made no showing that the reasons they failed to detect the planning of the recent attacks or any other terrorist attacks were the civil liberties compromised with the passage of USAPA.[46]

The EFF's chief concerns with the USAPA included:

1   Expanded surveillance with reduced checks and balances. USAPA expands all four traditional tools of surveillance – wiretaps, search warrants, pen/ trap orders and subpoenas. Their counterparts under the Foreign Intelligence Surveillance Act (FISA) that allow spying in the US by foreign intelligence agencies have similarly been expanded. This means:

   a   Be careful what you put in that Google search. The government may now spy on web surfing of innocent Americans, including terms entered into search engines, by merely telling a judge anywhere in the US that the spying could lead to information that is "relevant" to an ongoing criminal investigation. The person spied on does not have to be the target of the investigation. This application must be granted and the government is not obligated to report to the court or tell the person spied upon what it has done.
   b   Nationwide roving wiretaps. FBI and CIA can now go from phone to phone, computer to computer without demonstrating that each is even being used by a suspect or target of an order. The government may now serve a single wiretap, FISA wiretap or pen/trap order on any person or entity nationwide, regardless of whether that person or entity is named in the order. The government need not make any showing to a court that the particular information or communication to be acquired is relevant to a criminal investigation.
   c   ISPs hand over more user information.
   d   New definitions of terrorism expand scope of surveillance. One new definition of terrorism and three expansions of previous terms also expand the scope of surveillance. They are (1) § 802 definition of "domestic terrorism" (amending 18 USC §2331), which raises concerns about legitimate protest activity resulting in conviction on terrorism charges, especially if violence erupts; adds to 3 existing definitions of terrorism (int'l terrorism per 18 USC §2331, terrorism transcending national borders per 18 USC §2332b, and federal terrorism per amended

18 USC §2332b(g)(5)(B)). These new definitions also expose more people to surveillance (and potential "harboring" and "material support" liability, §§ 803, 805).

2   Over-breadth with a lack of focus on terrorism. Several provisions of the USAPA have no apparent connection to preventing terrorism. These include:

a   Government spying on suspected computer trespassers with no need for court order. Sec. 217.

b   Adding samples to DNA database for those convicted of "any crime of violence". Sec. 503. The provision adds collection of DNA for terrorists, but then inexplicably also adds collection for the broad, non-terrorist category of "any crime of violence".

c   Wiretaps now allowed for suspected violations of the Computer Fraud and Abuse Act. This includes anyone suspected of "exceeding the authority" of a computer used in interstate commerce, causing over $5000 worth of combined damage.

d   Dramatic increases to the scope and penalties of the Computer Fraud and Abuse Act.

3   Allows Americans to be more easily spied upon by US foreign intelligence agencies. Just as the domestic law enforcement surveillance powers have expanded, the corollary powers under the Foreign Intelligence Surveillance Act have also been greatly expanded, including:

a   General Expansion of FISA Authority. FISA authority to spy on Americans or foreign persons in the US (and those who communicate with them) increased from situations where the suspicion that the person is the agent of a foreign government is "the" purpose of the surveillance to anytime that this is "a significant purpose" of the surveillance.

b   Increased information sharing between domestic law enforcement and intelligence. This is a partial repeal of the wall put up in the 1970s after the discovery that the FBI and CIA had been conducting investigations on over half a million Americans during the McCarthy era and afterwards, including the pervasive surveillance of Martin Luther King in the 1960s. It allows wiretap results and grand jury information and other information collected in a criminal case to be disclosed to the intelligence agencies when the information constitutes foreign intelligence or foreign intelligence information, the latter being a broad new category created by this law.

c   FISA detour around federal domestic surveillance limitations; domestic detour around FISA limitations. Domestic surveillance limits can be skirted by the Attorney General, for instance, by obtaining a FISA wiretap against a US person where "probable cause" does not exist, but when the person is suspected to be an agent of a foreign government. The information can then be shared with the FBI. The reverse is also true.[47]

This supported the conclusion that the Patriot Act, like anti-terrorism legislation in Canada, Britain and elsewhere was cut from the same 'security over rights' cloth. Post September 11th in the United States represented a loss of basic human rights, many of them with very little to do with making America any more secure or fighting terrorism. Nothing under the subsequent Homeland Security Act 2002 altered this view.[48]

In January2002, the Homeland Security Bill was introduced into Congress. It immediately got bogged down in partisan fighting between Republicans and Democrats, largely over powers it afforded to the president; the Democrats had considerable support from a range of civil liberty, professional and media entities. When the Democrats lost seats in the November 2002 mid-term elections, the new Republican control of both Houses of Congress convinced Democrats to support the legislation. Its late November 2002 passage included 90–9 support in the Senate.

The Act defines terrorism as

> Any activity that involves an act that is dangerous to human life or poten-
> tially destructive of critical infrastructure or key resources; and is a violation
> of the criminal Code of the US or any state ... ; and appears to be intended
> to intimidate or coerce a civilian population; or to influence the policy of a
> government by intimidation or coercion; or to affect the conduct of a govern-
> ment by mass destruction, assassination or kidnapping.[49]

For Fiscal Year 2003, Congress allotted $37.45 billion to the new department. It is divided into four divisions:

1   Border and transportation security.
2   Emergency preparedness and response.
3   Chemical, biological, radiological and nuclear countermeasures.
4   Information analysis and infrastructure protection.

A variety of existing agencies – such as Immigration and Naturalization, Coast Guard, Customs, Border Patrol, Federal Emergency Management Agency, Secret Service, Transportation Security Administration, and the border inspection authority of the Animal and Plant Health Inspection Service were all moved to within the new department. Also Homeland Security will analyze intelligence from sources such as the Central Intelligence Agency, the National Security Agency, the Federal Bureau of Investigations, the Drug Enforcement Agency, as well as the Department of Energy, Customs Service and Department of Transportation.

Critics of the second piece of US anti-terrorism legislation mirrored complaints made in many other democracies about its scope:

> The Homeland Security Act that President Bush is poised to sign is sweeping
> in scope and will have big consequences, intended and unintended, on every-
> thing from civil liberties of Americans to due process for immigrants.

Some have little to do with homeland security, but emerged out of the intensive, last-minute bargaining that shaped this effort to refocus the nation's resources to defeat terrorism. As votes on the historic bill wrapped up this week, most lawmakers were still rifling through its 484 pages to find out what's there.

Its implications went considerably beyond specific anti-terrorism threats, including:

- New authority for agencies to collect and mine data on individuals and groups, including databases that combine personal, governmental, and corporate records – including e-mails and websites viewed.
- Limits on the information citizens can request under the Freedom of Information Act, and criminal penalties for government employees who leak information. This was a top priority for business groups, who worry that disclosing critical information to the new department could expose corporate secrets or vulnerabilities to competitors or terrorists.
- More latitude for government advisory committees to meet in secret – not subject to the requirements of the open meeting laws.
- Limits on liability for those who manufacture "antiterrorism technologies", including vaccines, gas masks, and baggage screening equipment. As a condition for their votes, several Senate moderates have an agreement from House leaders to revisit some of these provisions when the 108th Congress convenes in January.
- New powers to government officials to declare national health emergencies, including quarantines and forced vaccination.[50]

As a strategy for gathering legislative approval and co-opting opposition the Homeland Security Act was instructive: many US civil liberties groups 'welcomed' the withdrawal of a proposal by Attorney General John Ashcroft called the "terrorism information and prevention system" or TIPS. This allowed for a centralizing of all the 'snooping activities' allowed under the USA Patriot Act: Lisa Dean, Director of the Free Congress Foundation says Americans eventually "may find that their conversations have been monitored or [that they've been] caught walking past a surveillance camera and be outraged, but find they have no legal recourse".[51]

That this centralized information gathering and analysis activity would fall under the aegis of retired Admiral John Poindexter, originally convicted in the Iran-Contra affair, offered more pause to critics wondering whether abuses might occur beyond the task of fighting terrorist threats in the United States.

Among groups questioning the future impacts of the Homeland Security Act was the Electronic Frontier Foundation. Their concerns paralleled those asked by critics across the United States:

- Would law enforcement and the intelligence agencies use these new powers carefully and limit their use to bona fide investigations into acts of terrorism?

- Would, if these laws are misused to spy on innocent people, the courts appropriately punish those who misuse them and Congress re-examine its decision to grant such broad, unchecked powers?
- Would the courts refuse to allow evidence collected through these broad powers if these laws were misused to harm rights and in low level crimes unrelated to terrorism?

Here the answers seem unclear – unless past history offered any guide.

As 2003 rolled toward the second anniversary of the events of September 11, 2001, there was indication that the work of the 'securitivists' was far from done. Musings and legislative talk of a USA Patriot II Act, 2003 and other actions and legislative amendments came forward.

According to the Electronic Frontier Foundation, Patriot II legislative drafts included the following:

1   Privacy Invasions. USAPA II dramatically widens the powers of government to invade the privacy of Americans and others living here. This includes:

   - Broad new authority to compel information from ISPs, friends, relatives, businesses and others, all without informing you.
   - Immunity for businesses that voluntarily turn over your information to law enforcement.
   - Extra punishment for use of cryptography – no connection to terrorism needed.
   - Instant police access to your credit reports upon certification that they are sought "in connection with their duties" – again, with no connection to terrorism needed.
   - Relaxed requirement of specificity for warrants for multi-use devices like PDAs and computers with telephonic capabilities.
   - DNA collected from all terrorism suspects/DNA database information open to all law enforcement.
   - Less judicial oversight of surveillance.

2   More "end runs" around limitations on surveillance and information sharing. Federal, state and local officials can now freely share information, regardless of the original reason for gathering it. This includes information in your credit reports, educational records and visa records. It also includes information obtained by administrative subpoenas of any business, from your ISP to your credit card company to your grocer. It also includes DNA database information and information obtained through the secret court processes of the Foreign Intelligence Surveillance Act (FISA). Much of this sharing need not have any relationship to terrorism investigation.

3   Gag orders and increased governmental secrecy. The "sunshine of public review" is a key check on abuses of governmental power. But USAPA II makes it even harder for the public to evaluate what the government is doing with its broad new powers. USAPA II allows gag orders for subpoenas

that force third parties to turn over information about their friends, loved ones or customers while making it unlawful for them to tell anyone except their lawyers about the subpoena. In a similar vein, the law creates broad new exceptions to the Freedom of Information Act for terrorism detainee information, prevents the Environmental Protection Agency from warning the public about environmental dangers from chemical releases and reduces the ability of judges to force the government to present its evidence in open court.

4   Expanded reach of powers under the control of secret courts. The Foreign Intelligence Surveillance Act (FISA) was enacted more than 20 years ago to handle the special problem of non-criminal investigation of foreign intelligence activities in the United States. For this limited purpose, Congress established an unprecedented secret court system. USAPA expanded the reach of FISA and the secret court dramatically, and USAPA II goes even further. Under USAPA II, the secret court will be able to authorize searches of individuals with no connection to foreign governments or even terrorist organizations. It will increase the length of surveillance and decrease court oversight from the already low levels set by USAPA.

5   Not targeted to terrorism. As with its predecessor, USAPA II contains many provisions that appear to be nothing more than an opportunistic attempt to increase governmental powers in areas unrelated to terrorism. In other areas, while terrorism is included, the provisions are not limited to terrorism-related investigations. These include government access to credit reports, sentence enhancements for using encryption, and sharing of some FISA-obtained information.

The USAPA II, tentatively entitled the "Domestic Security Enhancement Act of 2003", "like its predecessor, is a grab bag of provisions spread throughout the legal landscape. One clear difference exists, however. Unlike USAPA, USAPA II has no provisions that 'sunset' after a certain time. All of its changes are permanent".[52] Even when changes in policy were – as regarding CIA assassination efforts – made permanent, these were not abided by. In summer 2009, Leon Panetta, President Obama's new CIA Director found out that former VP Dick Chaney had ordered the CIA not to report to Congress on the training of CIA assassination teams to target al-Qaeda leaders around the world – this despite an order made as far back as Gerald Ford in the 1970s for the CIA to cease any such activity.[53]

Conclusion

As former Canadian Privacy Commissioner George Radwanski has argued,

> One of the clearest lessons of history is that the greatest threats to liberty come not when times are tranquil and all is well, but in times of turmoil, when fidelity to values and principle seems an extravagance we cannot afford.

It is a similar sentiment expressed earlier by former US Supreme Court Justice Thurgood Marshall: "history teaches us that grave threats to liberty often come in times of urgency, when constitutional rights seem too extravagant to endure". Yet if we are to avoid "the curse of Osama" (who – in a televised statement in October 2001 – predicted that "freedom and human rights in America are doomed. The US government will lead the American people – and the West in general – into an unbearable hell and a choking life"), then some vigilance to excess must be encouraged.

Canada's Security Intelligence Review Committee recognizes that "in any democratic society security intelligence activities are among the most serious a government can undertake. They warrant the constant and meticulous attention of all who cherish democratic values and civil discourse in a turbulent and dangerous world."[54]

George Radwanski, Canada's former Privacy Commissioner, offered the most telling test: "If we react to terrorism by excessively and unreasonably depriving ourselves of privacy and the freedoms that flow from it, then terrorism will have won a great and terrible victory."[55] The deletion of significant data gathering and analysis in Canada's Public Safety Act allowed George Radwanski to conclude that "a precedent-setting and extraordinarily grave intrusion on privacy rights has been averted in Canada".[56] Their inclusion in American legislation and the significant rebalancing of security vs rights in the name of anti-terrorism in most Western democracies suggests that as the International Helsinki Federation for Human Rights concluded, "anti-terrorism measures introduced since September 11, 2001 … are severely curtailing human rights and civil liberties in much of the world. The measures often threaten freedoms because they are too broad, too vague and applied too arbitrarily".[57] At the start of the twenty-first century's second decade, these concerns remain.

Notes

1 Government of Canada, "Bill C-36". Available at: www2.parl.gc.ca/HousePublications/ Publication.aspx?pub=bill&doc=C-36&parl=37&ses=1&language=E, Accessed 1 July 2009.
2 Ibid.
3 Ibid.
4 Justice Canada "News Release: Government of Canada Introduces Anti-Terrorism Act", 15 October 2001. Available at: www.collectionscanada.gc.ca/webarchives/ 20071116041847/http://canada.justice.gc.ca/en/news/nr/2001/doc_27785.html, Accessed 1 July 2009.
5 John Dixon, "Repeat of McCarthy Era Would Imperil Democracy", *The Vancouver Sun*, 27 September 2001, p. A15.
6 David Beers, "The New McCarthyism", *The Vancouver Sun*, 6 October 2001, p. A6.
7 Patrick J. Smith, "Osama Wins? Resetting Agendas on Balancing Human Rights vs. Security: Canadian Perspectives, American and British Comparisons – Legislative Responses on Anti-Terrorism After 9/11", lecture/paper for the University of Puget Sound, 31 March 2003. An earlier paper on this theme in Canada was from the Fifth International Centre for Contemporary Middle Eastern Studies conference in North Cyprus, in Spring 2002; see Patrick J. Smith, "Anti-Terrorism and Rights

in Canada: Policy Discourse on the 'Delicate Balance'", *Arab Studies Quarterly*, 25(1–2) (2003): 137–158.

8 Bill C-36.

9 Editorial, "Revision Needed, Now, to Terrorist Legislation: Adequate Safeguards Must Control Potential for Abuse", *The Vancouver Sun*, 17 October 2001, p. A20. See also Daniel LeBlanc, "Senators Unite Against Anti-terror Bill", *The Globe and Mail*, 2 November 2001, p. A10.

10 See, for example, Janice Tibbetts, "Major Changes to Anti-Terrorism Legislation Hinted at by Ottawa: The Justice Minister Says 'We Are Listening to People's Concerns'", *The Vancouver Sun*, 2 November 2001, p. A9.

11 See LeBlanc, op. cit.

12 See, for example, Editorial, "Sunset's Good Sense", *The Globe and Mail*, 2 November 2001, A14. As noted in this editorial,

> There are provisions in this bill that should be accepted in the context of an emergency ... Those who value the liberties enshrined in the Charter and championed in earlier laws are unwilling to see their curtailment become the status quo, an accepted part of the legislative scenery.

13 See, for example, Jim McNulty, "Liberals to Amend Bungled Anti-Terrorism Act", *The Province*, 14 November 2001, p. A23.

14 Ibid.

15 In a brief presented to the House of Commons committee reviewing Bill C-36, Amnesty International Canada, 6 November 2001, Press release.

16 Ibid.

17 Ibid.

18 Ibid.

19 Canadian Press, "Festive Mood at Anti-Terrorism-Bill Sit-In", *The Province*, 9 December 2001, p. A25.

20 Department of Justice, Canada "Royal Assent to Bill C-36", 18 December 2001. Available at: www.canada.justice.gc.ca/en/news/nr2001/doc_28217.html, accessed 7 January 2002.

21 On these see, for example, www.caw.ca/visual+printlibrary/speeches+briefs/110901. asp; www.crr.ca/en/MediaCentre/NewsReleases/eMedCen_NewsRel20011119.htm; www.prochoice connection.com/pro-can/0102win.html#terrorism; www.rsf.org/rsf/uk/ html/ameriques/cplp01/lp01/121201.html; François Legras, "Canadian 'Anti-Terrorism' Law Attacks Democratic Rights", *World Socialist* website, 20 November 2001. Available at: www.wsws.org/articles/2001/nov2001/can-n20.shtml, accessed July 2009; www.arena. org.nz/canbil.htm; www.chrc-ccdp. ca/ar-ra/_AR2001RA/AR01RA/annualReport_1_ rapportAnnuel.asp; www.canadianliberty.bc.ca/liberty-vs-security/; George Radwanski, "Press Release", Office of the Privy Commissioner of Canada, 30 November 2001, www.privcom.gc.ca/media/nr-c/02_05_b_011130_e.asp, accessed July 2009; www. policyalternatives.ca; www.geocities.com/ericsquire/articles/np042502.htm; Jacquie Johnson, "Restricting Liberties: Canada Joins the Crowd", *Peace and Environment News*, February 2002, www.perc.ca/PEN/2002–02/s-johnson2.html, accessed July 2009; www.canadianactionparty.ca.

22 www.dnd.ca/eng/archive/2001/nov01/22NDA_b_e.htm.

23 Transport Canada: www.tc.gc.ca; accessed 12 April 2002.

24 Government of Canada, "Bill C-42", Parliament of Canada. Available at: www.parl. gc.ca/37/1/parlbus/chambus/house/bills/government/C-42/C-42_1/C-42TOCE.html, accessed July 2009.

25 James Travers, "Bill C-42 Replacement Is Less Offensive than Original", Torstar News Service, available at: www.hamiltonspectator.com/travers/562775.html, accessed July 2009.

26 David Collenette, Ministerial Statement on Bill C-55, 29 April House of Commons.
27 Attached backgrounders and information are available online at: www.canada.gc.ca.
28 Ibid.
29 www.tc.gc.ca/mediaroom/terrorism/faq.htm, accessed 4 May 2002.
30 www.canada.gc.ca/wire/2002/04/300402_e.html – accessed 30 April 2002.
31 See, for example, Jim Bronskill, "New Anti-Terrorism Bill Worries Privacy Chief: Provisions Would Allow Police to Check Air Travellers", *The Vancouver Sun*, 8 May 2002, p. A8, on Radwanski's letter to Minister of Transport David Collenette.
32 Ibid.
33 Ibid.
34 Editorial, *Ottawa Citizen*, 23 May 2002.
35 Jim Bronskill, "Passenger List Bill Draws Fire from Watchdog", *The Vancouver Sun*, 16 May, 2002, p. A8.
36 See Jim Bronskill, "Security Bill Watered Down: RCMP Would Have Had Increased Powers", *The Vancouver Sun*, 1 November 2002, p. A6. The changes accepted by the government will prevent the RCMP from combing airline passenger manifests according to changes tabled on 31 October 2002. but could screen passenger lists for transportation security; CSIS could do likewise for transportation or national security. The revised Public Safety Act would also provide some limits on designating security zones – now limited to established military areas – or 'on a case-by-case' basis (in ibid.)
37 See, for example, Canadian Press, "Canadians of Arab Origin Advised Not to Visit the U.S", *The Vancouver Sun*, 31 October 2002, p. A9.
38 See Mike Trickey, "U.S. to Ease Entry Rules for Us: Place of Birth No Longer an Automatic Trigger for Rigour, Cellucci tells Graham", *The Vancouver Sun*, 1 November 2002, p. A6.
39 Up to the summer 2002 recess, Bill C-55 was in Second Reading in the House of Commons – with Committee stage next. Information provided by Minister of Transportation's office, 12 June 2002. See also www.parl.gc.ca/bills. Accessed 12 June 2002.
40 There has been a broad discourse initially around terrorism generally, which supported governmental action on C-36 (Anti-Terrorism); then in 2002, much of this shifted to broader public safety issues, (Bills C-42 and C-55) such as bio-terrorism and cyber-terrorism. See, for example, Jeff Lee, "Reno Fears a Cyber Pearl Harbor: Former US Attorney-General Is Not Optimistic That Nations Are Ready for a Sustained Attack on Support Systems Like Food and Transportation", *The Vancouver Sun*, 1 May 2002, p. A9; Kathryn May and Jim Bronskill, "Canada Looking for a Few Good E-Spies: CSIS (and CSE) Launches Major Recruitment Drive", *The Vancouver Sun*, 13 May, 2002, p. A1; Joseph Brean, "Glory, Fighting Draw Recruits to Join Forces: There's No Doubt That Sending Troops to Afghanistan Was Very Popular", *National Post*, 4 May 2002, p. A10; and Bill Miller and Guy Gugliotta, "'Dirty' Bomb Meant to Cause Panic: US Authorities Foil Al-Qaida Operative's Plan to Detonate a Crude Radiological Weapon", *The Vancouver Sun*, 11 June 2002, pp. A1, A5.
41 See Jim Bronskill, "Privacy Watchdog Still Opposes Anti-Terror Bill: George Radwanski Says the Latest Changes Don't Allay His Fears of a 'Police State'", *The Vancouver Sun*, 2 November 2002, p. A6.
42 See George Radwanski, "News Release", Office of the Privy Commissioner of Canada, 1 November 2002. Available at: www.privcom.gc.ca/media/nr-c/02_05_b_021101_e.asp, accessed July 2009.
43 George Radwanski, "Privacy at the Crossroads", paper for The Frontiers of Privacy and Security: New Challenges for a New Century Conference, Government of British Columbia, 13 February 2003.
44 On this, see Electronic Frontier Foundation. Available at: www.eff.org/, accessed 12 April 2003.

45 Ibid.
46 Electronic Frontier Foundation, op. cit.
47 Electronic Frontier Foundation, "Analysis of the Provisions of the USA PATRIOT Act".
48 Susan Herman, "The USA Patriot Act and the US Department of Justice: Losing Our Balances?", *JURIST*, December, 2001.
49 Ibid., p. 7.
50 Ibid.
51 Cited in Gail Chaddock.
52 Electronic Frontier Foundation, op. cit.
53 See, for example, Alex Spillius, "Terrorism: CIA Operatives Secretly Targeted Al-Qaida Figures. Cheney Ordered Details Withheld from Congress", *The Vancouver Sun*, 14 July 2009, p. B5.
54 Security Intelligence Review Committee, *Annual Report, 1998–1999*, Government of Canada, 30 September 1999, p. 3.
55 Privacy Commissioner of Canada, *Annual Report, 2000–2001*, Privacy Commission, 2001, p. 4.
56 Jim Bronskill, "Database Changes Fair, Says Privacy Czar", *The Province*, 10 April 2003, p. A26.
57 "Anti-Terror Laws 'Curb Freedoms'", *The Province*, 17 April 2003, p. A4.

12 Huntington's "clash of civilizations"

Rumours and clarification

Glenn E. Perry

A recent best-seller in France provides advice on how to talk about books without actually reading them.[1] The impossibility of devouring every page of all important works may leave us depending on reviews or flipping through the pages. There are many rumours about what authors have said, sometimes inspired by reputations earned in writing about other matters. Even those who actually get around to reading a book may see it through the lenses of such rumours.

One of the most discussed, and perhaps also one of the most unread, books of recent times, Samuel P. Huntington's *Clash of Civilizations and the Remaking of World Order*[2]—which elaborated on the themes of an earlier article by the same author[3]—has evoked an extraordinary amount of negative reaction. Huntington's basic thesis is that in the immediate post-Cold War era the lines between broad cultural groups or civilisations ("culture and cultural identities, which at the broadest level are civilization identities"), of which he identifies seven or eight main ones, Western, Orthodox, Latin American, Islamic, Hindu, Sinic, Japanese, and possibly African, are shaping world politics.[4] Although he waffles on this matter,[5] he concludes that there is no major Buddhist civilisation as such. He believes that global politics is becoming multicivilisational as the recent period of Western hegemony makes way for other civilisations to resume their normal positions of equality. In the world that he sees emerging during the twenty-first century, the six great powers (China, Japan, India, Russia, the United States, and the European Union) will represent five different civilisations, meaning that "the rivalry of superpowers is replaced by the clash of civilizations".[6] He also points to the danger that small conflicts will spread as other peoples of the same civilisation will tend to be drawn in to support their "kin". He warns that other civilisations may not always tolerate Western arrogance.

Although this may partly be a matter of semantics, only a careful reader will notice that Huntington does not claim that there was an overall clash of civilisations at the time he was writing and that he is proposing a way to prevent such a clash from occurring. Although the title of his article was followed by a question mark, as only Antony T. Sullivan[7] seems to have noticed, Huntington did conclude that "The clash of civilizations will dominate global politics",[8] but in the enlarged study he is more cautious in speaking of the "potential" for such.[9]

He is not completely consistent on this matter, though, as he classifies both the Soviet war in Afghanistan and the Gulf War of 1991 as clashes across civilisational fault lines and calls the Bosnian War part of "the ongoing clash".[10] As he put the matter in his 1993 article,[11] conflicts in places such as the Caucasus, Bosnia, and the Persian Gulf provided evidence of what was "gradually emerging" but still did not constitute a "full-scale war between civilizations", something that he later deemed "highly improbable but not impossible".[12] He has also suggested that pointing to the danger of such a clash—a self-defeating prophecy, as it were—may have helped to avert it.

Huntington does not say that most conflicts are between civilisations but rather that those that do cut across the "fault lines" of civilisations are particularly dangerous, for they threaten to spread as other states ("kin countries") in each civilisation join in. He warns the West in particular that it must not intervene arrogantly in other civilisations and presents a plan for intercivilisational cooperation to prevent the "clash of civilizations". While recognizing that civilisations evolve and borrow from one another, he warns against attempts by any country to change its civilisational affiliation (although he thinks that Latin America might become part of the West) as well as against arrogant attempts by one civilisation to impose universalist standards on others.

Hatred of other civilisations indeed has a long pedigree both in the West (which to Huntington means the countries of Europe and overseas European settlement, not including Latin America, where Roman Catholicism and its Protestant offshoots prevail) and in the previous civilisation with which the West sees itself as being affiliated, namely the ancient Hellenic world.[13] It is manifested today particularly in the form of "Islamophobia".[14] That, however, is a different matter from Huntington's vision of renewed salience for boundaries among civilisations during the early twenty-first century as such. And in any case, it is not my purpose to evaluate the correctness of Huntington's ideas but rather to show—using both *Clash of Civilizations* and some of his subsequent writings and interviews in which he has clarified his ideas—that much of what he says continues to be widely misrepresented.

Some typical rumours

In some cases, one can read page after page of dialogue between brilliant scholars[15] on the alleged flaws in Huntington's theory and see that the authors are totally bypassing the ideas he has presented. Those intellectuals who wish the Islamic world well and deplore Western imperialism—and who would find themselves surprisingly in agreement with so much of what he says if they bothered to read his writings and various clarifications he has made in subsequent interviews—have almost without exception demonstrated a knee-jerk reaction to Huntington. The latter is rumoured to be calling for a clash of civilizations and egging his fellow Islamophobes on as he condemns other cultures and stresses the necessity of continuing Western supremacy over the world and particularly over an Islamic world that he labels as inherently bloody and dangerous.

Misrepresentation of Huntington's thesis can be found again and again in all kinds of writings, from popular magazines and blogs on the one hand to works by highly respected scholars. Among the latter, two typical examples picked at random should suffice. Hamid Dabashi,[16] a professor of Iranian Studies and Comparative Literature at Columbia University, casually lumps Huntington's *Clash* and Francis Fukuyama's *The End of History* together as representing pretty much the same point of view. According to Dabashi, Huntington agreed with Fukuyama's idea that history had ended with the victory of liberal democracy (the two writers are said to "complete and complement each other"), but Huntington had come up with a picture of the victorious ideology's opponents who "were resorting to their tribal affiliations" in a last desperate attempt to stop it. "Something, Huntington thought, ought to be done about this." While Fukuyama proclaimed that the final victory of the West had taken place, Huntington, according to Dabashi, "warn[ed] that still one more victory over 'Islam' was necessary".[17]

A second example of such misunderstanding is found in an important multi-authored volume on Islam published by Oxford University Press. Managing in fact to denounce in harsh tones almost exactly the ideas that Huntington also condemns, Yvonne Yazbeck Haddad dismisses the thesis of "The Clash of Civilizations?"[18]

> as a rehash of a century-old myth that undergirded European hegemonic policies justifying wars of colonial expansion and missionary crusades during the nineteenth century under the rubric of "civilizational mission", "white man's burden", or Manifest Destiny. It posited the superiority of "European man", the acme of human civilization, who willingly assumes the burden of sharing his values and achievements with the rest of the backward world. In the process, this myth justified the ransacking of the cultures of the conquered people and confining Muslim achievements to ethnological museums or the dustbin of history.[19]

No end to history

A careful reading of Huntington's actual words reveals much that contrasts with this image. Fukuyama's work proclaiming American triumphalism ("the end of history", representing the final triumph not only of liberal democracy but also the emergence of a unipolar world that would live happily ever after under the hegemony of the nation seen as that victorious ideology's incarnation) represented the Neocon response to the end of the Cold War, Fukuyama's later repudiation of this position aside. As some observers,[20] who correctly treat Fukuyama (before he renounced Neoconism) as an "alternative world" to Huntington, are well aware, the two "Philosophically and spiritually ... could hardly be more different."[21] The thrust of Huntington's *Clash* is the opposite of what, in reference to *The End of History*, he dismisses disparagingly as "endism" and in fact was written specifi-cally as a rebuttal of Fukuyama's "one harmonious world paradigm", described as "clearly far too divorced from reality".[22, 23] In the introduction to the final chapter of his book, Huntington warns that societies who "assume that their history has ended" are likely to be those who are "about to decline".[24]

While there is much room for criticising his ideas, Huntington stresses the need to recognise the reality that other civilisations, including Islam, are on the move and inevitably will enjoy a position of relative equality with the West, whose supremacy has been a mere recent oddity.[25] Huntington concludes that the West "will remain number one in terms of power and influence well into the twenty-first century"[26] but that "Gradual, inexorable, and fundamental changes … are also occurring" that will end its primacy and elevate the relative power of other civilisations. He thinks it is possible that this process will "speed up dramatically".[27] Pointing out that it was China, not the West, that had the largest economy in the past, he suggests that a mere "two-hundred-year Western 'blip' on the world economy will be over" by about 2050.[28]

Not only does Huntington think that the rest of the world is about to assert itself, but, while not explicitly stating such a preference, he actually seems to relish the emergence of this more equal world. At least one right-wing American commentator read *Clash* carefully enough to complain that he "does not seem to consider this [the end of Western dominance] is a subject for regret" or that "we Westerners ought to make a greater effort to win".[29] One of Huntington's main fears is that arrogant Westerners, particularly Americans, will not see the folly of continuing to pursue world domination. He advises us "not to attempt to stop the shift in power but to learn to navigate the shallows".[30] He implies support for the possession of nuclear weapons by one or two countries within each major civili-sation and clearly promotes the idea that each civilisation should have a perma-nent seat on the Security Council,[31] which would facilitate implementation of his second basic principle, "the *joint mediation rule*", whereby states representing all major civilisations would keep fault line wars from getting out of hand.[32]

Drawing on Oswald Spengler, Huntington calls for a Copernican view of the world, in which one's own civilisation is not the center, to replace the old Western-centered "Ptolemaic approach".[33] He warns that the old view has recently "blossomed forth in the widespread and parochial conceit that the European civilisation of the West is now the universal civilisation of the world".

Instead of calling for an aggressive Western policy toward Islam (and other civilisations), Huntington warns that Western aggressiveness is what poses a dire threat to the West itself. In his list[34] of what he considers most imperative for the survival of Western civilisation (which admittedly includes building its own strength), he concludes that the "most important" one is recognition "that Western intervention in the affairs of other civilizations is probably the single most dangerous source of instability and potential global conflict". In a dire imaginary scenario that Huntington presents,[35] the West (and almost everybody else in the Northern Hemisphere) suffers destruction not because of appeasing its enemies, as one might expect to hear from a hard-line imperialist, but rather from arro-gantly intervening in the affairs of another civilisation after 2010 A.D.

Consequently, "the first requirement of peace in a multicivilizational, multipolar world" that Huntington lays down for "core states"—expressing his fear that the United States in particular will not accept it—is the *abstention rule*"—i.e., a complete ban on "intervention in conflicts in other civilizations". In short, those who have reacted most negatively to the rumours about Huntington's *Clash of Civilizations* might find much to applaud if they read his writings carefully and without preconceived ideas.

Not simply a matter of mutual ethnocentrism

While Huntington emphasises the importance of culture in both domestic and international politics, the main thrust of his "clash of civilisations" thesis is not that conflict emerges because people are prejudiced against the way others live and worship. Nowhere does he suggest that there is a clash between civilisations based on dislike of the way people in other societies dress or what kind of music they listen to, or the patterns of marriage, courtship, and divorce that are followed, or the different types of political systems. He does suggest that cooperation is easier for members of the same civilisation and that the cultures of some peoples may be more conducive to economic development,[36] but he does not present this as the cause of his feared "clash of civilizations".

It is true that some of the civilisations Huntington discusses are identified along religious lines, but as Sullivan points out,[37] he is not talking about a clash of religions *per se*. The basic idea is rather that "cultural identity is what is most meaningful" today, with "the broadest level" of such identities being "civilization identities"[38] and with diverse peoples belonging to the same civilisation tending to support one another in conflicts with peoples of different civilisations ("kin-country rallying" in "fault-line wars"). It is rather a matter of what might be called "pan-civilisational loyalties", or perhaps a kind of "pan nationalism" that unites Westerners, Orthodox, or Muslims in conflicts with others of the same "supertribe". Huntington described a civilisation as "the broadest cultural entity" and as "the biggest 'we' ".[39]

Even where the fault line is based on the division between different religious sects, conflicts are about identity, not necessarily religion. As Huntington pointed out in relation to Bosnia,[40] which perhaps more than any other place provided the prototype for the "clash" thesis (although he considers the Muslim rallying against the Soviets in Afghanistan to be the first example of the "fault line clash" phenomenon), "Muslims ... were Bosnians who did not go to the mosque. Croats were Bosnians who did not go to the cathedral, and Serbs were Bosnians who did not go to the Orthodox church", although the conflict brought a resurgence of religion among the Muslims in particular. In effect, the clash in Bosnia was no more about religion than was the conflict between Protestants and Catholics in Ireland. What he is saying is that there are many conflicts within civilisations but that the most dangerous conflicts are those that cut across the "fault lines" because of "the potential for escalation as other states and groups ... rally to the support of their 'kin countries' ".[41]

Huntington recognizes the Islamic world's present clash with the West as a continuing struggle against colonialism. Thus, in an interview in 2006, he opined that:

> In large part, these difficulties are the result of the extent to which a good portion of the Muslim world was subject to Western colonialism. The peoples in those areas have now asserted themselves. So you have a natural tension and conflicts occurring between the gradually retreating imperial powers and the asserting native people.[42]

Admittedly, there is much to quarrel about in this statement. Instead of "gradually retreating", the American presence has been growing, since the 1970s, and particularly since 1990. Although that was itself a reaction to certain revolts against Western supremacy, it is the renewed Western presence that fuels further anti-imperialist revolts. Nevertheless, the way Huntington puts the struggle in the anti-colonial context sets him apart from the narrow-minded, chauvinist ("they hate us because of who we are" or "… because they hate freedom") line.

No claim that Islam is inherently hostile or bloody

It is widely understood that Huntington puts the onus for conflict and violence in the contemporary Islamic world on Islam itself. In *The Clash of Civilizations*, he indeed points to—but without endorsing— the argument that the Islamic world always has been particularly war-prone and that this is related to Islam's having "been a religion of the sword".[43] Referring to the disproportionate number of conflicts today that involve Muslims,[44] he reaffirms his famous statement first made in his *Foreign Affairs* article, that "Islam's [i.e., the Islamic world's] borders are bloody", adding "and so are its innards",[45] something that might have been said about Europe in, say, 1917 or 1942 and even more recently about much of non-Muslim Africa.

However, he argues that factors other than Islam as such are necessary to explain today's disproportionate number of conflicts in the Islamic world. In his more recent statements, he is particularly forthright about this. Thus, in his October 2001 interview he bluntly stated: "I don't think Islam is any more violent than any other religions, and I suspect if you added it all up, more people have been slaughtered by Christians over the centuries than by Muslims."[46] In his *Newsweek* article,[47] he reiterated his rejection of the idea that contemporary wars in the Islamic world relate to any "inherent nature of Islamic doctrine and beliefs".

After referring to the argument that Islam itself is to blame (which, as a careful reading will uncover, he never commits himself to), Huntington suggests several other possible causes of violence in the late twentieth century.[48] One that actually puts more of the onus on the Christian world is that Islam historically expanded by land, leaving "Muslims and non-Muslims living in close physical proximity", whereas the West expanded by sea, leaving conquered peoples "virtually decimated by Western settlers". He also points to the possibility that Muslims—because for Muslims national identity tends to be tied to religion—are less digestible, that is, less easy to assimilate to non-Muslim nationalities, and that Muslims in a disproportionate number of cases are victims (which he seems to reject as general explanation). Then he considers the possibility that the lack of a "core state" in the Islamic world is conducive to conflict.

Huntington places most of the responsibility for contemporary violence involving Muslims on demographic factors. In particular, he points to "the availability of large numbers of often unemployed males between the ages of fifteen and thirty", which he deems to be "a natural source of instability and violence" that "goes a long way in explaining" recent conflict but might be expected to disappear as the age structure changes by about 2020 and as economic development proceeds.[49]

Supporting Islamic power

While at least on one occasion qualifying his preference for the existence of a hegemonic power within each civilisation with the statement that it "depends on who that hegemonic leader is", Huntington pointed out that having a big regional power such as India or China facilitates dealing with regional problems.[50] This continues the thinking found in *Clash of Civilizations*, in which he points, as we saw above, to the absence of a "core state" in Islamic civilisation as one of the sources of conflict. In what might be labeled an endorsement of pan-Islamism and an implicit criticism of Western policies that have kept the Islamic world weak during the past century, Huntington reiterated the idea that the emergence of "one or two" powerful states in the Muslim world—he cites the Ottoman Empire as a past model for this—would be conducive to peace "among Muslims and, probably, between Muslims and non-Muslims".[51] This favorable attitude toward allowing a big power to emerge in the Islamic world puts Huntington at odds with the foreign policies of Western powers at least since World War I and in line with the demands of Islamists and Arab nationalists.[52]

Huntington's ideas about what is necessary for future world order involve several specific principles that sound as though they might have been proposed by nationalist movements in the Islamic world or by Islamists. His *"abstention rule"* would require core states in one civilisation not to intervene in conflicts within other civilisations, while his *"joint mediation rule"* would require collective efforts by core states to stop "fault line wars between states or groups from their civilization".[53] In order to implement this idea, he insists that each civilisation must have permanent membership in the Security Council of the United Nations (with rotating membership for member states of civilisations that lack core states, as now is the case with the Islamic world). He proposes that Western permanent membership be reduced from three to two for now, with French and British membership replaced by one European Union member chosen on a rotating basis, an arrangement he justifies as being based on "the distribution of people, wealth, and power".[54] Pointing to Iran's natural desire to emulate Pakistan as a nuclear power, he also believes that "one or two core states in each of the major civilizations"—he does not exclude the Islamic world—should have nuclear weapons in order to produce "a reasonably stable world".[55]

Elsewhere, Huntington clearly seems to think that the Islamic world needs to have a core state, and after considering several candidates for leadership he seems to settle on a future transformed—re-Islamicised—Turkey.[56] He suggests that one day this country will come back home to the civilisation it purported to tear itself off from—by renouncing "its frustrating and humiliating role as a beggar pleading for membership in the West and to resume its much more impressive and elevated role" and "reject Ataturk's legacy", comparing the way South Africa rejected apartheid and thus showed its qualifications "to lead Africa".[57] Whether or not one agrees with this, my point is that his ideas are far removed from what is so persistently and so widely rumoured about him. In effect, he is proposing a new version of pan-Islamism and a restored Ottoman Empire. More recently, he opined that, "Maybe Iraq will come back and become the dominant power among Arab countries."[58]

Opposing interventionism and Western or American hegemony

Far from calling for an aggressive Western, particularly American, policy toward the non-Western world ("the rest"), Huntington strongly stresses the dangers of such. Discussion of Huntington's "clash" thesis reveals a widespread notion that he is calling for a clash with—or hostility to—other civilisations. However, he has repeatedly made clear that he is warning about the danger of a clash of civilisations.

In his 1998 American Enterprise Institute address,[59] Huntington disputed the claim—essential to the Neocon scheme of unilaterally controlling the world—that the world had become unipolar (except for a "brief moment"). He insisted instead on describing the world at that time as uni-multipolar, that is, one in which there is one superpower but also "other major states" whose collaboration is necessary if actions are to be taken, and predicted that within "one or perhaps more" decades it would be multipolar.

In the same address, he warned his listeners about the way America is perceived. Reporting on what he had heard at an international conference held at Harvard the year before, he proclaimed—with an empathy that seems daring before a heavily Neocon audience—that most of the world then saw

> the United States as the single greatest external threat to their societies … as intrusive, interventionist, exploitative, unilateralist, hegemonic, applying double standards, engaging in "financial imperialism" and "intellectual colonialism", and with a foreign policy driven overwhelmingly by domestic politics, particularly the Israeli lobby.

He warned Americans to "stop acting and talking" as though they could "act as a global sheriff", concluding his lecture by predicting that life will be better for the

United States ("less demanding, less contentious, and more rewarding") once it takes its place as only one of several great powers.

Huntington's explanation for al-Qaeda's attack on the World Trade Center and the Pentagon stands in glaring contrast to what one usually hears in the United States. He is quite aware of the real reasons:

> America was targeted as the enemy because it was powerful, because it was Christian, and because it was deploying its military forces in the holy land of Islam and sustaining a corrupt Saudi regime, which was but "a branch or an agent of the U.S".[60]

Huntington's further analysis of the reasons for Muslim hostility to the United States contains much more that is more enlightened than what normally comes from establishment circles. He sees Muslim hostility as resulting "from American support for Israel" but more broadly from

> the fear of American power, envy of American wealth, resentment of what is perceived as American domination and exploitation, and [here he momentarily seems more hospitable to the Neocon/Bush line] hostility to American culture, secular and religious, as the antithesis of Muslim culture.[61]

He accepts the need to confront such hostility if it cannot be avoided[62] but—with the war in Iraq in mind—warns against the dangers of "extended war against one or more hostile states that had not attacked America directly and yet which did require high levels of mobilization".[63] In his *Newsweek* article,[64] he recognised that Muslim, and particularly Arab, hostility is related to "Western imperialism and domination of the Muslim world for much of the 20th century" and "particular Western policies, including American action against Iraq since 1991, and the continuing close relationship between the United States and Israel" as well as resentment against "corrupt, ineffective and repressive governments" and the Western powers "they [Muslims; Arabs] see supporting those regimes". He warned that use of force in the Islamic world would produce a "widespread and intense ... Muslim reaction" and even "Muslim unity". He opined that changes in "U.S. policies toward Israel" might alleviate "resentment and hostility".

In the sequel to *Clash of Civilizations*, Huntington outlines "three broad concepts" that might define "America in relation to the rest of the world".[65] He clearly opposes both "the cosmopolitan" approach, which he sees as subordinating its own national identity by opening its borders and becoming a multicultural country, with its "elites who increasingly identified with global institutions, norms and rules rather than national ones" and the "imperial alternative", in which "America remakes the world", that is, the kind of "imperial" policy that he describes conservatives (he means Neocons) as having endorsed at the beginning of the millennium, involving "the use of American power to reshape the world according to American values". He warns that, "In such a world America loses its identity as a nation and becomes the dominant component of a supranational empire"[66] and that neither of the two approaches "accurately reflects the state of the early-twenty-first-century world", as "there are other major powers" whose cooperation is required for the pursuit of important goals. "Their peoples normally feel deeply committed to their indigenous cultures, traditions and institutions, and hence fiercely resist efforts to change them by outsiders from alien cultures." While not suggesting that the rhetoric about spreading democracy might be hypocritical, he warns that success in this endeavor would bring "anti-American forces" to power.[67] Instead of these two approaches, Huntington comes down in favor of the "national approach" that "would recognize and accept what distinguishes America from" the rest of the world.[68]

> America cannot become the world and still be America. Other peoples cannot become American and still be themselves. America is different, and that difference is defined in large part by its Anglo-Protestant culture and its religiosity. The alternative to cosmopolitanism and imperialism is nationalism devoted to the preservation and enhancement of those qualities that have defined America since its founding.[69]

He goes on to blame elites for espousing the cosmopolitan and imperial ideas and believes that ordinary Americans support the national approach that "preserve[s] and strengthen[s] the American identity".

While Huntington endorsed the Bush Administration's immediate response to the September 11, 2001 attacks, he warned—in keeping with his opposition to arrogant intervention in the affairs of other civilisations—against further aggressive actions. In his 21 October 2001 interview, he spoke of calls some were making for broadening the response by attacking other groups and states, calling this "a danger" that, if it took place, "could broaden it [the U.S. response] into a clash of civilizations", which would be to the liking of Osama bin Laden.[70] While opining that there is a need to "try to understand" the concerns of the Islamic world and "try to accommodate their particular interests", he described himself at that time, with some apparent hesitation, as "reasonably satisfied" with Bush's "war on terrorism", if only because of fears that "it could have been much worse".[71]

Huntington repeatedly has been critical of the US invasion of Iraq. Apparently riled by hostile questions about his views on immigration, he bluntly told an interviewer for the *New York Times*[72] that, as "an old-fashioned Democrat", he "was dead-set against us going into Iraq", and that he was going to vote for John Kerry as president. In an interview in 2006,[73] he reiterated that while "Iraq is an important oil producer" and "we want to have stability in the Persian Gulf area", he "didn't see the need for us to go into Iraq" and advocated getting out "in a fairly responsible fashion that won't produce even worse consequences". He suggested the possibility of "setting a timetable ... of gradual withdrawal" that might include involvement of "other Gulf states, or the European Union".

Opposing Kemalism, supporting cultural authenticity

Just as he supports monoculturalism within each civilisation, Huntington sees the need for multiculturalism on a global level. He rejects universalism—and thus the ideas of imperialists and liberal interventionists—in favor of cultural relativism. He accepts the existence of only a "'thin' minimalist morality" shared by all cultures and calls for a search for "commonalities",[74] which leads him[75] to announce a third basic principle for future peace: "the *commonalities rule*".

Far from wanting to "relegate Islam to museums", as a prominent scholar described him above, Huntington believes that it is important for each civilisation, including the Islamic one, to preserve its own distinctiveness and not engage in the folly of Westernisation. He believes that attempts by a "member state" to be "torn" off from its own civilisation—except in rare cases in which the elites are enthusiastic and the masses are willing to "acquiesce", and the West is willing to accept the new member state[76]—are doomed to fail. Huntington[77] is confident that Europe will never accept Turkey as one of its own. For a non-Western country to be modern thus requires not trying to be Western.

Huntington points to Turkey as the classic case of a "torn country". He makes "Kemalism" a generic term for what he considers the "hubris" shown when any non-Western country confuses modernisation with Westernisation and tries to change its civilisational affiliation against the will of much of its public and the unwillingness of the West to accept it:

> the Western virus, once it is lodged in another society, is difficult to expunge. The virus persists but is not fatal; the patient survives but is never whole. Political leaders can make history but they cannot escape history. They produce torn countries; they do not create Western societies. They infect their country with a cultural schizophrenia which becomes its continuing and defining characteristic.[78]

Someone "of Ataturk's caliber and one who combined religious and political legitimacy", Huntington[79] opines, will be required to lead Turkey back to the right path.

Thus, for Huntington any Islamic country that has tried to Westernise must return to its own Islamic affiliation.[80] Quoting Regis Debray, he treats the revival of religion as "the vitamin of the weak" and calls it "a declaration of cultural independence from the West" but "not a rejection of modernity".

All of this is in line with what Huntington has been saying since the early 1970s. Going back at least to an important critique of modernisation and political development theory that pointed to an already-emerging body of writings on "modernization revisionism", Huntington[81] has stressed the fallacy of making indigenous practices ("tradition") the polar opposite of the "modern" and of failing "to distinguish between what is modern and what is Western" He says, in effect, that modernity does necessarily require Westernisation, for "traditional" patterns may actually be congruent with "modernity" and that a modernised world will not necessarily be a homogenous one, and that "modernization itself may strengthen tradition",[82] while "traditional attitudes and behavior may also help modernization".[83]

Not a Western chauvinist

In confronting the idea of permanent Western supremacy, Huntington is sometimes rather disparaging to the West. He makes clear that past Western dominance resulted not from the superiority of its culture in general ("its ideals or values or religion") but only from "its superiority in applying organized violence", something it tends to forget, although "non-Westerners never do".[84] He accepts the basic thesis of world-systems and dependency theorists that "the industrialization of the West led to the deindustrialization of the rest of the world".[85] He talks about Western "hypocrisy" and "double standards".[86]

Huntington suggests that bullying by the West is in danger of getting so egregious that it eventually will push the Sinic and Islamic worlds "to cooperate with each other against the West, even as the Allies and Stalin did against Hitler".[87] He approvingly quotes Graham Fuller's belief that Muslims and Confucians might decide that "they don't have to take it anymore".[88] He pointed to the West's failure to condemn members of its own supertribe, the Catholic Croatians, as much as it condemned the Orthodox Serbs.[89] He believes that the end of the West's political hegemony is bringing an end to its cultural hegemony as well, with the modernisation of non-Western societies "generating the revival of non-Western cultures throughout the world".[90]

Why the negative reaction?

The negative reaction to Huntington's "clash of civilizations" results from the convergence of several matters. It is not enough to dismiss the issue by saying that his critics just have not bothered to read him. It may also be true that many who do read sometimes start out with a preconceived idea of what they are reading. But why do so many people who would find some of Huntington's ideas appealing fail to understand him more than is the case with other writers? Even he has complained that all of his works "have been misinterpreted", suggesting that perhaps he just did not write clearly. But it might be more a matter of some readers' failure to pay attention to complex analysis or else that "people often project into a work what they think it should be saying".[91] As in the case of the phrase "bloody borders", he tends to use provocative language. While objectively true about the Islamic world at a particular point in time, such easily noticed sound bites can be misconstrued by most readers and cause them to overlook his elaborate, fair-minded analysis that puts matters in a totally different light from what they at first imagine. While Huntington's writing is clear, sometimes it is easy to miss the subtlety of his analysis when first reading it, as in the case of his discussion of the possible connections between Islam and violence.

Several Huntingtons?

Part of the explanation is that Huntington's ideas first appeared in abbreviated versions[92] in which his dovish attitude toward other civilisations is less obvious than in his later pronouncements and that many people made up their minds about him and failed to look further. I often have had people tell me they have not read the book but that they have read the *Foreign Affairs* article.

Sullivan maintains that the Huntington of later years has become "radically altered" compared with what he said in his *Foreign Affairs* article of 1993. The 1996 book is said to have served as a "watershed" that "foreshadowed Huntington's currently more sympathetic outlook toward Arabs and Islam". He is described indeed as having "repudiated his original hypothesis and emerged as an apostle of conciliation and a critic of U.S. foreign policy" to the extent that now "several Samuel Huntingtons exist".[93] There is some basis for this, as the book enlarges on some of the statements in the previous article that were so abbreviated as to be overlooked or at least not fully self-explanatory except in light of his more fully developed later work. In various interviews as well as in the Dubai address, which Sullivan cites, the thrust of his ideas are even clearer. To some extent, this is true, as he has presented various clarifications, particularly in rare interviews and in his *Newsweek* article, which surprised one reader[94] so much that he mistakenly thought Huntington was contradicting his earlier ideas. Admittedly, one must avoid the mistake of reading too much of his later analysis into his earlier writing. However, at several points in the 1993 article one can foresee what he says in the book. For example, in the last paragraph of the *Foreign Affairs* article,[95] he calls on the West "to accommodate" other civilisations and to develop a "profound understanding" of them. It is in his book that he fully lays out his scheme for a more egalitarian world order.

Equal but separate civilisations

Part of the explanation for his reputation as a bogeyman may relate to the fact that Huntington's support for the idea of a multicultural world is matched by a belief in the imperative of rejecting multiculturalism on a national level. As I previously put the matter, he is calling for an equal but separate world. He warns of the dangers that face a "cleft country",[96] that is, one that cuts across civilisational lines, such as Malaysia or the Sudan. Consequently, he warns countries not to accept such large numbers of immigrants from any one outside civilisation that they cannot be assimilated. This narrow position on immigration has kept many people from looking at his more enlightened position on world order.

Huntington's concept of American identity in particular strongly rejects multiculturalism on a national scale. American identity, he insists, is not mainly about people of diverse origins accepting a common American Creed (the salad bowl concept) but rather on acceptance of the Anglo-Protestant culture that British settlers (not immigrants, he stresses) brought with them, with later waves of alien immigrants being assimilated to this culture, which he describes as a kind of tomato soup that they have added some flavouring to but which has remained tomato soup. Even Catholic immigrants, he shows, have developed a kind of American Catholicism in keeping with the dominant Anglo-Protestant nation.[97] The best known part of this idea is Huntington's fear that that too many immigrants of one culture, Hispanics, are entering today to be assimilated.[98] It should be noted that while this may be made to look like a kind of Know-Nothingism, Huntington is not rejecting immigration *per se*, but rather the immigration of one group—particularly one that he defines as belong to a foreign civilisation—on such a scale that it might result in a country divided into two nations, Anglo-Protestant and Hispanic.

Huntington's past reputation: authoritarianism

Other past writings of Huntington, or at least widespread interpretations of them, helped to close minds with regard to what he was saying about the clash of civilisations. As Fukuyama states in his Foreword to the reprint of Huntington's 1968 classic, *Political Order in Changing Societies*,[99] the latter's stress on the need for "the 'authoritarian transition', whereby a modernizing dictatorship provided political order" helped to bring "considerable opprobrium on him".[100] Indeed, Huntington stressed that order is a first priority for many countries and that freedom has to await its establishment, as happened in the West.

In fact, Huntington presented Lenin's single-party regime, which he applauded as the greatest political invention of the twentieth century, as a model for non-communist countries to follow.[101] He stressed that such a monopolistic party provided a solution for countries where modernisation was producing demands for popular participation when institutions to facilitate such were not in place, allowing them to combine participation (highly regimented, but, according to Huntington, authentic) with order. Huntington and Nelson further developed the idea that "mobilized" participation is no less real than is the "autonomous" variety.[102] According to Ervand Abrahamian,[103] it was, in part, the influence of students who had studied in the United States and absorbed Huntington's ideas about this matter that led Muhammad Riza Shah to establish a single political organisation in Iran, the National Resurgence Party, which, "lacking popular support, would produce exactly what it was supposed to avoid—popular revolution". As Abrahamian notes,[104] Huntington's ex-students overlooked their former teacher's stress on the Leninist-style party's role as a conveyer of input from society—in effect, the more democratic side of Leninism—as well as its being an instrument of control.[105] Admittedly, by the early 1990s—immediately before he moved to the "clash of civilizations" idea—Huntington had joined the cause of democratisation,[106] presenting the story of a "third wave" of democratisation that had hit the world's shores since 1974 along with a relatively optimistic projection of the prospects that this wave would continue. But his earlier reputation would not die easily, although he served as an advisor to the military regime in Brazil on gradual liberalisation and, in 1981, urged the South African regime to carry out reforms.[107]

Accusations of authoritarian tendencies go back further than Huntington's 1968 book. Huntington relates that Carl Friedrich, who "led the opposition", made clear to him that his initial rejection for tenure at Harvard[108] (he was later invited back to Harvard after a stint at Columbia, as Friedrich changed his mind about him) resulted from the perception that his book, *The Soldier and the State*, published in 1957, "was basically an argument for authoritarianism"—something that he maintained at the time was a misinterpretation.[109] One reviewer compared him unfavorably with Mussolini.[110]

Huntington, the conservative anti-Neocon

More broadly, there is much in Huntington that one can easily recognise as a Burkean conservatism that tempers his fundamental liberalism. His stress on the importance of order provides one example of this, as does his belief that countries and peoples cannot easily—and in most cases must not try to—uproot themselves from the civilisations to which they have belonged for centuries. The realisation that one civilisation that has been dominant for only a few centuries must allow the world to resort to a more normal state of affairs in which civilisations are more equal in power also demonstrates his conservative stance. Even more clearly evincing conservatism are his warnings about the dangers of trying to reorder the world—and particularly to force democratisation—through military intervention.

But such conservatism should not be confused with "Neoconservatism". The latter is a movement founded by former leftists, mostly Jewish, closely aligned with the right wing, i.e., the Likud Party, in Israel. One is reminded of the way the formerly socialist and pacifist Benito Mussolini was transformed into the founder of a militant imperialist and anti-socialist movement during the First World War. Characterized by a kind of radicalism that reflects their origins and that some observers have labeled "Neo-jacobins", the Neocons are committed to American world supremacy—and engage in rhetoric about aggressively imposing democracy—as a way of supporting Israel.[111] It is rightist in the sense of promoting an imperialist policy but in many ways is the antithesis (particularly in its radical rhetoric about imposing democracy by force) of real conservatism in the European sense, of old-fashioned American-style conservatism (which is really classical liberalism), and the Paleo-conservatism that is represented by Pat Buchanan and his magazine, *The American Conservative*. (It is the latter whose ideas parallel Huntington's in opposing both imperialism and unlimited immigration.)

It is true, as Huntington pointed out in an address to the group in 1998,[112] that he has had longtime ties with the AEI (including membership in its Council of Academic Advisers), a well known bastion of the Neocons. He first aired his "clash" thesis in a Bradley Lecture at the AEI in 1992.[113,114] But he began his address by warning his listeners that "I do not exactly fit the AEI mold", that he considered himself "a conservative, but the old-fashioned Burkean sort of conservative rather than a modern Reaganite conservative", and expressed thanks for being welcomed despite being "a maverick Democrat and old-fashioned and unfashionable conservative". Referring particularly to Huntington's speech in Dubai in November 2001 in which he called on the United States to give up the idea that American ways should be universal, to end military intervention except when there is a threat to vital US interests, and "to distance itself from Israel,". Sullivan concluded that "Neoconservatives must be displeased by the trajectory of his thought" and that "American paleoconservatives ... should now not hesitate to embrace Huntington as one of their own"—indeed, that "Patrick J. Buchanan could not have said any of this better".[115]

Unlike the Neocons, Huntington's writings and public statements show no obsession with Israel. He has said that Stephen Walt and John Mearsheimer's thesis about the Israel Lobby is one that we "have to take seriously", although he opined that the Israel Lobby is only one of several ethnic interests and "is not unique", and that it "is focused on just one issue".[116] In his Dubai speech, he made strong statements about the Palestine question, calling for US actions "to bring about a Palestinian state", of which Jerusalem would be the shared capital, and to "secure the removal of Israeli settlements in Gaza and the West Bank". He called for self-determination for the Muslims of Chechnya and Kashmir as well as Palestine.[117]

Huntington long has been aware of the fallacy of the Neocon idea that forced "democratisation" of the Islamic world would produce governments favorable to American policies.[118] In a recent interview,[119] he responded to a question about recent victories of Islamist parties that this "did not surprise" him at all, as such elections could only be expected to reflect "nationalist sentiment" of peoples who, "for understandable reasons, are often rather anti-Western", and he expressed agreement that "there is a general failure on the part of many Americans", including "people in the Bush administration", in not foreseeing the victory for Hamas in recent Palestinian elections.

Association with the Vietnam War

Some writers' preconceptions may result from Huntington's past association with the US Government and its foreign policy, particularly during the Vietnam War. Even on this matter, he relates that a trip to Vietnam in 1967 led him to conclude that Washington's policies were "stupid".[120] He headed a task force on Vietnam for presidential candidate Hubert Humphrey in 1968 that drafted a speech calling for an end to the bombing.[121] While originally supporting the war in Vietnam, in a secret report he later argued for " 'accommodation' with local religious and political organizations, including even the Viet Cong", but he gained notoriety among opponents of the war when the Johnson Administration published an incomplete version of the report, making him a target of demonstrations on the Harvard campus.[122] Thus, when he was rejected (a second time) for membership in the prestigious National Academy of Sciences in 1987 (with opposition coming from natural scientists, purportedly on grounds of his using mathematical equations poorly, but with some believing that his "conservative" politics and particularly his association with the Vietnam War played a role[123]), a front-page editorial in the liberal American magazine, *The Nation*, applauded such treatment of "Mad Dog" (the epithet anti-war activists had hurled at him two decades earlier), declaring that not only was "his science pseudo" but that "His old adversaries, not to mention millions of Asians and Africans, know that his science was murderous as well."[124] Such a reputation in liberal circles, whether deserved or not, did not facilitate a willingness to listen to his ideas about a clash of civilisations with an open mind.

Confusion with Bernard Lewis's "Clash of Civilizations"

The closed-minded reaction may also have been a result of the fact that the phrase Huntington used—"clash of civilizations"—had recently been used by Bernard Lewis. As the rumours have it, Huntington is a virtual identical twin of Lewis.[125] Lewis's article appeared in 1990, and Huntington[126] cites it and apparently borrowed the term from him. Lewis presented a clash between Islam and the West that involved "a rejection of Western civilization as such, not only what it does but what it is, and the principles and values that it practices and professes".[127] Lewis discounted the obvious reasons for Muslim hostility to the West, although he admitted that "American support for hated regimes, seen as reactionary by radicals, as impious by conservatives, as corrupt and tyrannical by both" as having "some plausibility" but argued that "something deeper is involved than these specific grievances"[128] and presented strangely skewed arguments trying to undermine the idea that Western support for Israel is part of the problem (e.g., emphasising that Washington had opposed Israeli actions once, that is, in 1956), and arguing that for "fundamentalists" the explanation is "secularism and modernism".[129] Thus Lewis's "clash of civilizations" is simply "the perhaps irrational but surely historic reaction of an ancient rival against our Judeo-Christian heritage, our secular present, and the worldwide expansion of both".[130] In effect, it is "not our policies", Lewis was saying (and we have heard such crude versions of this theme many times recently) that trouble Muslims, but dislike of "who we are".

This is quite different from the "clash" that Huntington is talking about, one in which loyalties to the Islamic "supertribe" cause members of the *ummah* to rally in support of their fellow Muslims in Bosnia, Palestine, Afghanistan, Iraq, and Kashmir and in which unwarranted American intervention in the internal affairs of the Sinic or Islamic world is so dangerous. Lewis's presentation of secular nationalist Arabs as well as Islamists as enemies that the West must confront— and particularly taking the lead after September 11, 2001 in pushing for an invasion of Iraq—is matched by Huntington's call for staying out of the affairs of other civilisations lest the West's arrogance bring disaster on itself and others. Lewis's eagerness to impose the Ataturk model—also equated with democratisation, although that process did not begin in Turkey until well after Ataturk's death—on the Arab world through Ahmad Chalabi and the like, resulting in a "Lewis Doctrine" guiding the Bush Administration's policies,[131] is matched by Huntington's call for the renewed Islamicisation of Turkey to rid itself of the "sickness" of Kemalism. Whereas Lewis played a crucial role in inspiring the invasion of Iraq in 2003, Huntington, as shown elsewhere in this chapter, has been consistently critical of this action. While it is understandable that

Huntington's adoption of a phrase first popularized by Lewis would help create such a misunderstanding, it would be hard to imagine two versions of the "clash of civilisations" more different from each other than these two. Yet such an insightful writer as Mahmood Mamdani,[132] an anthropologist at Columbia University, dismissed Huntington's ideas as merely a "cruder version" of Lewis's "culture talk" simply on the basis of its global scope.

A mapmaker, not necessarily an oversimplifier

Finally, there is a failure to understand that Huntington is purporting to present a simplified map that he believes is useful for limited purposes. Like any "model" that a social scientist uses, maps "represent some features of the world and not others" and are useful for some but not all purposes".[133] He is merely proposing "a paradigm ... that will be meaningful to scholars and useful to policymakers", not one that "accounts for everything that is happening in global politics" and is applicable not to all periods of history but simply for "the late twentieth and early twenty-first centuries"[134] and will likely cease to be useful in the future, as came to be true of the "Cold War model during the late 1980s".[135] Such a map or paradigm "omits many things, distorts some things, and obscures others" but is necessary "if we are to think seriously about the world, and act effectively in it".[136] It needs to be realistic and parsimonious and to be useful for purposes of prediction.[137] Anyone who points to exceptions to the "clash" thesis is missing the point, as Huntington makes clear that this is only one theme among others in the contemporary world. He recognizes that *realpolitik* is a permanent force that will sometimes trump civilisational ties. An attempt to show statistically that most conflicts today are not related to civilisational differences is irrelevant, as is the commonly heard argument that conflict is mainly within rather than among civilisations. Any clash between a long hegemonic civilisation and one that has been subordinated is likely to involve a struggle—here I am using Toynbee's terms—between Herodian and Zealot elements in the latter. Even Huntington calculated that in 1993, when his paradigm was taking shape, clashes across civilisational fault lines accounted for slightly fewer than half of the world's conflicts.[138]

This misunderstanding has led to the idea that Huntington presents each civilisation as a monolithic entity. He rejects this as "totally false", suggesting that the Islamic world is particularly un-unified and that this is part of a "problem" that would be ameliorated if there were a dominant Islamic power.[139] As for the idea that civilisations are isolated, unchanging entities, Huntington rejects that too, fully understanding that "the lines between them are seldom sharp", that they "merge and divide" and "disappear", and that it is not even easy to determine how many there are.[140]

Conclusion

The thrust of Huntington's ideas about the post-Cold War world order diverges dramatically from what it is widely thought to be. He foresees a wide dispersion of power among the various civilisations during the twenty-first century that will not just end Western hegemony, which he portrays as having been a temporary phenomenon whose end it would be dangerous to resist. Further, instead of bewailing what he sees as the emerging equality of civilisations, he seems eager for the world to accept it as a reality. While seeing a need for the West to strengthen itself, he warns of the danger of arrogantly attempting to interfere in non-Western areas. And while he does not reject cultural borrowing, he maintains that modernisation for any country should not involve trying to tear itself away from its own civilisation and attempting to be part of another one. While his recipe for the West is the strengthening of its own religion, his advice to the Islamic world approximates that of Islamist movements both on the matter of seeking to restore the place of Muslims in the world and on strengthening the Islamic nature of its society. That might explain why, as Gilles Keppel[141] tells us, militant Muslims, who seem to have read the book more carefully than has Keppel (who imagines that Huntington and Islamic militants just "invert the signs of Good and Evil") are so "thrilled" by *The Clash of Civilizations*. After interviewing him, a Muslim graduate student at Harvard reported that what she had previously heard about "the 'clash of civilizations' may not be the thesis that Huntington originally conceived".[142]

It may be that the caricature of Huntington's "clash" carried by so many rumours inspires many whose outlooks are very different from his. As a critic of Huntington's "big idea",[143] put the matter:

> Now it may be a long way from the lecture halls of Harvard to Abu Ghraib prison but one has to wonder whether it wasn't some bastardized version of the "clash of civilizations" that motivated those Marine interrogators. Sam Huntington, an opponent of the Iraq intervention, would be appalled at such a suggestion but, again, once you rally the country around a "big idea" it's hard to control how it gets used.

Apparently influenced now by the usual rumours as his memory of what he perhaps once read (and particularly of the bad name he was called in *Clash of Civilizations*) was growing dim, a prominent observer whose career has benefitted greatly from taking the side of the enemies of the civilisation of his birth and who initially rejected Huntington's thesis, thus decided 15 years later that the latter was right after all.[144]

Contrary to the rumours, Huntington's fears of a clash on civilisational lines are accompanied by rather utopian-sounding proposals for "an international order based on civilizations" in which the diversity of the world is encouraged and there would be a restored equality of power among civilisations.[145] Disputes would be mediated by the joint efforts of major units representing all of the civilisations—as "the surest safeguard against war".[146] Huntington thinks the emergence of one big power in the Islamic world would facilitate his envisioned new order. He does not call this a caliphate, but that seems to be what he is pointing to. It would be a world in which no clash of civilisations would occur after all. Contrary to repeated rumours (and vagueness in some of his writings at times), Huntington has repeatedly agreed that a clash, though a danger, has not taken place yet and "is not inevitable".[147]

Notes

1 Pierre Bayard, *How to Talk About Books You Haven't Read*, trans. Jeffrey Mehlman, New York: Bloomsbury, 2007.
2 Samuel P. Huntington, *The Clash of Civilizations and the Remaking of the Modern World*, New York: Simon & Schuster, 1996.
3 Samuel P. Huntington, "The Clash of Civilizations?" *Foreign Affairs*, 73(3) (1993): 22–49.
4 Huntington 1996, op. cit., p. 20.
5 Ibid., pp. 27, 49–50.
6 Ibid., p. 28.
7 Antony T. Sullivan, "Has Samuel Huntington's Prediction Come to Pass", *Journal of the Historical Society*, 2(Spring) (2002): 170.
8 Huntington, 1993, op. cit., p. 22.
9 Huntington, 1996, op. cit., p. 28.
10 Ibid., pp. 247, 251, 291.
11 Huntington, 1993, op. cit., p. 35.
12 Huntington, 1996, op. cit., p. 312.
13 Robert Bevan, *The Destruction of Memory: Architecture at War*; London: Reakton Books, 2006, pp. 87ff.
14 Peter Gottschalk and Gabriel Greenberg, *Islamophobia: Making Muslims the Enemy*; Lanham, MD: Rowman & Littlefield, 2008.
15 Daisaku, Ikeda and Majid Tehranian, *Global Civilization: A Buddhist-Islamic Dialogue*, London and New York: British Academic Press, 2003, pp. 78ff.
16 Hamid Dabashi, *Iran: A People Interrupted*, New York and London: The New Press, 2007, p. 3.
17 Ibid., p. 212.
18 Yvonne Yazbeck Haddad, "The Globalization of Islam: The Return of Muslims to the West" in John L. Esposito (ed.) *The Oxford History of Islam*, Oxford: Oxford University Press, 1999, p. 632.
19 For other examples of such misrepresentation of the Huntington thesis, see my earlier article ("Huntington and His Critics: The West and Islam", *Arab Studies Quarterly*, 24 (Winter): 31–48; reprinted in *Islam and Globalization: Critical Studies in Islamic Studies*; Vol. III: *Global Order*; ed. Shahram Akbarzadeh, London and New York: Routledge, 2006, pp. 231–250), which, unlike this chapter, does not bring in much of what Huntington has said since the publication of *Clash of Civilizations* and does not attempt to explain the general predisposition to misrepresent Huntington's ideas on world order.
20 Stanley Kurtz, "The Future of 'History', Francis Fukuyama vs. Samuel P. Huntington", *Policy Review*, June/July (2002): 43–44 and *passim*.
21 Representing the typical bravado of the Neocons, at the time and in a telling attempt to reconcile Huntington's and Fukuyama's opposing views, Kurtz (ibid., pp. 43–58) goes on to opine that both writers nevertheless represent a kind of conservatism, with "unexpected areas of convergence", being "at once both complementary and irreconcilable", in the sense that a world so far correctly described by Huntington was making way, for the end of history after all as,

> Inevitably, our victories in the war against terror will give us greater and greater power within the Muslim world. We exercise that power now in Afghanistan; soon we are likely to hold it in Iraq. Should our policy be to spread democracy

[à la Fukuyama] to these newly conquered Muslim lands, or should we eschew cultural arrogance [à la Huntington] and thereby escape the danger of a traditionalist reaction?

22 Huntington, 1996, op. cit., p. 32.
23 After challenging Fukuyama's "one world", Huntington (*The Clash of Civilizations and the Remaking of the Modern World*, pp. 32ff), goes on to dispute other models of the post-Cold War world, including "Two Worlds: Us and Them", noting correctly the misleading residual nature of the term "non-West", stating his preference instead for "the rest", presumably allowing for references also to, say, "the Sinic world and the rest" or "the Islamic world and the rest". This has led to another misunderstanding, expressed over and over, namely that Huntington is presenting the whole "rest" as the inherent enemy of the West.
24 Huntington, 1996, op. cit., p. 301.
25 Huntington's statement (op cit. 1996, p. 51) that "For four hundred years intercivilizational relations consisted of the subordination of other societies to Western civilization" is in fact an overstatement. Although the West's supremacy on the seas goes back to the sixteenth century, its supremacy over Asian and Islamic land empires does not predate the eighteenth century. After all, the Ottomans were on the offensive against Christendom during much of the 1600s, nearly succeeding in their second attempt to conquer Vienna in 1683.
26 Huntington, 1996, op. cit., p. 82.
27 Ibid., p. 83.
28 Ibid., p. 88.
29 Robin Harris, review of "The Clash of Civilizations and the Remaking of World Order", *National Review*, 28 October 1996.
30 Huntington, 1996, op. cit., p. 311.
31 Ibid., p. 317.
32 Ibid., p. 316.
33 Ibid., p. 55.
34 Ibid., p. 312.
35 Ibid., pp. 313ff.
36 Ibid., pp. 28–29.
37 Sullivan, 2002, op. cit., p. 169.
38 Huntington, 1996, op. cit., p. 20.
39 Ibid., p. 43.
40 Ibid., p. 269.
41 Ibid., p. 28.
42 Samuel P. Huntington, "Question and Answer: Five Years After 9/11, The Clash of Civilizations Revisited". The Pew Forum on Religion & Public Life Transcripts, 18 August 2006. Available at: www.pewforum.org/events/?EventID=125, accessed 21 January 2008.
43 Huntington, 1996, op. cit., p. 263.
44 Ibid., p. 254ff.
45 Ibid., p. 258.
46 Samuel P. Huntington, "So, Are Civilisations at War?" (interview), *The Observer*, October, 2001a. Available at: www.guardian.co.uk/world/2001/oct/21/afghanistan. religion2, accessed 17 February 2008; also published as "A Head-On Collision of Alien Cultures?" *New York Times*, 20 October 2001, p. A11.
47 Samuel P. Huntington, "The Age of Muslim Wars", *Newsweek*, 138(25) (17 December 2001b). Available at: www.proquest.umi.com/pqdweb?index=0&did=94795405&Srch Mode=1&sid=1&Fmt=3&VInst=PROD&VType=PQD&RQT=309&VName=PQD& TS=1203111538&clientId=954, accessed 15 February 2008.
48 Huntington, 1996, op. cit., pp. 263ff.
49 Ibid., p. 265.

50 Samuel P. Huntington, "The Clash of Civilizations Revisited" (interview), *NPQ*, Winter 2007. Available at: http://www.digitalnpq.org/archive/2007_winter/14_huntington.html, accessed 12 November 2007.

51 Huntington, 2001b, op. cit.

52 This absence of an Islamic great power in recent times is also dealt with by Ian S. Lustick ("The Absence of Middle Eastern Great Powers: Political 'Backwardness' in Historical Perspective", *International Organization*, 51 (Autumn 1997): 653–683), who explains the situation in terms of the unavailability of the possibility of great power status such as had occurred in the West, including the "large-scale state-building wars" that would have been required for those "who still seek to enter the great club after its establishment" (ibid., p. 657), as a result of the way existing great powers "interrupt the dynamic interaction of war and state building that had helped bring them into existence" and also of the new "antibelligerency norms" (ibid., p. 660).

53 Huntington, 1996, op. cit., p. 317.

54 Ibid., p. 318.

55 Ibid., p. 317.

56 Ibid., pp. 174ff.

57 Ibid., pp. 178–179.

58 Amina R. Chaudary, "An Interview with Samuel Huntington", *Islamica Magazine*, 17 (2007). Available at: http://www.islamicamagazine.com/issue-17/an-interview-with-samuel-huntington.html, accessed 6 March 2008.

59 Samuel P. Huntington, "Global Perspectives on War and Peace or, Transiting a Uni-Multipolar World", AEI Bradley Lecture Series, 11 May 1998, posted 1 January 2000, American Enterprise Institute for Public Policy Research. Available at: www.aei.org/publications/pubID.16661,filter.all/pub_detail.asp, accessed 11 November 2007.

60 Here he seems to veer temporarily into a different sort of explanation, but it is presumably true that for a pan-Islamic ideologist such as Bin Laden America's military presence in the Arabian Peninsula would not necessarily be offensive if it too were a Muslim country. See Samuel P. Huntington, *Who Are We: The Challenges to America's National Identity*, New York: Simon & Schuster, 2004, p. 358, quoting an interview with Peter Arnett.

61 Ibid., p. 360.

62 Ibid., p. 361.

63 Ibid., p. 362.

64 Huntington, 2001b, op. cit.

65 Huntington, 2004, op. cit., p. 363.

66 Ibid., p. 364.

67 Ibid.

68 Ibid.

69 Ibid., p. 365.

70 Huntington, 2001a, op. cit.

71 Huntington, 2006, op. cit.

72 Debrah Solomon, "Questions for Samuel P. Huntington", *New York Times*, 5 February 2004.

73 Huntington 2006, op. cit.

74 Ibid., p. 318.

75 Ibid., p. 320.

76 Huntington, 1996, op. cit., p. 139.

77 Ibid., pp. 145–146.

78 Ibid., p. 154.

79 Ibid., p. 197.

80 Ibid., p. 101.

81 Samuel P. Huntington, "From Change to Change: Modernization, Development, and Politics". *Comparative Politics*, 3 (January 1971): 294.

82 Ibid., p. 295.
83 Ibid., p. 296.
84 Huntington, 1996, op. cit., p. 51.
85 Ibid., p. 87.
86 Ibid., p. 184.
87 Ibid., p. 185.
88 Ibid., p. 239.
89 Ibid., p. 38.
90 Ibid., p. 92.
91 Gerardo L. Munck and Richard Snyder, *Passion, Craft, and Method in Comparative Politics*, Baltimore, MD: Johns Hopkins University Press, 2007.
92 Huntington, 1993, op. cit.
93 Sullivan, 2002, op. cit., p. 170.
94 Engin I. Erdem "The 'Clash of Civilizations': Revisited after September 11", *Alternatives: Turkish Journal of International Relations*, 1(2) (2002). Available at: www.alternativesjournal.net/volume1/number2/erdem.htm, accessed 24 February 2008.
95 Huntington, 1993, op. cit., p. 49.
96 Huntington, 1996, op. cit., p. 137.
97 See Huntington, 2004, op. cit., *passim*.
98 Ibid., pp. 222ff.
99 Francis Fukuyama, "Foreword", in Samuel P. Huntington, *Political Order in Changing Societies*, New Haven, CT: Yale University Press, 2006, p. xiii.
100 See Robert Putnam, "Samuel P. Huntington: An Appreciation", *PS*, 19(4)(1986): 838–839, on Huntington's shift during the early Cold War years to "an appreciation for order and stability" in response to "external threats" and to McCarthyism as well as to General MacArthur's "insubordination"—involving a stress on conservative institutions such as the military as protectors of liberalism.
101 Samuel P. Huntington, *Political Order in Changing Societies*, New Haven, CT: Yale University Press, 1968, *passim*.
102 Samuel P. Huntington and Joan M. Nelson, *No Easy Choice: Political Participation in Developing Countries*, Cambridge, MA: Harvard University Press, 1967, pp. 7–10 and *passim*.
103 Ervand Abrahamian, "Structural Causes of the Iranian Revolution", *MERIP Reports*, 87 (1980): 25 (note).
104 Ervand Abrahamian, *Iran between Two Revolutions*, Princeton, NJ: Princeton University Press, 1982, p. 441.
105 Leonard Binder ("The Natural History of Development Theory"; *Comparative Studies in Society and History*, 28 (January 1986): 31) wryly comments that "Some will regret that advisors of the shah of Iran seem to have read Huntington rather than [Theda] Skocpol."
106 Samuel P. Huntington, *The Third Wave: Democratization in the Late Twentieth Century*, Norman, OK: University of Oklahoma Press, 1991, *passim*.
107 Putnam, op. cit., p. 824.
108 Munck and Snyder, 2007, op. cit., p. 275.
109 Putnam, op. cit., p. 840.
110 Huntington, 2006, op. cit.
111 Ilan Peleg and Paul Scham, "Israeli Neo-Revisionism and American Neoconservatism: The Unexplored Parallels", *Middle East Journal* 61 (Winter 2007), *passim*.
112 Huntington, 1998, op. cit.
113 Huntington, 1996, op. cit., p. 14.
114 I know of no analysis of how this has evolved, but the AEI has not always been dominated by the ideas promoted by the Neocons. For example, it published a series entitled "United States Interests in the Middle East", edited by George Lenczowski,

during 1968 that generally emphasized the need for a more balanced policy in the area, notably warning that support for Israel was undermining American interests and providing an opening for Soviet penetration. See, in particular, Lenczowski's introductory volume to the series, also entitled *United States Interests in the Middle East* (American Enterprise Institute (ed.), Washington, D.C: American Enterprise Institute, 1968, especially pp. 110–112). In some circles, opposition to Washington's pro-Israel position then was regarded as a conservative stance. The whole AEI series was made available, at subsidized prices, by Americans for Middle East Understanding, typically regarded as a "pro-Arab" group. The inside front cover of the introductory volume reveals that the AEI's advisory board included such people as Lenczowski, and also Loy W. Henderson, a *bête noir* of the Zionist movement during the late 1940s, and that William J. Baroody, an Arab-American not known as a militant pro-Zionist served as president of the organization. In fact, the Neocon movement was only is the process of formation at that time. Although the phenomenon of leftist Jewish Americans' morphing into rightists, which the term purports to describe, had its beginnings in the 1960s, the first appearance of the word "Neoconservative" in print is said to have been in an article by Michael Harrington in *Dissent Magazine* in Fall 1973 (Benjamin Ross, "Who Named the Neocons?" *Dissent Magazine*, Summer (2005); Jonah Goldberg, "The Neoconservative Invention: No New Kid on the Block", *National Review*, 20 May, 2003).

115 Sullivan, 2002, op. cit., pp. 171–172, citing Staff Writer, "US Should Distance Itself from Israel—Harvard Academic", *Arab News* (Jiddah, Riyadh, Dhahran), 14 November 2001. Available at: http://www.arabnews.com/?page=9&section=0&article=10490& d=14&m=11&y=2001.
116 Huntington, 2007, op. cit., and Chaudary, 2007, op. cit.
117 Sullivan, 2002, op. cit., p. 172.
118 Huntington, 1996, op. cit., p. 198.
119 Huntington, 2006, op. cit.
120 Munck and Snyder, 2007, op. cit., p. 223.
121 Putnam, 1986, op. cit., p. 841.
122 Ibid., pp. 842–843.
123 Philip M. Boffey, "Prominent Harvard Scholar Barred by Science Academy", *New York Times*, 29 April, 1987.
124 "Scholars Bite Mad Dog", *The Nation*, 244(18) (9 May 1987): 605.
125 Dabashi, 2007, op. cit., p. 9.
126 Huntington, 1993, op. cit., p. 32.
127 Bernard Lewis, "The Roots of Muslim Rage", *Atlantic Monthly*, September (1990): 48.
128 Ibid., pp. 52–53.
129 Ibid., p. 59.
130 Ibid., p. 60.
131 See Michael Hirsch, "Bernard Lewis Revisited", *Washington Monthly*, November (2004), and Peter Waldman, "Containing Jihad: A Historian's Take on Islam Steers U.S. in Terrorism Fight: Bernard Lewis's Blueprint: Sowing Arab Democracy Is Facing a Test In Iraq–The 'Clash of Civilizations'", *Wall Street Journal*, 3 February 2004.
132 Mahmood Mamdani, *Good Muslim, Bad Muslim: America, the Cold War, and the Roots of Terror*. New York: Doubleday, 2004, p. 20.
133 See Kevin A. Clark and David M. Primo, "Modernizing Political Science: A Model-Based Approach", *Perspectives on Politics*, 5 (December 2007): 742.
134 Huntington, 1996, op. cit., pp. 13–14.
135 Ibid., p. 37.
136 Ibid., p. 29.
137 Ibid., p. 36.

138 Ibid., p. 37.
139 Huntington, 2001 and 2007, op. cit.
140 Huntington, 1996, op. cit., pp. 34–43.
141 Gilles Keppel, *Bad Moon Rising: A Chronicle of the Middle East Today*, trans. from the French by Pascale Ghazaleh, London: Saqi Books, 2003, p. 133.
142 Chaudary, 2007, op. cit.
143 "A Pontius Pilate for Our Age", *New Internationalist*, 369 (July 2006). Available at: www.newint.org/columns/worldbeaters/2004/07/01/samuel-p-huntington/, accessed 21 January 2008.
144 Fouad Ajami, "The Clash", *New York Times Book Review*, 6 January 2008, p. 10.
145 Huntington, 1996, op. cit., p. 321.
146 Ibid., p. 310.
147 Huntington, 2001b, op. cit.

13 Getting it wrong yet again
America and the Islamic mainstream

Raymond W. Baker

I began my serious study of Islam and Islamic societies as a graduate student at Harvard in the mid-1960s. With the course work for my doctorate completed, I set out in 1968 to engage the world I was studying at one of the West's great learning centers. My preparation, or so I thought, was excellent. In my course work I drew on the proud Gibb legacy of Islamic studies at Harvard, represented for me by Nadav Safran, a student of Gibb and then a leading figure in Middle Eastern studies. To this work in the classics I married what I took to be the best of the new social scientific studies in modernization. In Safran's courses I began my reading in the burgeoning 'development' literature focused on the Middle East. My major guide, though, was Samuel Huntington who became my academic mentor and thesis advisor. Huntington was exceptionally well known even then as a major conservative intellectual. I had prepared myself to witness the intellectual, moral, economic, and political transformation of backward societies into modernized states, or so the syllabi encouraged us to believe. Egypt, as the lead society in the Arab world, would be my case study in political development and my vantage point from which to witness up close this march of history.

Now, I do not mean to say that I accepted these perspectives uncritically. Quite the contrary, as a working-class boy from Jersey City I brought a very strong set of progressive intellectual and moral commitments to Harvard which allowed a critical stance to both the old Islamic studies tradition and the new development literature. From the first, I understood both approaches as mainstream and my own positions as critical. In formulating my independent stance, I drew on dependency and world system critiques of dominant approaches, as well as the varieties of Marxism and phenomenology that suffused the New Left political and intellectual movements in which I was active, all centered on opposition to the American assault on Vietnam.

Though fortified with the critical perspectives of the left, my encounter with Cairo was a major shock. The Islamic world laid out so completely and so transparently in Cambridge, whether by the mainstream or its critics, simply did not exist. One part of my Harvard experience, however, did prove helpful. My supplemental studies in Arabic language, literature, and philosophy had taken on a life of their own. In the long run, they proved to be the only indispensable subjects I studied at Harvard. At the time, though, I thought of these classic cultural studies as a kind of reward for slogging through the oppressive social science literature, not realizing then that I had mistaken the main course for dessert. From the fragments we novices could read from the splendid Arab travel and philosophical literature of the golden age in my Arabic tutorial (in those days there were only two or three students in the advanced Arabic courses), I caught my first glimpses of the richness, complexity, and diversity of Islamic and Arab culture. It was the human element that touched me most. The openness and wonder of an Ibn Battuta, that great Arab traveler and raconteur of the fourteenth century, stood in such sharp contrast to the closed, self-referential attitude of the Western specialists who dominated my formal studies at Harvard and made Arab societies available to me. While Ibn Battuta did occasionally whisper in my ears his doubts that another cultural world could really be so transparently available, it was unfortunately the development literature that I packed for my trip to Cairo.

Is it any wonder that I, like so many of my Western counterparts, only caught glimpses of the Islamic Awakening, in retrospect the major development of the late 1960s and early 1970s? Throughout the area at that time new Islamist intellectuals and movements were emerging to reshape the Middle East in ways completely at odds with Western expectations, not to mention those of the Egyptian left. In my political study of Egypt written during that period, I focused instead on the secular forces, nationalist and leftist, that were driving Nasser's revolution. I juxtaposed the views of Egyptian leftists and their impressive critique of the Nasserist experience with the truths I had acquired at Harvard. I still reassure myself that this intellectual exercise helped to make my first book a better one, though it could not overcome its inattention to Islam and its political impact. I regrettably left the Islamic movements, notably the Muslim Brotherhood, in the shadows. However, I do note with some small pleasure that even then I could never quite manage the hostility to all things Islamic that animated the work of my mentors at Harvard and of my new friends on the Egyptian left. It took some time and a great effort of unlearning before I could get a reasonable grasp on the Islamic Awakening and develop an appreciation of just why Egypt has been so central to it.

However, what concerns me in this chapter is less my own earlier experience of disillusionment with so much of Western scholarship on the Islamic world, whether taken directly from its sources or indirectly from Westernized Arab intellectuals. Rather, I want to share my very vivid sense that we are not doing much better today. In fact, the rampant hostility in the wake of September 11, 2001 to all things Islamic has made the situation much worse, though President Obama has begun the serious work of changing those attitudes. My courses for the last few years have been flooded with students motivated by a 'know thy enemy' impulse that I had seen only once before as a student myself of the Soviet Union. The enemy in those days was Soviet communism and our 'totalitarian' models explained it fully. During the long Bush years the enemy was defined in broad strokes as 'Islamo-facism' with pretty much the same model in play, tinted green instead of red, though equally abstract, self-serving, and unrelated to realities on the ground.

In the 1960s, the area studies programs for the Soviet Union and the Middle East in which I was trained were motivated by a sense that the United States was an emerging superpower with global responsibilities. We needed people to understand the world beyond our borders to help facilitate its economic and political transformation along the modern lines we, rather than the Soviets, had pioneered. The rhetoric of global responsibility screened a rising imperial assertiveness and talk of underdeveloped countries slid easily into condescending assumptions of underdeveloped peoples. Yet, however unhappy these pretensions and their racist implications in the 1960s, things are worse today. Now, the call is for terror specialists, fluent in Arabic, to serve national security interests. In my worst moments, I wonder whether my recommendations of students for language study programs now simply increase the crop of Arabic speakers for interrogation and eaves-dropping purposes. The terror specialists, with their special focus on the Arab world, are preparing themselves to face a vast and nameless army of Islamic extremists that must be confronted abroad, they are told, with as much violence as is needed, in order to avoid another September 11 at home. America's putative aim now is not to develop backward societies but rather to demolish imagined Islamist enemies and protect the 'homeland'. The old centers for development and modernization now take a back seat to a new generation of centers for Terror Studies at some of the West's most prestigious universities. Convinced of history's direction, my generation of graduate students believed that our Western, secular experience, from which abstract and ahistorical models of development were extracted, provided a mapping of the future of the Arab Islamic world. With eyes riveted on an imported, inevitable future for the Arab societies, we missed the importance of the Islamic wave then emerging to shape important dimensions of political and social life. Today, with our gaze firmly fixed on the criminal, extremist Islamist minorities represented by al-Qaeda and on the violence and mayhem they cause, we pay almost no attention at all to the centrist Islamist mainstream that has made itself the driving force of the Islamic Awakening.

During all these many years of my Cairo connection hardly a day has gone by without two or three Middle East stories in the major American news outlets. Over these four decades my American family, friends, and students repeatedly and always with a sense of the novelty of the moment have commented on "what a fascinating time to be living and working in the Middle East" – responding always to media reports of the latest disaster, upheaval or war.

Yet, consistently, from the vantage point of my direct experience, the most important developments in the region today make almost no impression at all. Real struggles for freedom and social justice with reasonable prospects for success are underway and they go unnoticed or misrepresented. For too many in the West, they are screened from view simply because they are waged under Islamist banners. All we see is terrorism or extremism in clever, moderate disguise. In fact, the Islamic mainstream has been gaining strength everywhere since the late 1960s and has been establishing itself as the major opposition to currently existing regimes and as the inspiration for resistance to foreign invaders. The story of these struggles and the successes registered should be of interest to all who share democratic and anti-imperialist commitments. These values still represent an important part of the legacy of the American people, though they have often all too often been badly compromised, not least since 2001. However, we should not forget that these same years have also witnessed impressive efforts – originating from American civil society – to resist empire and protect American civil liberties. It is imperative that those thousands and thousands who took to the streets recognize potential allies in Islamic lands and among Islamic centrists for the advancement of these anti-imperialist and democratic aims.

Arab peoples, in particular, groan under authoritarian rule while facing foreign assault on several fronts. These realities of everyday life, so completely outside the experience of Westerners, inevitably mean that the struggle just to live an ordinary life takes place in quite extraordinary circumstances. Battles for normalcy in such circumstance generate a surprising capacity for resistance, including forceful resistance. It makes no sense at all to criticize the 'duplicity' of mass Islamist movements because they are committed both to social welfare projects for their people and to assertive resistance to occupiers. The first is not a mere screen for the second. The identity of Islamist resistance movements codifies both sets of commitments. Circumstances require no less, as the experiences of the routinely demonized movements of Hamas and Hizbullah make clear. Both are movements of national resistance that arose to confront foreign occupation. They are also social movements that strive to meet the pressing social needs of the people from whom they have arisen. They have also evolved into political movements that are important players in their respective national settings. Ordinary citizens throughout the Arab world have an acute sense that the immediate enemies of freedom and the prospects of a decent life, represented by the repressive governments under which they live, are not the only, nor always the most serious threat they face. In this assessment they are absolutely correct. There are indeed enemies from afar, with Israel and the United States in the front rank. Memories of direct foreign occupation are fresh and cutting throughout the region, revived continuously over four decades in a particularly vivid way by the oppressive Israeli occupation and unrelenting colonization of the West Bank and Gaza.

These everyday horrors of national displacement and dispossession in the battered and besieged remnants of historic Palestine provided the backdrop for the American assault on Afghanistan first in 2001 and then Iraq in 2003. Many Americans regard the attack on Afghanistan as an appropriate response to the events of September 11, 2001. That view is questioned throughout the region, and with good cause. None of the actual perpetrators of September 11th were Afghanis nor is there any evidence of the complicity of the Afghani regime in the planning and execution of the attack on the Twin Towers of the World Trade Center and the Pentagon. It is true that al-Qaeda had found refuge in the mountains and caves of Afghanistan. I am not persuaded that this fact justifies the full force military assault on Afghanistan with all its consequences for the people of Afghanistan. Yet, however one judges that matter, it is now quite clear that the attack did nothing to weaken al-Qaeda. On the contrary, it quite clearly increased the pool of anti-American extremists in Afghanistan and throughout the Islamic world. The subsequent war on Iraq and the appalling devastation it has caused even more decisively turned a major Arab country that had previously not been the site of Islamist extremism into an open field for international extremist movements. Iraq has proved to be an even greater failure for the US than Afghanistan and the deliberate destruction of Iraq has served as a major recruitment tool for al-Qaeda.

It should not be forgotten that the Afghan war also represented the first time that the United States directly made war on an Islamic country. The rhetoric of American empire in the Bush Jr. years was all about a democratic remaking in the region and a global war against terror. However, it was the Afghan and Iraqi wars and the death and destruction they brought that, from the vantage point of ordinary citizens of the Islamic world, defined the American version of the "foreigner's gift".[1] There have been very few signs that these essentials will change much with the new president. Even the withdrawal of American troops from Iraq is far from a certainty, given the loophole of substantial forces left ostensibly to train Iraqis. All indications also point to the continuation and probable expansion of the war that cannot be won in Afghanistan and Pakistan. On the ground the rhetoric of these long years of a global war on terror, renamed but not yet repudiated, has translated into colonization, apartheid, collective punishment, and periodic open war against the civilian subject population in the Israeli-occupied territories, a full-scale Israeli assault on Lebanon, American support for dictatorships elsewhere, and death and destruction on a mind-numbing scale, first in Afghanistan and then in Iraq. Thanks to the Information Revolution the sounds and images of these travails come directly into ordinary households on a daily basis. On the Arab satellite channels over the last several years it has often been hard to tell if the latest images of the violence of the occupiers depict Americans in Iraq and Afghanistan or Israelis on the West Bank.

None of this is meant as a blanket whitewash of Islamist resistance movements. There is no question that there have been excesses, at times criminal excesses, by both Hamas and Hizbullah. My argument is simply that the policies of the United States and Israel have made the violent excesses of Islamist extremists more probable and more sustainable. However, it is also not my intention to reduce extremist actions to mere echoes of past acts of ours. To think in this way is to portray the people committing those acts as non-persons – mere forces of nature. It makes it impossible to understand the motivations behind their actions today and likely future actions. What makes *us* so special that we can have commitments, including commitments to violent pre-emptive wars, for which we are accountable whereas violent others are mere products of their environment? My point is rather that we should recognize that extremist violence is connected to the efforts to overthrow oppressive rulers and to expel foreign occupiers, efforts that often include cruel means. Extremist violence should be understood as the expression of commitments (commitments that our actions have made far more compelling) rather than as the blind reflex to a force that originally came from us. Understanding of the roots of an action, especially a condemnable criminal action, in the commitments of others in no way justifies that action. To understand is not to approve.

The matter of the Islamic character of the resistances should not really require further comment. Should we really be surprised that, at a time when everyday dreams are contradicted by violence and despair, people turn to their faith to sustain them? In American inner cities, the 'package stores' that peddle alcohol on every corner just barely outnumber the store-front churches, at least that is so in Hartford's inner city where my college is located. What we are witnessing in the turn to faith is clearly a global and not a purely Islamic phenomenon. When all else fails, ordinary people turn to their religious tradition and its leadership and institutions to find some relief from intolerable, oppressive conditions. Recently, the red-clad, barefoot Buddhist monks reminded us of this fully understandable response on the streets of Myanmar's new capital. Jesse Jackson in America, Bishop Desmond Tutu in South Africa, the Ayatollah Khomeini in Iran, Hizbullah in southern Lebanon, and Hamas in the Israeli-occupied territories – all these figures and movements have more in common than we in the West are prepared to recognize. With the exception of the Iranian Islamic Revolution with its distinctive Shi'ite features, in no other case did these figures seek to create religious societies. Most everywhere, as in Myanmar today, their aim is to create more just civil societies and civil states. When it comes to the Islamic world, almost none of the rather ordinary shadings of these events are noticed in the West.

This inattention to the struggles to live ordinary lives in extraordinary circumstance and the turn to Islam to inspire them has taken an enormous toll in incomprehension and missed opportunities. More importantly for our purposes, these neglected realities on the ground hold out the real possibility that even the worst of our recent policies, such as US support for Israeli collective punishment of the 1.5 million tormented people of Gaza, might be less damaging to our global standing than we have any right to expect. I move freely as an American throughout the Arab Islamic world, including places like Damascus, note the rising anti-Americanism everywhere and *never* encounter it on a personal level anywhere. Arab people are smart. They know the difference between citizens and governments. They have their own direct experience with governments ignoring citizens.

Even more to the point, we are missing the fact that we Americans have potential partners in the Arab Islamic world, notably in our anti-imperial and democratic commitments and, surprisingly perhaps, especially among Islamist centrists who now play such an important part in the on-going struggles for freedom and resistance. Centrist Islamists share commitments to which we *as Americans* hold ourselves accountable. They are our commitments as well as theirs. These include commitments to promoting democracy and human rights, protecting freedom of speech and assembly, promoting literacy, helping the poor, avoiding wars and achieving peace on a world scale. There is also a more focused convergence between anti-imperialist movements in American civil society and those in Islamic lands. We need to remind ourselves that struggles against American wars are not by that fact alone anti-American struggles. We need to remind the world that not all Americans support the empire. In fact, anti-imperialist and anti-war sentiment is strong and growing in the United States. American citizens across the political spectrum have adopted anti-war positions. Important Islamist centrist intellectuals have often taken note of the importance of these sentiments and the actions they have stimulated, especially in the United States.[2] Here again common cause with Islamist centrists is quite reasonable to imagine. In a global age anti-war movements must have a global reach and that should include a reach from and into the Islamic lands.

Yet, intellectually and psychologically we are not yet prepared for such break-throughs. To the limited degree that we Americans have faced our own most recent failings, the focus has been on the shortfalls of the military and the intel-ligence effort in the context of inept, ideologically-driven political leadership. These are important beginnings. Yet, it seems deeply regrettable that so little attention has been paid to the colossal intellectual failure that underlies all else: our consistent failure to recognize possible partners for American critics of empire and advocates for democracy in mainstream Islamist movements. America is larger than any particular government and it is certainly more generous and more pacific than the incumbents of the Bush years. Our situation as a nation, after all, is that we now find ourselves a massive presence in an Islamic world we do not understand, where we cannot distinguish our friends from our enemies unless they are shooting at us. It is time for the social movements that animate civil society and have been responsible for the most important democratic advances America has achieved to make the intellectual, moral and political effort to look beyond our shores and beyond our fears to find partners, like the mainstream Islamists, who share the best of our commitments.

Empires inevitably generate some version of the white man's burden, just as they always conjure up some horrific threat to civilization, emanating from the 'natives', by which to cow their own population and justify the terrible violence, for the most part against civilians, used to achieve their ends in distant lands. Yet, empires also inevitably create domestic critics, especially when losses in treasure and lives mount. Opposition to empire takes root first in these narrow nationalist terms as imperial excesses come to be seen as a threat to the national interest. Invariably, there are also prophetic minorities from the metropole who see further and recognize a common human interest in resistance to imperial projects and the violence they entail, whatever their national origins. These individuals and groups based in the imperial center are open, in theory at least, to cooperation in resistance to empire and in the building of a better, more equitable and more democratic world.

Openings to Islamist centrists must be made in a spirit of complete mutuality. It is absolutely critical that overlapping commitments be recognized precisely as such. Our aim must be to identify goals that are genuinely shared, rather than to attempt to impose commitments. Even in these cases where common beliefs and aims are discovered, American civil society as the stronger party must make every effort to nurture genuine cooperation, while being sensitive to the danger

of making centrists out to be agents or puppets of Western power. Real partner-
ships require mutual respect. It is the role of humanistic scholarship to provide
the knowledge base for such cooperative efforts in the human interest. There
have been some important beginnings to generate scholarship of this kind, but
the record thus far remains unimpressive. Most effort has been invested in decon-
structive critique. The work of positive, humanistic scholarship has hardly begun.

The place to start is contextual, grounded understanding of the actual circumstances within which ordinary people in the Arab Islamic world live their lives.
The first lesson of such an approach is awareness that the West and its Israeli ally
play a decisive role in defining those circumstances. The second lesson, no less
important, is that local regimes share responsibility for degrading the possibilities
of ordinary people to live decent lives. To make the point that there is plenty of
blame to share with local tyrants does not diminish the fact that America is an
empire with imperial interests in the region and not just a great power. Nor does
it downplay the importance of America's Israeli partner. Israel, to put the matter
bluntly, is the dominant regional power, expansionist in its strategic goals, and
with nuclear arsenal and a world class military to back its aspirations. Israeli
actions confirm the intent to colonize as much of the West Bank as possible while
expanding its other borders, notably into Lebanon and Syria, as opportunities
arise. The American notion of Israel as a besieged, vulnerable ally is a purely
American fantasy, nowhere put forward more effectively than in Nadav Safran's
classic, *Israel, the Embattled Ally*. This work, by my graduate school mentor, is
still in print after all these years. The powerful myth of the 'embattled ally' that
Safran helped create still dominates our thinking.

It is really quite absurd to write about the Middle East region today as though
the Israeli unimpeded colonization of historic Palestine is not proceeding apace,
as though America did not initiate a new era in relations with the Islamic world
by its criminal attacks on Afghanistan and Iraq. How can one understand a region
and its people without paying attention to the foreign pressures, incursions, and
outright assaults that block their prospects for a self-determined future?

There is a tendency today to attribute the shortcomings of Western scholarship
to the deadly influence of the unrepentant, neo-conservative thinkers like Bernard
Lewis and Fouad Ajami, who played so large a part in rationalizing and defending the George W. Bush agenda for remaking the Middle East by force. There is
much to be said for the argument, but in the end it should be resisted. It is too
easy to lay all our problems at the feet of the neo-cons. Our moral and intellectual
failure is much larger in scope.

On both the theoretical and policy levels, there is less that is new in the
contemporary American imperial project and its rationalizations in the alleged
animus of Islam toward democracy than is sometimes supposed. In the rush to
critique the neo-conservative version of empire, we should not forget the broader
continuities of the American imperial project and of the structures of attitude and
settled beliefs that sustain it. The roots of American empire, as Chalmers Johnson
and others have shown, extend deep into the Cold War era.[3] A consensus of
liberals and conservatives, from Roosevelt to Clinton, from Reagan to Bush has

sustained it. Such scholars as Mahmood Mamdani have usefully documented the origins of the intellectual justifications for neo-con militarism in Reagan-era thinking.[4] The 'evil empire' and 'the war on terror', to cite just two examples, are refurbished ideological relics of the Reagan era that in turn had their origins in the Cold War thinking of Truman and Eisenhower. It is also true, however, that although the liberal legacy identified with the Democrats has emphasized economic and political tools of empire, highlighted in particular by Clinton, liberals supported, without reserve, the consensus view that the contest for global hegemony requires military exertions. On both intellectual and policy levels Bush Jr. inherited an on-going, robust imperial project. Whether shaded in conservative or liberal tones, it came complete with well-established bi-partisan ideological justifications, notably invocations of democratic transitions beyond the borders under benevolent American tutelage. What Bush Jr. did on the policy level was simply to take *existing* trends of imperialist militarism and push them to the extreme in the wake of September 11th. The skillful exploitation of that crime against humanity provided the rationale and necessary climate of fear for a heightened militarization of imperial policy along aggressively expansionist lines that the neo-conservatives had been planning for years. There is no need to adopt conspiracy theories to register the usefulness of September 11th to the neo-conservatives. The heart of their well-documented policy prescriptions, including its critical linkage to the Israeli right, was already long in place before the Bush team redirected American foreign policy from the emphasis on the economic and diplomatic instruments of the Clinton era to an almost exclusive reliance on military means in the wake of the al-Qaeda attacks. In parallel fashion, the Bush era scholarship on Islam and democracy, used to rationalize empire, simply took existing conservative and liberal theoretical formulations and gave them a simplifying clarity and certitude that only extremist thought can manage.

It is now perfectly clear that the Bush policies pursued toward the Islamic world have been monstrously destructive in Palestine, Afghanistan, and Iraq. Studies of Islam and democracy produced by embedded scholars of the neo-conservative right, nestled comfortably in such think tanks as the American Enterprise Institute, the Washington Institute for Near East Policy, the Jewish Institute for National Security Affairs, and the Hudson Institute, have not surprisingly had a largely apologetic character, quite explicitly serving the imperial project. As on a host of other issues, these scholars dominated the national debate. Failures on the ground have not altered this reality. The neo-conservative pundits and the right wing scholars who provide them with intellect support are still taken seriously by the mainstream media and scholarly community and their strategies to rescue their flawed and dangerous analyses have surprising traction. The electoral defeat of George W. Bush has not changed this situation. All of this suggests quite clearly that the neo-conservatives have firmly rooted their presence in the official structures of American political life. They will not fade away with the passing of a discredited George W. Bush.

The issue of Islam and democracy remains at the heart of the debate between imperial scholarship and its critics. The inability of the Islamic world to generate democracy, by neo-conservative lights, compelled a strategy of using over-whelming military force to clear the inhospitable Islamic ground for the planting of democratic seeds from abroad. This characteristic was apparent years ago in the leading scholars on whom the worker bees in the think tanks rely, notably Bernard Lewis and Fouad Ajami. When the grandiose and misguided plans for remaking dissolved in death and destruction, the blame for the failures was then placed squarely on Islam's shoulders. Noble dreams of remaking the Middle East along democratic lines faltered, we are told by the same Ajami, when the damaged human material of these transformations, especially in Iraq, failed to live up to imperial expectations and to assume their proper responsibilities as the "shocked and awed" country descended into devastating chaos and the "noble experiment" suffered blameless failure.[5] For our purposes Bush-era studies of Islam and democracy are of importance only for what they reveal of neo-conservative American thinking. They have no relationship at all to actual struggles for democracy in the Islamic world. Nor are they intended to. They quite unabash-edly transcend mere realities on the ground to serve the higher purposes of empire by riveting attention on the alleged dangers that a failed Islamic civilization poses for the West.

The historic complicity of the liberal establishment in the imperial project prevented the emergence of an effective liberal alternative to this analysis and to the war on terror under a democratic banner that lead us into Iraq. It proved impossible for liberals to generate either an effective policy alternative or world-view to halt the march to Baghdad. The liberals had pioneered in the formulation of the binary oppositions of good and evil, freedom and tyranny. They had of course actively participated during the long Cold War years in the cynical manip-ulation of democratic symbols for imperial purposes throughout the Third World. Liberals, no less than conservatives, bought fully into the Orientalist idea that Islam blocks the development of democracy in Islamic lands.

Meanwhile, even those on the political and cultural left who have engaged issues of Islam and democracy have not gone beyond the critique of distorted ideas of Islamic realities. They have skillfully exposed the ways in which these ideas and their institutional affiliations have misrepresented and 'covered' Islam and Islamist movements. The left has also played a large and important leadership role in mobilizing domestic opposition to the ravages of the Bush policies. Yet, the task of lifting that ideological cover that rationalizes the imperial project has yet to be fully engaged. Notions of Islam as both incapable and resistant to modernity hold sway, as much on the left as with the liberals. There have been almost no efforts at all to seriously evaluate the emancipatory potential of centrist Islamist movements, including their contributions to both imperial resistance and democratic theory and practice.[6]

These underlying continuities in neo-conservative and liberal thinking about Islam, combined with the inattention of the left to Islamist resistance and demo-cratic struggles, have yielded a very large body of Western scholarship that is surprisingly homogeneous and consistently deeply flawed on issues of Islam and democracy. For the dominant neo-conservatives, Islam as failed faith and civilization stands revealed as a colossal threat, precisely because of its inherent flaws and the rage and jealousy those irreparable defects stimulate when juxtaposed to the beautiful West. Moreover, not only is Islam evil, it is evil on a global scale that demands a military riposte around the globe. Liberals tend to adopt a somewhat softer view that focuses on cultural deficiencies rather than violent rage as the character of the Islamic threat. By these lights, Muslims everywhere are carriers of flawed cultural genes that make them, whatever their intentions or surface behavior, the carriers of irrationality, anti-Enlightenment, and anti-secular values. In short, they lack the liberal gene. Whatever the emphasis, the conclusion is the same. It is the cultural deficiencies of Muslims or the jealous rage they experience facing a superior Western civilization and *not* rapacious US or Israeli policies that create the dangers that threaten to engulf the civilized world in flames.

In my view, neither blaming Islam as failed civilization nor blaming Western policies and the reactions they generate represents a productive approach. Neither conceives Islamists as actual persons struggling to deliver on intelligible commitments. The second option focusing on Western policies can be retrieved, however, by recasting it in terms that mean our actions have put Muslims in a deplorable situation. We can then examine the ways they have chosen to act and the reasons behind their actions. There is a tendency among critics of US policies to locate all responsibility on the shoulders of the US. This position only appears to be the most forceful stance. In fact, it drains agency, and thus personhood, away from all other players on the field. In daily life, it is belittling to be told, in response to an apology, "No it's my fault. I *made* you act that way." Yet, somehow this insulting way of framing things is supposed by many progressive critics of US foreign policy to be the right way to talk when we're describing the failed and destructive policies of the West in Islamic lands. Part of creating a more just and humane world must be figuring out a way to talk about the humiliation the West has inflicted on the Islamic domains that is not in itself humiliating to Muslim peoples.

In fairness to Americans, the absurdities of such imperial thinking do not exceed that of the British 'white man's burden' nor of the French 'civilizing mission'. Nor are the required suspensions of rational understanding and fellow feeling for the victims of such projects any more demanding of Americans than those required earlier of British and French publics. The American historic sensibility as a settler society facing hostile indigenous people has helped enormously in the stereotyping of Arabs and Muslims. So too has the calculated drum beat of fear of the 'natives' fostered by the state and media monopolies to provide essential cover for the dirty work of empire.

Large imperial projects in a global age require even larger purposes to justify them. The advocates of Imperial America know that it will not do to speak simply of oil and strategic dominance. Carrying the flag of democracy gives American empire a far more worthy, far more uplifting goal. Once it is accepted that Islam precludes development of democracy, taken as the defining characteristic of civilization itself, the way is open to use massive force to rescue Muslims from their self-imposed barbarism. In the poor cultural soil of the Islamic world democracy simply cannot take root. The Islamic world must be remade and that task requires massive force. Democratic development from within the Islamic world is simply ruled out by the very nature of Islam itself.

Violent, criminal minorities in the Islamic lands and the insurgency they have mounted against the American regional presence have been invaluable allies in making this imperial agenda seem reasonable. In contrast, mainstream Islamists have been singularly unhelpful to this imperial project. Their words and actions contravene the notion of an anti-democratic Islamic threat. They have launched a substantial rethinking of the heritage, revealing important Islamic sources of democratic precedents and possibilities of elaboration of democratic practices attuned to our time. Moreover, they have been singularly uncooperative by participating wherever possible in democratic openings, playing by the rules of the game and achieving some remarkable successes as in Jordan, Turkey, and Egypt.

While Western scholars can pass over this record of active mainstream Islamist engagements on behalf of democracy lightly, it is impossible to ignore it altogether. There are ways, however, of voiding these democratic experiences of the mainstream of their real weight and importance. Typically, liberal Western scholars include Islamist centrists in their narratives and analyses only as stand-ins for the absent, Westernized liberals for whom they endlessly search. For leftist scholars, if the Islamist centrists appear at all, they are invoked as blank slates on which their own leftist version of such Western values of justice and human rights can be inscribed.[7]

This deficiency argument would not be an easy one to make if scholars and journalists in the West had even a cursory familiarity with the writings and practice of any of the major centrist Islamist thinkers and the movements and parties they have created. For the most part, they do not.[8] Neo-conservative thinkers of course deride the very notion of an Islamic center. Mainstream liberal scholarship treats Islamist centrists with excessive skepticism, while the left for the most part is either actively hostile or simply ignores the Islamists. Therefore, the standard arguments about the incompatibility of Islam and democracy flow with unperturbed confidence: Islam is a flawed faith and Islamic civilization a failed civilization with no hope of democratic development. One can only imagine the impact of a serious engagement with the intellectual work in which centrist intellectuals have been engaged for decades, exploring the roots in Islamic conceptions of reason and culture for democratic development. Such an engagement has yet to take place.

In this regard, even the most interesting work of both liberal and leftist scholars writing for Western audiences falls short of a serious engagement of the centrists as important, even decisive actors in their own right for the future of their societies. Willful inattention is required to maintain this posture. Consider, for example, the work of the 'intellectual school' of the New Islamists that has been active since the 1970s. These Egyptian centrists have produced a full-blown body of collective work that addresses the most important issues facing the Islamic world, ranging from the rights of women and minorities to the modalities of resistance to Western and especially American imperialism. Out of their ranks have come some of the most important figures on the Islamist moderate landscape, such as the late Muhammad al-Ghazali and Yusuf al Qaradawi, arguably the two most influential Islamist thinkers of our time.[9] Their work has been a major factor in moderating the positions of the influential Egyptian Muslim Brotherhood and it has provided inspiration for centrist movements throughout the Islamic world.

In Egypt, the attitudes of secular scholars and journalists toward the *Wassatteyya* vary widely. As the school has grown in stature, it has become impossible to ignore their presence as intellectuals with an important role in Egypt and the Islamic world. Secularists unfailingly shape their assessments with the Americans clearly in view. In the Bush era, some, like Abdul Moneim Said and Hala Mustafa of the al Ahram Center for Political and Strategic Studies, unabashedly courted the American neo-conservatives, even when that support undercut their ties to the regime. For the Egyptian public these figures describe their orientation as liberal. In fact, they offered themselves as advocates for Bush era, neo-conservatives politics on the ground, treating American peace initiatives on Palestine as serious, supporting privatization, and displaying an understanding attitude toward the burdens of American imperial projects like Iraq. Scholars of this type display a monochromatic hostility to Islamists, lumping them together as constituting a threat of violent take-over no matter how moderate their rhetoric. Others who also claim the secular liberal label like Saad Ibrahim, position themselves as advocates for democracy, human rights and a more open political regime, though with differences over time as to just what these commitments mean in practical terms. Ibrahim has taken a variety of positions, cooperating closely with the regime and its talk of political reforms in earlier times, especially through his linkages to Suzanne Mubarak but later incurring regime wrath and imprisonment, for his outspoken, courageous criticisms of regime abuse of power and his attempts to monitor elections. For Ibrahim, the Islamic mainstream represents an ambiguous force. He has been willing at times to recognize differences in the Islamist camp and, in recent years, even to support inclusion of centrist Islamists in a democratic opening. However, Ibrahim has periodically questioned just how deep the distinctions between moderates and extremists really go. He is concerned that the centrists are merely providing cover for the same goals in the end as the extremists, i.e. some form of theocracy. Thus, Ibrahim's position is marked by a pronounced ambivalence toward the Islamists that threatens at any point to dissolve into mistrust and an unwillingness to regard them as reliable partners. This sentiment, as we have seen, finds strong echoes in the West. In contrast to his skepticism about Islamists, Ibrahim has consistently supported the idea of US intervention to pressure the Egyptian government on democratic reforms, taking American pro-democracy sentiments at face value despite the clear evidence of their insincerity.

The work of liberal and leftist scholars, no less than those of such neo-conservative analysts such as Cheryl Benard, all take as their starting point the assumption, whether stated as deep skepticism or outright certainty, that an

Islamic cultural context precludes democratic development. Meanwhile, events on the ground make it perfectly clear that Islamic democracy is very much a real possibility. Democracy is in fact on the agenda of Islamic centrist movements throughout the Islamic world. At the same time, prominent Islamist scholars of the center have made major contributions to the theorization of democracy on Islamic ground. The *Wassatteyya*, the Islamic mainstream, addresses the issue with three distinctive questions: Does the *Ummah* require democracy in order to flourish in the late modern world? What are the intellectual and practical resources on which Islamic movements of the center can draw to realize democracy? How likely are centrist Islamists to succeed in their on-going struggles for democracy in sites around the Islamic world?

These questions are framed in ways that reflect the treatment of the issue of Islam and democracy by mainstream Islamists themselves who today take a leadership role in that struggle in sites throughout the Islamic world. The New Islamists of Egypt, to cite the most encouraging example, have developed an extremely sophisticated and comprehensive rethinking of Islam in all its dimensions, with notable attention to the question of Islam and democracy. While the Egyptian New Islamist School has never been able to form a political party, they have been active for decades in Egyptian civil society. They have exercised considerable influence on the moderation of the Muslim Brotherhood and have had an even more decisive impact on a younger generation of centrist Islamist activists, most notably those who have organized since 1996 around the al Wassat Party. Parallel developments of centrist movements have occurred elsewhere in the Arab Islamic world, notably the Renaissance Party in Tunisia, the Justice and Development Party in Morocco, the Reform Party in Algeria, the Jordanian Islamic Action Union, the *Ummah* Party in Kuwait, and the Yemeni Reformist Union. For the last two decades at least, it is possible to speak of an informal network of centrists with Egypt as its hub that shares an Islamic civilizational world-view combined with a commitment to a gradualist, democratic politics and a foreign policy of vigilant, lawful resistance to Western, especially American, intrusions in the Islamic world. In the West, these centrist groups and parties have attracted nowhere near the attention of the violent extremists with whom they compete, although their weight in their respective societies is far greater.

The approach of centrist Islamists to democracy departs in significant ways from the standard treatments in the West. The whole issue of the compatibility of Islam and democracy that dominates Western discussions is pushed into the background. Islam as understood by the mainstream is capable of generating a wide variety of political systems, including democratic ones. The issue for serious consideration, particularly in the decades since the 1970s, has been whether or not a democratic system should be a priority for the Islamic world. Influential Islamic thinkers of the center, including such figures as Fahmy Huwaidy, Muhammad al-Ghazali, and Selim al Awa of Egypt and Yusuf al-Qaradawi, based in Qatar, have argued unequivocally that democracy is absolutely imperative. Collectively, these activists and scholars have produced an impressive body of literature and a related record of practical achievements, for the most part ignored in the West but circulated widely in centrist networks, that makes a compelling Islamic case for democracy.

In this way, the New Islamists quite consciously have cultivated a clear sense that there are parallels and compatible achievements in other cultural settings of the most prized dimensions of their own Islamic culture. Their historical memory of the development of the Islamic heritage includes productive encounters with Greek philosophy, with Iranian literature, with Chinese and Indian technologies. All such connections provide a glimpse into what might be called universal human attainments. In the current age, the New Islamists have no trouble at all recognizing some dimensions of the political genius of the American experience that have a universal importance, including relevance to the Islamic world. Such appreciation for the transcending achievements of other cultural communities does not of course mean that their own culture has nothing of value to contribute on the all-human scale. Nor does it imply any sense at all of excessive deference to external cultural attainments. For example, an appreciation for the historic contribution of American thinking and practice to the quest for democracy, such as the idea of term limits for the executive, does not preclude in any way the toughest criticism of the anti-democratic policies abroad. The New Islamists consistently denounce the US and other democratic Western powers for their anti-democratic policies in Islamic lands and elsewhere in the Global South.

Given these impressive resources of reason and culture that can be drawn from Islam and turned to the purposes of democratic development, it should come as no surprise that the worldly Islam of the *Wassatteyya* has contributed in especially significant ways to the growing Islamist literature and record of concrete achievements in the quest for democracy. In the decades since the 1970s, the New Islamists of Egypt have actively supported movements to limit the arbitrary power of Egypt's president and to make Egypt a society of laws, always grounding their positions in a reading of the Islamic heritage that highlights the possibilities for its development along democratic lines. Whenever openings for democratic practice have occurred in civil society, notably in the professional syndicates, they have encouraged and honored democratic practices. Above all, the centrists have worked to create avenues for popular participation in social and economic work that serves the common good, most often in the face of bureaucratic and political obstacles. Very little of this record is known or appreciated in the West.[10] Unfortunately, that ignorance has been turned, especially in the most recent years, to the purposes of empire.

The American empire requires the notion that democracy cannot come to the Islamic world from internal resources of reason and culture, like those highlighted by the New Islamists. The centrist Islamists seize opportunities for practical democratic advancement in their diverse circumstances, however circumscribed. In place of focusing on whether Islamic movements should be democratic or not, they ask more grounded questions about the precise character democracy should take in different settings. They interrogate the heritage to assess how it can be interpreted to support the forms of democracy required. They circulate among themselves insights gleaned from the practical experiences of struggles for democracy in particular settings, with Egyptian centrists playing a particularly important role in this effort to share experiences and lessons learned.

Real histories, our own and other people's, are the best antidotes to the distortion of the idea of democracy that inevitably flow from the use of the concept as a tool of empire as the US has done in Iraq. Their history and ours makes it clear that democracies are built slowly over decades and even centuries. Lived experiences that curtail arbitrary power, generate just rules to govern the common life, and the creation of broader and broader opportunities for the people themselves to take part in determining these rules are generic characteristics of the struggle for democracy everywhere. Viewed in this light, the battle is far from won in America, where arrogant plutocratic forces, a nearly unchallengeable military-industrial complex, and an overtly imperial foreign policy threaten hard won democratic gains. Viewed in the same light, it is easy to put to rest once and for all the patently false thesis of an Islamic exceptionalism that precludes engagement in battles for democracy in the Islamic world. Such struggles are part of the history of movements dominated by secularists in some of the most important Islamic countries in the region, notably Turkey, Iran, and Egypt. They are being waged today and some of the most promising in the Arab Islamic world, such as those in Morocco, Jordan, Egypt, Yemen, and Kuwait, now have an Islamic coloration. Repression of Islamists elsewhere, notably in Tunisia and Algeria, has been especially severe. When noting the shortcomings of efforts waged in such very difficult conditions so often with unbearable levels of violence and hated, we might at least have the good grace to note our own. Our own democracy has clearly suffered egregious blows in recent years that would have greatly alarmed the Founding Fathers.

Nevertheless, for all our problems of democracy at home, the limitations of democratic struggles in the Islamic world do rightfully engage our attention. Extremist groups like al-Qaeda have made spectacular use of violence and linked it with decidedly undemocratic political visions. The Taliban drew on extremist interpretations of Islam to create a brutal dictatorship that worsened the legendary suffering of the Afghan people. But it is just as true and worthy of attention that, just below the surface of unattractive authoritarian regimes and alongside the headline grabbing actions of the violent minorities, very real struggles for democracy are being waged in the Islamic world and some of the most important are engaged in explicitly centrist, Islamic terms.

Should we be surprised, especially given the undeniable role of outside forces in supporting the authoritarianism prevalent in the Islamic world, that these struggles have had only limited successes? How can it possibly make sense to generalize those limitations into some kind of permanent barrier between Islam and democracy?

It is time to change the subject from illusory, inhibiting essences to the actual histories of struggles for freedom in the Islamic world. It is time, at a minimum, to stop obstructing those struggles. Without a consistent rethinking of our policies we will quite assuredly turn potential partners into probable enemies. When it comes to democracy, John Dewey, that great American progressive reformer and pragmatist, said it best: A central message of the corpus of John Dewey's intellectual and practical work was the conviction that the greatest gift America could give the world was the earnest development of its own democratic experiment. The prospects for democracy around the world today would be so much stronger if the biggest, richest democracy in the world offered an appealing example, if its culture were more worthy of esteem, if its policies were more worthy of respect. It is highly unlikely that these changes will come any time soon from the US government, whether liberal democratic or neo-conservative republican. At a minimum, then, the powerful forces of civil society should aim to engage more assiduously our own battles for democracy at home, while pressuring the government to do less damage to the real struggles for freedom in which others are engaged, including those promising democratic projects of Islamist centrists in the Arab Islamic world.

Acknowledgments

The author was a Carnegie Scholar 2006–2008. The research on which this chapter is based was completed in the context of on-going book project made possible (in part) by a grant from Carnegie Corporation of New York. The statements made and views expressed are solely the responsibility of the author. In finalizing this chapter I have benefitted greatly from conversations with two colleagues, Dr. Manar Shorbagy from the American University in Cairo and Alex Henry with whom I have co-authored a second chapter in this book. My gratitude is expressed in the influence both have had on the ideas expressed here.

Notes

1 Fuad Ajami, *The Foreigner's Gift: The Americans, the Arabs and the Iraqis*, New York: Free Press, 2006.
2 R. Bishry, *The Arabs in Facing the Enemy*, Cairo: Dar al Sharouq, 2002.
3 C. Johnson, *Sorrows of Empire: Militarism, Secrecy, and the End of the Republic*, New York: Metropolitan Books, 2004.
4 M. Mamdani, *Good Muslim, Bad Muslim*, New York: Pantheon Books, 2004.
5 L.C. Brown, "The Dream Palace of the Empire: Is Iraq a 'Noble Failure'?", *Foreign Affairs*, September/October (2006).
6 See the insightful study by Mamdani (op. cit.) of the Cold War origins of the war on terror. Mamdani correctly draws a parallel between Islamist radicals who would "forever close 'the gates of ijtihad,' and the neo-Reaganite talk of 'good' and 'evil' [that] closes the door to political reform" (ibid., p. 259). But Mamdani's work tells us nothing about the work of those in the Islamic world who resist those calls, often heroically. One of the rare studies that does is A.S. Tamimi, *Rachid Ghannouchi: A Democrat within Islamism*, Oxford: Oxford University Press, 2001.
7 See Amr Hamzawy, *The Key to Arab Reform: Moderate Islamists*, Carnegie Endowment Policy Brief 40, 2005 and Stephen Zunes, *Tinderbox: US Middle East Policy and the Roots of Terrorism*, Monroe, ME: Common Courage Press, 2003.

8 There are exceptions of course, like the work of Marshall Hodgson, Roy Mottahedeh, John Esposito, John Voll and a number of others.
9 Raymond W. Baker, *Islam Without Fear: Egypt and the New Islamists*, Cambridge, MA: Harvard University Press, 2004.
10 For a detailed treatment of this positive record on behalf of democratic goals, see Baker, op. cit., Chapter 5, pp. 165–211.

Index